GCSE German

Complete Revision and Practice

Contents

Section One — General Stuff

Section Two — Lifestyle

Section Three — Leisure

Section Four — Holidays

Contents

Section Five — Home and Environment

Section Six — Education and Work

Section Seven — Grammar

Do Well in Your Exam

Published by CGP

Editors: Paul Jordin, Hayley Thompson

Contributors: Diana Berry, Jan Greenway, Peter Tyson, Katharine Wright

With thanks to Esther Bond, Glenn Rogers and Janet Sheldon for the proofreading.

Audio CD produced by Naomi Laredo of Small Print and recorded, edited and mastered at The Speech Recording Studio by Graham C. Williams, featuring the voices of Bileam Bader, Maike Heuer, Benjamin Mayr and Ramona Wallner.

ISBN: 978 1 84762 433 8

Website: www.cgpbooks.co.uk
Printed by Elanders Ltd, Newcastle upon Tyne.
Clipart from CorelDRAW®

Based on the classic CGP style created by Richard Parsons.

Useful Information for GCSE German

Here are a few bits and pieces you'll need to know for GCSE German.

Tricky things to pronounce

German bits	How they're pronounced
'z'	a very sharp 'ts', as in 'Mozart'
'ch'	as in 'Loch Ness'
'v'	'f'
'w'	'v'
'ei'	an 'i' sound, as in 'pine'
'ie'	an 'e' sound, as in 'me'

These trip loads of people up — learn them.

Understanding plurals

A lot of the time, you just add a letter or two on the end of a German noun to make it plural. We've put these plural endings in brackets.

Learn the plural when you learn the noun — it's the only way.

E.g. *potato:* die Kartoffel (-n)
one potato: eine Kartoffel *two potatoes:* zwei Kartoffeln

(-) means you don't add anything to make the plural.

E.g. *cake:* der Kuchen (-)
one cake: ein Kuchen *47 cakes:* 47 Kuchen

A few plurals are more complicated — we've written these out in full.

E.g. *sausage:* die Wurst (die Würste)
one sausage: eine Wurst *144 sausages:* 144 Würste

For singular nouns the word for 'the' can be 'der', 'die' or 'das' — but for plurals it's always 'die'.

Wie schreibt man das? — How do you spell that?

You may have to spell your name and home town letter by letter in your speaking assessment or listen to someone spell something in the listening exam.

Kannst du das buchstabieren? = Can you spell that?

That means you have to be able to pronounce the German alphabet — here's how:

A — ah (as in 'car')	***H*** — hah	***O*** — oh	***T*** — tay
B — bay	***I*** — eeh (as in 'me')	***P*** — pay	***U*** — ooh
C — tsay	***J*** — yot	***Q*** — coo	***V*** — fow (as in 'fowl')
D — day	***K*** — cah (as in 'car')	***R*** — air	***W*** — vay
E — ay	***L*** — ell	***S*** — ess	***X*** — ix
F — eff	***M*** — em	***ß*** — ess tset (or scharfes ess)	***Y*** — oopsilon
G — gay	***N*** — en		***Z*** — tset

Stop — read this page before you turn over

Useful stuff this. Learn how to pronounce those letters now — you'll sound much more like a real German in your speaking if you do. And make sure you understand how those plurals work too.

Numbers and Amounts

No two ways about it, you've got to know the numbers — so get cracking.

Eins, zwei, drei — One, two, three...

0	null
1	eins
2	zwei
3	drei
4	vier
5	fünf
6	sechs
7	sieben
8	acht
9	neun
10	zehn
11	elf
12	zwölf

1. It all starts off easy enough. Learn zero to twelve — no probs. Watch out though — you might hear people on the phone say 'zwo' instead of 'zwei'.

13	dreizehn
14	vierzehn
15	fünfzehn
16	sechzehn
17	siebzehn
18	achtzehn
19	neunzehn

2. You can work out the teens using numbers one to ten — for example thirteen is just 'three' and 'ten' stuck together (drei+zehn). BUT 16 and 17 are different — they lose the '-s' and '-en' from the ends of 'sechs' and 'sieben'.

20	zwanzig	60	sechzig
30	dreißig	70	siebzig
40	vierzig	80	achtzig
50	fünfzig	90	neunzig

3. After dreißig all the ten-type numbers are easy.

21	einundzwanzig	24	vierundzwanzig	27	siebenundzwanzig
22	zweiundzwanzig	25	fünfundzwanzig	28	achtundzwanzig
23	dreiundzwanzig	26	sechsundzwanzig	29	neunundzwanzig

4. The in-between numbers are the tricky ones. For these you say the numbers backwards.

Say 'two and thirty' instead of 'thirty-two'.

= Thirty-two

100	hundert
1000	tausend
1,000,000	eine Million

5. When you get to hundreds and thousands it's simple again — thousands come before hundreds, and hundreds before the rest of the numbers.

= 1532

1000 500 32

It's as easy as 1, 2, 3...

You might already know great chunks of this — that's great. But it's not hard to make silly mistakes with numbers that could cost you easy marks in an exam or assessment. So make sure you learn them.

Numbers and Amounts

OK, it gets a bit more complicated now — still nothing too taxing though...

Erste, zweite, dritte — First, second, third...

1st	das erste	8th	das achte
2nd	das zweite	9th	das neunte
3rd	das dritte	10th	das zehnte
4th	das vierte	20th	das zwanzigste
5th	das fünfte	21st	das einundzwanzigste
6th	das sechste	100th	das hundertste
7th	das siebte		

1. For numbers between 1 and 19, add '-te' to the number in German. The four exceptions are in green.
2. From 20 onwards, just add '-ste' to the German number.
3. '1st' is written '1.' in German.

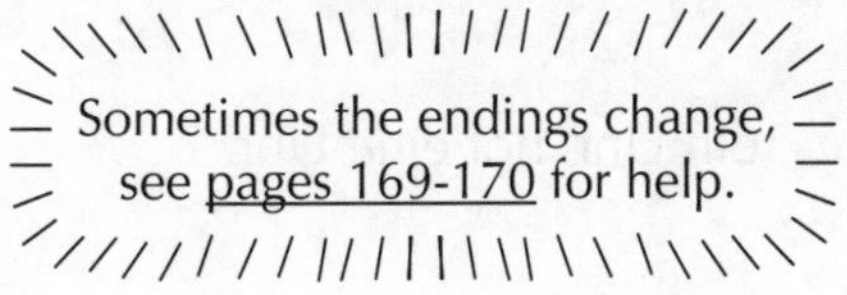
Sometimes the endings change, see pages 169-170 for help.

The word for 'the' that goes before 'erste'/'zweite'/'dritte', etc. could be 'das', 'der' or 'die' — it depends on what object you're talking about.

Nehmen Sie die erste Straße links. = Take the first street on the left.

Wie viel? — How much?

Little words for 'how many' or 'how much' are really vital. There are a lot of them to learn down there, but don't skimp — write each one out in different sentences and make sure you don't miss any.

Ich habe beide Äpfel. = I have both apples.

all:	alle	*some:*	manche
other:	andere	*several:*	mehrere
one and a half:	anderthalb	*many:*	viele
no:	keine	*few:*	wenige

See page 171 for more on 'jeder'.

Jeden Tag fahre ich Rad. = I go cycling every day.

Ich weiß nichts darüber. = I know nothing about it.

lots: viel *little:* wenig

Remember: 'erste', 'dritte', 'siebte' and 'achte' are the exceptions

Learn how to say first, second, third, etc. in German. Make sure you know all of those words about amounts too. The best way to check is to cover up the page, and then try to write them down.

Times and Dates

Knowing how to say the time is vital — examiners love it.
When you think about it, it's also pretty useful in real life.

Wie viel Uhr ist es? — What time is it?

There are loads of ways of saying the time in German — just like English.
You need to learn 'em all of course.

Wie viel Uhr ist es? ← = What time is it?  ***Wie spät ist es?***

1) Something o'clock:

It's 1 o'clock:	(Es ist) ein Uhr
It's two o'clock:	(Es ist) zwei Uhr
It's 8pm:	(Es ist) zwanzig Uhr

← ein Uhr, not eine Uhr.

2) Quarter to and past, half past:

quarter past two:	Viertel nach zwei
half past two:	halb drei
quarter to three:	Viertel vor drei

Be careful with 'halb': 'halb drei' means 'half to three' (i.e. half past two), not half past three.

3) '... past' and '... to':

twenty past seven:	zwanzig nach sieben
twelve minutes past eight:	zwölf nach acht
ten to two:	zehn vor zwei

4) The 24-hour clock:
They use it a lot in Germany — and it's easier too.

03.14:	drei Uhr vierzehn
20.32:	zwanzig Uhr zweiunddreißig
19.55:	neunzehn Uhr fünfundfünfzig

'Viertel nach' means 'quarter past', 'Viertel vor' means 'quarter to'

Most of this is pretty straightforward. Excellent news. Just remember to get 'halb' straight in your head — they like to try and catch you out with that one in exams. Practise your 24-hour clock too.

Times and Dates

You've got to know this stuff. Where would you be in general conversation without a gem like 'on Mondays I play football'? Exactly. So get learning this little lot...

Die Woche — The week

This is 'must-learn' stuff — it'll gain you simple marks in your assessments.

Days of the Week

Monday:	Montag
Tuesday:	Dienstag
Wednesday:	Mittwoch
Thursday:	Donnerstag
Friday:	Freitag
Saturday:	Samstag/Sonnabend
Sunday:	Sonntag

Days of the week are all masculine. If you want to say 'on Monday', it's either 'Montag' or 'am Montag', but not 'an Montag'.

Dienstags gehe ich einkaufen.

= I go shopping on Tuesdays (every Tuesday).

Dienstag fahre ich weg. = I'm going away on Tuesday.

Remember, plurals are always 'die'.

Some Useful Words About the Week

today:	heute	*the day before yesterday:*	vorgestern
tomorrow:	morgen	*week:*	die Woche (-n)
yesterday:	gestern	*weekend:*	das Wochenende (-n)
the day after tomorrow:	übermorgen	*on Mondays:*	montags

You don't need a capital letter here.

Januar, Februar, März, April...

German month names are blummin' similar to the English — make sure you learn what's different.

1. Like the days, the months are masculine. Say 'Januar' or 'im Januar', not 'in Januar'.

Er fährt Juli / im Juli weg.

= He's going away in July.

January:	Januar	*July:*	Juli
February:	Februar	*August:*	August
March:	März	*September:*	September
April:	April	*October:*	Oktober
May:	Mai	*November:*	November
June:	Juni	*December:*	Dezember

2. The seasons are masculine too.

The Seasons: Die Jahreszeiten

spring:	Frühling
summer:	Sommer
autumn:	Herbst
winter:	Winter

Learn these time phrases now — you'll use them a lot

In the mark schemes they specifically mention being able to say when you do things — and you can't do that if you don't know how to say the days of the week and things like 'tomorrow' or 'weekend'.

Times and Dates

Still not quite finished, I'm afraid. Here are a few more time phrases for you to learn...

Im Jahre zweitausendelf — In the year 2011

Write the date out like this for an informal letter... and like this for a formal letter.

See page 15-16 for letters.

den 5. März = 5th March

den 12.11.2011 = 12th November, 2011

Here's how to say the date — it's a bit different because you have to pronounce all the numbers. In German you NEVER say 'In 2011...' like we do in English, you say:

Im Jahre zweitausendelf ... = In the year 2011.

Ich komme am zwanzigsten Oktober. = I am coming on the 20th of October.

The special endings are because this is the dative case, see pages 167 and 170.

Like in English, the year is 'neunzehnhundert...' rather than 'tausendneunhundert...'.

Ich wurde am dritten März neunzehnhundertfünfundneunzig geboren.

= I was born on the 3rd of March 1995.

Morgen — Tomorrow... Gestern — Yesterday

Was machst du heute Abend ? = What are you doing this evening?

tomorrow:	morgen
yesterday:	gestern
this morning:	heute Morgen
this afternoon:	heute Nachmittag
tonight:	heute Nacht
tomorrow morning:	morgen früh
this week:	diese Woche
next week:	nächste Woche
last week:	letzte Woche
every two weeks:	alle zwei Wochen
every day:	jeden Tag
at the weekend:	am Wochenende
recently:	neulich

i.e. not 'morgen Morgen' even though the word for tomorrow is 'morgen' as well.

always:	immer
never:	nie
often:	oft, häufig
sometimes:	manchmal

Ich fahre selten Ski. = I seldom go skiing.

More important time phrases to learn

This stuff is absolutely crucial. It's got to be worth making the effort to learn it — it'll get you loads more marks. And as an added bonus, it's not that hard. Hurrah.

Asking Questions

You've got to be able to understand questions. You might have to ask them too.

Wann — when... warum — why... wo — where

when?:	wann?
why?:	warum?
why?:	wieso?
where?:	wo?
where (to)?:	wohin?
where (from)?:	woher?
how?:	wie?
how much?:	wie viel?
how many?:	wie viele?
who/whom?:	wer/wen/wem?
what?:	was?
which (one)?:	welche/r/s?

It's really important that you learn these question words.

Wann kommst du wieder nach Hause?

= When are you coming back home?

Wie viele Karotten möchten Sie?

= How many carrots would you like?

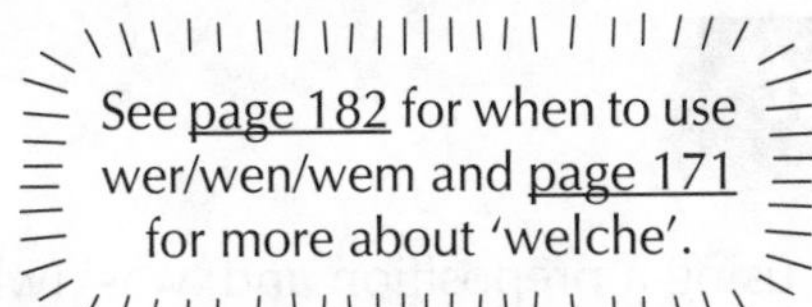

See page 182 for when to use wer/wen/wem and page 171 for more about 'welche'.

Reverse word order to ask a question

In English you change 'I can go' to 'Can I go?' to make it into a question — you can in German too.

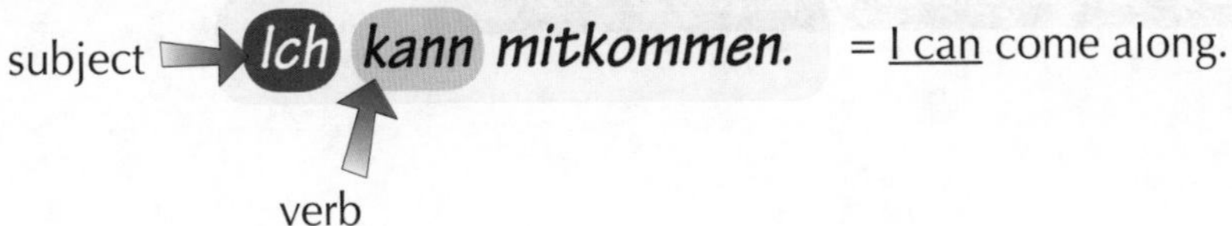

Ich kann mitkommen.

= I can come along.

Put the verb first and then the verb's subject to show it's a question:

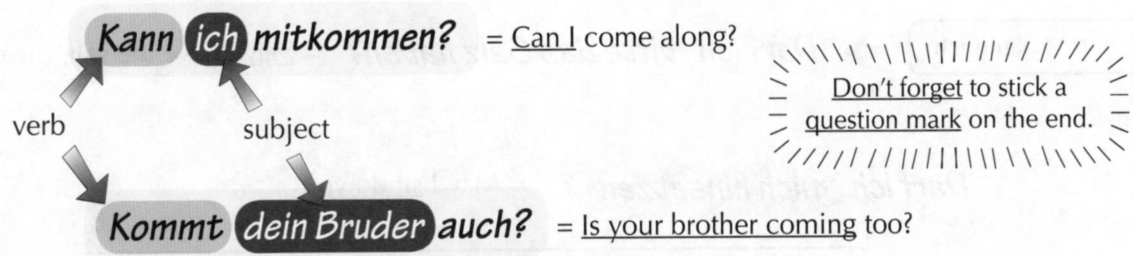

Kann ich mitkommen?

Kommt dein Bruder auch?

= Can I come along?

= Is your brother coming too?

Don't forget to stick a question mark on the end.

You need to know those question words

The secret to most of GCSE German is to learn a phrase, and learn the words you can change in it, and what you can change them to. You can learn how to ask quite a few questions like that.

Asking Questions

More questions you need to know. Nothing too difficult here.

Learn how to say 'isn't it?'

The most common words used for this are 'nicht (wahr)?', 'ja?' and 'oder?'. Just stick them on the end of a statement with a comma first and bung a question mark on the end — lovely.

Gut, nicht ? = Good, isn't it?

Es ging gut, ja ? = It went well, did it?

Du warst auch da, oder ? = You were there too, weren't you?

Add 'wo' to a word to mean 'what'

Instead of saying 'mit was' or 'auf was' or anything else using a preposition and 'was' (what), you can make a handy little word to do the whole thing. Add 'wo(r)' to the preposition and use that.

What are you writing with?:	Womit schreibst du?
What ... on?:	Worauf ... ?
What ... about?:	Worüber ... ?
What ... for?:	Wozu ... ?

If the preposition starts with a vowel you need to add an 'r' between it and the 'wo'.

Prepositions are words like 'with', 'from', 'at' or 'to'. There's more about them on pages 177-179.

Darf ich — May I

Here's how to ask for something. Use 'May I?' to be more polite.

Can I?: Kann ich?

Darf ich bitte das Salz haben? = May I have the salt, please?

Darf ich mich hinsetzen ? = May I sit down?

use the toilet:	die Toilette benutzen
please have something to drink:	bitte etwas zu trinken haben

Asking questions is pretty straightforward

I love this kind of thing — you know, stuff that will actually come in useful in real-life situations. But even if you never plan on going to Germany, you still need to know this stuff for your GCSE. So learn it.

Being Polite

You've absolutely got to know these phrases. You need to be able to say them, and to understand them. It's utterly crucial — so make sure you know these inside out.

Guten Morgen! — Good Morning!

To reply to 'Guten Tag', simply say 'Guten Tag' back. Do the same with 'Guten Abend'.

Good day / hello:	Guten Tag
Good evening:	Guten Abend
Hello (informal):	Grüß dich!

Wie geht's? — How are you?

How are you?:	Wie geht es dir?
How are you? (formal):	Wie geht es Ihnen?
How are you? (informal plural):	Wie geht es euch?

'Wie geht es (dir)?' is often shortened to 'Wie geht's?'.

This is how you'd reply: ***Mir geht's gut, danke.*** = I'm fine thanks.

not too well:	nicht so gut
ill:	schlecht
great:	klasse/super
OK:	OK

You could just say 'Gut, danke' (you'll sound more impressive if you say the whole thing, though).

Darf ich Petra vorstellen? — May I introduce Petra?

Dies ist Petra. = This is Petra.

you (formal): Sie

Nice: Schön

Es freut mich, dich kennen zu lernen.

= I'm pleased to meet you.

you (plural, informal): Kommt herein. Setzt euch.

Remember: Sie = formal, dich = informal

Komm herein. Setz dich. = Come in. Sit down. (Informal)

Kommen Sie herein. Setzen Sie sich. = Come in. Sit down. (Formal)

you (singular & plural formal): Ihnen *you (plural, informal):* euch

Vielen Dank. Das ist sehr nett von dir. = Thank you. That is very nice of you. (Informal)

Learn these phrases and sound like a real German

Little niceties will help you to excel as a social butterfly in Germany... oh yes, and they'll help shedloads when it comes to those speaking assessments.

Being Polite

This stuff is dead important — without it you'll lose marks and sound rude — 'nuff said.

Bitte — Please... Danke — Thank you

Easy stuff — probably the first German words you ever learnt.
When someone says 'danke' it is polite to say 'bitte' or 'bitte schön'.

please:	bitte	*you're welcome:*	bitte schön/bitte sehr
thank you:	danke/danke schön	*it was nothing:*	nichts zu danken

Ich hätte gern — I would like

It's more polite to say 'ich hätte gern' (I would like) than 'ich will' (I want).

1. Here's how to say you would like a thing:

   I would like: Ich möchte → ***Ich hätte gern das Salz.*** = I would like the salt.

2. Here's how to say you would like to do something:

   Ich würde gern singen. = I would like to sing.

   I would like: Ich möchte

See pages 206-207 for more info on the grammar behind these phrases and pages 25-27 for help on asking for things.

Es tut mir leid — I'm sorry

Learn both these ways of apologising — and how they're used.

I'm sorry (when you've done something wrong):	Es tut mir leid
Sorry! (to a friend):	Entschuldige!

Don't just barge in and demand things — it'll lose you marks, and friends.

Excuse me! (e.g. wanting to ask someone the way): Entschuldigung! / Entschuldigen Sie!

More key phrases here

It's a bit boring, I know. But grin, bear it, and most of all learn it, and you'll be fine. Not only that, if you ever go to Germany, everybody will think you're lovely and want to be your friend. Aww.

Quick Questions

OK, let's see what you've learnt. Have a go at these Quick Questions. *

* You'll find the answers in the back of the book.

Quick Questions

1) Write out the following numbers in words, in German:
   a) 7
   b) 17
   c) 23
   d) 34
   e) 396
   f) 1472

2) How would you say the following in German?
   a) the first
   b) the third
   c) the eighth
   d) the twenty-ninth

3) Write out the following times in full in German:
   a) 3 o'clock
   b) half past nine
   c) quarter to seven
   d) twenty-two minutes past six
   e) 20.45
   f) 13.58

4) Translate the following into English:
   a) Mittwochs spiele ich Fußball.
   b) Heute gehe ich in die Stadt.
   c) Vorgestern war ich krank.
   d) Er fährt im März weg.
   e) Mein Geburtstag ist im Frühling.
   f) Im Jahre zweitausendzwölf.

5) Translate the following questions into English:
   a) Wann spielst du Tennis?
   b) Wie viele Äpfel möchten Sie?
   c) Was machst du?
   d) Wohin gehst du?

6) Change the word order in these German sentences to form a question:
   a) Steve kann mitkommen.
   b) Sie können kochen.
   c) Hannah spielt Klavier.
   d) Du möchtest eine Tasse Tee.
   e) Du gehst aus.

7) You're at a party in Germany. How would you say the following?
   a) Good evening
   b) Hello (informal)!
   c) I'm pleased to meet you (formal).
   d) How are you (informal)?
   e) please
   f) thank you
   g) I would like to sing.
   h) May I use the toilet?

Opinions

To get a decent mark, you need to be able to say what you think about things.

Magst du...? — Do you like...?

Magst du diese Band ? = Do you like this band?

this film:	diesen Film
this newspaper:	diese Zeitung
this book:	dieses Buch

This needs to be in the accusative case, see the grammar section page 156.

Ich mag diese Band nicht. Ich finde sie schlecht . = I don't like this band. I think it's bad.

These are linked. If the first bit is feminine, then the second bit must be feminine too.

it: ihn/sie/es

There are more opinion words on pages 13-14.

These are good, all-purpose ways of asking whether somebody agrees with what you've just said:

Ich denke, diese Zeitung ist langweilig. Und du? = I think this newspaper is boring. What about you?

Denkst du das auch? = Do you agree? (Literally: 'Do you think that too?')

Ich mag... — I like...

Liking things

I like ... :	Ich mag ...
I like ... :	... gefällt mir
I love ... :	Ich liebe ...
I'm interested in ... :	Ich interessiere mich für ...
I find ... great:	Ich finde ... toll
I like ... :	Ich habe ... gern

Disliking things

I don't like...:	Ich mag ... nicht
I don't like....:	... gefällt mir nicht
... doesn't interest me:	... interessiert mich nicht
I find ... awful:	Ich finde ... furchtbar

Tischtennis gefällt mir , aber Fußball interessiert mich überhaupt nicht . = I like table tennis, but football doesn't interest me at all.

Watch out — say 'ich mag Hermann' if you want to say you like him. If you say 'Hermann gefällt mir', it means you fancy him.

Other Useful Phrases

It's all right:	es geht
I don't mind/care:	es ist mir egal
I prefer to do ...:	ich mache lieber

You'll be expected to give opinions all the time

This is another must-know topic. It's one of those that they specifically mention in the mark schemes — now don't say I didn't warn you. Get these phrases learnt for loads of marks.

Opinions

You'll get given other people's opinions in your exams and you'll need to give some of your own in the speaking and writing tasks. This page gives you loads more ways to tell the world what you think...

Wie findest du...? — What do you think of...?

Look out for these words, they all mean the same thing — 'what do you think of ...?'. If you can use loads of these then your German will be dead interesting — that means more marks of course. But be really careful about 'ich meine' — it means 'I think', not 'I mean'.

Finding out Someone's Opinion

What do you think of... ?:	Was hältst du von...?
What do you think of...?:	Wie findest du...?
What do you think of...?:	Was denkst du über...?
What's your opinion of that?:	Was ist deine Meinung dazu?
What do you think?:	Was meinst du?

I think...

In my opinion ... :	Meiner Meinung nach ...
I think that ... :	Ich meine, dass ...
I think that ... :	Ich denke, dass ...
I think ... is ... :	Ich halte ... für ...

Wie findest du meinen Freund? = What do you think of my boyfriend?

Meiner Meinung nach ist er interessant. = In my opinion he's interesting.

See page 12 for how to ask if somebody agrees.

Ich halte ihn für verrückt. = I think he's mad.

This is in the accusative case — see page 156.

Ich finde es... — I think it's...

You might have to say whether you like something or not.

Ich finde diese Band gut. = I think this band is good.

this team:	diese Mannschaft
that magazine:	das Magazin
this music:	diese Musik

bad:	schlecht
excellent:	ausgezeichnet
terrible:	schrecklich
boring:	langweilig
quite good:	ziemlich gut

See page 14 for more opinion words.

Ich finde diese Musik schrecklich. = I think this music is terrible.

Ich denke, dass dieses Buch wunderbar ist. = I think that this book is wonderful.

'Dass' sends the verb to the end of the sentence (like 'weil' on the next page).

The more ways you can give an opinion, the better

Giving your opinion about things gets you big marks in speaking and writing. It's quite easy to say whether you like something or not, so you've got no excuses — just learn these phrases.

Opinions

After you've impressed the examiners by saying you like or hate something, really knock their socks off by explaining why.

Toll — Great... Furchtbar — Terrible

Here are some words you can use to describe things you like or don't like. They're really easy to use, so it's worth learning them.

great:	toll / prima	*excellent:*	ausgezeichnet	*not nice (person):*	unsympathisch
	super / klasse	*fantastic:*	fantastisch	*bad:*	schlecht / schlimm
good:	gut	*fabulous:*	fabelhaft	*terrible:*	furchtbar / schlimm
lovely:	schön	*interesting:*	interessant		fürchterlich
beautiful:	wunderschön	*nice (person):*	nett	*awful:*	mies
friendly:	freundlich		sympathisch	*ugly:*	hässlich

Bob ist toll. = Bob is great.

Tennis ist furchtbar. = Tennis is terrible.

Weil — Because

'Weil' is ultra-important — it's the main German word for because.
When you use 'weil' the verb in that part of the sentence gets shoved to the end.

Remember: a verb is a doing word.

This means that...

Der Film gefällt mir. Er ist interessant. = I like the film. It is interesting.

... becomes: (verb)

Der Film gefällt mir, weil er interessant ist. = I like the film, because it is interesting.

Ich finde sie sehr nett, weil sie freundlich ist. = I think she's very nice because she is friendly.

There's always a comma before 'weil'.

See page 166 for other words like 'weil'.

Ich mag ihn nicht, weil er langweilig ist. = I don't like him, because he is boring.

Denn — Because

It's handy to know that 'denn', like 'weil', means 'because'.
'Denn' is dead useful, cos it doesn't change the word order.

Don't confuse 'denn' with 'dann', which means 'then'.

Ich mag ihn nicht, denn er ist langweilig. = I don't like him, because he is boring.

Remember: 'weil' changes word order

It's no good only knowing how to ask someone else's opinion, or how to say 'I think', without being able to say what you think. Just don't say something daft like 'I like it because it's boring'.

Writing Informal Letters

You might have to write a letter in German at some point.
So learn how to lay out a letter and how to say Dear Bill, and all the stuff like that.

Lieber Hermann — Dear Hermann

You've got to be able to start and end a letter properly.
OK, this one's a bit short, but it shows you how to start and end it, and where to put the date.

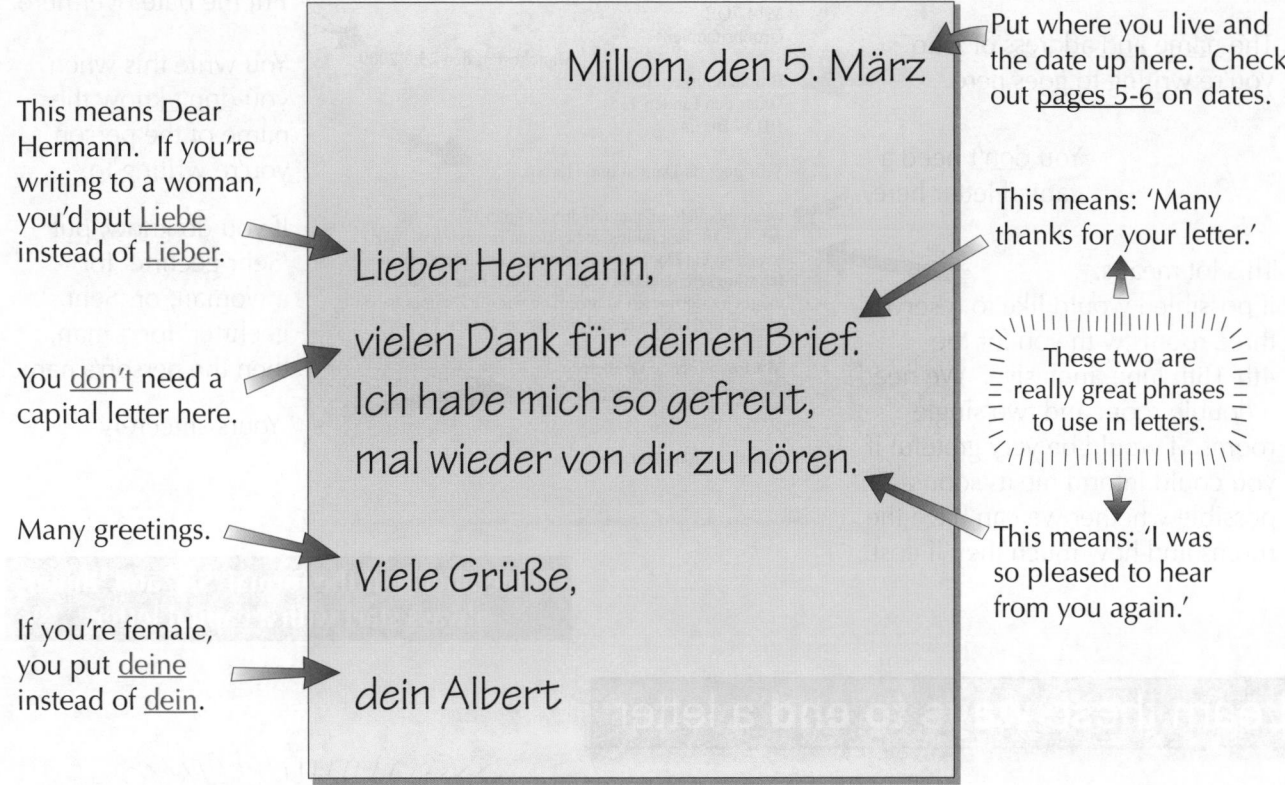

Millom, den 5. März

Lieber Hermann,

vielen Dank für deinen Brief.
Ich habe mich so gefreut,
mal wieder von dir zu hören.

Viele Grüße,

dein Albert

Put where you live and the date up here. Check out pages 5-6 on dates.

This means Dear Hermann. If you're writing to a woman, you'd put Liebe instead of Lieber.

You don't need a capital letter here.

This means: 'Many thanks for your letter.'

These two are really great phrases to use in letters.

This means: 'I was so pleased to hear from you again.'

Many greetings.

If you're female, you put deine instead of dein.

Use these **phrases** in your **letters**

One thing that you can use for just about every informal letter is asking how the person is:

Wie geht's? = How are you?

You can use this one to start a letter, just after Dear whoever.

And here are a couple of things that are good to put just before you sign off:

Ich freue mich schon darauf, dich wieder zu sehen. = I'm already looking forward to seeing you again.

Ich hoffe, bald wieder von dir zu hören. = I hope to hear from you again soon.

German letters — keep them Brief...

This is pretty easy stuff, but it could well help with your writing assessment.
Make sure you can use the German stock phrases — then your letter will sound authentic.

Writing Formal Letters

It might not be fair, but they expect you to be able to write a formal letter as well.

Put your **name** and **address** at the top

Put your name and address up here.

Aleesha Thompson
16 Rusland Drive
Manchester
M14 7QE
Großbritannien

Put the date over here.

Manchester, den 23.6.2009

The name and address of who you're writing to goes here.

Brandenburger Hotel
Unter den Linden 115
10159 Berlin

You write this when you don't know the name of the person you're writing to.

If you do know, put 'Sehr geehrte' for a woman, or 'Sehr geehrter' for a man, then the person's name.

Sehr geehrte Damen und Herren,

You don't need a capital letter here.

wenn möglich möchte ich drei Zimmer für den 4. - 18. Juni inklusive bei Ihnen reservieren. Wir brauchen ein Doppelzimmer und zwei Einzelzimmer. Ich wäre sehr dankbar, wenn Sie mich bitte so bald wie möglich informieren könnten, ob wir die Zimmer haben können und auch wie viel sie kosten werden.

This lot means:
If possible I would like to reserve three rooms with you for the 4th-18th June, inclusive. We need a double room and two single rooms. I would be very grateful if you could inform me as soon as possible whether we can have the rooms and how much they'll cost.

Mit freundlichen Grüßen

Yours sincerely

A. Thompson

Aleesha Thompson

Remember that the formal 'Sie' and 'Ihnen' always start with a capital letter.

Learn these **ways to end** a letter

Hochachtungsvoll = Yours faithfully/sincerely

You can use the ending from the letter above, as well.

Vielen Dank im Voraus für alle Ihre Bemühungen = Many thanks in advance for all your efforts

Use '**entschuldigen**' to apologise

You might find you have to apologise for something. This is the phrase you'll need:

Ich möchte mich bei Ihnen entschuldigen. = I would like to apologise.

You might also have to complain about something:

Ich möchte mich über Ihr Hotel beschweren. = I would to complain about your hotel.

Formal 'your'. Put whatever you need in here.

You might have to write a formal letter of complaint too

OK, there's a lot to learn for these, but they might come in pretty handy.
There are set polite phrases for formal letters in German just like there are in English.

Quick Questions

A few more Quick Questions for you here. Don't skip them — they really are the best way to make sure you've taken in everything you've just learnt. It's no good just reading everything through and hoping it's all going to stick. You need to practise using your new-found knowledge.

Quick Questions

1) How would you say the following in German?
   a) I like sport.
   b) I like tennis. (Try to use a different phrase for 'I like'.)
   c) I don't like this book.
   d) I'm interested in football.
   e) It's all right.

2) Your German friends are having a conversation about likes and dislikes. Translate it into English.

Emilie: Hanna, was hältst du von Schwimmen?

Hanna: Ich halte Schwimmen für langweilig, aber ich finde Squash ausgezeichnet.

Alex: Meiner Meinung nach ist Sport furchtbar. Ich habe das Theater gern.

Hanna: Es geht. Was denkst du über das Theater, Emilie?

Emilie: Ich liebe das Theater auch. Es ist fabelhaft!

3) Translate these opinions into German:
   a) Lena is nice.
   b) Heike is very friendly.
   c) Daniel is awful.
   d) This band is terrible.
   e) German is fantastic.

4) Join these sentences together, using the word 'weil'.
   Remember, you'll have to change the word order of the second sentence.
   a) Die Landschaft gefällt mir. Sie ist wunderschön.
   b) Ich mag den Film nicht. Er ist langweilig.
   c) Ich finde ihn sehr unsympathisch. Er ist wirklich hässlich.
   d) Ich mag dieses Buch. Es ist sehr interessant.
   e) Ich finde Bergsteigen toll. Es ist aufregend.

5) How might you start an informal letter to your German pen friend Georg?

6) How might you end an informal letter to Georg?

7) How would you write the date 'the 9th of February' in an informal German letter?

8) How would you write 'the 9th of February 2011' in a formal German letter?

9) How would you start a formal German letter to someone you didn't know?

10) How might you end a formal German letter?

11) How could you say 'I would like to complain about your hotel' in German.

Listening Questions

So. You've reached your first lot of Listening Questions. That's what the CD's for incidentally — just in case you thought it might be something more interesting. Take a deep breath and dive in. Remember: you get to hear each track twice, so take your time.

Track 1

1 Stefan is talking about his parents.

Which of these statements expresses what Stefan says?

A His parents don't have much time for him.

B He thinks his parents are too strict.

C He gets on well with his parents.

Write the correct letter in the box. ☐

Track 2

2 Anna is talking about her plans for the coming week.

Which of the following statements are true?

A Tomorrow is Monday.

B Anna is going to the doctor's at 11 o'clock on Monday.

C On Tuesday she's meeting friends to go shopping.

D On Wednesday she has to visit her grandmother.

E On the 22nd she's going to the cinema with her sister.

F She's going out for a meal on Friday at half past eight.

G On Sunday, she's relaxing.

Write the correct letters in the boxes.

Example: **A** ☐ ☐ ☐

Reading Question

1 You're working in the German youth hostel 'Kalte Dusche' for the summer and receive this letter.

Christine Smith
34 Coppice Road
Midsommer
MR6 9HG
Großbritannien

Midsommer, den 18.11.2010

Jugendherberge Kalte Dusche
Nordseeallee
59835 Kleinstadt

Sehr geehrter Jugendherbergsvater,

mein Sohn und fünf seiner Freunde fahren am einunddreißigsten Juli nach Kleinstadt, um zwei Wochen dort zu verbringen. Sie freuen sich sehr darauf, aber ich habe einige Sorgen. Könnten Sie bitte meine Fragen beantworten?

Wie viele Betten gibt es im Schlafsaal? Müssen die Jungen ihre eigene Bettwäsche mitbringen?

Gibt es einen Laden, wo sie Lebensmittel kaufen können und eine Küche oder einen Grill, wo sie ihre Mahlzeiten vorbereiten können?

Was gibt es in der Nähe zu sehen und zu tun? Gibt es viele Sehenswürdigkeiten oder andere Aktivitäten für Jugendliche?

Mit freundlichen Grüßen,

Christine Smith

a) When are the boys going to Kleinstadt and how long will they spend there?

....

b) What two questions does Mrs Smith ask about the sleeping arrangements?

....

....

c) What does she ask about the surrounding district?

....

....

Speaking Question

Right, here's your first chance to practise for your speaking assessment. Get someone else to read the teacher's part. You might have to talk about pretty much any of the topics in this guide in the real task, but you'll always be expected to give opinions and, whenever possible, your reasons for having them.

Task: Leisure activities
You are talking with your exchange partner about what you like doing in your spare time. Your teacher will play the part of your exchange partner.

Make sure you give plenty of opinions and try to back them up with reasons why.

Your teacher will ask you the following:
- What sort of television programmes do you enjoy and which do you not?
- How long do you spend watching television at home?
- Do you go to the cinema often?
- What sort of films do you like to see and which can you not stand?
- What was the last film you watched?
- What sort of music do you like to listen to?
- Do you play a musical instrument?
- !

Flick forward to Section Three for more on topics like television, films and music.

! Remember that the exclamation mark means you'll have to answer a question that you won't have prepared an answer to.

The whole conversation should last about five minutes.

Notes for Teachers
You need to ask the student the following questions:
- Was für Fernsehsendungen siehst du gern und welche siehst du nicht gern?
- Wie viele Stunden siehst du zu Hause fern?
- Gehst du oft ins Kino?
- Was für Filme siehst du gern und welche kannst du nicht leiden?
- Was war der letzte Film, den du gesehen hast?
- Was für Musik hörst du gern?
- Spielst du ein Musikinstrument?
- !

! The unpredictable question could be: Was für Bücher liest du gern?

Writing Questions

Speaking German's not the only skill you're going to have to practise for your coursework. You'll also be assessed on how well you can write — so have a go at these example writing tasks.

Task 1: You're sending an e-mail to a German friend. You want to tell him or her a bit about your school and social life.

You should write an e-mail in the same way you would an informal letter.

You could write about the following:

- What time you get up on school days
- How you get to school
- What time school starts and ends
- How many lessons you have
- When you have breaks and lunch
- What you like to do at weekends

Again, you should give plenty of opinions — and justify them.

Remember: to score the highest marks you need to answer the task fully (for grades C and above you will need to write 200-300 words).

Task 2: Write a review of a book you have read recently, or your favourite book. You could write about the following:

- What genre of book it is and why you decided to read it
- The plot
- The central characters
- What you particularly liked about it and why
- Anything you didn't like and why
- Whether you think it would make a good film

Remember: to score the highest marks you need to answer the task fully (for grades C and above you will need to write 200-300 words).

Revision Summary

This section contains the absolute basics that you need to have totally sorted come exam time. The stuff on your opinions, and on times (including today, tomorrow, every week, on Mondays etc.), can make a really big difference to your marks. The only way to make sure that you've got it sorted is to do all of these questions. Go over the section again and again (and again) until you know it.

1) Count out loud from 1 to 20 in German.

2) How do you say these numbers in German? a) 22 b) 35 c) 58 d) 71 e) 112 f) 2101

3) What are these in German? a) 1st b) 4th c) 7th d) 19th e) 25th f) 52nd

4) What do these words mean? a) alle b) manche c) viel d) wenig

5) Give two ways to ask 'What time is it?' in German.
Look at your watch, and say what time it is, out loud and in German.

6) How would you say these times in German? a) 5.00 b) 10.30 c) 13.22 d) 16.45

7) Say all the days of the week in German.

8) How do you say these in German? a) yesterday b) today c) tomorrow

9) Say all of the months of the year in German.

10) How do you say the date of your birthday (including the year) in German?

11) 'Was machst du heute Abend?' means 'What are you doing this evening?'
How would you say 'What are you doing a) this afternoon?' b) tonight?' c) next week?'

12) 'Ich fahre selten Ski' means 'I seldom ski.'
How would you say: a) 'I never ski.' b) 'I often ski.' c) 'I sometimes ski.'

13) 'Du singst' means 'You sing' or 'You are singing'. What do these questions mean?
a) Wann singst du? b) Wo singst du? c) Was singst du?
d) Wie singst du? e) Warum singst du? f) Wie viel singst du?

14) How do you say these in German? a) Please b) Thank you c) How are you?

15) Here are some phrases: 'ich hätte gern', 'ich möchte', 'ich würde gern'.
Which two could you use to say you'd like a) some coffee? b) to dance?

16) How would you ask someone what they think of Elvis Presley? (In German.)
Give as many ways of asking it as you can.

17) How would you say these things in German? Give at least one way to say each of them.
a) I like Elvis Presley. b) I don't like Elvis Presley. c) I find Elvis Presley interesting.
d) I love Elvis Presley. e) I find Elvis Presley awful. f) I think that Elvis Presley is fantastic.

18) To win this week's star prize, complete the following sentence in 10 words or less (in German): 'I like Elvis Presley because...'

19) To win last week's potato peelings, complete the following sentence in 10 words or less (in German): 'I don't like Elvis Presley because...'

20) Which of the following phrases would you use to start a formal letter in German?
a) Sehr geehrter Herr Presley, b) Lieber Elvis, c) Yo Elvis.

Mealtimes

This page is full of stuff that you can use all the time — not just at mealtimes. Use it to say what you like, and to ask people politely for things. You've just got to know it.

Ich mag... — I like...

These expressions aren't just for food — use them to talk about anything you like or dislike.

Ich mag Äpfel.
bananas: Bananen
cream: Sahne

= I like apples.

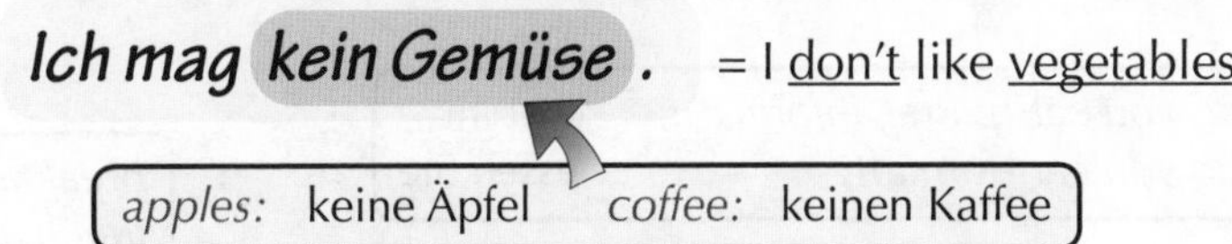
Ich mag kein Gemüse.
apples: keine Äpfel
coffee: keinen Kaffee

= I don't like vegetables.

Remember: Add the '-in' to the end of 'Vegetarier' for women and girls.

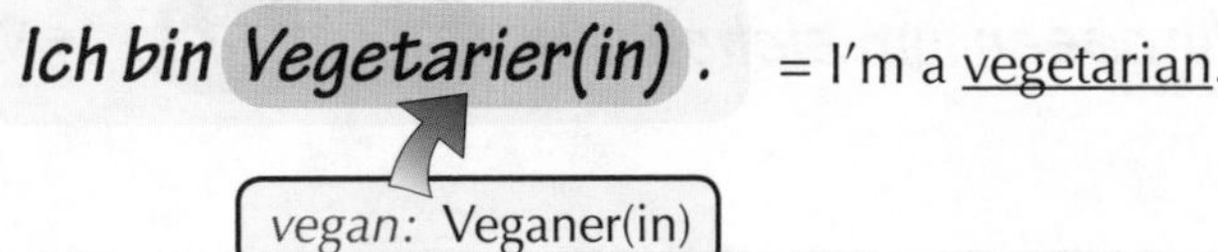
Ich bin Vegetarier(in).
vegan: Veganer(in)

= I'm a vegetarian.

Ja bitte — Yes please

It doesn't come any easier than this.

Ja bitte. = Yes, please.

Nein danke. = No thanks.

Important: Always say 'Ja bitte', not 'Ja danke'.

Könnten Sie...? — Could you...?

Two mega-important phrases that you've got to learn and be able to use properly.

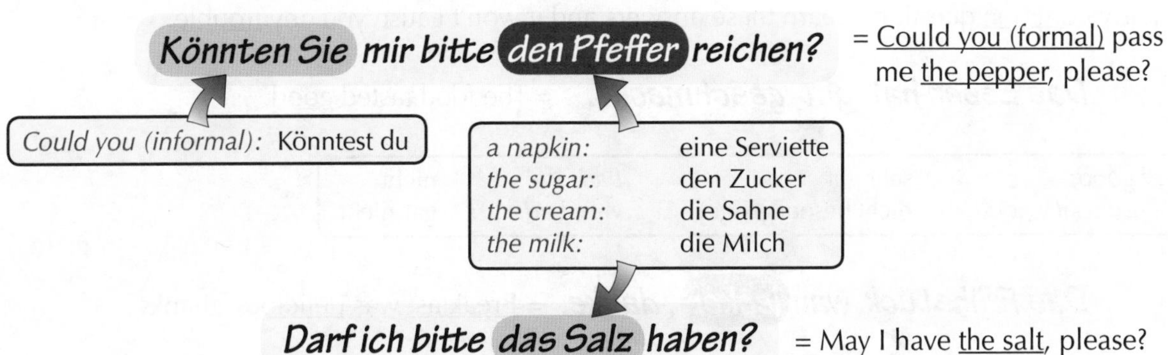
Könnten Sie mir bitte den Pfeffer reichen?
Could you (informal): Könntest du
a napkin: eine Serviette
the sugar: den Zucker
the cream: die Sahne
the milk: die Milch
Darf ich bitte das Salz haben?

= Could you (formal) pass me the pepper, please?

= May I have the salt, please?

You need to know these basic phrases

This is pretty easy. They're bound to ask what you like and don't like — so you need to know what to say. And make sure you can ask questions politely... so you don't go offending anyone.

Mealtimes

Yup, more mealtimes stuff, I'm afraid. You've just got to crack on with it...

Wann isst du...? — When do you eat...?

Meals are important — so get learning these phrases.

Wann isst du zu Abend? = When do you eat dinner?

do you eat (plural, informal):	esst ihr
do you eat (formal):	essen Sie

breakfast:	das Frühstück
lunch:	zu Mittag
supper:	das Abendbrot

See page 4 for more times.

Wir essen um sieben Uhr zu Abend. = We eat dinner at seven o'clock.

Hast du Hunger oder Durst? — Are you hungry or thirsty?

Common enough questions. Make sure you can answer them.

Hast du Hunger? = Are you hungry?

thirsty: Durst

Both mean the same thing

Ich habe Hunger. ***Ich bin hungrig.*** = I'm hungry.

thirsty: Durst

thirsty: durstig

Nein danke, ich habe keinen Hunger. = No thanks, I'm not hungry.

Hat das geschmeckt? — Did that taste good?

Again, a fairly common question. Learn these answers and it won't cause you any trouble.

Das Essen hat gut geschmeckt. = The food tasted good.

very good:	sehr gut	*bad:*	nicht
not especially good:	nicht besonders gut	*very bad:*	gar nicht

Das Frühstück war lecker, danke. = Breakfast was delicious, thanks.

Lunch: Das Mittagessen *Dinner:* Das Abendessen

Learn how to ask these questions — and answer them

Not only could these nifty little question-answer-combos come in really useful in an exam or a speaking assessment, say — they could also really help you out if you're ever on a German exchange. Cool.

Mealtimes

This is stuff you should know — especially if you want a top grade. Again, a lot of it could be used in different sorts of situations — not just in conversations at the dinner table.

Möchten Sie...? — Would you like...?

It's that word 'möchten' again. These sentences are dead important — you can use them to make different sorts of offers, not just ones about food.

Möchten Sie das Salz haben? = Would you like the salt?

the pepper:	den Pfeffer
the red wine:	den Rotwein
the butter:	die Butter

This is similar to what's on page 25.

Kann ich Ihnen eine Serviette reichen? = Can I pass you a napkin?

Ein wenig... — A little...

These quantity words are dead useful. There'll be loads of times in your speaking and writing tasks that you can use them and bag yourself more marks.

Ich möchte viel Zucker, bitte. = I would like lots of sugar, please.

a bit: ein bisschen/ein wenig

See page 3 for more on quantities.

Ich möchte ein großes Stück Torte. = I would like a big piece of cake.

Ich habe genug gegessen, danke. = I've eaten enough, thanks.

Ich bin satt. = I'm full.

You'll find this stuff useful in loads of situations

These quantity words are really handy — learn them and you're cooking on gas. There are loads of ways you can use this stuff, so get cracking and make sure you know it inside out. Sorted.

Household Chores

This is all useful stuff for if you're staying with a German family.

Musst du zu Hause helfen? — Do you have to help at home?

Even if you never help at home — learn these words.

Ich wasche zu Hause ab. = I wash up at home.

I tidy my room:	Ich räume mein Zimmer auf.
I make my bed:	Ich mache mein Bett.
I vacuum:	Ich sauge Staub.
I clean:	Ich putze.
I dust:	Ich wische Staub.

'Abwaschen' and 'aufräumen' are separable verbs. If you don't know much about these, have a look at pages 201-202.

Ich muss abwaschen. = I have to wash up.

clean:	putzen
dust:	Staub wischen
tidy up:	aufräumen
make my bed:	mein Bett machen
empty the dishwasher:	die Spülmaschine leeren

Brauchst du etwas? — Do you need anything?

These are easy phrases — so there's no excuse for not knowing them.
Remember to use the formal 'Sie' if you're asking someone older.

Darf ich mich duschen? = May I have a shower?

a bath: baden

Kann ich bitte etwas Zahnpasta haben? = Can I have some toothpaste please?

a towel:	ein Handtuch
some soap:	etwas Seife

Haben Sie Zahnpasta? = Have you any toothpaste?

Have you (informal): Hast du

Separable verbs aren't as scary as they look

Those separable verbs might well take a bit of getting used to. Learn one though, and thankfully all the others will follow the same pattern. Phew. It's almost as fun as washing up...

Quick Questions

Right, here we go, a few Quick Questions just to check you've been <u>learning</u> this stuff <u>properly</u> and whatnot. This should get the old <u>brain juices</u> flowing nicely...

Quick Questions

1) Name these vegetables in English:
   a) die Kartoffel
   b) die Zwiebel
   c) die Möhre
   d) die Gurke
   e) der Kohl

2) Give the names of these fruits in German:
   a) apple
   b) banana
   c) strawberry
   d) raspberry
   e) peach

3) You're in a German restaurant with your family.
   Translate the following meals from the menu into English to help them out:

   - Bockwurst mit Sauerkraut und Kartoffeln
   - Rindfleisch mit Knödeln
   - Hähnchen mit Nudeln und Tomaten

4) Your sister has decided to become a vegetarian. How would she say this in German?
   How would she say she doesn't like meat?

5) How would you ask your German friend to pass you the salt?

6) You're staying with your German exchange partner.
   How would you ask him when he eats dinner?

7) You get the reply 'Wir essen um halb sieben zu Abend'.
   What does this mean in English?

8) Your friend's mum asks if you want something to eat now.
   How would you say 'No thanks, I'm not hungry' in German?

9) How would you tell your friend's mum that 'Lunch was delicious, thanks'?

10) Translate the following quantity words into German:
    a) lots
    b) a bit
    c) a big piece
    d) enough

11) Translate the following sentences into German:
    a) I tidy my room.
    b) I must tidy up.
    c) I dust.
    d) I must empty the dishwasher.

12) How would you say 'Can I have a towel please?' in German?

13) How would you say 'May I have a bath?' in German?

About Yourself

You'll probably have to give all sorts of personal details about yourself in your speaking and writing tasks. You should know all this already, so just make sure you really know it backwards.

Erzähl mir etwas von dir... — Tell me about yourself...

You might need to answer these questions in your speaking assessment:

Wie heißt du? = What are you called?

Ich heiße George. = I'm called George.

Wie alt bist du? = How old are you?

Ich bin fünfzehn Jahre alt. = I'm 15 years old.

Wann hast du Geburtstag? = When is your birthday?

Ich habe am 12. Dezember Geburtstag. = My birthday is on the 12th of December.

Wo wohnst du? = Where do you live?

Ich wohne in Lancaster. = I live in Lancaster.

See page 111-112 for where you live, page 2 for more numbers and page 6 for more dates.

Was magst du? = What do you like?

Use this to say you like or dislike any person or thing, e.g. I like you: ich mag dich.

Ich mag Fußball. = I like football.

Get practising your alphabet

'Excellent', I hear you cry, 'I've been answering questions like these since I was knee-high to a grasshopper'. That's true, but it means you'll be expected to answer them really well. So get practising.

Describing People

You might have to describe how gorgeous you are as well — shouldn't be too hard. Just make sure you learn these key bits of vocab...

Wie siehst du aus? — What do you look like?

Ich habe braune Augen. = I have brown eyes.

blue: blaue
green: grüne

Ich trage eine Brille. = I wear glasses.

Ich habe lange Haare. = I have long hair.

short:	kurze	*dark:*	dunkle
shoulder-length:	schulterlange	*light:*	helle
quite long:	ziemlich lange	*blond:*	blonde
straight:	glatte	*red:*	rote
wavy:	wellige	*brown:*	braune
curly:	lockige	*black:*	schwarze

Ich bin groß. = I am tall.

medium height:	mittelgroß
small:	klein
fat:	dick
thin:	dünn
slim:	schlank

Ich habe einen Bart. = I have a beard.

OK — so you might not have a beard, but you might have to describe someone who does.

moustache: Schnurrbart

Wie sieht er aus? — What does he look like?

If you want to describe other people (like your friends and relatives, see page 32) then use these sentences:

Er ist zwölf Jahre alt. = He's 12 years old.

Er hat blaue Augen. = He has blue eyes.

Er trägt eine Brille. = He wears glasses.

Sie hat glatte Haare. = She has straight hair.

You can stick the words above in the green boxes.

Sie ist groß. = She is tall.

You never know when you'll need to fill in a missing persons report

Learn how to describe how scrumptious you look — so you can do it without a second thought. You have to be able to describe how other people look too. If I were you I'd get practising now.

Family and Pets

You might have to talk about your family or pets in your speaking assessments or writing tasks.

Meine Familie — My family

OK, first up: the basics — a who's who of your nearest and dearest.

If you're talking about more than one person, use 'heißen', not 'heißt'.

Remember, it's 'meine' for plurals.

Meine Mutter heißt Janet. = My mother is called Janet.

My father:	Mein Vater	*My uncle:*	Mein Onkel (-)
My brother:	Mein Bruder (Meine Brüder)	*My female cousin:*	Meine Cousine (-n)
My sister:	Meine Schwester (-n)	*My male cousin:*	Mein Cousin (-s)
My stepmother:	Meine Stiefmutter	*My grandmother:*	Meine Großmutter (Meine Großmütter)
My stepfather:	Mein Stiefvater	*My grandfather:*	Mein Großvater (Meine Großväter)
My stepsister:	Meine Stiefschwester (-n)	*My male friend:*	Mein Freund (-e)
My half brother:	Mein Halbbruder (Meine Halbbrüder)	*My female friend:*	Meine Freundin (-nen)
		My siblings:	Meine Geschwister
My aunt:	Meine Tante (-n)	*My parents:*	Meine Eltern

'Freund' and 'Freundin' can also mean 'boyfriend' and 'girlfriend'.

Ich habe eine Schwester. = I have one sister.

Ich habe einen Bruder. = I have one brother.

Ich bin ein Einzelkind. = I am an only child.

Hast du Haustiere? — Have you any pets?

Ich habe einen Hund. = I have a dog.

a dog:	einen Hund (-e)	*a rabbit:*	ein Kaninchen (-)
a cat:	eine Katze (-n)	*a snake:*	eine Schlange (-n)
a budgie:	einen Wellensittich (-e)	*a horse:*	ein Pferd (-e)
a guinea pig:	ein Meerschweinchen (-)	*a goldfish:*	einen Goldfisch (-e)

Swap in any descriptive word here.

Er ist gelb. = He is yellow.

See page 68 for colours and page 31 for sizes and things like fat and thin.

Mein Hund heißt Rudi. = My dog is called Rudi.

Use 'meine' for female relations and 'mein' for male relations

Most of this page is basic stuff you have to know — like how to say what relations you have (or don't have). If you don't already know it like the back of your hand — get learning.

Personality

Personality, character, whatever you want to call it, I'm sure you've got bags of it. It'd probably be useful if you could talk about it in German though...

Meine Persönlichkeit — My personality

You might have to describe your personality in one of your speaking assessments — here's how...

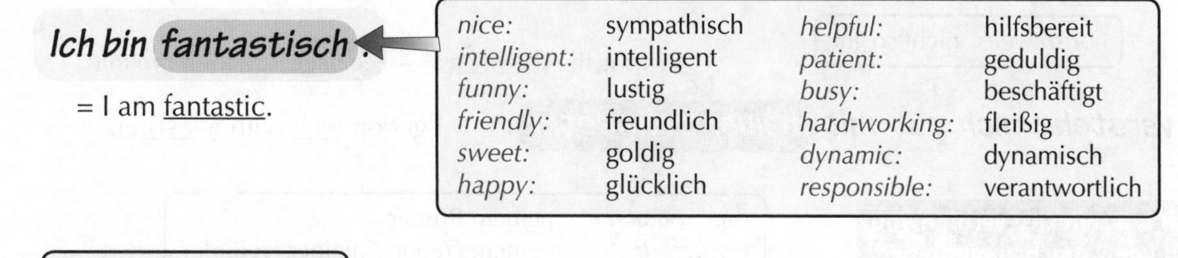

Ich bin fantastisch.

= I am fantastic.

nice:	sympathisch	*helpful:*	hilfsbereit
intelligent:	intelligent	*patient:*	geduldig
funny:	lustig	*busy:*	beschäftigt
friendly:	freundlich	*hard-working:*	fleißig
sweet:	goldig	*dynamic:*	dynamisch
happy:	glücklich	*responsible:*	verantwortlich

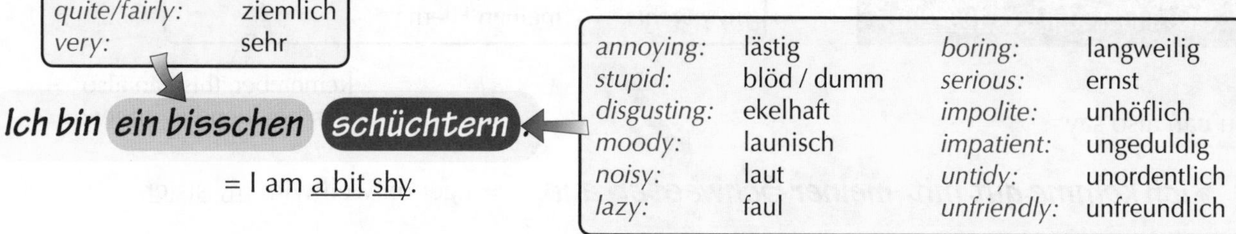

quite/fairly:	ziemlich
very:	sehr

Ich bin ein bisschen schüchtern.

= I am a bit shy.

annoying:	lästig	*boring:*	langweilig
stupid:	blöd / dumm	*serious:*	ernst
disgusting:	ekelhaft	*impolite:*	unhöflich
moody:	launisch	*impatient:*	ungeduldig
noisy:	laut	*untidy:*	unordentlich
lazy:	faul	*unfriendly:*	unfreundlich

Die Persönlichkeiten anderer Leute — Other people's personalities

So you know how to talk about yourself, here's how to talk about other people...

Mein kleiner Bruder ist sehr lästig. = My little brother is very annoying.

Meine Schwester ist wirklich sympathisch, aber sie kann ein bisschen ernst sein. = My sister is really nice, but she can be a bit serious.

You can put any of the personality traits above in the coloured boxes.

Mein Vater ist oft beschäftigt, aber er ist auch sehr lustig und immer glücklich. = My father is often busy, but he is also very funny and always happy.

Using words like 'very' or 'a bit' makes sentences more interesting

Try not to just say 'my sister is loud' — liven up your sentences a bit by saying whether she's very loud, sometimes loud or always loud. You'll sound much more impressive that way. Honest.

Relationships

OK, we're about to get all deep and meaningful here.
Tissues at the ready? Let's plough on...

Wir verstehen uns gut — We get on well

Now's your chance to pour out all your relationships woes in German.

not so well: nicht so gut

This is the dative case — see page 157 for more info.

Ich verstehe mich gut mit meiner Schwester. = I get on well with my sister.

This is a reflexive verb. If you don't know much about these, take a look at pages 199-200.

my brother:	meinem Bruder
my friend:	meinem Freund / meiner Freundin
my parents:	meinen Eltern

Remember, this can also mean boyfriend / girlfriend.

You can also say:

Ich komme gut mit meiner Schwester aus. = I get on well with my sister.

'Auskommen' is a separable verb. Take a look at pages 201-202 to find out more.

Ich streite mich oft mit meinem Bruder. = I often argue with my brother.

Wir streiten uns oft. = We often argue.

Get more marks, say **why**...

Really impress by saying why you do or don't get on with your loved ones...

Ich streite mich oft mit meinem Bruder, weil er so unordentlich ist. = I often argue with my brother because he's so untidy.

You can put any of the personality words from page 33 in the green box.

Use this lot to say how you get on with work or school mates too

OK, so this page might involve you thinking a bit, but once you've learnt a few key phrases you should be just fine. You know what I'm going to say: look, cover, scribble... Lovely jubbly.

Relationships and Future Plans

You might have to talk about different people's relationships with each other — as well as what your future relationship plans might be.

Ist er verheiratet? — Is he married?

Here's some more fancy stuff to learn...

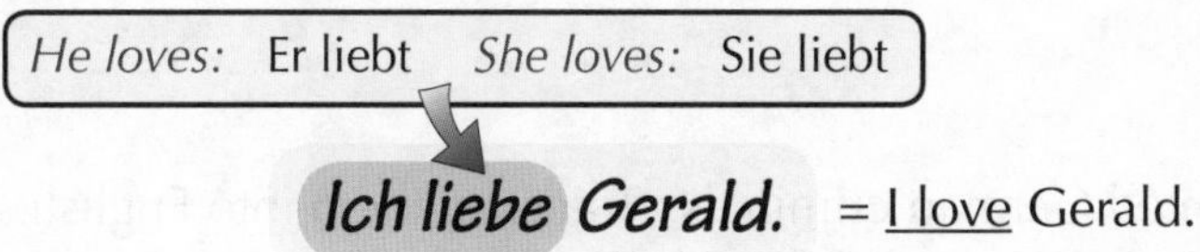

He loves: Er liebt *She loves:* Sie liebt
Ich liebe Gerald.

= I love Gerald.

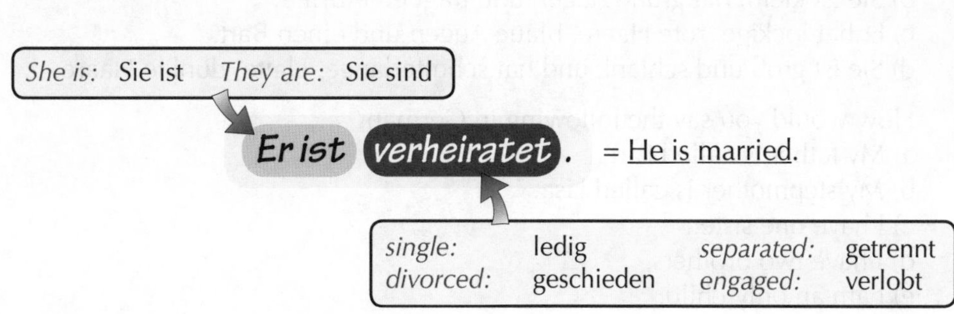

She is: Sie ist *They are:* Sie sind
Er ist verheiratet.
single: ledig *separated:* getrennt
divorced: geschieden *engaged:* verlobt

= He is married.

In der Zukunft — In the future

You need to be able to say what your relationship plans for the future are in German. If you don't have any yet, learn how to say so.

Ich möchte heiraten. = I would like to get married.

to get engaged:	mich verloben
to have a family:	eine Familie haben
to be in a relationship:	in einem Verhältnis sein

Im Moment, weiß ich nicht.

= At the moment, I don't know.

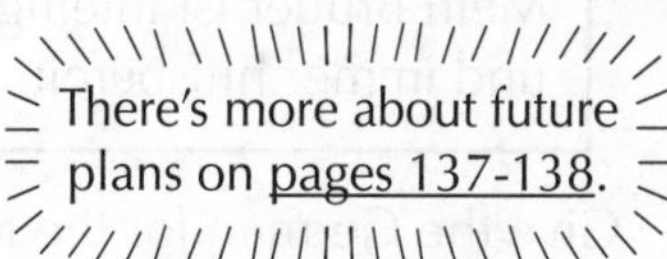

There's more about future plans on pages 137-138.

Get thinking about those future plans

Luckily, there's not too much vocab on this page — hoorah. You really just need to learn a few key phrases and you're sorted. Just make sure you get those sentence structures right.

Quick Questions

Time to find out if you've really been paying attention. You should be able to answer these questions, no probs. If not, go back and take another look at the bits you're struggling with.

Quick Questions

1) Answer the following questions in German:
a) Wie heißt du?
b) Wie alt bist du?
c) Wann hast du Geburtstag?
d) Wo wohnst du?
e) Was magst du?

2) Here are some descriptions of wanted German criminals. Translate them into English.
a) Er ist mittelgroß und dick.
b) Sie ist klein, hat grüne Augen und trägt eine Brille.
c) Er hat lockige, rote Haare, blaue Augen und einen Bart.
d) Sie ist groß und schlank und hat schulterlange, glatte, dunkle Haare.

3) How would you say the following in German?
a) My father is called Paul.
b) My stepmother is called Lisa.
c) I have one sister.
d) I have two brothers.
e) I am an only child.

4) Translate the following sentences into German:
a) I have a dog.
b) I have a cat.
c) I have a rabbit.
d) I have a guinea pig.

5) Write two or three sentences in German, describing members of your family or your pets.

6) Give the German for the following personality words:
a) nice
b) funny
c) friendly
d) stupid
e) disgusting
f) impolite

7) Anna is telling you about her family. Translate what she is saying into English.

> Ich habe eine kleine Schwester und einen älteren Bruder. Meine Schwester ist ein bisschen lästig, aber sie kann auch sehr goldig sein. Mein Bruder ist intelligent und ziemlich ernst, aber er ist sehr geduldig und immer hilfsbereit. Ich komme gut mit meinem Bruder aus.

8) Give the German for the following:
a) He loves Maria.
b) She is married.
c) He is single.
d) They are divorced.

9) Write a couple of sentences in German about your plans for the future.

Social Issues and Equality

Argh, social issues... Talking about them can seem daunting enough in your own language, let alone another one, but keep a cool head and don't start anything you can't finish.

Die Arbeitslosigkeit und die Obdachlosigkeit — Unemployment and Homelessness

There's not really very much that needs saying here. These things suck whichever way you look at it.

homeless people: Obdachlose
Es gibt viele Arbeitslose in meiner Stadt.
few: wenige
some: einige
area: Gegend
city: Großstadt

= There are lots of unemployed people in my town.

Homelessness: Die Obdachlosigkeit

Die Arbeitslosigkeit in Großbritannien ist ein großes Problem heutzutage.

no: kein

= Unemployment in Britain is a big problem nowadays.

Es geht mir auf die Nerven. = It gets on my nerves.

Young: Junge *Some:* Einige

Viele Leute haben ein Problem Arbeit zu finden.

= Many people have a problem finding work.

You might have to talk about topical subjects like this

This page covers a really important topic that examiners just love testing you on. It could come up anywhere from speaking and writing to reading and listening too, so make sure you learn this vocab.

Social Issues and Equality

Take a deep breath... I've a few more social issues for you to get your head around here...

Die Gleichberechtigung — Equal Opportunities

This is your chance for a good rant — in German of course.

unimportant: unwichtig

Ich halte Gleichberechtigung für sehr wichtig . = I think equal opportunities are very important.

nasty:	böse
unfriendly:	unfreundlich

am a girl:	ein Mädchen bin
wear glasses:	eine Brille trage
am foreign:	ausländisch bin

Manche Leute sind gemein zu mir, weil ich aus Indien komme .

= Some people are mean to me because I come from India.

For more countries see pages 79-80.

Useful Vocab

poverty:	die Armut
vandalism:	der Vandalismus
discrimination:	die Diskriminierung
AIDS:	das AIDS
violence:	die Gewalt
racism:	der Rassismus

unfair: unfair
sexist: sexistisch

Das ist rassistisch . = That's racist.

You can put any of the words from the Useful Vocab box above in here — you don't need the 'der/die/das' bit though.

Ich denke, dass Rassismus ein großes Problem in unserer Gesellschaft ist.

= I think that racism is a big problem in our society.

You really need to know this vocab

OK, I know this stuff isn't easy, but if you learn all the vocab on this page, then you'll be halfway there. Show off where you can, but don't make life too complicated. Stick to stuff you know you can say.

Feeling Unwell

You've got to be able to tell the doctor what's wrong with you. To do that, you've got to know the names of all the parts of your body in German. It's not hard, so get learning.

Der Körper — The body

Der Kopf — The head

Remember, plurals are always 'die'.

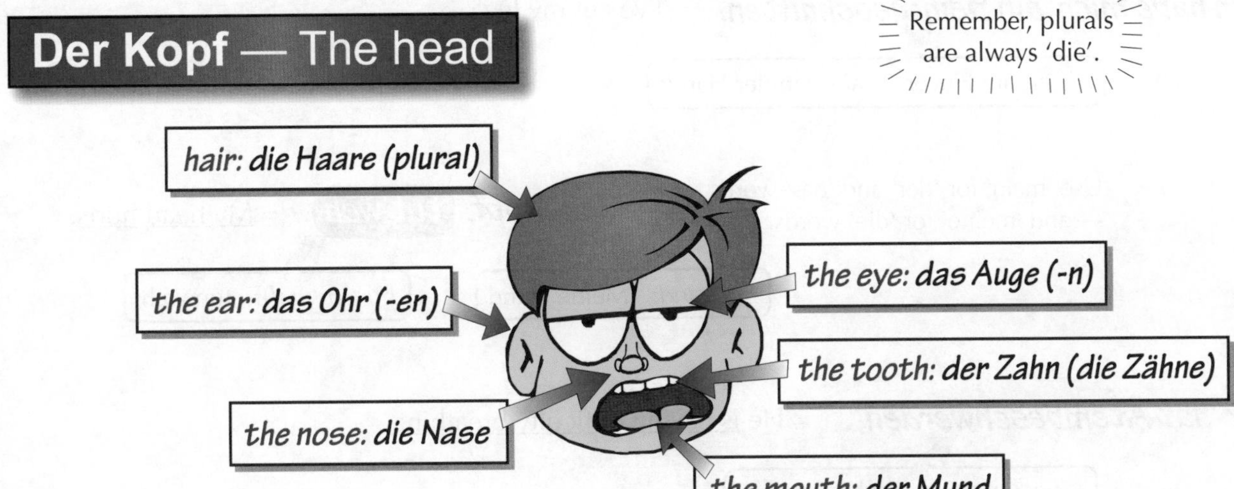

Make sure you learn the plurals too

When you think you know all those body parts, cover the page and scribble down a rough body picture with all the German words — with the der, die or das. Keep learning till you can get them all.

Feeling Unwell

Pain, illness and suffering... ah, it's all good fun. OK, roll your sleeves up and get stuck in.

Wie fühlen Sie sich? — How do you feel?

Mir ist schlecht. = I am ill.

hot:	heiß
cold:	kalt

The alternative words you can use in each sentence here are different.

Ich bin krank. = I am ill.

hungry:	hungrig
thirsty:	durstig
tired:	müde

Ich muss zum Arzt gehen. = I need to go to the doctor's.

to the hospital:	ins Krankenhaus	*to the chemists:*	zur Drogerie
to the pharmacy:	zur Apotheke	*to the dentist:*	zum Zahnarzt

Was ist los? — What's wrong?

If you want to say your stomach aches, you stick '-schmerzen' ('pains') on the end of the word for stomach and make one long word. Bauch+schmerzen = Bauchschmerzen.

Ich habe Bauchschmerzen. = I have stomach ache.

a headache:	Kopfschmerzen	*a stiff neck:*	einen steifen Hals
earache:	Ohrenschmerzen	*a sore throat:*	Halsschmerzen
flu:	die Grippe	*backache:*	Rückenschmerzen
a cold:	eine Erkältung	*a temperature:*	Fieber

The German words for neck and throat are the same — 'der Hals'. You need to learn the difference between 'Halsschmerzen' and 'ein steifer Hals'.

Ich habe mich am Bein geschnitten. = I've cut my leg.

finger: am Finger *hand:* an der Hand

Use 'mein' for 'der' and 'das' words — and 'meine' for 'die' words.

Mein Kopf tut weh. = My head hurts.

My hand: Meine Hand

hurt (plural): tun weh

Er hat Atembeschwerden. = He is having difficulty breathing.

is unconscious: ist bewusstlos

Say 'Mir ist heiß', not 'ich bin heiß'

It's not the most pleasant page in the world, but you've got to learn it.
You know the score — cover the page, scribble it down, and check you've got it right.

Health and Health Issues

First up, how to live a healthy lifestyle. Ah the joys of GCSE German. There's a fair bit to say on this topic, mind...

Diät — Diet

No, I'm not talking about any ridiculous lettuce-only, weight-loss diet. This is about your normal everyday diet and how healthy it is, or isn't.

Isst du gesund ? = Do you eat healthily?

unhealthily: ungesund

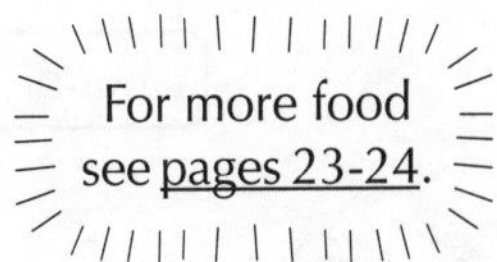
For more food
see pages 23-24.

NEIN!

Nein, ich esse Pommes fast jeden Tag und ich trinke nur Cola.

= No, I eat chips almost every day and I only drink cola.

Nein, ich bin wahrscheinlich ein bisschen übergewichtig.

= No, I'm probably a bit overweight.

JA!

organic food: Biokost

Ja, ich esse viel Salat und frisches Obst .

= Yes, I eat a lot of salad and fresh fruit.

Ja, ich mache eine relativ fettarme Diät.

= Yes, I'm on a relatively low fat diet.

Ja, ich versuche zu viel Fett und Zucker zu vermeiden.

= Yes, I try to avoid too much fat and sugar.

Bewegung — Exercise

It doesn't matter if you don't do any, just be able to say so.

For more sports see page 49.

Was machst du, um fit zu bleiben?

= What do you do to stay fit?

Ich treibe viel Sport. = I play a lot of sport.

Ich bin sehr aktiv und ich spiele regelmäßig Fußball und Tennis.

= I am very active and I regularly play football and tennis.

Ich mache oft Aerobic, weil es sehr gut für das Herz ist.

= I often do aerobics because it's very good for the heart.

Ich spiele Rugby gewöhnlich zweimal in der Woche.

= I usually play rugby twice a week.

There are more foods at the start of this section

There's loads you might want to say about these exciting things, but learning the stuff on this page is a good start. Think about what else you might want to say, write it down, and practise it.

Health and Health Issues

This bit's all about smoking, drugs, alcohol and rock 'n' roll. All right. I'm lying about the rock 'n' roll part. It's still pretty interesting though and you'll probably already have some sort of opinion on it.

Rauchen und Trinken — Smoking and drinking

Was ist deine Meinung über Rauchen ? = What do you think about smoking?

alcohol: Alkohol *drugs:* Drogen

Ich rauche nicht. = I don't smoke.

drink: trinke

Ich rauche gern. = I like to smoke.

Rauchen ist widerlich. Ich hasse es wenn andere rauchen, es stinkt so. Es verursacht auch Krebs. = Smoking is disgusting. I hate it when others smoke, it really stinks. It also causes cancer.

Rauchen ist cool. Mir ist es egal, ob es ungesund ist, Image ist alles. = Smoking is cool. I don't care if it is unhealthy, image is everything.

Ich rauche, aber ich würde nie Drogen nehmen, weil es zu gefährlich ist. = I smoke, but I would never take drugs because it's too dangerous.

Drogen — Drugs

drugs/narcotics are: Rauschgifte... sind *alcoholism is:* Alkoholismus... ist

Ich glaube, dass Drogen immer noch ein großes Problem in unserer Gesellschaft sind . = I think that drugs are still a big problem in our society.

an alcoholic: Alkoholiker

Man kann abhängig werden. = You can become dependent.

Man könnte eine Überdosis nehmen. = You could take an overdose.

Es gibt Drogenberatungsstellen. Hier kann man sich über Drogen und Entziehungskuren informieren. = There are drug advice centres. Here, you can get information about drugs and withdrawal treatments.

Don't be afraid to give your opinion

I admit, this page is pretty heavy going, but at least it's interesting. Again, there's plenty more to say about this lot — so get your thinking cap on. And learn as much of the tricky vocab as you can.

Quick Questions

Okey-doke, this is your last lot of Quick Questions before the Exam Practice. This doesn't mean you can just skim through them though — you need to make sure you're <u>really comfortable</u> answering <u>every single one</u> before you move on.

Quick Questions

1) Give the German for the following:
   a) homelessness
   b) unemployment
   c) discrimination
   d) poverty
   e) violence
2) Translate these sentences into German:
   a) Young people have a problem finding work.
   b) I think equal opportunities are very important.
   c) AIDS is a big problem nowadays.
   d) I think that vandalism is a big problem in my town.
   e) That's unfair. It gets on my nerves.
3) Give the names of the following body parts in English:
   a) der Rücken
   b) der Hals
   c) die Zehen
   d) das Knie
   e) das Ohr
4) Give the names of the following body parts in German:
   a) the head
   b) the stomach
   c) the leg
   d) the hand
   e) the mouth
5) How would you say the following in German?
   a) I am ill.
   b) I am hot.
   c) I am thirsty.
   d) I need to go to the hospital.
   e) I need to go to the dentist.
6) You're on a school trip to Germany and just about everyone has something the matter with them. Translate these sentences into English to find out what.
   a) Meine Beine tun weh.
   b) Ich habe Halsschmerzen.
   c) Ich habe die Grippe und Fieber.
   d) Ich habe mich an der Nase geschnitten.
7) You decide to do a survey into the lifestyle of the average German teenager. Translate the answers you're given into English.
   a) Ich esse nur Biokost und mache Aerobic zweimal in der Woche.
   b) Ich esse viel Obst und Gemüse und ich treibe regelmäßig Sport.
   c) Ich versuche Pommes zu vermeiden und ich bin ziemlich aktiv.
   d) Ich bin ein bisschen übergewichtig. Ich spiele keinen Sport.
   e) Ich trinke nicht, aber manchmal rauche ich. Ich würde nie Drogen nehmen.
   f) Ich trinke nie, weil mein Onkel Alkoholiker ist.

Listening Questions

Track 3

1 Karin is talking about her family.

She says that her brother is:

A patient **B** moody **C** friendly

Write the correct letter in the box. ☐

Track 4

2 Andreas and Maria are both ill.

A **B** **C** **D**

What is the matter with each of them? Write the correct letters in the boxes.

Andreas: ☐

Maria: ☐

Track 5

3 Peter is talking to his exchange partner's mum about dinner this evening.

Example: What time is dinner?

six o'clock

a) What doesn't Peter like to eat?

....

b) Which vegetables does he particularly like?

....

c) What does he want for dessert?

....

Reading Question

OK, a nice, straightforward Reading Question for you to have a go at here.

1 Kurt is writing about himself.

Grüße! Ich heiße Kurt und ich bin fünfzehn Jahre alt. Mein Geburtstag ist am neunten Juli. Ich bin mittelgroß, mit roten welligen Haaren und blauen Augen und ich trage eine Brille. Ich interessiere mich für Sport und spiele Fußball dreimal in der Woche. Meistens bin ich freundlich und hilfsbereit, aber manchmal kann ich ungeduldig sein.

Ich wohne mit meiner Familie an der Küste in Norddeutschland. Mein Stiefvater arbeitet als Apotheker in der Stadt. Meine Mutter ist Geschäftsfrau und arbeitet zu Hause. Ich habe eine Stiefschwester, die Laura heißt, und sie wohnt auch bei uns. Laura ist achtzehn Jahre alt und studiert sehr ernst für ihre Prüfungen. Sie ist klein und schlank und hat lockige, blonde Haare.

glasses a moustache impatient wavy businesswoman

eighteen a beard housewife impolite serious irresponsible

lazy ~~fifteen~~ chemist curly friendly sixteen

Complete the sentences with the words or phrases from the box.

Example: Kurt is ***fifteen*** years old.

a) Kurt has ....

Remember: use the questions to help you understand the text.

b) He can sometimes be ....

c) His mum is a ....

d) His stepsister is a .... student.

e) Laura's hair is blonde and ....

Speaking Question

So, for your speaking assessment, you could well find yourself having to talk about some aspect of a healthy lifestyle. Get some practice by having a go at this task. Remember, the unseen question will be on a related topic — so think about what it might be when you're preparing your answers.

Task: Health
You are visiting your pen friend's school.
You are being interviewed for the school newspaper for an article on health.
Your teacher will play the part of the reporter.

Your teacher will ask you the following:
- Do you eat healthily?
- How could you improve your diet?
- Are you a vegetarian? Why/why not?
- When were you last ill? What was wrong?
- What do you do to keep fit?
- Do you drink alcohol?
- Do you smoke?
- !

! Remember that the exclamation mark means you'll have to answer a question that you won't have prepared an answer to.

The whole conversation should last about five minutes.

Notes for Teachers
You need to ask the student the following questions:
- Isst du gesund?
- Wie könntest du besser essen?
- Bist du Vegetarier(in)? Warum/warum nicht?
- Wann warst du zum letzten Mal krank? Was war los?
- Was machst du, um fit zu bleiben?
- Trinkst du Alkohol?
- Rauchst du?
- !

! The unpredictable question could be: Was denkst du über Drogen?

Writing Questions

Ah, the writing task — always a favourite. Have a go at these two little gems. And remember to write in full sentences please — you'll get marks for the accuracy of your grammar.

Task 1: You have been asked by your exchange school to write an article for their school paper about social problems in your home town.

You could write about the following:

- Unemployment
- Homelessness
- Racial problems
- What there is to do for young people
- Problems with drugs / alcohol
- What you would do to improve your home town

Remember: to score the highest marks you need to answer the task fully (for grades C and above you will need to write 200-300 words).

Task 2: Your pen friend is doing a survey of teenagers. He has asked you to help him by writing about your relationships with others.

You could write about the following:

- How you get on with family members
- How you get on with teachers at school
- How you get on with your classmates
- Your social life
- What you could do to improve your life / relationships

Remember: to score the highest marks you need to answer the task fully (for grades C and above you will need to write 200-300 words).

Revision Summary

The idea isn't that you just do these questions and stop. To really make sure you've learnt this stuff, you need to go back through the section and look up the ones you couldn't do. Then try them all again. Your aim is to eventually be able to glide through them all with the greatest of ease.

1) You're making a fruit salad for a party. Think of the German words for as many fruits as you can to put in it — at least 5. Make a list of 5 drinks you could offer people at the party.

2) Write down how you'd say that you like vegetables but don't like sausage. Also that you're very hungry.

3) You're staying with a German family. Thank your hosts for the meal, say you enjoyed it and it was delicious. Offer to pass your hostess the milk (remember to use the right form of 'you').

4) You're telling your host family about your home life. Say that you make your bed and sometimes vacuum and clean at home. You have breakfast at 8 o'clock and lunch at 1 o'clock.

5) Introduce yourself to someone in German. Tell them your name, age and when your birthday is.

6) In German, describe three of your friends and say how old they are. Spell out loud their names and the names of the towns where they live.

7) Tell your German pen friend what relations you have — including how many aunts, cousins etc.

8) Your animal-loving friend has six rabbits, a budgie, a guinea pig and two cats. How will she say what these are in her German speaking assessment?

9) Describe in German the personalities of two of your family members. Say how well you get on with them.

10) A German news reporter asks your opinion on unemployment in the UK. What would you say to them?

11) Say in German that you feel ill. You have a temperature and your arms, back and legs hurt.

12) Do you play a lot of sport? Why? Why not? Write down how you'd explain this to your German friend.

13) What's your opinion on smoking? Give your answer in German.

Sports and Hobbies

Lots of useful vocab here. Look back to this page if you need to know the name of a sport.

Treibst du Sport? — Do you do any sport?

Quite a lot of the stuff you'll be expected to say about yourself will be to do with sport. Even if you're no demon on the pitch, you need to be good at talking about it.

Verbs for outdoor sports

to fish:	angeln	*to ski:*	Ski fahren
to go out:	ausgehen	*to go for a walk:*	spazieren gehen
to run:	laufen	*to play:*	spielen
to cycle:	Rad fahren	*to walk, hike:*	wandern
to swim:	schwimmen	*to jog:*	joggen

Names of sports

badminton:	das Badminton
football:	der Fußball
tennis:	das Tennis
table tennis:	das Tischtennis
squash:	das Squash
hockey:	das Hockey

Usually when you talk about sports you just say their name, e.g. 'Fußball', not 'der Fußball'.

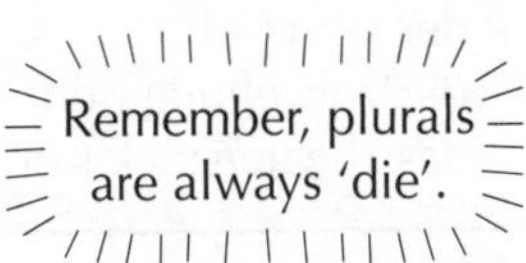

Remember, plurals are always 'die'.

Places you can do sports

fitness centre:	das Fitnesszentrum (-zentren)
open-air pool:	das Freibad (die Freibäder)
swimming pool:	das Schwimmbad (die Schwimmbäder)
indoor swimming pool:	das Hallenbad (die Hallenbäder)
sports field:	der Sportplatz (die Sportplätze)
sports centre:	das Sportzentrum (die Sportzentren)
bowling alley:	die Kegelbahn (-en)
park:	der Park (-s)

Get thinking about what sports you play and when you play them:

Ich spiele am Wochenende Fußball. = I play football at the weekend.

every day:	jeden Tag
every week:	jede Woche
twice a month:	zweimal im Monat

badminton:	Badminton
tennis:	Tennis

For more about times, see pages 4-6.

Don't just learn the sports you do — you'll need to know them all

This is dead important. Cover up the German bits and scribble down the ones you know. Then look back, find out the ones you don't know and try again... and again... and again...

Sports and Hobbies

There are plenty of <u>other things</u> to do apart from sports...

Hast du ein Hobby? — Do you have a hobby?

Learn this <u>dead handy</u> vocab:

General but vital

hobby:	das Hobby (-s)
interest:	das Interesse (-n)
fan (supporter):	der Fan (-s)
club:	der Club / Klub (-s)
member:	das Mitglied (-er)
game:	das Spiel (-e)

Verbs for indoor activities

to meet:	(sich) treffen
to dance:	tanzen
to sing:	singen
to collect:	sammeln
to bowl:	kegeln
to read:	lesen

To see how to use verbs with different people, see <u>pages 187-195</u>.

Musical instruments

violin:	die Geige
flute:	die Querflöte
drums:	das Schlagzeug
clarinet:	die Klarinette
guitar:	die Gitarre
trumpet:	die Trompete
piano:	das Klavier
cello:	das Cello

Musical words

band, group:	die Band (-s)
CD:	die CD (-s)
instrument:	das Instrument (-e)
cassette:	die Kassette (-n)
concert:	das Konzert (-e)
stereo:	die Stereoanlage (-n)

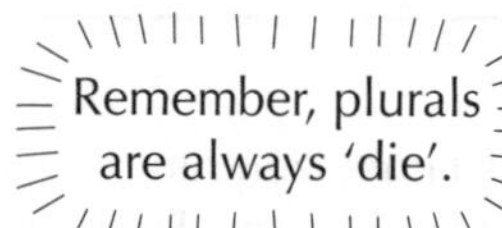

Other important nouns

chess:	das Schach
film:	der Film (-e)
performance:	die Vorstellung (-en)
play (in a theatre):	das Theaterstück (-e)

Was machst du in deiner Freizeit? — What do you do in your free time?

You'll get asked this question <u>a lot</u> — so <u>learn it</u>.

Put any of the instruments above in here.

Ich spiele Klavier. = I play the <u>piano</u>.

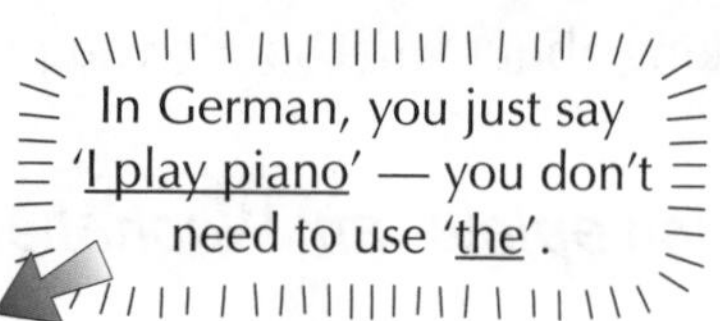

In German, you just say 'I play piano' — you don't need to use 'the'.

Ich bin Mitglied eines Tennisklubs. = I'm a member of a <u>tennis club</u>.

chess club:	Schachklubs
squash club:	Squashklubs

The '<u>-s</u>' on '<u>-klubs</u>' isn't to make a plural — it's the <u>genitive case</u> (see <u>pages 157 and 159</u>). This is a little bit tricky because the plural of 'der Klub' is also 'Klubs' — be careful.

Make revision your new hobby

Right-o, more things to learn. Get your head round how to say <u>what you do</u> in your free time and what <u>hobbies</u> you have. And <u>don't forget</u> to learn how to say <u>when</u> you do them.

Sports and Hobbies

Those examiners like to know your opinion on everything — sports and hobbies are no different. Learn this page — it could come in pretty handy in your speaking assessments and writing tasks.

Wie findest du Fußball? — What do you think of football?

Here's how to say what you think of different hobbies — learn these phrases.

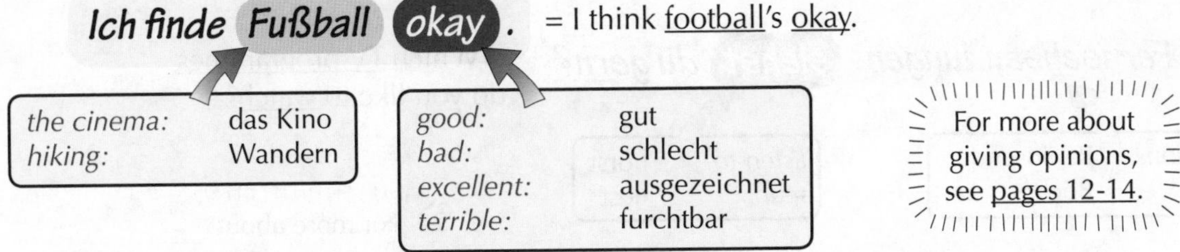

Ich finde Fußball okay. = I think football's okay.
the cinema: das Kino
hiking: Wandern
good: gut
bad: schlecht
excellent: ausgezeichnet
terrible: furchtbar

For more about giving opinions, see pages 12-14.

Put 'gern' here if you like doing something, or 'nicht gern' if you don't.

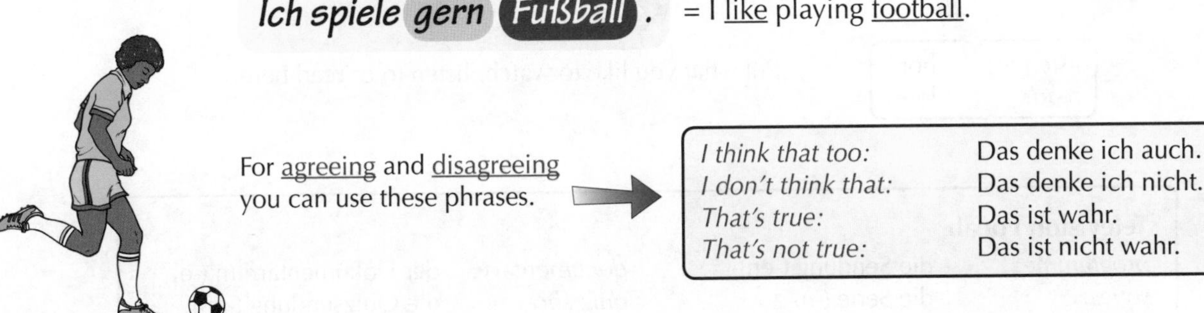

Ich spiele gern Fußball. = I like playing football.
For agreeing and disagreeing you can use these phrases.
I think that too: Das denke ich auch.
I don't think that: Das denke ich nicht.
That's true: Das ist wahr.
That's not true: Das ist nicht wahr.

Warum denkst du das? — Why do you think that?

You'll really impress the examiners if you can back up your opinion with a reason why.

difficult: schwierig
tiring: anstrengend
interesting: interessant
exciting: aufregend
Ich jogge nicht gern, weil es langweilig ist. = I don't like jogging because it's boring.
like: gern

For more on using 'weil' see page 14.

You need to be able to give an opinion — and not just on football

You might well be asked to say what you think about a range of hobbies — not just the ones you do. So make sure you've got a fair few different opinions (both positive and negative) up your sleeve.

Television

A nice easy page about television for you here. Lovely.

Meine Lieblingssendung ist... — My favourite programme is...

You've probably got quite a bit to say about television — here's how to do it auf Deutsch.

Welche Fernsehsendungen siehst du gern? = Which TV programmes do you like to watch?

radio stations:	Radiosender
books:	Bücher

listen to:	hörst
read:	liest

For more about giving opinions, see pages 12-14.

Ich sehe gern Westenders. = I like to watch Westenders.

listen to:	höre
read:	lese

Put what you like to watch, listen to or read here.

Television vocab

programme:	die Sendung (-en)	*documentary:*	der Dokumentarfilm (-e)
series:	die Serie (-n)	*quiz show:*	die Quizsendung (-en)
weather report:	der Wetterbericht (-e)	*comedy:*	die Komödie (-n)
news:	die Nachrichten (plural)	*cartoon:*	der Zeichentrickfilm (-e)
soap opera:	die Seifenoper (-n)	*feature film:*	der Spielfilm (-e)

Remember, plurals are always 'die'.

Wann fängt sie an? — When does it start?

Die Sendung fängt um acht Uhr an und endet um halb zehn.

= The programme starts at 8 o'clock and finishes at half past nine.

For more on telling the time, see page 4.

Learn this vocab — you never know when you might need it

OK, so it turns out that talking about television in German isn't quite as much fun as actually watching it in real life. But (you guessed it) you've got to learn it anyway. Better get cracking.

Film and Television

OK, start paying attention — this page covers explaining the kind of things you've done recently and giving your opinion on films, books and TV programmes.

Was hast du neulich gemacht? — What have you done recently?

This past tense stuff is really important — to get top marks, you have to be able to use it. See pages 192-194 for more info.

last week:	letzte Woche
two weeks ago:	vor zwei Wochen
a month ago:	vor einem Monat

heard:	gehört
read:	gelesen

Ich habe neulich Godzilla gesehen. = I saw Godzilla recently.

the new song by Antarctic Apes:	das neue Lied von Antarctic Apes
a great book:	ein tolles Buch

For more about times and dates, see pages 4-6.

Wie fandest du den Film? — What did you think of the film?

You're bound to get asked for your opinion at some point — so get learning these little gems... There's more on giving opinions on pages 12-14.

Was hielst du vom Film? = What did you think of the film?

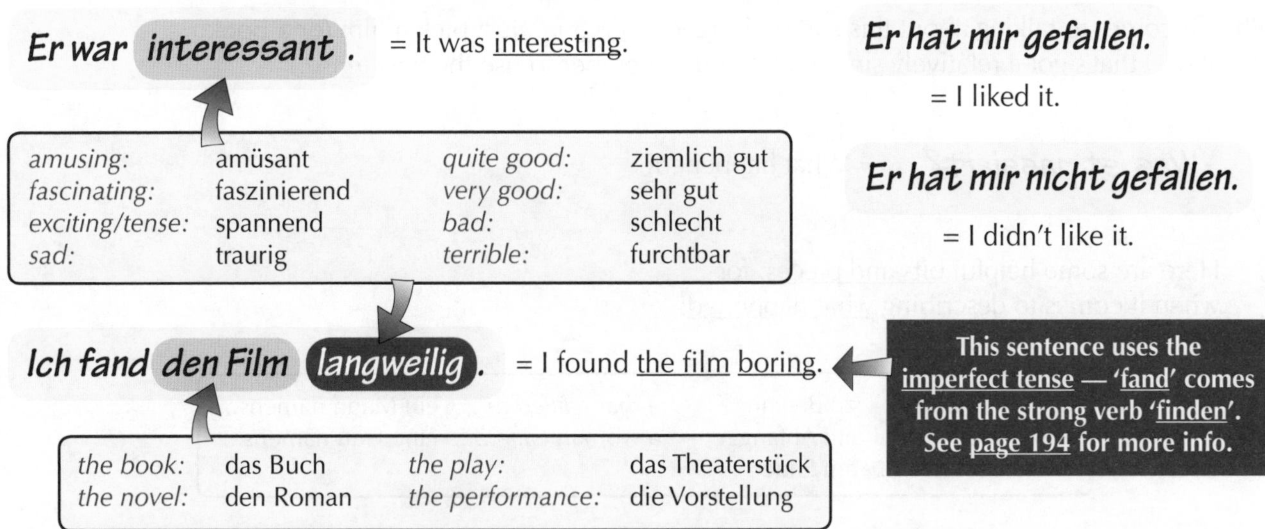

Er war interessant. = It was interesting.
amusing: amüsant
fascinating: faszinierend
exciting/tense: spannend
sad: traurig
quite good: ziemlich gut
very good: sehr gut
bad: schlecht
terrible: furchtbar
Er hat mir gefallen.
= I liked it.
Er hat mir nicht gefallen.
= I didn't like it.
Ich fand den Film langweilig. = I found the film boring.
This sentence uses the imperfect tense — 'fand' comes from the strong verb 'finden'. See page 194 for more info.
the book: das Buch
the novel: den Roman
the play: das Theaterstück
the performance: die Vorstellung

When you use the past tense, make sure you get it right

The past tense and giving opinions are ultra-important topics in GCSE German — which makes learning this page ultra-important too. If you need help, check out the grammar section at the end of this book.

Talking About the Plot

It could be last night's Westenders episode or the twists and turns of the last book you read, but you might well get asked to talk about the plot.

Welche Filme hast du neulich gesehen?

— Which films have you watched recently?

Another great opportunity to practise using the past tense. If you need some help, see pages 192-194.

Letzte Woche habe ich 'Pirates of the Mediterranean' gesehen.

= I saw 'Pirates of the Mediterranean' last week.

Was für ein Film ist das? = What sort of film is that?

Das ist ein Abenteuerfilm. = It is an adventure film.

a horror film:	ein Horrorfilm
a comedy:	eine Komödie
a romance:	ein Liebesfilm *(literally: a love film)*
a crime drama:	ein Krimi
a love story:	eine Liebesgeschichte

Kannst du den Film beschreiben?

— Can you describe the film?

When it comes to talking about this sort of thing, don't panic. Just pick a film (or a book, or a play...) that's got a relatively simple plot and remember to use the past tense.

Was ist passiert? = What happened?

Here are some helpful bits and pieces, for when it comes to describing what happened:

at the beginning:	zu Beginn	*a man called...:*	ein Mann namens...
at the start:	am Anfang	*a woman called...:*	eine Frau namens...
at the end:	am Ende		

Using the past tense properly will grab you loads of marks

Learn the vocab on this page — even if it doesn't come up in a speaking assessment or writing task, you could well end up with, say, a film review in your reading exam. This little lot will come in handy then.

Quick Questions

There's been quite a bit of vocab to learn on these last few pages — and the best way to make sure you know it all is to test yourself. I've put in these lovely Quick Questions to help you. So get to it.

Quick Questions

1) Give the German for:
   a) football
   b) badminton
   c) table tennis
   d) squash
   e) hockey
2) How would you say 'I go for a walk every day' in German?
3) Name three places you can do sport. Give the names in German.
4) Translate the following into English:
   a) Zweimal im Monat spiele ich Tennis mit meinem Freund im Sportzentrum.
   b) Am Wochenende fahre ich im Park Rad.
   c) Ich schwimme jeden Tag im Hallenbad.
   d) Abends laufe ich auf dem Sportplatz.
5) Give the German for:
   a) violin
   b) flute
   c) guitar
   d) piano
6) Tell your German pen friend that you play the clarinet.
7) Now tell your friend that you're a member of a film club.
8) Your friend asks you what you think of chess.
   Tell him (in German) that you think chess is excellent.
9) Your friend disagrees. How would he say 'I don't think that'?
10) How would you say 'I don't like playing squash because it's tiring' in German?
11) Translate the following into English:
   a) Ich sehe gern Zeichentrickfilme.
   b) Ich höre gern eine Seifenoper im Radio.
   c) Die Nachrichten fangen um sechs Uhr an.
   d) Der Wetterbericht endet um halb sieben.
12) How would you say 'I read a great book last week' in German?
13) Give the German for:
   a) an adventure film
   b) a romance
   c) a horror film
   d) a crime drama
14) Translate this short film review into German:

> Last weekend I saw 'The Adventures of George and Betty'.
> It's a comedy about a man called George and a woman
> called Betty. It was amusing. I liked it.

Music

Whether it's Kylie or Bach, everybody likes a bit of music. You need to be able to talk about your musical preferences, as well as saying where and when you listen to it.

Was für Musik magst du? — What sort of music do you like?

This bit's about giving your opinion again.
Try and find something a bit interesting to say and jazz up those sentences.

For more about giving opinions, see pages 12-14.

Ich höre gern Popmusik. = I like listening to pop music.

rock music:	Rockmusik
rap music:	Rapmusik
modern music:	moderne Musik

Volksmusik gefällt mir nicht. = I don't like folk music.

Ich spiele klassische Musik am Klavier, aber ich höre lieber modernere Musik. = I play classical music on the piano, but I prefer listening to more modern music.

Like in English, you can add '-er' onto the end of an adjective to mean 'more', e.g. small → smaller, klein → kleiner — 'moderner' just means 'more modern' (the extra '-e' on the end is because 'Musik' is feminine). See page 175.

Wo magst du Musik hören? — Where do you like listening to music?

This is all about how and where you listen to music. Easy peasy.

on my iPod®:	auf meinem iPod®
on my MP3 player:	auf meinem Mp3-Player/Mp3-Spieler
on CD:	auf CD

Examiners will love it if you talk about the latest technologies.

Ich höre gern Musik im Radio, wenn ich in meinem Zimmer bin. = I like listening to music on the radio when I'm in my room.

in the shower:	in der Dusche
in the car:	im Auto

Try and make your sentences as original as possible

Tip: if you happen to have heard any German pop music then say so. Not only does it make life more interesting, the examiners will be over the moon that you've taken an interest in German culture.

Famous People

You might not want to discuss celebrities with your German exchange partner, but you could end up talking about them with your teacher in a speaking assessment. This page'll give you a few tips.

Welche berühmten Persönlichkeiten findest du gut? — Which celebrities do you like?

Talking about celebrities and famous people you admire mostly involves all the same old straightforward stuff that you need to talk about yourself and your family.
Start with their name, then what they do, and follow that up with why you like them.

WHO

Put the name of the person you like here.

Meine Lieblingssängerin ist Beyoncé. = My favourite (female) singer is Beyoncé.

my favourite (male) singer:	Mein Lieblingssänger
my favourite group:	Meine Lieblingsgruppe
my favourite actor:	Mein Lieblingsschauspieler
my favourite actress:	Meine Lieblingsschauspielerin

For more about giving opinions, see pages 12-14.

Ich finde Beyoncé fantastisch. = I think Beyoncé is fantastic.

Sie ist eine berühmte amerikanische Popsängerin.
= She is a famous American pop singer.

Beyoncé sieht so hübsch aus und trägt immer schicke modische Klamotten.
= Beyoncé looks so pretty and always wears smart trendy clothes.

Noch dazu singt sie wie ein Engel. = She sings like an angel as well.

Sie ist meine absolute Heldin. = She is my absolute heroine.

Always back up your opinions with a reason why

This doesn't have to be too complicated. You probably already know how to describe family and friends, and this is pretty much the same thing. If you're stuck, see pages 31 and 33 for a few pointers.

Famous People

Celebrities are often role models for young people. You may be expected to have an opinion on this and the role the media plays in the whole cult of celebrity.

Der Einfluss berühmter Persönlichkeiten — The influence of celebrities

Sollten berühmte Persönlichkeiten als positive Beispiele für junge Leute dienen? = Should celebrities serve as positive examples for young people?

JA!

Sicher. Sie sind erfolgreiche Menschen. = Of course. They are successful people.

Sie sind Vorbilder für viele Jugendliche. = They are role models for a lot of young people.

Man kann sie bewundern. = You can admire them.

NEIN!

Keineswegs. Sie sind gar keine normale Menschen. = No way. They aren't normal people.

Manche Mädchen glauben sie müssen so dünn wie die 'Supermodels' sein. Dann kommen oft Probleme mit Magersucht oder Bulimie vor. = Some girls think they have to be as thin as the 'Supermodels'. Then problems with anorexia or bulimia often occur.

Pretty useful vocab: Relativ nützliche Vokabeln

famous:	bekannt / berühmt	*celebrity (person):*	die berühmte Persönlichkeit
pop singer:	Popsänger / Popsängerin	*responsibility:*	die Verantwortung
on the stage:	auf der Bühne	*hero / heroine:*	Held / Heldin
anorexia:	die Magersucht	*the media (plural):*	die Medien
bulimia:	die Bulimie	*influence:*	der Einfluss
role model:	das Vorbild (-er)	*admire:*	bewundern
example:	das Beispiel (-e)	*responsible:*	verantwortlich
actor / actress:	Schauspieler / Schauspielerin	*occur:*	vorkommen

This sort of thing could come up in a speaking assessment...

... or even a writing task. If it does, don't panic. Again, you don't have to make life too complicated for yourself — but you could use it as a chance to really show off all that vocab you've been learning.

New Technology

Computers are taking over the world, or so they say.
They'll almost definitely be cropping up somewhere in GCSE German.

Computer und das Internet — Computers and the internet

It's a good idea to be able to talk about what you use computers for...

Ich habe eine Website für meinen Schachclub gemacht. = I have made a website for my chess club.

my football team:	meine Fußballmannschaft
my band:	meine Band

Ich will meine Fotos downloaden. = I want to download my photos.

download:	herunterladen
upload:	hochladen

Ich surfe im Internet. = I surf the internet.

Wir chatten über MSN®. = We chat over MSN®.

Your writing task might involve you writing a blog:

You can also just say 'ein Blog'.

Ich schreibe ein Online-Tagebuch seit zwei Jahren.

= I've been writing a blog for two years.

Here's some more useful vocab for you:

Computer hardware

computer:	der Computer
printer:	der Drucker
screen/monitor:	der Bildschirm
keyboard:	die Tastatur

Internet-speak

website:	die Website
webpage:	die Webseite / die Internetseite
server:	der Server
search engine:	die Suchmaschine

Technology's no substitute for good, old-fashioned learning

Make sure you can say what you use computers for. The stuff on this page could come in pretty useful when you're talking about what you do in your spare time too — so learn it well.

New Technology

More opinions I'm afraid, as well as a little bit about text messaging.

Technologie: Vorteile und Nachteile — Technology: Advantages and Disadvantages

There are lots of things you can say about the pros and cons of computers.
Here are a few to get you started:

Computer sind wirklich nützlich. Ohne Computer könnte ich meine Schularbeit nicht machen.

= Computers are really useful. Without a computer I couldn't do my schoolwork.

Computer können viel Zeit sparen. = Computers can save a lot of time.

Man kann zu viel Zeit vor dem Computer verbringen. Es ist nicht gut für die Gesundheit.

= You can spend too much time in front of the computer. It's not good for your health.

Simsen — To text — eine SMS — A text message

Text messages could crop up anywhere. You might get asked to write a text message in one of your writing tasks, or read one in the reading exam.

If you do get asked to write a text, don't panic. You probably send them all the time in English — just think about the sort of things you'd normally say to your friends and remember to use the informal 'du'.

The same goes for e-mails (see page 61).

16:04
Hallo Berta. Wie geht's? Möchtest du heute Abend mit mir ins Kino gehen? Der neue Film von Danny Kraig beginnt um 20h00. Bis später. Alex.

=

16:04

Hello Berta. How's it going? Do you want to go to the cinema with me tonight? The new Danny Kraig film starts at 8 o'clock. See you later. Alex.

Learn these words, they might come in handy:

text message:	die SMS, die (SMS-)Mitteilung
mobile phone:	das Handy

Don't be afraid to come up with a few pros and cons of your own

You're probably familiar with the arguments for and against modern technology — just think about what you'd say in English. Oh, and don't try and use text speak in your writing assessment or the exam.

E-mail and Blogging

Ah, the joys of digital communication. Exam boards like to move with the times, so here's a bit about blogging and electronic-post. Great stuff.

Ich möchte eine E-Mail senden — I would like to send an e-mail

Ich werde eine E-Mail schicken. = I'm going to send an e-mail.

my inbox: meinen Posteingang

Ich muss meine E-Mails abrufen.
Darf ich deinen Computer benutzen, bitte?

= I need to check my e-mails. Please may I use your computer?

Some more useful words to look out for when e-mailing:

sender:	der Absender	*attachment:*	der Anhang
subject:	der Betreff	*reply, reply to all:*	antworten, allen antworten

You can write an e-mail in pretty much the same way as an informal letter — see page 15.

Ich blogg, du bloggst... — I blog, you blog...

A blog is basically just 'a day in the life of...'. Here's an example to get you started:

Cumbria den 11. Mai 22h15

Heute habe ich einen tollen Tag gehabt. Ich bin mit meinen Freunden ins Kino gegangen und wir haben den neuen Film von Danny Kraig gesehen. Normalerweise mag ich keine Abenteuerfilme, aber er war eigentlich sehr lustig. Ich würde diesen Film bestimmt empfehlen!

Cumbria 11th May 22h15

Today I've had a great day. I went to the cinema with my friends and we saw the new Danny Kraig film. Normally I don't like adventure films, but it was actually very funny. I would definitely recommend this film!

This blog is written (mainly) in the perfect tense.
See pages 192-193 for help.

You'll probably come across e-mails quite a bit

This is the sort of stuff that might appear in one of your writing tasks, so it's important you're familiar with it. Be warned though: your e-mail, text or blog could be about a whole host of different topics.

Shopping

This is bread-and-butter stuff and you really have to know it. Basically, if you learn this stuff, you'll be able to use it when it comes up.

Wo ist...? — Where is...?

A dead useful question — and luckily the word order is the same in English and German.

Wo ist der Supermarkt, bitte? = Where is the supermarket, please?

the butcher's:	die Metzgerei (-en)
the bakery:	die Bäckerei (-en)
the grocer's:	der Lebensmittelgeschäft (-e)
the greengrocer's:	der Gemüsehändler (-)

Remember, plurals are always 'die'.

Wann...? — When...?

To say when a shop is open or closed, you need these handy little phrases. Chances are they'll come up at some point — so make sure you know them like the back of your hand.

Wann hat der Supermarkt auf? = When is the supermarket open?

...Or any other shop.

shut: zu

These verbs are separable — see pages 201-202 for more info.

Wann macht der Supermarkt zu? = When does the supermarket close?

open: auf

For times, see page 4.

Der Supermarkt macht um neunzehn Uhr zu. = The supermarket closes at 7:00 pm.

Andere Läden — Other shops

The words 'der Laden' and 'das Geschäft' both mean 'shop'.
You'll often find them stuck to other words telling you what type of shop it is.

pharmacy:	die Apotheke (-n)
chemist's:	die Drogerie (-n)
bookshop:	die Buchhandlung (-en)
stationer's:	die Schreibwarenhandlung (-en)
department store:	das Kaufhaus (die Kaufhäuser) das Warenhaus (die Warenhäuser)
fishmonger's:	der Fischladen (die Fischläden)
market:	der Markt (die Märkte)
electrical shop:	das Elektrogeschäft (-e)
cake shop:	die Konditorei (-en)
shopping centre:	das Einkaufszentrum (-zentren)

Note: you pick up prescriptions from the Apotheke, but buy your toothpaste from the Drogerie.

If you need help with asking questions, see Section 1

Asking where things are and when they open isn't too difficult, so get those questions learnt.
Try and remember as many of those shops as possible too — they could well come up in an exam.

Shopping

Lots of useful shopping-related vocab for you to get your teeth into here.
First up, how to talk about your shopping habits...

Ich gehe gern einkaufen — I like going shopping

Ich gehe einmal pro Woche einkaufen. = I go shopping once a week.

Ich kaufe oft in der Bäckerei ein. = I often shop in the bakery.

Ich kaufe besonders gern Bücher ein. = I particularly like shopping for books.

You'll need this sales vocab if you want to grab yourself a bargain:

IMPORTANT: In German, 'per cent' is 'Prozent'. So, '10% reduction' = 'zehn Prozent Ermäßigung'.

Sales vocab

end-of-season sale:	der Schlussverkauf (die Schlussverkäufe)
special offer:	das Sonderangebot (-e)
reduction:	die Ermäßigung (-en)
sale:	der Ausverkauf (die Ausverkäufe)

And just in case you want to ask for your money back at the end of it all...

Ich hätte gern mein Geld für dieses Hemd zurück.

= I'd like a refund on this shirt.

Deutsches Geld — German money

German money's easy. There are 100 cents in a euro, like there are 100 pence in a pound.

This is what you'd see on a German price tag:

This is how you'd say the price: *'Fünf Euro fünfzig Cent'* = 5 euros 50 cents

See page 2 for numbers.

It pays to get your head around German money

Lots of bits and pieces here, I know. The thing is they're all really useful — so make sure you're prepared for anything and learn them properly. You'll thank me for it in the long run. Honest.

Shopping

More important phrases that you might well need to know. They're not difficult — and the standard questions and answers will save you having to think.

Ich möchte... — I would like...

You'll be using this all the time. You should be pretty comfortable with 'Ich möchte' by now.

Ich möchte ein großes Stück Brot , bitte. = I'd like a big piece of bread, please.

Another good way to say 'I would like' is 'Ich hätte gern'.

Ich hätte gern eine Tüte Bonbons , bitte. = I'd like a bag of sweets, please.

Kann ich Ihnen helfen? — Can I help you?

Ich hätte gern fünfhundert Gramm Zucker, bitte. = I'd like 500 g of sugar, please.

1 kg: ein Kilo
2 kg: zwei Kilo

1. You don't need to make words like 'Gramm' and 'Kilo' plural. Just say, 'Ein Kilo...', 'Zwei Kilo...' and so on.
2. In German, you can also just say '500 g sugar' — you don't need to use 'of'.

Useful vocab

several:	mehrere
a dozen:	ein Dutzend
a tin/box of:	eine Dose
a bottle of:	eine Flasche
a jar of:	ein Glas
a slice of:	eine Scheibe
a piece of:	ein Stück
a bag of:	eine Tüte
a bar of:	eine Tafel

The shop assistant may say:

Sonst noch etwas? ...or... ***Sonst noch einen Wunsch?***

= Will there be anything else?

You could reply:

Nein danke. = No thank you.

...or...

two apples: zwei Äpfel *three pears:* drei Birnen

Ja, ich möchte auch eine Kartoffel , bitte.

= Yes, I'd like a potato as well, please.

See page 2 for numbers.

This might be fairly basic stuff, but you need to know it

There's lots of important stuff here. Remember, you don't have to make those 'quantity words' like 'Gramm' and 'Kilo' plural — just use them as they are. Also, you don't need to use 'of' like in English.

Shopping

Ahh. A nice, easy page before the next lot of Quick Questions. Shouldn't take long, this.

Haben Sie...? — Do you have...?

Maybe you're not sure this shop will have what you want — in which case, you'll have to ask.

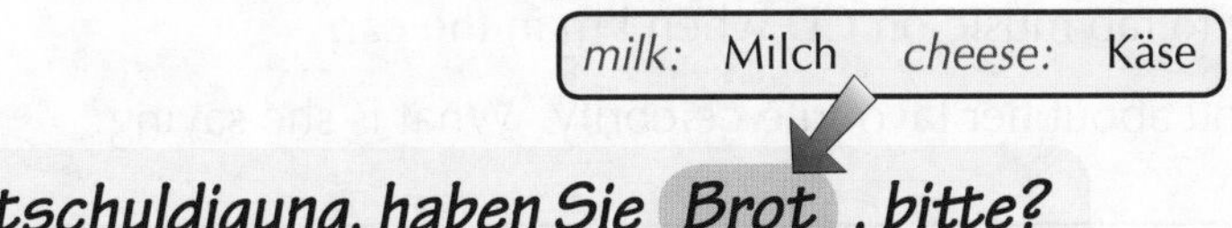

milk: Milch *cheese:* Käse

Entschuldigung, haben Sie Brot, bitte?

= Excuse me, do you have any bread, please?

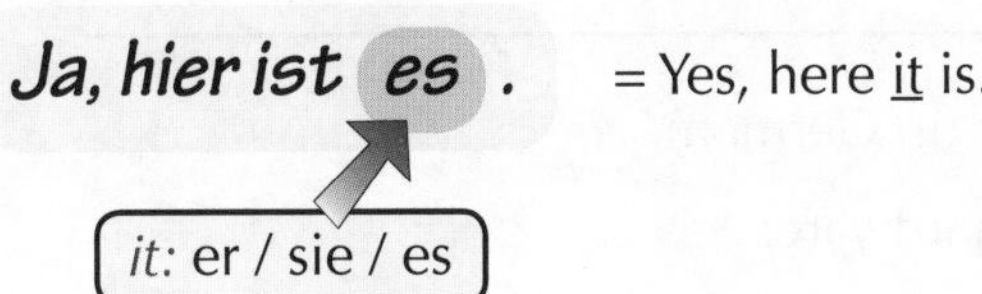

Ja, hier ist es. = Yes, here it is.

it: er / sie / es

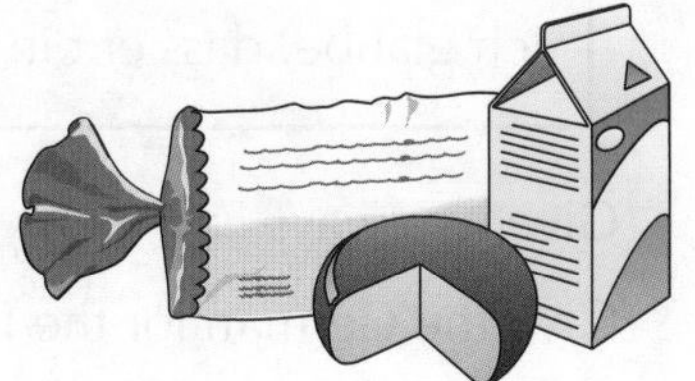

Nein, haben wir nicht. = No, we don't.

Nehmen Sie das? — Will you be taking that?

Decision time. It happens every time you go into a shop. Make sure you know these.

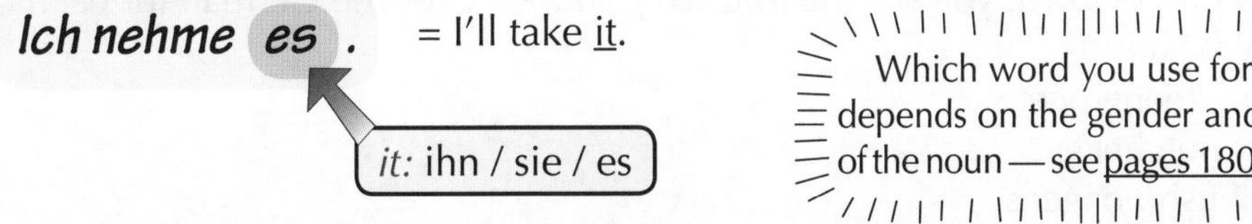

Ich nehme es. = I'll take it.

it: ihn / sie / es

Which word you use for 'it' depends on the gender and case of the noun — see pages 180–181.

Ich lasse es. Die Farbe gefällt mir nicht. = I'll leave it. I don't like the colour.

It's the wrong size: Es ist die falsche Größe
It's too expensive: Es ist zu teuer

A pretty straightforward page — so no excuses for not learning it

This little lot might not seem important, but it could well come up in a listening exam or speaking assessment. You might even want to use it in real life. Amazing. So get learning it.

Quick Questions

Don't skip these questions. If you can answer all of them now, it'll really help with the Exam Practice at the end of the section. If there's one you can't answer, go back over the relevant page until you can.

Quick Questions

1) How would you say the following in German?
a) I like listening to rock music.
b) I don't like pop music.
c) I like listening to rap music on CD when I'm in the car.

2) Erika is telling you about her favourite celebrity. What is she saying?

> 'Ich finde Karl Traumboot total fantastisch. Er ist ein berühmter deutscher Schauspieler. Karl sieht so cool aus und trägt immer schwarze, modische Klamotten. Ich habe ihn auf der Bühne gesehen und er war ausgezeichnet. Ich glaube, dass er ein gutes Vorbild für junge Leute ist.'

3) Give two ways in which you use computers (in German).

4) Give the German for the follwing items of hardware:
a) computer
b) printer
c) monitor
d) keyboard

5) Do you think computers are a good or a bad thing? Give a short answer in German.

6) What's 'eine SMS-Mitteilung' in English?

7) How would you say 'I'm going to send an e-mail' in German?

8) You're visiting your German exchange partner and offer to go into town to do some shopping. Ask your exchange partner where the supermarket is.

9) You get to the supermarket and it's closed. Ask a passer-by what time it opens.

10) They reply 'Der Supermarkt macht um halb neun auf'. What does this mean?

11) While in town, you see the following shops. Give the German for each one.
a) bakery
b) greengrocer's
c) butcher's
d) fishmonger's
e) chemist's

12) You buy a shirt, but later decide to take it back. How would you ask for a refund?

13) How would you say 'I particularly like shopping for shoes' in German?

14) Translate these prices into English.
a) 'Neun Euro fünfundneunzig Cent'
b) 'sechsunddreißig Cent'
c) 'Hundert Euro'

15) How would you say you'd like the following items in German?
a) 1 kg of sugar
b) a dozen apples
c) a bar of chocolate
d) a jar of jam

Clothes

Don't be put off by the big vocab box in the middle of the page — you should find most of the words pretty easy to learn. Good job really, 'cos this is another topic you definitely need to know.

Die Kleidung — Clothing

Most of this stuff is pretty common — so you need to know it.

Dieser Mantel gefällt mir (nicht). = I (don't) like this coat.

Dieser Mantel ist wirklich bequem. = This coat is really comfortable.

fashionable: modisch *old-fashioned:* altmodisch

Remember, plurals are always 'die'.

Clothing

shirt:	das Hemd (-en)	*suit:*	der Anzug (die Anzüge)
blouse:	die Bluse (-n)	*jacket:*	die Jacke (-n)
trousers:	die Hose (-n)	*scarf:*	der Schal (-e)
skirt:	der Rock (die Röcke)	*glove:*	der Handschuh (-e)
miniskirt:	der Minirock (die Miniröcke)	*tie:*	die Krawatte (-n), der Schlips (-e)
dress:	das Kleid (-er)	*tights:*	die Strumpfhose (-n)
coat:	der Mantel (die Mäntel)	*shorts:*	die Shorts (plural), die kurze Hose (-n)
hat:	der Hut (die Hüte)	*sock:*	die Socke (-n)
cap:	die Mütze (-n)	*a pair of socks:*	ein Paar Socken
T-shirt:	das T-Shirt (-s)	*shoe:*	der Schuh (-e)
jumper:	der Pullover (-)		

Watch out: 'die Hose' is feminine singular, not plural as in the English 'trousers'. Same with 'die Strumpfhose'.

Die Mode — Fashion

Examiners love it if you talk about fashion too...

Es ist sehr schwierig richtig individuell zu sein. = It's very difficult to be truly individual.

fashionable clothes: die modischen Klamotten

Man muss immer die Markenklamotten tragen und die sind wirklich teuer.

= You always have to wear brand-named clothes and they are really expensive.

You need to know your 'Krawatte' from your 'Strumpfhose'

Lots of these clothes are pretty easy to remember — Schuh, Socke, Hut, Bluse and so on. Others (like 'Strumpfhose') need a bit more effort. It's important stuff though, so it's worth it. Honestly.

Clothes

More pretty darn important vocab to learn here, so get stuck in...

Größen — Sizes

Ich möchte eine Hose. Meine Größe ist zweiundvierzig.

= I'd like a pair of trousers. I'm size 42.

Continental sizes

size:	die Größe / die Nummer
dress size 10 / 12 / 14 / 16:	36 / 38 / 40 / 42
shoe size 5 / 6 / 7 / 8 / 9 / 10:	38 / 39 / 41 / 42 / 43 / 44

Welche Farbe...? — What colour...?

Another vital little topic...

Colours: Die Farben

black:	schwarz	*green:*	grün	*pink:*	rosa
white:	weiß	*blue:*	blau	*purple:*	lila
red:	rot	*brown:*	braun	*light blue:*	hellblau
yellow:	gelb	*orange:*	orange	*dark brown:*	dunkelbraun

For adjective endings, see pages 169-170.

Ich möchte eine blaue Jacke. = I'd like a blue jacket.

The colours 'rosa', 'lila' and 'orange' don't take endings.

Ich möchte einen rosa Rock. = I'd like a pink skirt.

Es besteht aus... — It's made out of...

Ich hätte gern eine neue Jacke aus Leder. = I'd like a new leather jacket.

wool: Wolle

Other materials: Andere Stoffe

iron:	das Eisen	*paper:*	das Papier
wood:	das Holz	*plastic:*	das Plastik
metal:	das Metall	*silver:*	das Silber
silk:	die Seide	*cotton:*	die Baumwolle

You might know your colours, but you need to learn materials too

Colours are bound to pop up all over the place — so if you don't already know them, it'd be a great idea to learn them all now. Make sure you learn the rest of the vocab on this page while you're at it.

Inviting People Out

As well as finding out how much things cost, when they're open and where they are, you've got to learn how to ask someone to come with you.

Gehen wir aus — Let's go out

These are all really useful phrases, so get them learnt.

Gehen wir ins Schwimmbad. = Let's go to the swimming pool.

to the theatre:	ins Theater
to the park:	zum Park

For other places you might want to invite someone to, and more activities or sports, see pages 49-50.

Ja, gern. = Yes, I'd love to.

Good idea.:	Gute Idee.
Great!:	Prima!

Nein, danke. = No, thank you.

I'm sorry:	Es tut mir leid.
Unfortunately I can't:	Ich kann es leider nicht.
I don't have enough money:	Ich habe nicht genug Geld.

If you can learn this and use it in the right way you'll score loads more marks — worth it even though it's a bit tricky.

Ich würde lieber Fußball spielen. = I'd prefer to play football.

to go for a walk:	spazieren gehen
to go cycling:	Rad fahren

Wo treffen wir uns? — Where shall we meet?

Now to sort out the details of where and when to meet.
The verb 'sich treffen' is reflexive. For more on this, see page 199.

Wir treffen uns vor dem Rathaus. = We'll meet in front of the town hall.

at your house:	bei dir zu Hause
next to the church:	neben der Kirche

For other places, see pages 106-107. For more on 'in front of'/ 'at'/ 'next to' etc. see pages 177-179.

Um wie viel Uhr treffen wir uns? = What time shall we meet?

Wir treffen uns um 10 Uhr. = We'll meet at 10 o'clock.

two thirty:	vierzehn Uhr dreißig
half past three:	halb vier

For more about times, see page 4.

I'm not going out till I've learnt this German

Now you've got that sorted you should be able to ask Boris Becker out to the theatre or arrange to meet Claudia Schiffer in front of the park. If you can't then go back over it until you darn well can.

Going Out

You're going to need this stuff — you may need to talk about it and you'll definitely have to be able to understand it all. Don't just sit there, get into gear and get down to it.

Was gibt es hier in der Nähe? — What is there near here?

Gibt's hier in der Nähe ein Theater ? = Is there a theatre near here?

a sports field:	einen Sportplatz
a bowling alley:	eine Kegelbahn

For hobbies & more places, see pages 49-50.

Kann man hier in der Nähe schwimmen ? = Can people swim near here?

play tennis:	Tennis spielen
go for walks:	spazieren gehen

Wann macht das Schwimmbad auf? — When does the swimming pool open?

close: macht ... zu

For more on verbs like 'aufmachen', see pages 201-202.

Wann macht das Schwimmbad auf ? = When does the swimming pool open?

the gallery:	die Galerie
the sports centre:	das Sportzentrum

This is in the present tense, but it's talking about something that's going to happen in the future. For more info. see page 191.

Es macht um halb zehn auf. = It opens at half past nine.

Es macht um fünf Uhr zu. = It closes at five o'clock.

For more times, see page 4.

Ich möchte bitte eine Karte . = I'd like one ticket, please.

two tickets: zwei Karten

Opening times could crop up in a listening exam

Before you move on, make sure you can ask when something opens and if something's nearby. Cover the page and see if you've got it all sussed out. Testing yourself's the only way.

Going Out

It's important to find out how much everything'll cost...

Wie teuer ist es...? — How expensive is it...?

Wie viel kostet es, schwimmen zu gehen ? = How much does it cost to go swimming?

to go cycling:	Rad zu fahren
to play tennis:	Tennis zu spielen

For other sports and activities, see pages 49-50.

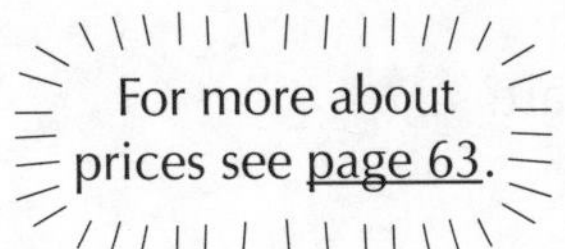
For more about prices see page 63.

Es kostet 2 Euro . = It costs 2 euros.

Es kostet 5 Euro pro Stunde. = It costs 5 euros per hour.

Was läuft im Kino? — What's on at the cinema?

Some useful cinema-related phrases for you:

Wie viel kostet eine Eintrittskarte ? = How much does one entry ticket cost?

How much do two entry tickets cost?:
Wie viel kosten zwei Eintrittskarten?

Plural ending — see page 188

'Eintrittskarte' means 'entry ticket' and 'Karte' means 'ticket', so they're basically the same thing. You'll get more marks if you can use the longer word, but you need to understand it.

Eine Karte kostet 10 Euro. = One ticket costs 10 euros.

Ich möchte zwei Karten , bitte. = I'd like two tickets, please.

one ticket:	eine Karte
three tickets:	drei Karten

You should be familiar with asking questions by now

So, you should now be able to ask for tickets and find out how much they cost. If you're a bit rusty on the old numbers, now might be the time for a quick recap (see page 2). Excellent stuff.

Going Out

Almost everyone likes the cinema, and whatever kind of films tickle your fancy you'll need to know how to arrange going there with someone else. Away you go.

Um wie viel Uhr...? — At what time...?

It's no good if you don't know what time the film starts.
You'll miss all the nice adverts at the beginning for one thing...

Um wie viel Uhr beginnt die Vorstellung? = What time does the performance begin?

'fängt ... an' comes from 'anfangen', which is a separable strong verb. See pages 201-202 for more info.

Wann fängt die Vorstellung an? = When does the performance start?

the film: der Film *the play:* das Theaterstück *the concert:* das Konzert

Wann endet die Vorstellung ? = When does the performance end?

Es beginnt um... — It begins at...

'Anfangen' again. Well the more you see it, the more likely you are to use it, right?

The film: Der Film *The concert:* Das Konzert

Die Vorstellung fängt um acht Uhr an. = The performance starts at 8 o'clock.

For more about times, see page 4.

You use 'sie' here because 'die Vorstellung' is feminine.
For 'der Film' use 'er' and for 'das Konzert' use 'es'.

Sie endet um halb elf. = It finishes at half past ten.

If you want to know how to describe a film you've seen, see pages 53-54.

Get your head around these separable verbs

'Anfangen' is a separable verb. It means pretty much the same thing as 'beginnen', but it looks much more impressive if you use it in a sentence. You've got to get it right though — see pages 201-202 for help.

Quick Questions

Lots more thrilling questions to make sure you know the contents of these last few pages like the back of your own hand. Preferably better. Let's see what you've learnt then...

Quick Questions

1) Give the German for the following items of clothing:
a) shirt
b) dress
c) trousers
d) jumper
e) scarf
f) a pair of socks

2) How would you say 'I like this dress' in German?

3) How would you say 'This dress is really fashionable' in German?

4) Translate the following sentences into English:
a) Diese Jacke gefällt mir nicht. Sie ist ein bisschen altmodisch.
b) Ich glaube, dass es wichtig ist, individuell zu sein.
c) Markenklamotten können wirklich teuer sein.

5) What are the German words for the colours red, orange, yellow, green, blue and purple?

6) Name three colours which don't need adjective endings in German.

7) How would you say 'I'd like a silk shirt' in German?

8) What are the names of the following materials in English?
a) das Eisen
b) das Holz
c) das Plastik
d) die Baumwolle

9) Suggest to your German friend that you both go to the cinema (in German).

10) Your friend says he doesn't have enough money and would rather go cycling.
How would he say this?

11) You go to the tourist office.
How would you say 'Can people go cycling near here?' in German?

12) Sadly, cycling is forbidden. Ask if there's a swimming pool nearby.
Ask what time it opens.

13) You ask your other German friend to go to the cinema.
She says yes. Tell her 'we'll meet at your house'.

14) The film you want to see is pretty popular. You decide to ring up and book the tickets beforehand. How would you say the following sentences in German?
a) 'How much does one entry ticket cost?'
b) 'I'd like two tickets please.'
c) 'What time does the film start?'
d) 'What time does it (the film) end?'

15) Here are some of the answers you get to the questions above.
Translate them into English.
a) Eine Karte kostet fünf Euro.
b) Der Film fängt um halb acht an.
c) Der Film endet um zehn Uhr.

Listening Questions

Before answering, remember to read each question and the instructions through carefully.

Track 6

1 Jonas and Heidi are arranging to go out.

a) When are they going out?

A Friday afternoon **B** Saturday afternoon **C** Friday evening

Write the correct letter in the box.

b) Why don't they go to the disco?

A it's expensive **B** Heidi's hurt her leg **C** Heidi can't dance well

Write the correct letter in the box.

c) Where do they arrange to meet?

A the marketplace **B** Heidi's house **C** the cinema

Write the correct letter in the box.

Track 7

2 Fritz, Katja and Sabine are discussing what they like to do in their spare time.

a) Who likes to play the piano?

....

b) Who doesn't like classical music?

....

c) Who likes historical novels?

....

d) Who likes watching soap operas?

....

Reading Question

1 Sharon is writing a blog about her recent shopping trip to Freiburg.

Lahr den 27. Oktober 20h30

Grüße! Ich heiße Sharon. Wir machen einen Austausch mit unserer Partnerschule im Schwarzwald — wir verbringen zehn Tage in Lahr. Heute sind wir in Freiburg einkaufen gegangen. Freiburg, eine malerische historische Stadt nicht weit von Frankreich und der Schweiz, hat ein sehr gutes Einkaufszentrum in der Fußgängerzone.

In Freiburg kann man alles kaufen. Zuerst haben wir „Douglas" besucht, wo ich Schminke und Parfüm für meine Schwestern billig gekauft habe. Dann haben wir ein großes Kaufhaus besucht, aber eine Jeansjacke hat zweihundertfünfundsiebzig Euro gekostet — viel zu teuer! Ich mag Designerkleider, aber ich habe das Lotto nicht gewonnen!

Am Mittag haben wir ein kleines Café am Münsterplatz gefunden. Ich hatte eine Forelle mit Salzkartoffeln und meine Freundin Tracey hatte eine Riesenbockwurst mit Sauerkraut. Wir haben Traubensaft getrunken.

Später am Nachmittag haben wir Souvenirs gekauft. Für meinen Bruder, der sich für Formel-1-Rennen interessiert, habe ich eine Sebastian-Vettel-Mütze gekauft. Mein Vater ist Fußballfan und ich habe ihm einen Bayern-München-Bierkrug gekauft. Ich hatte nicht viel Geld übrig und für meine Mutter habe ich glücklicherweise eine Schachtel schweizerische Pralinen in einem Schlussverkauf gefunden.

Um sechzehn Uhr haben wir uns alle am Bahnhof getroffen und sind wieder mit dem Zug nach Lahr gefahren. Wie immer in Deutschland war der Zug pünktlich und sauber.

Circle the correct answer.

a) The exchange school is in: the Black Forest / Switzerland / Freiburg.

b) Sharon bought her sisters perfume and: jewellery / make-up / designer clothes.

c) The denim jacket cost: €257 / €275 / €265.

d) Sharon ate: a jumbo sausage / roast potatoes / trout.

e) They drank: grape juice / wine / blackcurrant cordial.

f) Sharon was pleased with the chocolates because: they were her favourites / they were on sale / it was a big box.

Speaking Question

OK, here's another juicy little speaking task for you to get your teeth into. The more you practise this kind of stuff, the better you'll be when it comes to the real thing. Honest.

Task: New Technology
You are being interviewed by a German radio station for a programme about new technology. Your teacher will play the role of the show's presenter.

Your teacher will ask you the following:

- How important are computers for you? — *You could take this as an opportunity to say what you use them for.*
- What do you think of computer games?
- Do you have a laptop? — *Don't just answer yes or no — give a bit more detail.*
- What is your favourite website?
- Are computers bad for your health?
- Has new technology ever caused you problems?
- Are mobile phones allowed in your school?
- !

! Remember that the exclamation mark means you'll have to answer a question that you won't have prepared an answer to.

The whole conversation should last about five minutes.

Notes for Teachers
You need to ask the student the following questions:

- Wie wichtig sind Computer für dich?
- Wie findest du Computerspiele?
- Hast du einen Laptop?
- Was ist deine Lieblingswebsite?
- Sind Computer schlecht für die Gesundheit?
- Hat neue Technologie jemals Probleme für dich verursacht?
- Sind Handys in deiner Schule erlaubt?
- !

! The unpredictable question could be: Könntest du ohne Handy leben?

Writing Questions

Try and make your written work as interesting as possible — use lots of vocab, vary your sentence structures and try and get more than one tense in there if you can. But remember to stay relevant to the task — it's no good rabbiting on about your favourite food if you've been asked to write about holidays.

Task 1: You've been asked by your exchange school to write an article for their school paper on a local celebrity.

You don't have to actually interview a real person for this if you don't want to, as long as you can make up something plausible and write some decent German.

Write the article in the form of an interview.

You could ask the following questions:

- Where do you come from?
- Was it difficult becoming famous?
- What's your greatest achievement?
- Do you know many other famous people?
- What sort of house do you live in?
- What are your plans for the future?

Remember: to score the highest marks you need to answer the task fully (for grades C and above you will need to write 200-300 words).

Task 2: Your pen friend is doing a survey of leisure facilities in England and has asked you to help out.

Write about the leisure facilities in your town.

You could write about the following;

Hint: if your home town doesn't have any of these things, you could talk about how boring it is to live there and what you'd introduce to make it better.

- Sports facilities
- Availability of cinemas, theatres, restaurants etc.
- Tourist attractions
- Outdoor amenities, e.g. parks, gardens
- Clubs or facilities for young people
- How your home town could be improved

Remember: to score the highest marks you need to answer the task fully (for grades C and above you will need to write 200-300 words).

Revision Summary

These questions really do check what you know and don't know — which means you can spend your time learning the bits you're shaky on. But it's not a good idea to do this one day, then forget about it. Come back to these a day later and try them again. And then a week later...

1) Franz asks Christine if she has a hobby. She says that she plays the guitar, plays football and reads books. Write down their conversation in German.

2) Hermann and Bob are having an argument. Hermann says that he likes tennis because it's exciting. Bob finds tennis boring and tiring. Write down their conversation in German.

3) You're talking to your German pen friend. How do you tell her what TV programmes you like to watch?

4) Tell your German friend you went to see 'Night of the Zombie-Mummies 26' at the cinema last week. Tell her it was a horror film and that you thought it was very sad.

5) You and your pen friend are having an unlikely conversation about where and how you listen to music. Your friend says she listens to her iPod® when she's in the car. How did she say that in German?

6) Nadja thinks she's fallen in love with Justin Timberlake. Write a paragraph in German to her saying what you think of him, and telling her which celebrities you admire. Don't forget to give reasons.

7) Give one advantage of using a computer and one disadvantage. Don't cheat — give them in German.

8) Write out a text message in German asking your friend Joe if he wants to go swimming with you on Saturday. Don't forget to be a good friend and ask how he is.

9) What are the German names for the shops where you'd buy: paper, a cake, some sausages, some soap? (And don't just say 'Supermarkt' for all four.)

10) You need to buy a brown jumper, size 48, and three pairs of socks in Munich. How do you say this to the shop assistant?

11) Dave wants to see 'Romeo und Julia' at the cinema, but Gabriela says they should see 'Otto — der Katastrophenfilm'. They arrange to meet in front of the cinema at 8pm. Write down their conversation in German. *(Watch out for word order here.)*

12) You're in Germany and you want to play squash. Ask when the sports centre is open and how much it costs to play squash. Ask for two tickets.

Holiday Destinations

I know there's a lot to learn on this page, but it's really pretty important. It could come up anywhere.

Learn these foreign places

You need to understand where other people are from when they tell you. And you're bound to have to talk about holidays and trips abroad at some point. So get learning this little lot:

	Place	People (male/female)	Adjective
Germany:	Deutschland	Deutscher/Deutsche	deutsch
France:	Frankreich	Franzose/Französin	französisch
Italy:	Italien	Italiener(in)	italienisch
Spain:	Spanien	Spanier(in)	spanisch
Austria:	Österreich	Österreicher(in)	österreichisch
Holland:	Holland	Holländer(in)	holländisch
Greece:	Griechenland	Grieche/Griechin	griechisch
America:	Amerika	Amerikaner(in)	amerikanisch
Belgium:	Belgien	Belgier(in)	belgisch
Denmark:	Dänemark	Däne/Dänin	dänisch
Russia:	Russland	Russe/Russin	russisch
Africa:	Afrika	Afrikaner(in)	afrikanisch
Ireland:	Irland	Ire/Irin	irisch
India:	Indien	Inder(in)	indisch
Poland:	Polen	Pole/Polin	polnisch
China:	China	Chinese/Chinesin	chinesisch
Australia:	Australien	Australier(in)	australisch

An adjective is a describing word. See pages 169-170.

When you use adjectives in German, you often need to put endings on them. See pages 169-170.

So your (male) German friend might say:

Ich bin Deutscher. Ich komme aus Deutschland.

= I am German. I come from Germany.

And you'd describe him as:

This is a nominative adjective ending (see page 170).

Mein deutscher Freund.

= My German friend.

Women and girls need the feminine versions — usually that just means adding '-in' to the end.

E.g. ***Ich bin Französin.*** = I am French (female).

For more on talking about where you're from, including countries in the UK, see page 111.

Watch out for similar spellings in German and English

You've got to learn all those countries and nationalities. There's a pretty ridiculous amount of vocab here, but keep testing yourself until you know it back to front. It's really the only way.

Holiday Destinations

We're not done with those countries just yet. Here are a few more for you to learn...

Some countries are a bit more **tricky**...

1 Watch out: you have to put 'die' before these countries:

	Place	People (male/female)	Adjective
Turkey:	die Türkei	Türke/Türkin	türkisch
Switzerland:	die Schweiz	Schweizer(in)	schweizerisch
The Netherlands:	die Niederlande	Niederländer(in)	niederländisch
The USA:	die USA, die Vereinigten Staaten	Amerikaner(in)	amerikanisch

Don't forget — Holland and the Netherlands are the same place.

There's no people/adjective to go with 'the USA', so just use these.

2 BUT after 'aus', the 'die' changes to 'der' for Turkey and Switzerland (because they're singular and feminine) and 'den' for the others (cos they're plural).

Ich komme aus den USA. = I come from the USA.

See page 167 and page 178 for stuff about 'die' and 'aus'.

You need to know these **holiday destinations**

Um... not that I'm really suggesting you go on holiday in the Channel Tunnel, but I'm sure you catch my drift — learn this little lot, they just might come in handy:

the English Channel:	der Ärmelkanal
the Channel Tunnel:	der Tunnel
the Alps (plural):	die Alpen
the Black Forest:	der Schwarzwald
Lake Constance:	der Bodensee
Bavaria:	Bayern
the Rhine:	der Rhein
the Danube:	die Donau

Some German-speaking cities have different names in German and English. Learn them and really impress the examiners.

Cologne:	Köln	*Geneva:*	Genf
Munich:	München	*Vienna:*	Wien

There's some important grammar on this page

At first glance, this page may look a bit tricky, but it's a lot more straightforward than it seems. Honest. Learn which countries need 'die', and while you're at it learn those holiday destinations too.

Catching the Train

Trains, planes and automobiles... Well, just trains for now. You'll need loads of vocab if you want the best marks. And you must know a few bog-standard sentences — things you'll always need.

Ich möchte mit dem Zug fahren — I'd like to travel by train

Fährt ein Zug nach Berlin? = Is there a train to Berlin?

Cologne: Köln *Munich:* München

return(s): hin und zurück

Einmal einfach nach Berlin, erste Klasse. = One single to Berlin, first class.

Two: Zweimal
Three: Dreimal

second class: zweite Klasse

There's another word for 'return ticket' — 'die Rückfahrkarte':

Eine Rückfahrkarte nach Berlin, bitte. = One return ticket to Berlin, please.

Learn this trains vocab

More vocab... Yes, it's as dull as a big dull thing, but it's also vital to know as much as you can.

Remember, plurals are always 'die'.

to depart:	abfahren	*timetable:*	der Fahrplan
to arrive:	ankommen	*to get on:*	einsteigen
to change (trains):	umsteigen	*to get out:*	aussteigen
platform:	das Gleis (-e)	*through train:*	der D-Zug
departure:	die Abfahrt	*fast-stopping train:*	der Eilzug
arrival:	die Ankunft	*regional train:*	der Nahverkehrszug
the waiting room:	der Warteraum	*suburban train:*	die S-Bahn
ticket:	die Fahrkarte (-n)	*intercity express train:*	der ICE-Zug
ticket window:	der Fahrkartenschalter	*cross-country train:*	der Interregio-Zug
ticket machine:	der Fahrkartenautomat		

The separable bits of verbs are shown in green.

This stuff could actually come in useful

Be careful with verbs like 'abfahren' and 'einsteigen'. They're 'separable' — you say 'der Zug fährt ab', not 'der Zug abfährt'. There's more on separable verbs on pages 201-202. Easy peasy.

All Kinds of Transport

More transport for you — first, a bit extra on trains...

Wann fahren Sie? — When are you travelling?

This stuff is a bit complicated, but it's still dead important.

Ich möchte am Samstag nach Köln fahren. = I would like to travel to Cologne on Saturday.

today:	heute
next Monday:	nächsten Montag
on the tenth of June:	am zehnten Juni

Wann fährt der Zug nach Köln ab? = When does the train for Cologne leave?

Wann kommt der Zug in Köln an? = When does the train arrive in Cologne?

Von welchem Gleis fährt der Zug ab? = Which platform does the train leave from?

'Abfahren' and 'ankommen' are separable verbs. See pages 201-202 for more info.

Wie kommst du dahin? — How do you get there?

You won't always be travelling by train, so here's how to talk about all kinds of transport.

Use the verb 'fahren' with most vehicles, but 'gehen' if you're on foot.
Also, you have to use 'mit...' with vehicles — but if you're on foot, say 'zu Fuß'.

Ich gehe zu Fuß. = I'm going on foot.

Ich fahre mit dem Zug. = I'm travelling by train.

by bus:	mit dem Bus
by tram:	mit der Straßenbahn
on the underground:	mit der U-Bahn
by bike:	mit dem Fahrrad
by car:	mit dem Auto / mit dem Wagen
by motorbike:	mit dem Motorrad
by coach:	mit dem Reisebus
by boat:	mit dem Boot

Normalerweise fahre ich mit dem Bus in die Stadt. = I normally go into town by bus.

You can't use 'Ich fahre...' for travelling by plane. Instead, you can use one of these:

Ich reise mit dem Flugzeug. = I'm travelling by plane.

Ich fliege. = I'm flying.

Always say 'zu Fuß' for on foot

Remember, if you want to say 'I go by bus/plane/train etc.' you use 'fahren' and 'mit'. If you want to say 'I go on foot' you use 'gehen' and 'zu Fuß'. Simple. Now that's sorted, we can move on...

All Kinds of Transport

Here's the rest of what you need to know about transport.
There's a bit more vocab I'm afraid, but you do need to know it.

Abfahrt und Ankunft — Departure and arrival

These are the kinds of questions you'd have to ask at a station.

Fährt ein Bus nach Mannheim? = Is there a bus that goes to Mannheim?

a tram: eine Straßenbah *a coach:* ein Reisebus

Wann fährt der nächste Bus nach Stuttgart ab? = When does the next bus to Stuttgart leave?

the (next) coach: der (nächste) Reisebus
the (next) boat: das (nächste) Boot

Wann kommt das Flugzeug in Frankfurt an? = When does the plane arrive in Frankfurt?

Welcher Bus...? — Which bus...?

No doubt about it — you need to be able to ask which bus or train goes where. Just learn this.

Which tram: Welche Straßenbahn
Which underground line: Welche U-Bahn-Linie

Welcher Bus fährt zum Stadtzentrum, bitte? = Which bus goes to the town centre, please?

to the bus stop: zur Bushaltestelle
to the airport: zum Flughafen
to the harbour/port: zum Hafen

You need to know your public transport

Nothing too tricky here, but do watch out for 'abfahren' (to leave) — remember it's a separable verb.
If you've already learnt all the vocab on the last couple of pages, then this lot shouldn't be too hard.

Planning Your Holiday

So you've finally made it to your destination. Now you need to know what there is to do. Unfortunately there are quite a lot of things to learn about this. Better get started then...

Das Verkehrsamt — The Tourist Information Office

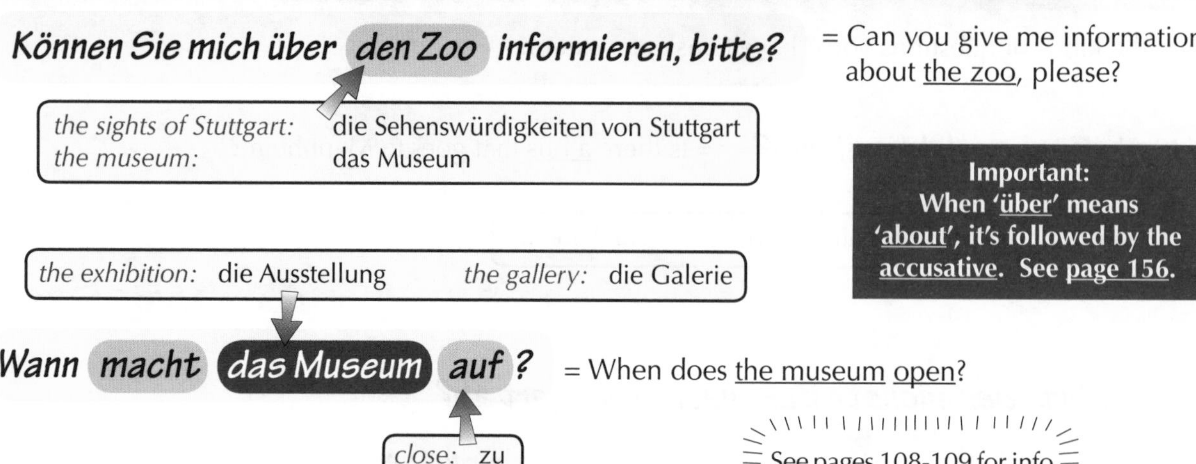

Können Sie mich über den Zoo informieren, bitte? = Can you give me information about the zoo, please?

the sights of Stuttgart:	die Sehenswürdigkeiten von Stuttgart
the museum:	das Museum

Important: When 'über' means 'about', it's followed by the accusative. See page 156.

the exhibition:	die Ausstellung	*the gallery:*	die Galerie

Wann macht das Museum auf? = When does the museum open?

close: zu

See pages 108-109 for info on asking for directions.

Ausflüge — Excursions

Learning this lot'll get you big bonus marks.

Haben Sie Broschüren über Ausflüge von München aus? = Do you have any leaflets about excursions from Munich?

the museums in Cologne: die Museen in Köln

Was für einen Ausflug würden Sie gern machen? = What kind of excursion would you like to go on?

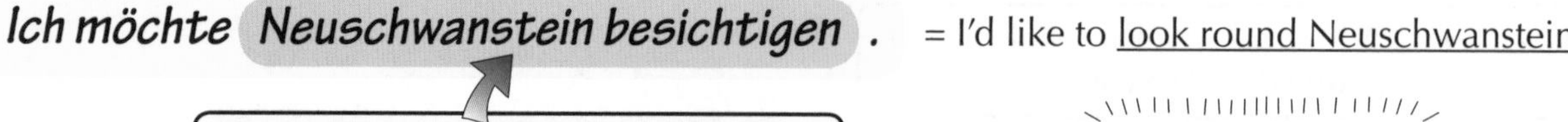

Ich möchte Neuschwanstein besichtigen. = I'd like to look round Neuschwanstein.

go to a museum:	in ein Museum gehen
see the castle:	das Schloss sehen

See page 71 for how to ask about prices.

Dieser Bus fährt nach Neuschwanstein.
Der Bus fährt um halb drei vom Rathaus ab.
= This bus goes to Neuschwanstein. The bus leaves from the town hall at half past two.

2 pm:	vierzehn Uhr
3.15 pm:	fünfzehn Uhr fünfzehn

from the church:	von der Kirche
from the marketplace:	vom Marktplatz

Learn how to ask these questions — and how you might answer them

You might have to answer questions about a tourist brochure in the reading exam, or you could end up writing a letter to a tourist office in the writing assessment. Either way, this stuff's dead useful.

Quick Questions

These Quick Questions aren't here to make the page look nice. Oh no. They're here to help you find out what you know. Then you can concentrate on revising the bits you're not so hot at. So don't skip 'em — give them a go. It's for your own good, honestly.

Quick Questions

1) Give the names of the following countries in German:
a) France
b) Germany
c) Denmark
d) Italy
e) Spain
f) Poland

2) Your male Austrian friend tells you, 'I am Austrian. I come from Austria.' How would he say this in German?

3) If you wanted to describe him in German as 'my Austrian friend', what would you say?

4) If your friend's sister told you she was an Austrian, what would she say (in German)?

5) Name four countries that you generally have to put 'die' before in German.

6) How would you say 'I come from Switzerland' in German?

7) Translate the following into English:
a) der Ärmelkanal
b) der Schwarzwald
c) der Rhein
d) die Donau
e) Bayern
f) Wien

8) You're in a German train station. How would you ask, 'Is there a train to Munich?'

9) How would you ask for a return ticket to Munich, second class, in German?

10) You're looking for the waiting room. What would the sign outside say?

11) How would you say the following sentences in German?
a) I'm going on foot.
b) I'm travelling by boat.
c) I'm travelling by car.
d) I normally go into town on the underground.

12) Translate the following questions into English:
a) Von welchem Gleis fährt der Eilzug nach Stuttgart ab?
b) Wann fährt der nächste Reisebus nach Frankfurt ab?
c) Wann kommt das Flugzeug in Berlin an?
d) Welche Straßenbahn fährt zum Flughafen, bitte?

13) You're in a tourist information office in Cologne. How would you say: 'Can you give me information about the museums in Cologne please?'

14) How would you say 'What time does the museum open?' in German?

15) How would you ask, 'Do you have any leaflets about the sights of Cologne?'

16) You decide to get the bus into town. The woman in the tourist office says: 'Der Bus fährt um halb eins von der Bushaltestelle ab.' What does this mean in English?

Holiday Accommodation

Okay, this page has all the words you need to know about hotels, hostels and camping. You may not find it exactly riveting, but it is dead useful. Better get learning then...

Der Urlaub — Holiday

They like to test you on booking the right kind of room in the right kind of hotel — learn it...

General vocabulary

holiday:	der Urlaub (-e)
abroad:	im Ausland
person:	die Person (-en)
night:	die Nacht (die Nächte)
overnight stay:	die Übernachtung (-en)

Verbs used in hotels

to reserve:	reservieren
to stay the night:	übernachten
to stay:	bleiben
to cost:	kosten
to leave:	abreisen/abfahren

Things you might ask for

room:	das Zimmer (-)
double room:	das Doppelzimmer (-)
single room:	das Einzelzimmer (-)
place/space:	der Platz (die Plätze)
room service:	der Zimmerservice (-s)

Types of accommodation

full board:	die Vollpension
half board:	die Halbpension
bed and breakfast:	Übernachtung mit Frühstück

For more on meals see pages 91-93.

guest house: das Gasthaus (die Gasthäuser)

campsite: der Campingplatz (die Campingplätze)

hotel: das Hotel (-s)

youth hostel: die Jugendherberge (-n)

Remember: plurals are always 'die'.

Die Rechnung — The bill

After all that, you need to be able to ask about your room, where things are... and paying the bill.

Parts of a hotel

reception:	der Empfang (die Empfänge)
restaurant:	das Restaurant (-s)
dining room:	der Speisesaal (die Speisesäle)
lift:	der Aufzug (die Aufzüge)
stairs:	die Treppe (-n)
car park:	der Parkplatz (die Parkplätze)
games room:	der Aufenthaltsraum (die Aufenthaltsräume)

Other hotel vocab

key:	der Schlüssel (-)
balcony:	der Balkon (-e)
bath:	das Bad (die Bäder)
shower:	die Dusche (-n)
washbasin:	das Waschbecken (-)

Paying for your stay

bill:	die Rechnung (-en)
price:	der Preis (-e)

Learn this vocab now — it'll really help you later

A page bristling with vocab — learn all the stuff on this page and you're well away if anything on hotels comes up. Check you know the words by covering the page and scribbling them down.

Booking a Room / Pitch

Looking for a relaxing post-exam break this summer? Here's how to book yourself a room in Deutschland.

Haben Sie Zimmer frei? — Do you have any rooms free?

You'll have to say what sort of room you want and how long you'll be staying.

Ich möchte ein Einzelzimmer. = I'd like a single room.

double room: Doppelzimmer

You could be a bit more specific and use these:

room with a bath: Zimmer mit Bad
room with a balcony: Zimmer mit Balkon

Ich möchte zwei Nächte hier bleiben. = I'd like to stay here for two nights.

If you're staying for one night, use 'eine Nacht' (not ein Nacht). See page 2 for more numbers.

Was kostet es pro Nacht für eine Person? = How much is it per night for one person?

two people: zwei Personen
three people: drei Personen

Ich nehme es. = I'll take it.

Ich nehme es nicht. = I won't take it.

Kann man hier zelten? — Can I camp here?

Whether you like the outdoor life or not — you'll need these phrases.

Ich möchte einen Platz für drei Nächte, bitte. = I'd like a pitch for three nights, please.

Put how long you want to stay here.

You might need these phrases too:

Is there drinking water here?:	Gibt es hier Trinkwasser?
Can I light a fire here?:	Kann man hier Feuer machen?
Where can I get...?:	Wo bekomme ich...?

And these verbs:

to camp:	zelten
to pitch the tent:	das Zelt aufstellen

Remember, plurals are always 'die'.

pitch (place for a tent): der Platz (die Plätze)

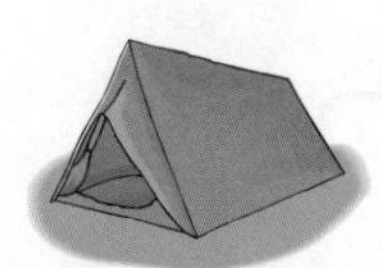

tent: das Zelt (-e)

caravan: der Wohnwagen (-)

sleeping bag: der Schlafsack (die Schlafsäcke)

Lots more important vocab here

Going to a hotel or campsite could well come up somewhere like your listening exam. So even if you're never going to go on holiday to Germany, get this page learnt.

Where / When is... ?

Being able to <u>ask questions</u> is pretty darn useful — as is <u>understanding</u> the answers. This lot'll also help when you go on holiday...

Wo ist... ? — Where is... ?

Knowing how to ask <u>where</u> things are is essential — get these <u>learnt</u>:

Wo ist der Speisesaal, bitte? = Where is <u>the dining room</u>, please?

the car park:	der Parkplatz (die Parkplätze)
the games room:	das Spielzimmer (-)
the play area:	der Spielplatz (die Spielplätze)
the toilet:	die Toilette (-n)
the loo:	das Klo (-s)

See <u>page 86</u> for more things you might need to ask about.

Remember, plurals are always 'die'.

The floor number takes a <u>dative</u> ending here. See <u>page 170</u>.

Er ist im dritten Stock. = It's on the <u>third floor</u>.

For higher floor numbers, see <u>page 3</u>.

fourth floor:	vierten Stock
second floor:	zweiten Stock
first floor:	ersten Stock
ground floor:	Erdgeschoss

These are other words you might need when you describe where something is.

outside:	draußen
on the left / right:	links / rechts
upstairs:	oben
downstairs:	unten
at the end of the corridor:	am Ende des Ganges

Wann ist... ? — When is... ?

And then when you've found out <u>where</u> everything is, you'll need to know <u>when</u> things happen...

Wann wird das Frühstück serviert, bitte? = When is <u>breakfast</u> served, please?

lunch:	das Mittagessen (-)	*evening meal:*	das Abendessen (-)

For more times, see <u>page 4</u>.

Es wird um acht Uhr serviert. = It's served at <u>eight o'clock</u>.

You should be able to use 'wo' and 'wann'

That stuff on <u>1st floor</u>, <u>2nd floor</u> etc. comes up for <u>other</u> things, like <u>shops</u> — so it's well worth <u>learning</u>. You need to <u>know</u> all of this vocab. Cover up the page and try to <u>scribble</u> the words down.

Problems with Accommodation

Whatever your problem, sometimes it's good to get it all off your chest. Nobody wants their holiday ruined by dodgy plumbing and itchy sheets, so here's how to make yourself heard auf Deutsch...

Es gibt ein Problem mit... — There's a problem with...

Here are a few common complaints to be getting on with:

The room: Das Zimmer → ***Das Wasser ist kalt.*** = The water is cold.

too hot: zu heiß

soap: Seife

Es gibt keine Handtücher in meinem Zimmer. = There are no towels in my room.

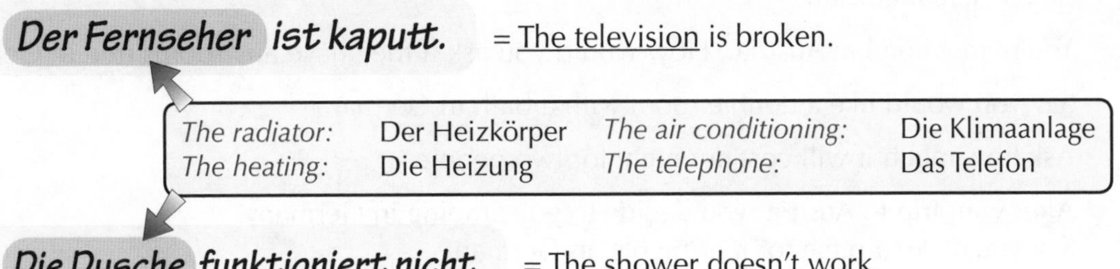

Der Fernseher ist kaputt. = The television is broken.

The radiator:	Der Heizkörper	*The air conditioning:*	Die Klimaanlage
The heating:	Die Heizung	*The telephone:*	Das Telefon

Die Dusche funktioniert nicht. = The shower doesn't work.

Es ist zu laut. Ich kann nicht schlafen.

= It's too loud. I can't sleep.

Das Zimmer ist schmutzig. = The room is dirty.

The bath: Das Bad *The bed linen:* Die Bettwäsche

Können Sie mir helfen, bitte? — Can you help me, please?

So you've told them what the problem is, now you need to get it fixed.

Ich brauche neue Handtücher. = I need new towels.

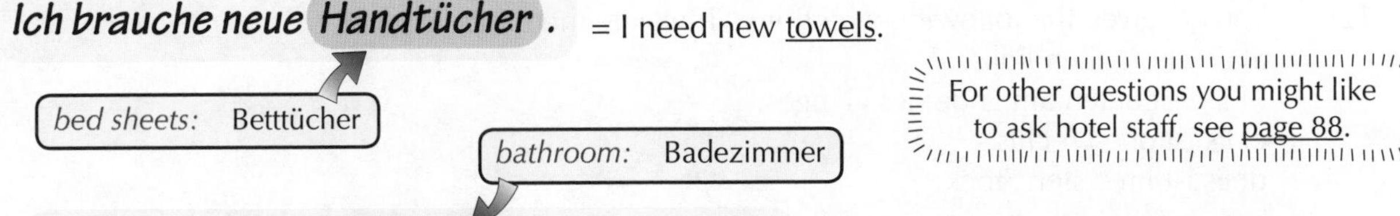

bed sheets: Betttücher

bathroom: Badezimmer

For other questions you might like to ask hotel staff, see page 88.

Können Sie mein Zimmer putzen, bitte? = Can you clean my room please?

Ich möchte ein neues Zimmer. = I would like a new room.

Learning this lot should be no problem

This sort of thing could come in really useful if you ever find yourself in a dodgy German hotel. Even if you don't, I'd still suggest learning this page. You never know when it'll come in handy.

Quick Questions

These questions aren't here to make your life miserable (I promise). They're just to check you've really learnt everything on the last few pages. Which will only help you in the long run.

Quick Questions

1) What's the word for 'holiday' in German?
2) Give the German for:
   a) hotel
   b) guest house
   c) campsite
   d) youth hostel
3) Translate the following parts of a hotel into English:
   a) der Empfang
   b) der Speisesaal
   c) die Aufzüge
   d) der Aufenthaltsraum
4) You're in a hotel in Austria. How would you ask if they have any rooms free in German?
5) Say you would like a double room with a bath in German.
6) Ask how much it will cost per night for two people.
7) After your trip to Austria, you decide to go camping in Germany.
   Say you'd like a pitch for four nights, in German.
8) How would you ask 'Is there drinking water here?' in German?
9) How would you ask 'Can I pitch the tent here?' in German?
10) How would you say the following in German? Give their plurals too.
   a) pitch (place for a tent)
   b) tent
   c) caravan
   d) sleeping bag
11) It's bucketing it down with rain, so you decide to go and stay in a hotel.
   How would you ask where...
   a) the car park is?
   b) the toilet is?
   c) the restaurant is?
   d) the games room is?
12) You get given the following directions. Translate them into English.
   a) Er ist draußen links.
   b) Sie ist unten am Ende des Ganges.
   c) Es ist oben rechts.
   d) Es ist im ersten Stock.
13) How would you ask when lunch is served in German?
14) There are a few problems with your room. Tell the hotel staff in German that:
   a) The heating doesn't work.
   b) There are no towels in my room.
   c) The bath is dirty.
15) Tell a member of staff (in German again) that you need new towels.
   Ask the person to clean your bathroom.

At a Restaurant

All this restaurant stuff's not hard — but your exam could well be if you don't make an effort to memorise it.

Haben Sie einen Tisch frei? — Do you have a table free?

This part's easy, so it's definitely worth learning.

Einen Tisch für vier Personen, bitte. = A table for four, please.

two: zwei *three:* drei

two: zu zweit *three:* zu dritt

Wir sind zu viert. = There are four of us.

See page 2 for more about numbers.

outside:	draußen
on the terrace:	auf der Terrasse

Wir möchten drinnen sitzen. = We'd like to sit inside.

Im Restaurant — At the restaurant

This is what you'd use to call the waiter or waitress over...

Entschuldigen Sie! = Excuse me!

...and these are the names of the jobs.

waiter:	der Kellner (-)
waitress:	die Kellnerin (-nen)

Darf ich bitte die Karte haben? = May I have the menu, please?

the menu of the day: die Tageskarte

See page 88 on 'hotels' for asking where things are.

Wo ist die Toilette, bitte? = Where's the toilet, please?

the phone: das Telefon

Practise using these helpful phrases

These important phrases are just the sort of thing your exam board loves, so get cracking and learn them now. You could even test some of them out on your mum at tea time... on second thoughts maybe not.

At a Restaurant

You might've seen some of these sentences before in different situations and with different vocabulary. That's because they're important, so get them learnt.

Die Speisekarte — The Menu

It's always handy to know which bit of the menu you're looking at.

Courses — Die Gänge

starter:	die Vorspeise (-e)
main course:	das Hauptgericht (-e) / der Hauptgang (die Hauptgänge)
dessert:	der Nachtisch (-e)

Ich hätte gern... — I'd like...

This stuff could be used in other situations too, like shops — so learn it well.

Haben Sie Bockwurst ? = Do you have boiled sausage?

fried sausage:	Bratwurst
German noodles:	Spätzle

See pages 23-24 for more food vocab.

the steak:	das Steak
the chicken:	das Hähnchen

Ich hätte gern das Schnitzel mit Pommes . = I'd like the schnitzel with chips.

rice:	Reis
pickled cabbage:	Sauerkraut

Wie schmeckt es? — What does it taste like?

Wie schmeckt Sauerkraut ? = What does Sauerkraut taste like?

German Christmas cake:	Stollen

Wie schmecken Leberwürste? = What do liver sausages taste like?

Learn how to say 'I would like...' — it crops up all the time

Being at a restaurant could easily come up somewhere, so you need to know all about it. If you've learnt all the stuff on this page, then it'll be easy. So no skiving out of anything.

At a Restaurant

Just a few more restaurant-related phrases for you to learn here.
Then you'll be able to go and have a nice meal out in Berlin somewhere.

Ich bin nicht zufrieden — I'm not satisfied

Once you've learnt this first phrase, you can complain about anything. Useful.

Ich möchte mich beklagen. = I'd like to make a complaint.

Das Rindfleisch ist nicht gar. = The beef is underdone.

The steak:	Das Steak
The pork:	Das Schweinefleisch
The soup:	Die Suppe
The sausage:	Die Wurst

overcooked:	verbraten
too hot:	zu heiß
too cold:	zu kalt
too salty:	zu salzig

See pages 23-24 for more food vocab.

Sind Sie fertig? — Are you finished?

There's no getting away from having to know this. You can't leave without paying.

Die Rechnung, bitte. = The bill, please.

Darf ich bitte zahlen? = May I pay, please?

Ist die Bedienung inbegriffen? = Is service included?

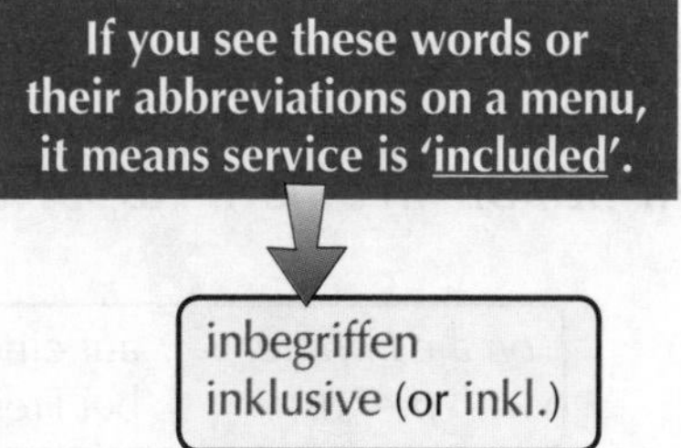

If you see these words or their abbreviations on a menu, it means service is 'included'.
inbegriffen
inklusive (or inkl.)

Lots of handy bits and pieces here

'Ich möchte mich beklagen' is a pretty useful little phrase — learn it and you can complain everywhere from restaurants to shops and hotels. Remember it if you ever have to write a letter of complaint too.

Talking About Your Holiday

When you've been on holiday you want to tell everyone all about it. After this page you'll be able to bore... I mean, tell... people in German too. And get good marks.

Wohin bist du gefahren? — Where did you go?

Talking about your holiday is a great place to use the perfect tense.
Get it right and the examiners will be dead impressed. For help, see pages 192-193.

Ich bin vor zwei Wochen nach Amerika gefahren. = I went to America two weeks ago.

a week ago:	vor einer Woche
last month:	letzten Monat
in July:	im Juli
in the summer:	im Sommer

Spain:	Spanien
France:	Frankreich
Ireland:	Irland

When 'vor' means 'ago', you need the dative case. See page 179.

For other dates and times: pages 4-6.
For points of the compass: page 111.
For a bigger list of countries: page 79.

Mit wem warst du im Urlaub? — Who did you go on holiday with?

a fortnight:	zwei Wochen
a month:	einen Monat

Use the dative case after 'mit'. See page 179.

Ich war eine Woche lang mit meiner Familie im Urlaub. = I went on holiday with my family for a week.

my brother:	meinem Bruder
my friends:	meinen Freunden

For friends and family — see page 32.

For past tenses, see pages 192-195.

Wir haben in einem Hotel übernachtet. = We stayed in a hotel.

on a campsite:	auf einem Campingplatz
with friends:	bei Freunden

Another great chance to use the past tense — and pick up marks

You need to be able to talk about holidays in your speaking and writing tasks, and understand other people going on about their holidays. Cover up the page and see how much you can remember.

Talking About Your Holiday

The things you could say about your last holiday are positively endless — so make sure you learn all the stuff on this page. It'll help you no end come the speaking assessment or writing task.

Wie bist du dorthin gekommen? — How did you get there?

'Dorthin' means 'there' when you're going 'to' a place. It's a useful one.

Wir sind mit dem Wagen dorthin gekommen. = We went there by car.

boat: dem Boot
bike: dem Fahrrad
train: dem Zug

For more types of transport, see page 82.

You could also say: ***Wir sind mit dem Auto gefahren.*** = We travelled by car.

Or even: ***Wir sind geflogen.*** = We flew.

Was hast du gemacht? — What did you do?

You need to be able to say what you did on holiday — learn it well.

Ich bin an den Strand gegangen. = I went to the beach.

to a disco: zu einer Diskothek
to a museum: in ein Museum

Ich habe mich entspannt. = I relaxed.

sunned myself: mich gesonnt
played tennis: Tennis gespielt

See page 98 for how to talk about what the weather was like on your holiday.

Wie fandest du deinen Urlaub? — How was your holiday?

Giving your opinion is a great way to impress those examiners. See pages 12-14 for more on opinions.

Er hat mir gefallen. = I liked it.

Er hat mir nicht gefallen. = I didn't like it.

'Urlaub' is masculine — that's why it's 'er war', not 'es' or 'sie'.

Er war in Ordnung. = It was OK.

The more interesting things you can say, the more marks you get

You need to know all this vocab for writing and talking about holidays. You can always make up a holiday you didn't have, if you know the German words for it. Smile — it could be worse. Just.

Talking About Your Holiday

Why stop at just one tense? Start talking about future travel plans and a whole world of extra marks will open up to you...

Wohin wirst du fahren? — Where will you go?

You've got to be able to talk about the future — things that you will be doing. These are the sorts of questions you might get asked. They're all in the future tense...

Wohin wirst du fahren? = Where will you go?

Mit wem wirst du in den Urlaub fahren? = Who will you go on holiday with?

Wie wirst du dorthin kommen? = How will you get there?

Was wirst du machen? = What will you do?

For more about the future tense, see page 191.

... and so are these answers...

Ich werde in zwei Wochen nach Amerika fahren. = I'm going to America in two weeks.

Ich werde einen Monat lang mit meiner Familie in den Urlaub fahren. = I'm going on holiday for a month with my family.

Ich werde mit dem Wagen fahren. = I'm going there by car.

Ich werde an den Strand gehen. = I'm going to the beach.

The future tense is another impressive one to use

If you're not too well up on your future tense, then now's probably the time to take a quick look at the grammar section. Whatever you say, you'll get the most marks for getting the sentence right.

Talking About Your Holiday

Finally, you might want to talk about an exchange visit you did with school.
It's the sort of thing that makes an exam board go weak at the knees...

Ein deutscher Austausch — A German Exchange

Letztes Jahr bin ich nach Deutschland gefahren, um meinen Brieffreund zu besuchen. = Last year I went to Germany in order to visit my pen friend.

my pen friend (female): meine Brieffreundin

For more about 'um... zu...' ('in order to') see page 209.

Ich habe Deutschland mit der Schule besucht. Ich habe bei einer deutschen Familie gewohnt. = I visited Germany with school. I stayed with a German family.

host family: Gastfamilie

Während meines Austausches habe ich die Schule meines Freundes besucht. = During my exchange I visited my friend's school.

my (female) friend: meiner Freundin

This is the genitive case. For more info see page 157.

Wir haben uns sehr gut verstanden. = We got on really well.

Find a way to sneak in the **future tense**

The more tenses you show you can use, the more impressive you'll sound and the more marks you'll pick up.

Diesen Sommer wird mein Brieffreund nach England kommen. = This summer my pen friend will come to England.

It's usual to use the accusative here, so it's 'diesen' not 'dieser'.

More tenses = more marks — but get them right

So, that just about wraps up talking about your holiday. There's loads of stuff you can say, which makes this a really important topic. Make sure you know it well. I mean ultra-well.

The Weather

You may well have to talk about the weather yourself, or understand a forecast in your listening exam. But don't worry — just learn this lot and the stuff on the next page.

Wie ist das Wetter? — What's the weather like?

These short phrases are the ones you definitely can't do without — luckily, they're easy.

Es regnet. = It's raining.

It's snowing:	Es schneit	*There's lightning:*	Es blitzt
It's thundering:	Es donnert	*It's hailing:*	Es hagelt

Die Sonne scheint. = The sun's shining.

Es ist kalt. = It's cold.

hot:	heiß	*cloudy:*	bewölkt	*warm:*	warm
humid:	feucht	*rainy:*	regnerisch	*dry:*	trocken
windy:	windig	*overcast:*	bedeckt	*foggy:*	nebelig
sunny:	sonnig	*wet:*	nass	*cool:*	kühl

Wie ist die Temperatur? = What's the temperature?

You can also say 'Wie viel Grad ist es?' — it means the same thing.

Es ist siebzehn Grad Celsius. = It is 17 °C.

You can also say 'Es ist siebzehn Grad.' — it means the same thing.

Wie war das Wetter? — How was the weather?

You'll need to be able to talk about the weather in the past tense too — especially useful when you're discussing your last holiday.

Die Sonne schien und es war heiß. = The sun shone and it was hot.

It rained:	Es hat geregnet
It snowed:	Es hat geschneit

cold:	kalt
rainy:	regnerisch

You could use the perfect tense (see pages 192-193) and say 'die Sonne hat geschienen' for 'the sun shone', but it's more normal to say 'die Sonne schien' — that's the imperfect tense (see page 194).

You need to know all this vocab

All I want to know is "Do I need a coat?" and "Will I get a tan?" Still, this stuff comes up in the exams so you've got to do it — luckily it's not that hard. Learn the vocab and the main sentences. Sorted.

The Weather

Thought you'd seen the last of weather? Oh no. There's plenty more where that came from. I could do this for days, I really could...

Wie wird das Wetter morgen? — What will the weather be like tomorrow?

You'll be dead impressive if you know this — and it's fairly easy. Ideal.

Next week: Nächste Woche
On Tuesday: Am Dienstag

Morgen wird es schneien. = Tomorrow it will snow.

rain:	regnen	*be cold:*	kalt sein
thunder:	donnern	*be windy:*	windig sein
be hot:	heiß sein	*be cloudy:*	bewölkt sein

See pages 5-6 for more on times and dates, and page 191 for using 'werden' to talk about the future.

Die Wettervorhersage — The weather forecast

This is the crunch — a real weather forecast. You might not know all the words, but you don't need to. Look at the bits of words you do know and have a guess.

Work through this one, and see if you can figure out what each bit means. Any words you don't know will be in the dictionary at the back of the book.

Der Wetterbericht für heute
Heute wird es in Deutschland warm sein. Morgen wird es im Süden windig und im Norden bewölkt sein. An der Küste wird es regnen.

today:	heute
in the south:	im Süden
in the north:	im Norden

When you've translated it as well as you can, check it against this:

Today's Weather Report
Today it will be warm in Germany. Tomorrow it will be windy in the South and cloudy in the North. It will rain on the coast.

You could easily get a weather report in your listening exam

Now, luckily for you, there's not too much extra vocab on this page, so all you have to do is learn the sentence structures. Get to it and you'll be working for the Met Office in no time...

Quick Questions

Hurrah! The last set of Quick Questions before the Exam Practice bit kicks in. Make sure you can answer these really, really well. Not long now till the end of the section...

Quick Questions

1) You go to a restaurant in Germany. Ask for a table for four, in German. Say you'd like to sit on the terrace.
2) You get shown to your seats. How would you ask to see the menu of the day?
3) You see the following words on the menu. What do they mean in English?
   a) der Nachtisch
   b) die Vorspeise
   c) das Hauptgericht
4) It's time to order. Say that you would like the fried sausage with chips.
5) Your friend is having German noodles. Ask her in German what they taste like.
6) When your sausage arrives, it's overcooked. Attract the waiter's attention and tell him this.
7) It's time to pay. Ask for the bill.
8) Ask if service is included.
9) You're telling your German exchange partner all about your recent holiday. Tell him that you went to France last month.
10) Say that you went on holiday for a fortnight with your friends and that you stayed on a campsite.
11) How would you tell your friend 'We went there by boat'?
12) How would you tell your friend 'I went to the beach and I played tennis'?
13) Your friend is going on holiday too. Translate the following sentences about what he will be doing into English.
    a) Ich werde in einem Monat in die Schweiz fahren.
    b) Ich werde eine Woche lang mit meiner Familie in einem Hotel bleiben.
    c) Wir werden mit dem Flugzeug dorthin kommen.
14) Give the German for the following:
    a) pen friend (male)
    b) pen friend (female)
    c) a German exchange
    d) host family
15) How would you say the following in German:
    a) It's raining.
    b) The sun's shining.
    c) It's hot and humid.
    d) It was overcast.
    e) It snowed.
    f) It's 18 °C.
16) Translate this German weather report into English.

> Heute wird es in Deutschland nass und nebelig sein. Morgen wird es im Süden donnern und im Norden hageln. In Berlin wird es kühl und windig sein.

Listening Questions

Here you go, a few Listening Questions to start off your Exam Practice. Question 2 might look tricky, but don't forget, you get to hear each track twice. You might find it helps to make notes after the first recording, then write your final answer down after the second.

Track 8

1 Four people are discussing different ways of getting around. Match each speaker to a mode of transport by writing the correct letter in the box.

Example: Max	C		A	tram
a)	Anna		B	underground
b)	Paul		C	bicycle
c)	Julia		D	train
			E	plane
			F	car

Track 9

2 You're listening to today's weather report for Germany on the radio.

a) What's the temperature going to be today in North Germany?

....

b) What's the weather going to be like today on the North Sea coast?

....

c) Where will it be both hot and dry today?

....

d) What's the weather going to be like tomorrow in the West?

....

Reading Question

1 You're on holiday and read this restaurant review in the local paper.

Das Gasthaus „zur Krone"

Das Gasthaus „zur Krone", das in der schönen Altstadt liegt, hat ein großes historisches Restaurant mit dreißig Tischen drinnen und zehn Tischen draußen.

Ich bin um acht Uhr angekommen. Als Vorspeise hatte ich mein Lieblingsgericht Gulaschsuppe und meine Freundin hatte ein Champignonomelett. Die Suppe hat sehr gut geschmeckt, aber das Omelett war zu salzig.

Meine Freundin, die Vegetarierin ist, war enttäuscht, weil es nur wenige Hauptgerichte für sie gab. Sie hat Pizza Margherita gewählt. Ich habe Brathähnchen mit Pommes frites und Salat gegessen.

Als Nachtisch hatten wir Schwarzwälder Kirschtorte — sie war lecker!

a) How many tables does the restaurant have outside?

....

b) Why did the reviewer choose goulash soup as a starter?

....

c) What was wrong with the omelette?

....

d) Why was the reviewer's girlfriend disappointed with the menu?

....

e) What was the Black Forest gateau like?

....

Speaking Question

Yup, another speaking task I'm afraid. It might seem like a lot of effort to do one of these right now, but you'll thank me in the long run. I promise.

Task: Holidays
You are talking with your exchange partner about your holiday last year.
Your teacher will play the part of your exchange partner.

Your teacher will ask you the following:

- Where did you go on holiday last year?
- How did you get there? What was the journey like?
- Where did you stay?
- What did you do in the daytime?
- What was the food like?
- Did you have any problems during your stay?
- What would you like to do next year?
- !

! Remember that the exclamation mark means you'll have to answer a question that you won't have prepared an answer to.

The whole conversation should last about five minutes.

Notes for Teachers
You need to ask the student the following questions:

- Wohin bist du letztes Jahr in den Urlaub gefahren?
- Wie bist du dorthin gekommen? Wie war die Reise?
- Wo hast du gewohnt?
- Was hast du während des Tages gemacht?
- Wie war das Essen?
- Hattest du Probleme während des Urlaubs?
- Was möchtest du nächstes Jahr machen?
- !

! The unpredictable question could be: Wenn du das Lotto gewonnen hättest, wo würdest du in den Urlaub fahren?

Writing Questions

Look upon the writing tasks as a chance to really show off what you know. Include as much good grammar and vocab as you can — and try and keep your work as accurate as possible.

Task 1: You have been asked by your exchange school to write an article for their website describing your recent visit.

You could write about the following:

- The journey
- Where you stayed
- What you did during the day
- The trips you went on
- What you did in the evening
- What you are going to do when your exchange partners come to England

You don't necessarily need to have done an exchange to do this task — write about an imaginary one.

Remember: to score the highest marks you need to answer the task fully (for grades C and above you will need to write 200-300 words).

Task 2: You have just visited Germany, but were disappointed by your hotel. Write a letter of complaint to the hotel.

Again, you can use your imagination for this task.

You could write about the following:

- Who you are and when / how long you stayed
- The room
- The hotel facilities
- The food
- If you would return in the future

This is a letter of complaint, so you need to write about the problems you had, but you could also mention things you liked about your stay.

Remember: to score the highest marks you need to answer the task fully (for grades C and above you will need to write 200-300 words).

Revision Summary

These questions are here to make sure you really know your stuff. Work through them all, and make a note of the ones you couldn't do. Look back through the section to find out how to answer them. Try those problem questions again. Then look up any you still can't do. Keep at it until you can do them all — cos that'll mean you've really learnt it.

1) Write down ten countries in German.
How would you say that you came from each one of these countries?

2) Ask for three return tickets to Dresden, second class.
Ask what platform the train leaves from and where the waiting room is.

3) Say in German that you go to school by car, but your friend walks.
(Make sure you use the right verb for these.)

4) You've missed the bus to Frankfurt.
Ask when the next bus leaves and when it arrives in Frankfurt.

5) You arrive in Tübingen and go to the tourist information office.
Ask for information about the sights.

6) There's an excursion to a nearby museum. Ask for a leaflet about the excursion.
Ask what time the bus departs from the town hall.

7) You get to a hotel in Germany. Ask them if they have any free rooms.

8) Say you want one double room and two single rooms. Say you want to stay five nights.
Say you'll take the rooms.

9) Ask where the games room is.

10) Ask the staff in your German hotel when breakfast is served.

11) You get to your room and find that's it's dirty and the shower doesn't work.
Tell the hotel staff this and say that you would like the room cleaned.

12) You're going out for a meal. Ask if you can have a table for two and ask where the toilet is.

13) Order steak and chips for you, and roast chicken with potatoes for your friend.
Attract the waitress's attention and tell her that the potatoes are cold.

14) Attract the waiter's attention and say that you'd like the bill.

15) You've just been on holiday to Italy. You went for two weeks with your sister. You went there by plane. You relaxed and sunned yourself. The weather was hot and sunny. You enjoyed the holiday and are going to go to Spain next year. Phew — say that lot in German.

16) Your German pen friend wants to know what the weather is like where you are.
Say that it is cloudy and raining, but that tomorrow the sun will shine.

Names of Buildings

You'll be able to talk about your town much better if you know what buildings there are in it — and the examiners will think you're pretty cool too. Which means bucketloads of marks.

Die Gebäude — Buildings

These are the basic, bog-standard 'learn-them-or-else' buildings. (Building = das Gebäude.) Don't go any further until you know all of them.

the bank:
die Bank (-en)

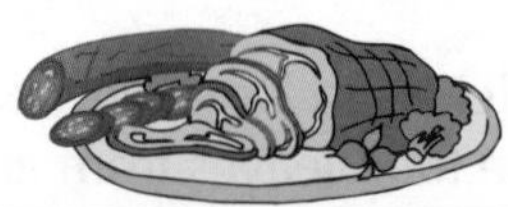

the butcher's:
die Metzgerei (-en)

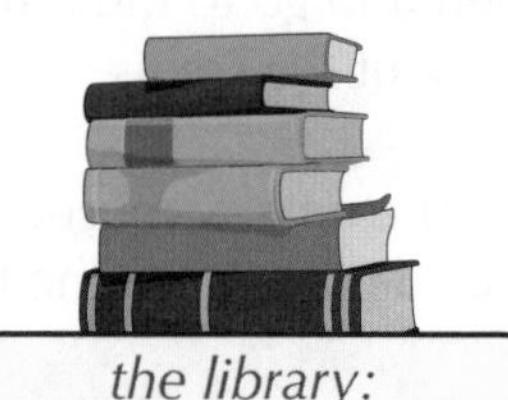

the baker's:
die Bäckerei (-en)

the theatre:
das Theater (-)

the post office:
die Post (die Postämter)

the library:
die Bibliothek (-en)

the railway station:
der Bahnhof (die Bahnhöfe)

the cinema:
das Kino (-s)

the supermarket:
der Supermarkt (die Supermärkte)

the castle:
das Schloss (die Schlösser)

the marketplace:
der Marktplatz (die Marktplätze)

the church:
die Kirche (-n)

Learn the genders of these buildings now — you'll need 'em later

You'll probably find yourself writing a lot of sentences like 'I visited the castle' and 'I'll meet you in the library'. To get top marks, you need to get your grammar right — and that means knowing your genders.

Names of Buildings

It might seem silly, learning endless lists of buildings, but not only might you have to write or talk about them yourself in your coursework, they could well crop up in a listening or reading exam too.

Andere Gebäude — Other buildings

OK, I'll come clean. There are absolutely loads of buildings you need to know...

Touristy Bits

the hotel:	das Hotel (-s)
the youth hostel:	die Jugendherberge (-n)
the restaurant:	das Restaurant (-s)
the tourist information office:	das Verkehrsamt (die Verkehrsämter)
the museum:	das Museum (die Museen)
the zoo:	der Zoo (-s)

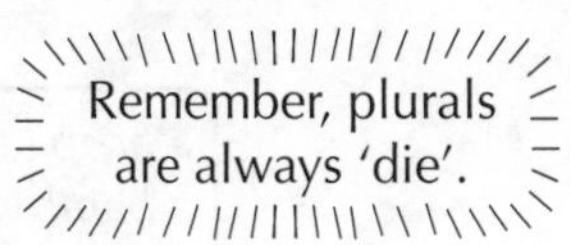
Remember, plurals are always 'die'.

Shops

the shop:	der Laden (die Läden)
the pharmacy:	die Apotheke (-n)
the chemist's:	die Drogerie (-n)
the department store:	das Kaufhaus (die Kaufhäuser)
the cake shop:	die Konditorei (-en)
the market:	der Markt (die Märkte)

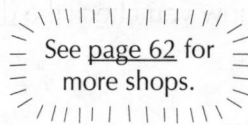

See page 62 for more shops.

Other Important Places

the hospital:	das Krankenhaus (die Krankenhäuser)
the town hall:	das Rathaus (die Rathäuser)
the cathedral:	der Dom (-e)
the park:	der Park (-s)
the airport:	der Flughafen (die Flughäfen)
the university:	die Universität (-en)
the swimming baths:	das Schwimmbad (die Schwimmbäder)
the indoor swimming pool:	das Hallenbad (die Hallenbäder)
the sports centre:	das Sportzentrum (die Sportzentren)
the stadium:	das Stadion (die Stadien)
the school:	die Schule (-n)

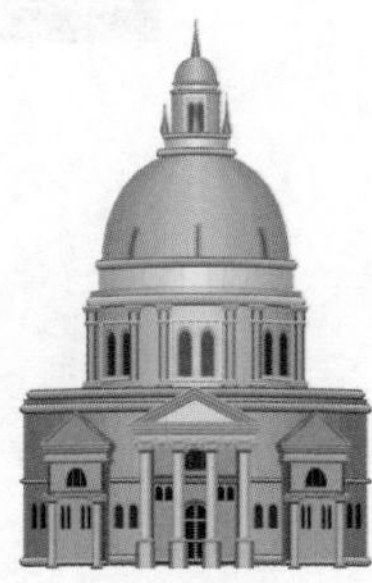

You won't learn this page just by reading it

There are lots of words to learn here. The best way to do it is to turn over the page and see if you can write them all down, have a look and then have another go... It's boring, but it works.

Asking Directions

You're probably going to get at least one question about asking directions. So this page is going to be really important. Start learning this stuff and get these phrases between your ears.

Wo ist... ? — Where is... ?

It's dead easy to ask where a place is — say 'Wo ist...' and stick the place on the end. No dodgy word order — say it how you would in English.

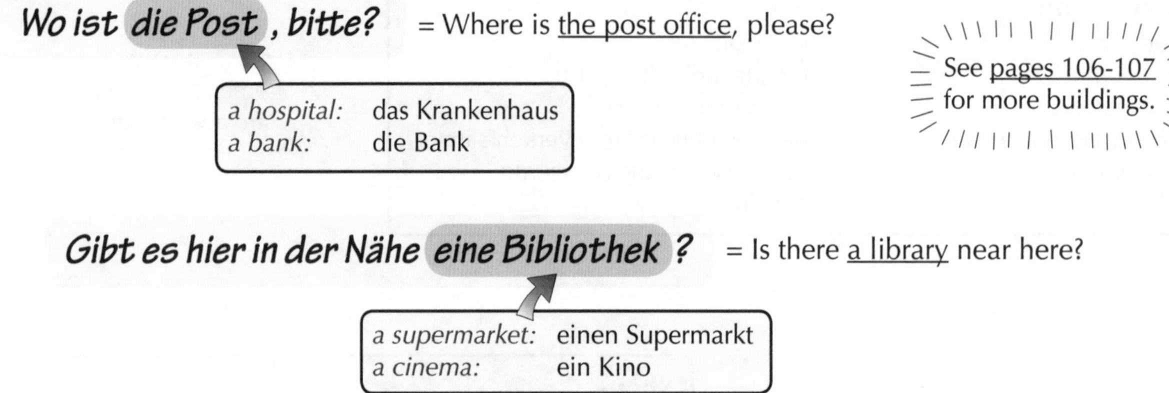

Wo ist die Post, bitte? = Where is the post office, please?
a hospital: das Krankenhaus
a bank: die Bank
Gibt es hier in der Nähe eine Bibliothek? = Is there a library near here?
a supermarket: einen Supermarkt
a cinema: ein Kino

See pages 106-107 for more buildings.

Wie weit ist es? — How far is it?

The place you're looking for might be too far to walk — you might need a bus or tram instead. Here's how you check the distance, before you let yourself in for a 3-hour trek to the airport.

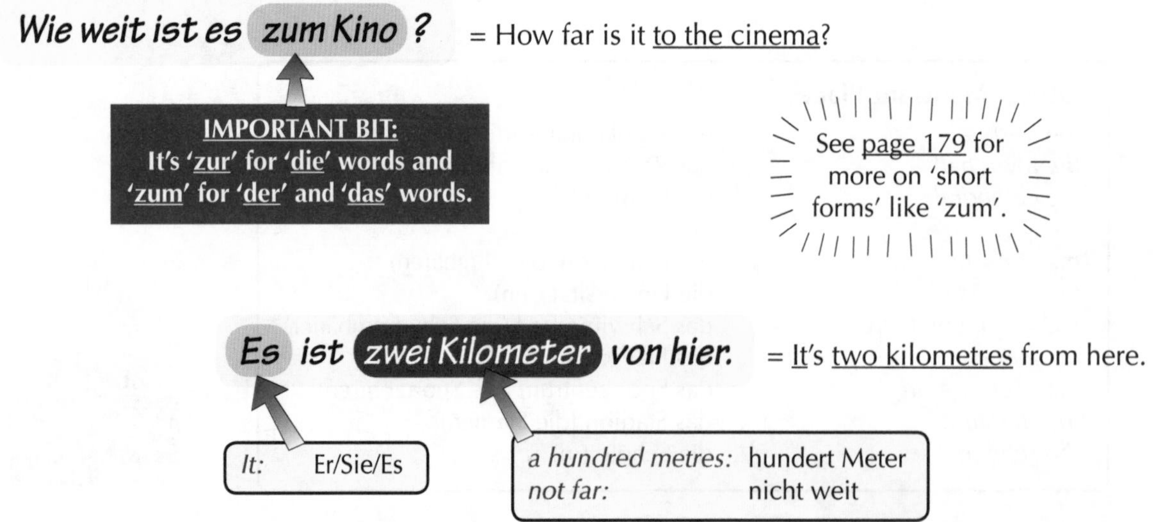

Wie weit ist es zum Kino? = How far is it to the cinema?
IMPORTANT BIT:
It's 'zur' for 'die' words and 'zum' for 'der' and 'das' words.
Es ist zwei Kilometer von hier. = It's two kilometres from here.
It: Er/Sie/Es
a hundred metres: hundert Meter
not far: nicht weit

See page 179 for more on 'short forms' like 'zum'.

Practise using these phrases with all that buildings vocab

You could well hear someone asking for or giving directions in a listening exam, so you need to know your stuff. There's more on the next page, but make sure you're happy with this first.

Asking Directions

Here's the rest of what you'll need to know about asking directions...

Wie komme ich zu...? — How do I get to...?

If you're not standing right in front of it, you'll need directions.
Here's how you ask for them...

to the station:	zum Bahnhof
to the library:	zur Bibliothek
to the castle:	zum Schloss

Entschuldigen Sie bitte, wie komme ich zur Bank?

= Excuse me please, how do I get to the bank?

IMPORTANT BIT:
Swap this for any place, using 'zum' for 'der' and 'das' words and 'zur' for 'die' words.

You can add 'am besten' into the sentence (before the building) to ask the best way to get there.

Wie komme ich am besten zum Bahnhof?

= What's the best way to the station?

You'll need all this vocabulary to understand any directions you're given:

go straight on:	gehen Sie geradeaus
go right:	gehen Sie rechts
go left:	gehen Sie links
on the corner:	an der Ecke
round the corner:	um die Ecke
over there:	dort drüben/da drüben

Look at page 3 for more stuff on 1st, 2nd, etc.

take the first road on the left:	nehmen Sie die erste Straße links
right at the traffic lights:	rechts an der Ampel
straight on, past the church:	geradeaus, an der Kirche vorbei
on the right-hand/left-hand side:	auf der rechten/linken Seite

You'll need to know your left from right

It's time to cover up the page and see how much of the vocab you can remember — and keep going until you know it all. Use the phrases on all the buildings you can remember from pages 106-107.

Quick Questions

You might think that a good revision session involves leisurely skimming through the pages of this book, occasionally stopping to gaze out of the window / help yourself to a biscuit / flick through the TV guide. Well, it doesn't. Harsh, I know. You need to do some active learning to really make sure you're taking things in. Which is where these Quick Questions come in...

Quick Questions

1) Give the names of these buildings in German:
   a) the bank
   b) the butcher's
   c) the baker's
   d) the railway station
   e) the church
   f) the marketplace
   g) the cinema

2) The following German sentences all contain the name of a building. For each sentence, give the name of the building in English.
   a) Das Hallenbad ist sehr kalt.
   b) Ich fahre zum Flughafen.
   c) Ich muss ins Krankenhaus gehen.
   d) Ich habe in einem schönen Hotel gewohnt.
   e) Die Fußballmannschaft spielt im Stadion.
   f) Wir treffen uns vor dem Dom.
   g) Es ist meine Lieblingskonditorei.
   h) Ich habe einen fantastischen Mantel im Kaufhaus gefunden.

3) You're lost in a German town. How would you ask a nice friendly policeman the following questions?
   a) Where is the town hall please?
   b) Is there a pharmacy near here?
   c) How far is it to the tourist information office?

4) In answer to your last question, the policeman replied, 'Es ist zweihundert Meter von hier'. What did he say in English?

5) You make it to the tourist information office. Once you're there, how would you ask 'What's the best way to the castle?'

6) The man in the tourist office is only too happy to help. You receive the following very detailed directions. Well you did ask. Translate them into English.

> Gehen Sie geradeaus, an der Kirche vorbei, dann nehmen Sie die erste Straße links. Gehen Sie rechts an der Ampel, um die Ecke und es ist auf der linken Seite.

7) When you get out onto the street, someone asks you where the pharmacy is. Good job you asked that policeman earlier. How would you say 'it's over there on the corner' in German?

Where You're From

At some point, you're probably going to get asked about where you're from. And you're going to have to be able to answer. So it's a good job you're reading this page.

Woher kommst du? — Where do you come from?

Get this phrase learnt off by heart — if the country you're from isn't here, look at pages 79-80, or go look it up in a dictionary.

Ich komme aus England. Ich bin Engländer(in). = I come from England. I am English.

Wales:	Wales
Northern Ireland:	Nordirland
Scotland:	Schottland
Great Britain:	Großbritannien

Welsh:	Waliser(in)
Northern Irish:	Nordirländer(in)
Scottish:	Schotte/Schottin
British:	Brite/Britin

IMPORTANT BIT:
You must add '-in' on the end for women and girls.

With 'Schotte' and 'Brite' you also have to remove the '-e' from the end before you add on the '-in' to make the feminine versions.

Wo wohnst du? = Where do you live?

Ich wohne in England. = I live in England.

Wo wohnst du? — Where do you live?

You're bound to get asked this at some point — so get your answer ready.

Ich wohne in Barrow. = I live in Barrow.

Barrow liegt in Nordwestengland. = Barrow's in the north-west of England.

in the north:	im Norden	*in the south:*	im Süden	*in south-east England:*	in Südostengland
in the east:	im Osten	*in the west:*	im Westen	*in north Scotland:*	in Nordschottland

a city: eine Großstadt *a village:* ein Dorf

Barrow ist eine Stadt mit ungefähr 60 000 Einwohnern und viel Industrie. = Barrow is a town with about 60 000 inhabitants and a lot of industry.

See page 159 for an explanation of the '-n' on the end of 'Einwohner'.

Nationalities have masculine and feminine versions

This page is fairly straightforward, which — after all that asking for directions stuff — is quite nice. It's so straightforward in fact that you'd be a fool not to learn it. So I suggest you get to it...

Talking About Where You Live

Whether you like where you live or not, you can still find plenty to say about it.

Die Gegend von Plymouth... — The Plymouth area...

Come up with this little lot and you'll knock your teacher for six...

Plymouth liegt am Meer. = Plymouth is by the sea.

in the countryside:	auf dem Land	*on the Scottish border:*	an der schottischen Grenze
by a river:	an einem Fluss	*on the coast:*	an der Küste
near London:	in der Nähe von London	*in the mountains:*	in den Bergen

Dative plural — noun adds '-n'. See page 159.

Die Landschaft um Plymouth ist sehr schön und grün. = The landscape around Plymouth is very beautiful and green.

More really important stuff — you'll need to be able to talk about the place where you live, where your home is and what it looks like.

In deiner Stadt — In your town

This sort of thing is easy marks. Make sure you can reel off those buildings at the drop of a hat.

Was gibt es in deiner Stadt? = What is there in your town?

You need the accusative case (see page 156) after 'Es gibt'.
Es gibt einen Markt. = There's a market.
a cathedral: einen Dom
a park: einen Park
a university: eine Universität
a sports centre: ein Sportzentrum
See pages 106-107 for more buildings.

Wohnst du gern in Barrow? = Do you like living in Barrow?

Ich wohne gern in Barrow. = I like living in Barrow.

don't like: nicht gern

Yep, you've got to give an opinion again

Make sure you learn these phrases, then you can happily regurgitate them in your speaking and writing tasks. Try and come up with something a little bit interesting to say about your home town too.

Talking About Where You Live

As always — when you give an opinion, try to back it up with a reason why.

Was für eine Stadt ist Hull? — What kind of town is Hull?

If you want a really good mark, make sure you're ready to give more details.
It's always best if you can give an opinion and then say why.

Die Stadt ist sehr interessant. = The town is very interesting.

boring:	langweilig
great:	klasse/prima
dirty:	schmutzig
clean:	sauber
quiet/peaceful:	ruhig/still

See pages 12-14 for more on opinions.

Es gibt viel zu tun. = There's lots to do.

nothing:	nichts
enough:	genug
not much/little:	wenig
always something:	immer etwas

Ich mag Hull, weil... — I like Hull because...

Put them all together and make a longer sentence — you'll get extra marks if you get it right.

'Weil' sends the verb to the end of the sentence. See page 166.

Put the name of your town in here.

Ich wohne gern in Hull, weil es immer viel zu tun gibt. = I like living in Hull, because there's always lots to do.

Ich wohne nicht gern in Hull, weil es nichts zu tun gibt. = I don't like living in Hull, because there's nothing to do.

Learn how to describe your town

If you think you come from a really dreary place which has nothing going for it, you can make things up (within reason) — but chances are there'll be something to say about a place near you.

Your House

Being able to talk about where you live is really important...

Beschreib dein Haus... — Describe your house...

Watch out — in German addresses, the house number comes after the street name, and the street name is joined to the word 'Straße'.

Ich wohne in der Magdalenstraße 24 in Lancaster.

= I live at 24 Magdalen Street, in Lancaster.

Ich wohne in einem kleinen, alten Haus. = I live in a small old house.

big:	großen	*modern:*	modernen
new:	neuen	*cold:*	kalten

See pages 169-170 for more on adjective endings.

Remember, plurals are always 'die'.

Types of House

house:	das Haus (die Häuser)
flat:	die Wohnung (-en)
semi-detached house:	das Doppelhaus (die Doppelhäuser)
detached house:	das Einfamilienhaus (die Einfamilienhäuser)
terraced house:	das Reihenhaus (die Reihenhäuser)

My house: Mein Haus

Meine Wohnung liegt in der Nähe von einem Park. = My flat is near a park.

See page 179 for 'in' and 'von' with the dative.

the town centre:	der Stadtmitte
the motorway:	der Autobahn
the shops:	den Geschäften
a shopping centre:	einem Einkaufszentrum
a bus stop:	einer Bushaltestelle
a train station:	einem Bahnhof

These are all in the dative case.

Hast du einen Garten? — Have you got a garden?

Mein Haus hat einen Garten.

= My house has a garden.

My flat: Meine Wohnung

Wir haben Blumen in unserem Garten.

= We have flowers in our garden.

a tree:	einen Baum (die Bäume)
a lawn:	einen Rasen

Lots more vocab for you to learn here

This is stuff they could easily chuck at you. You really need to know how to describe your house and garden and you should definitely be able to understand all the words if you read or hear them.

Inside Your Home

You've got to be able to describe what's in your home. It may not look exciting, but ignore it at your peril.

Wie ist dein Haus? — What's your house like?

Whether or not you need to ask where rooms are in your exchange partner's home, you do need to know this stuff for the exams. To make the second question a bit more polite, just add 'bitte' on the end — easy.

Wie sieht die Küche aus? = What does the kitchen look like?

the living room:	das Wohnzimmer (-)	*the dining room:*	das Esszimmer (-)
the bathroom:	das Badezimmer (-) / das Bad (die Bäder)	*the bedroom:*	das Schlafzimmer (-)

Wo ist die Küche? = Where is the kitchen?

small: klein *huge:* riesig *tiny:* winzig

Ist die Küche groß? = Is the kitchen big?

Wie ist dein Schlafzimmer? — What's your bedroom like?

Was für Möbel hast du im Schlafzimmer? = What kind of furniture do you have in the bedroom?

Im Schlafzimmer habe ich ein Bett, zwei Stühle und einen kleinen Tisch. = In the bedroom I have a bed, two chairs and a small table.

You can use any of these words in the coloured boxes above, but you need to get the right endings for 'ein' — the accusative case is used after 'habe'. See pages 156 and 168 for more info.

Things in the Home

armchair:	der Sessel (-)	*carpet:*	der Teppich (-e)
sofa:	das Sofa (-s)	*ceiling:*	die Decke (-n)
lamp:	die Lampe (-n)	*wardrobe:*	der Kleiderschrank (die Kleiderschränke)
table:	der Tisch (-e)	*wallpaper:*	die Tapete
chair:	der Stuhl (die Stühle)	*bed:*	das Bett (-en)
cupboard:	der Schrank (die Schränke)	*double bed:*	das Doppelbett (-en)
wall:	die Wand (die Wände)	*curtains (plural):*	die Vorhänge

Remember, plurals are always 'die'.

You might want to look up adjectives and their endings

Get learning the words above for what's in your room — and remember that if your room doesn't have any of these things in it, you can always lie — as long as you get the vocab right.

Quick Questions

You really do need to know all the stuff you've read on the last few pages — so here are a few Quick Questions, to make absolutely sure that you do.

Quick Questions

1) Write out three sentences (in German), saying the following:
   a) where you come from
   b) what nationality you are
   c) what country you live in

2) Translate the following sentences into English:
   a) Ich wohne in Newcastle in Nordostengland.
   b) Ich wohne in Cardiff in Südwales.
   c) Ich wohne auf dem Land in der Nähe von Bristol.
   d) Mein Dorf liegt in Nordirland an einem Fluss.
   e) Oban liegt an der schottischen Küste.
   f) Meine Stadt liegt in den walisischen Bergen.

3) You're describing the picturesque market town of Boddley-Bibbington to your German friend. How would you say the following in German?
   a) There's a market, a church and a library.
   b) The town is clean and peaceful.
   c) There's not much to do.
   d) I don't like living in Boddley-Bibbington because it's boring.

4) Translate these sentences into English:
   a) Ich wohne in einem modernen Einfamilienhaus.
   b) Wir wohnen in einem alten Reihenhaus.
   c) Meine Wohnung liegt in der Nähe von den Geschäften.
   d) Das Doppelhaus liegt in der Nähe von der Autobahn.
   e) Mein Haus hat einen kleinen Garten mit einem großen Baum.

5) This is a bit of an e-mail sent to you by your German friend, briefly describing her house. Translate it into English.

> Ich wohne in einem neuen Doppelhaus in der Stadtmitte. Es gibt ein großes Wohnzimmer, ein Esszimmer, eine Küche, drei Schlafzimmer und ein winziges Badezimmer. Mein Haus hat einen Garten, aber keinen Rasen. Mein Schlafzimmer ist klein und die Wände sind gelb.

6) Name the following items of furniture in German:
   a) armchair
   b) lamp
   c) table
   d) bed
   e) wardrobe

7) Write a few sentences describing the following in German:
   a) your home
   b) your garden (if you have one — if not, make one up)
   c) your bedroom

Celebrations

Time to get the party poppers out — this page is gonna be a hoot...
Now where did I put my balloon animals...

Wann feierst du? — When do you celebrate?

There are loads of things you can celebrate — any excuse for a party and all that. Here are just a few:

Put the date you celebrate here. For more on dates see page 6.

Wir feiern Weihnachten am fünfundzwanzigsten Dezember.

= We celebrate Christmas on the 25th of December.

Christmas Eve:	Heiligabend	*Hanukkah:*	Chanukka
New Year's Eve:	Silvester	*Ramadan:*	Ramadan
New Year:	Neujahr	*Easter:*	Ostern
my birthday:	meinen Geburtstag		

Mit wem feierst du? — Who do you celebrate with?

Well it's no fun celebrating alone — it also wouldn't give you much to talk about in a speaking assessment, say.

my friends:	meinen Freunden
my parents:	meinen Eltern

Ich feiere meinen Geburtstag mit meiner Familie.

= I celebrate my birthday with my family.

Normalerweise habe ich eine Party zu Hause. = Normally I have a party at home.

in the restaurant:	im Restaurant
at a hotel:	in einem Hotel

Learn these celebrations

Even if you don't celebrate it, it's a good idea to know what 'Christmas' is in German — this sort of thing could just as easily come up in a listening or reading exam as a coursework assessment piece.

Celebrations

This page is all about how people celebrate their festivals...

Wie feierst du? — How do you celebrate?

These examiners want to know everything, the nosy beggars...

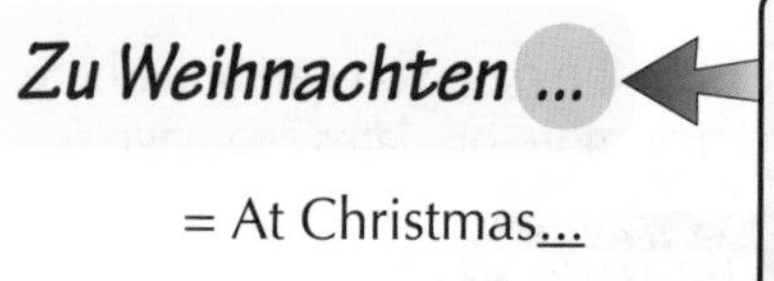

= At Christmas...

...we have a Christmas tree:	...haben wir einen Weihnachtsbaum
...we send Christmas cards:	...senden wir Weihnachtskarten
...we give presents:	...geben wir Geschenke
...we sing carols:	...singen wir Weihnachtslieder

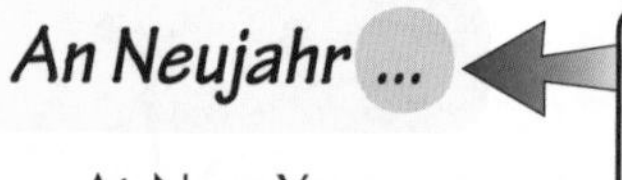

= At New Year...

...we have fireworks:	...haben wir Feuerwerk
...we dance:	...tanzen wir
...we have fun:	...machen wir uns Spaß

Deutsche Feste... — German Festivals...

You'll really impress those examiners if you know anything about German festivals and how they celebrate them.

Letztes Jahr war ich in Köln für Rosenmontag.
Es gab große Umzüge mit Singen und Tanzen.
Es hat viel Spaß gemacht.

= Last year I was in Cologne for Rosenmontag.
There were giant parades with singing and dancing.
It was a lot of fun.

'Rosenmontag' is the high point of the German Catholic festival season, 'Karneval' (also called 'Fasching'). It's the day before Shrove Tuesday (Pancake Day).

The main Karneval celebrations take place in the weeks leading up to Lent (Jan-Feb), but in some places start as early as November. There are parades, street parties, dances and much more.

Talk about German festivals to really impress

Well, that was fun... Admittedly not as fun as actually celebrating something, but still...
There's loads you can say about festivals and the like — just make sure you've cracked this lot first.

The Environment

Things get serious when the environment comes up, and you're supposed to have an opinion. It's a chance for you to write or say what you think about something real and important — not just what colour velour jumpsuit you'd like to buy in the sale.

Ist die Umwelt wichtig für dich..? — Is the environment important to you..?

Ja, ich halte die Umwelt für total wichtig. = Yes, I think the environment is very important.

Always give a reason why — it'll make your teacher go all tingly inside...

Ich habe große Angst um die Umwelt wegen des Treibhauseffekts. = I'm really worried about the environment because of the greenhouse effect.

because of the hole in the ozone layer:	wegen des Ozonloches
because we don't recycle enough:	weil wir nicht genug recyceln

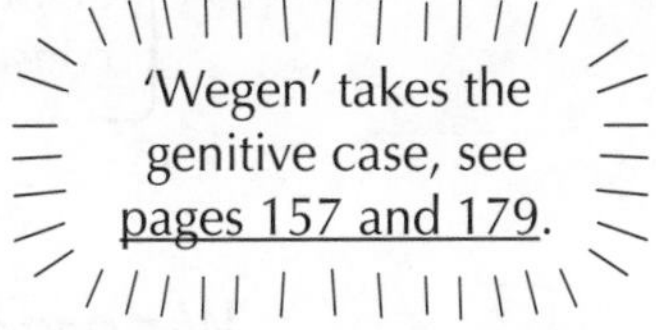
'Wegen' takes the genitive case, see pages 157 and 179.

Wir müssen die Umwelt schützen oder unsere Kinder werden leiden.

= We must protect the environment or our children will suffer.

Hast du Angst um die Umwelt..? — Do you worry about the environment..?

Nein, ich interessiere mich ganz und gar nicht dafür.

= No, I'm not at all interested in it.

Es geht mich nichts an. Ich bin sehr beschäftigt und ich habe keine Zeit zu recyceln.

= It doesn't concern me. I am very busy and I don't have time to recycle.

Blumen und die Natur sind todlangweilig. Ich mag lieber Computerspiele. = Flowers and nature are dead boring. I prefer computer games.

You don't have to love all things green — just be able to say so

There are so many different aspects of the environment you could choose to talk about — as always, be wise and learn the basics. There's more of this to come, so learn this lot before turning over...

The Environment

Yep, more on the environment I'm afraid. It is a pretty big topic after all.
There's lots more vocab to be learnt on this page, so be prepared...

Es gibt schwere Umweltprobleme...
— There are serious environmental problems...

You might get asked about, or hear people talking about, problems with the environment.
Here are some of the biggies...

Es gibt zu viel Verschmutzung. = There is too much pollution.

noise pollution:	Lärmbelästigung
water pollution:	Wasserverschmutzung
deforestation:	Abholzung
consumption:	Verbrauch

Wir produzieren zu viel Müll. = We produce too much rubbish.

greenhouse gases like carbon dioxide:	Treibhausgase wie Kohlendioxyd
CFCs:	FCKWs

Chemische Pestizide und Insektizide schaden der Umwelt.

= Chemical pesticides and insecticides damage the environment.

Luftverschmutzung durch Abgase gefährdet die Umwelt.

= Air pollution through exhaust fumes endangers the environment.

Saurer Regen kommt von Gasen wie Schwefeldioxyd.

= Acid rain comes from gases like sulphur dioxide.

Learn this environment-related lingo

If you learn all this vocab, you'll be halfway there when it comes to talking about the environment.
And whatever your opinion is, you'll have a hard job giving it if you don't know the right words.

The Environment

So, you know what the problems are — what can you do about them?

Wie kann man mehr umweltfreundlich sein? — How can you be more environmentally friendly?

IMPORTANT:
'Umweltfreundlich' means 'environmentally friendly' — 'umweltfeindlich' means 'environmentally unfriendly'. Don't mix them up.

Jeder kann mehr umweltfreundlich sein.

= Everyone can be more environmentally friendly.

Zum Beispiel fahre ich mit dem Rad in die Schule.

= For example, I travel to school by bike.

recycle our waste paper:	unser Altpapier recyceln
recycle packaging:	Verpackungen recyceln
use fewer fossil fuels:	weniger fossile Brennstoffe benutzen
use less water:	weniger Wasser benutzen

Wir sollten mit öffentlichen Verkehrsmittel fahren.

= We should travel using public transport.

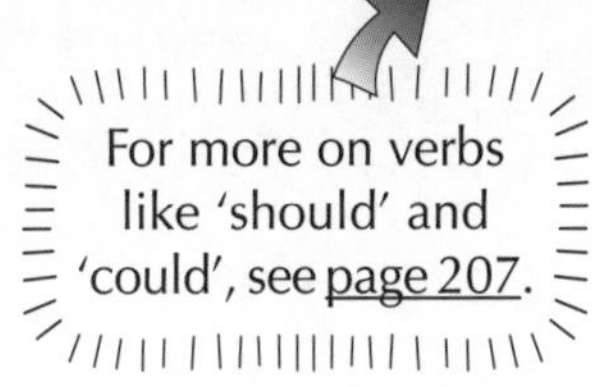
For more on verbs like 'should' and 'could', see page 207.

If you're really up on green matters then you could get well stuck into this, but if you're not then say so. You'll get as many marks for saying why you're not interested as you would for enthusing about Greenpeace.

This sort of stuff could easily be sneaked into a reading comprehension or a listening conversation, so make sure you're familiar with it.

Have a few of these stock phrases up your sleeve

If you get asked a question about the environment in your speaking assessment, look on it as an opportunity to really show off. There's some pretty mark-worthy vocab on this page — so learn it.

Quick Questions

As if this section just couldn't get <u>any better</u> — here are a few <u>Quick Questions</u> for you...

Quick Questions

1) Give the German for:
   a) Christmas
   b) Christmas Eve
   c) New Year's Eve
   d) New Year
   e) Hanukkah
   f) Ramadan

2) How would you say "We celebrate my birthday on the 23rd of May" in German?

3) What does "Wir haben Ostern am vierten April gefeiert" mean in English?

4) You're talking to your German exchange partner about how you celebrate Christmas and New Year. How would you say "At Christmas we have a Christmas tree"?

5) Your exchange partner tells you, "Wir geben Geschenke und senden Weihnachtskarten". What does this mean in English?

6) How would you say "I celebrate New Year with my family and friends" in German?

7) Translate the following sentence into English:
   "Normalerweise haben wir eine Party zu Hause mit Tanzen und Feuerwerk".

8) Translate these words to do with the environment into English:
   a) das Ozonloch
   b) der Treibhauseffekt
   c) die Lärmbelästigung
   d) die Wasserverschmutzung
   e) das Schwefeldioxyd
   f) das Kohlendioxyd
   g) die fossile Brennstoffe
   h) der Müll

9) Write out the following sentences in German:
   a) I think the environment is very important.
   b) Everyone can be more environmentally friendly.
   c) We should recycle our waste paper.
   d) We should use less water.

10) Heinz is telling you what he thinks about the environment. Translate what he says into English.

> Ich interessiere mich ganz und gar nicht für die Umwelt. Ich bin sehr beschäftigt und ich habe keine Zeit zu recyceln. Ich fahre nie mit öffentlichen Verkehrsmittel, weil ich absolut keine Angst vor dem Treibhauseffekt oder dem Ozonloch habe. Die Umwelt ist total langweilig.

Listening Questions

Track 10

1 Three of your friends are giving you directions for where to meet them.

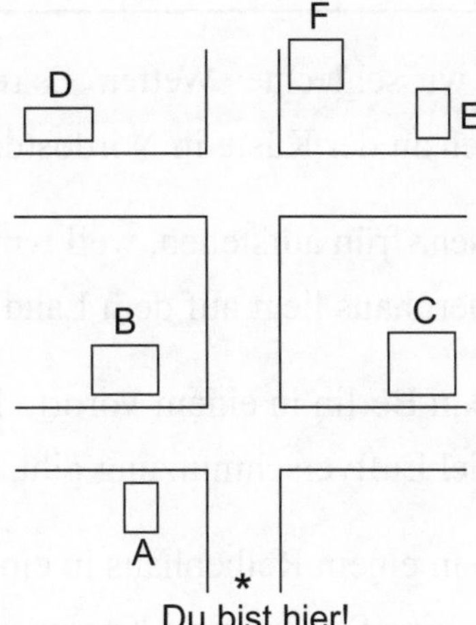

For each person, write the correct letter in the box.

a) Johanna ☐

b) Alexander ☐

c) Lena ☐

Track 11

2 Karl is telling you about his home town.
Which three of the statements below are true?

A Karl lives in a small industrial town.

B Unemployment is a big problem in his town.

C There is a new car factory there.

D The town has an excellent transport system.

E The airport is less than 20 kilometres from the town.

F There's plenty for young people to do.

Write the correct letters in the boxes. ☐ ☐ ☐

Reading Question

1 These students are all writing about where they live.

Andreas:	Oft haben wir schlechtes Wetter. Es regnet und ist stürmisch. Wir wohnen an der Küste in Nordostdeutschland.
Monika:	Ich muss sehr früh aufstehen, weil wir viele Tiere haben. Unser Bauernhaus liegt auf dem Land.
Thomas:	Ich wohne in Berlin in einem Vorort. Ich mag Berlin nicht, da es zu viel Luftverschmutzung gibt.
Hanna:	Ich wohne in einem Reihenhaus in einem kleinen Dorf. Es gibt nur eine Straße, zwei Kneipen und einen Laden.
Bernd:	Wir haben ein Hotel in den Bergen. Wir bekommen viele Touristen, die wandern und Ski laufen.
Vanessa:	Ich wohne in Norddeutschland an der dänischen Grenze. Wir fahren oft auf Urlaub in Skandinavien.
Matthais:	Wir wohnen in Oberfell an einem Fluss. Es ist sehr ruhig, obwohl wir viele Besucher bekommen.
Selina:	Ich wohne im Schwarzwald. Die Landschaft ist wunderschön. Unser traditionelles Haus liegt im Wald.

Example: Who lives in the mountains? ***Bernd***

a) Who lives on a border? ....

b) Who lives in a village? ....

c) Who lives in a suburb? ....

d) Who lives by the sea? ....

e) Who lives by a river? ....

Speaking Question

The writing task isn't the only place where you should be thinking about showing off all that excellent grammar and vocab you've learnt — that sort of thing really needs to come across in your speaking assessment too.

Task: The Environment
You are talking to a German magazine about environmental issues near you.
Your teacher will play the part of the magazine's writer.

Your teacher will ask you the following:

- Where do you live?
- What environmental problems are there in your town?
- Are there any environmental problems outside the town?
- Do you think these problems will get worse in the future?
- Are you environmentally friendly?
- What do you do in school for the environment?
- Is noise pollution a problem in your town?
- ! — *Plan in advance what you could say to this. You need to think about what would be a good question to ask, but which hasn't come up yet.*

! Remember that the exclamation mark means you'll have to answer a question that you won't have prepared an answer to.

The whole conversation should last about five minutes.

Notes for Teachers
You need to ask the student the following questions:

- Wo wohnst du?
- Was für Umweltprobleme gibt es in deiner Stadt?
- Gibt es Umweltprobleme außerhalb der Stadt?
- Glaubst du, dass diese Probleme in der Zukunft verschlechtern werden?
- Bist du umweltfreundlich?
- Was macht ihr in der Schule für die Umwelt?
- Ist Lärmbelästigung ein Problem in deiner Stadt?
- !

! The unpredictable question could be:
Was kann man für die Umwelt in deiner Stadt machen?

Writing Questions

These tasks aren't just here for you to have a look at, you know. Try planning and writing your own responses to them — it's great practice for the real thing.

Task 1: You are writing an article for your exchange school's magazine on celebrations in Britain and Germany.

You could write about the following:

In the writing tasks, you don't have to use the suggestions in the bullet points — so if you don't celebrate Christmas you can write about something else. Just keep it relevant.

- What you do at Christmas
- What the people in Germany do at Christmas
- Any celebrations that are specifically British
- Any festivals they only have in Germany
- Whether you prefer celebrating in Britain or Germany
- Your favourite celebration

Remember: to score the highest marks you need to answer the task fully (for grades C and above you will need to write 200-300 words).

Task 2: You are e-mailing your new pen friend, describing where you live.

You could write about the following:

- Where your house is
- Who lives there
- What the house is like
- Your bedroom
- Whether you intend to stay in your home town

Remember: to score the highest marks you need to answer the task fully (for grades C and above you will need to write 200-300 words).

Revision Summary

The thing with doing GCSE German is that it's mainly about learning a few phrases, being able to change a few words in them, and stringing some of those phrases together. But if you don't <u>know the phrases</u>, you've got a problem. These questions will check you know what you need to know about this section. <u>Keep trying</u> them until you can do them <u>all</u>.

1) You've just arrived in Heidelberg and are writing to your pen friend about the sights. How do you say that there is a castle, a swimming pool, a university, a zoo, a museum and a theatre?

2) You need to go to the pharmacy in Germany. Ask where it is, and how far away it is.

3) A German tourist has come to see your home town and is looking for the youth hostel. Tell him to go straight on, turn left at the traffic lights and the youth hostel is on the right.

4) Tell your German pen friend where you live and whereabouts it is (which country and whether it's north-east etc.).

5) Say in German that you like living in your town, there's loads to do and it's quite clean. Say there's a sports centre and a cinema.

6) Say your address in German and describe the place where you live — is it a town or a village, is the landscape nice, and how many people live there?

7) Julia lives in a big house with a garden. It's near a shopping centre, a bus stop and a motorway. How would she say this in German?

8) Give the names of the rooms in your home in German and say how many bedrooms it has.

9) Tom has red wallpaper and a brown carpet in his bedroom. He has a bed, two lamps, a wardrobe and a cupboard. He doesn't have a sofa. How will he say all this in German?

10) You and Erika are talking about her birthday. She tells you that it's on the 24th of July, and that she and her family celebrate with a big party at her house. How would she say this in German?

11) Your German pen friend is writing an article about the environment for his school newspaper. He wants to know whether or not the environment is important to you. In German, tell him whether it is or isn't and make sure you give a reason why.

12) Your German pen friend is really struggling with this newspaper article. Now he wants to know two environmental problems and two things that we can do to be more environmentally friendly. Give him these in German. Honestly, you might as well be writing this thing for him...

School Subjects

School and jobs — maybe not what thrills you most in life. But never mind — this stuff's really important, so learn it well and you'll have less to stress about.

Welche Schulfächer hast du? — What school subjects do you do?

Go over each group of subjects until you can write them all out without looking.

Humanities

English:	Englisch (das)
history:	Geschichte (die)
geography:	Erdkunde/Geografie (die)
philosophy:	Philosophie (die)
social sciences:	Sozialwissenschaften (die)
religious studies:	Religion (die)
media studies:	Medienwissenschaften (die)

Languages

German:	Deutsch (das)
French:	Französisch (das)
Spanish:	Spanisch (das)
Italian:	Italienisch (das)

Normally these words are adjectives, so they don't have capitals (see page 79). When they're used as names of languages, they become nouns (see page 158) — so they need a capital letter.

Numbers and Stuff

maths:	Mathe(matik) (die)
ICT:	Informatik (die)

Physical Education

PE:	Sport (der)

Sciences

science:	Naturwissenschaften (die)
physics:	Physik (die)
chemistry:	Chemie (die)
biology:	Biologie (die)

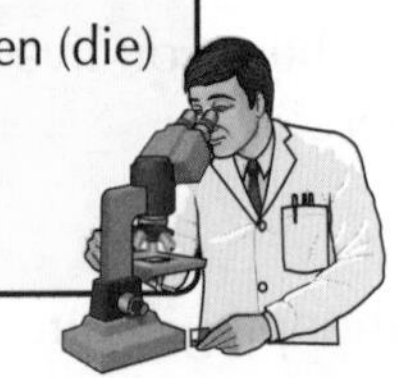

Arts and Crafts

theatre studies:	Theaterwissenschaften (die)
art:	Kunst (die)
music:	Musik (die)
design technology:	Werken (das)
home economics:	Hauswirtschaft (die)

Welche Fächer sind dir lieber? — Which subjects do you prefer?

Was ist dein Lieblingsfach? = What is your favourite subject?

Deutsch ist mein Lieblingsfach. = German is my favourite subject.

Biologie gefällt mir mehr. = I prefer biology.

Ich mag Mathe. = I like maths.

Ich hasse Sport. = I hate PE.

There's more on how to say what you like and don't like on pages 12-14.

Make sure you learn these lessons...

Make sure you can say all the subjects you do, and at least understand the ones you don't do. You don't need to use 'der', 'die' or 'das' when you're talking about a school subject — phew.

The School Routine

This isn't the most thrilling set of sentences, but when it comes to the exams they're gold dust.

Wie kommst du in die Schule? — How do you get to school?

This could come up in the reading or listening exam, so make sure you learn the lot.

Ich fahre mit dem Auto in die Schule. = I go to school by car.

car: dem Auto/dem Wagen
bus: dem Bus
bike: dem Fahrrad

Use 'in die Schule' for 'to school'. 'Gehen' means 'to go' only for 'on foot', so use 'fahren' if you have any kind of transport.

Ich gehe zu Fuß in die Schule. = I go to school on foot.

Der Stundenplan — The timetable

Write out all these sentences and slot in the right times and numbers for your school.

Die Schule fängt um neun Uhr an. = School begins at 9.00.

Die Schule ist um halb vier aus. = School ends at 3.30.

Um elf haben wir Pause. = We have break at 11.

Lunch break: Mittagspause

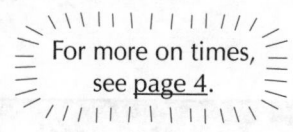

For more on times, see page 4.

Wir haben acht Stunden pro Tag. = We have 8 lessons per day.

Watch out — 'Stunde' can mean 'lesson' or 'hour'. Sneaky.

Jede Stunde dauert vierzig Minuten. = Each lesson lasts forty minutes.

Wir machen eine Stunde Hausaufgaben pro Tag. = We do one hour of homework every day.

Timetable this lot into your revision...

This is all useful stuff and you'll feel like a right lemon if you don't know it when you need to. Remember the handy phrase 'pro Tag' — it'll come in useful.

The School Routine

This page is full of extra little bits that could crop up in both the exams and things like the speaking and writing tasks — without them you'll miss out on some easy marks.

Die Ferien — The holidays

Es gibt drei Trimester. = There are three terms.

If there are two terms, you say 'zwei Semester'.

Wir haben im Sommer sechs Wochen Ferien. = We have six weeks' holiday in the summer.

at Christmas:	zu Weihnachten
at Easter:	zu Ostern

eight weeks':	acht Wochen
five days':	fünf Tage

Die Regeln — The Rules

Die Regeln sind streng. = The rules are strict.

In der Schule müssen wir eine Uniform tragen. = We must wear a uniform at school.

Unsere Uniform ist ein roter Pulli, eine graue Hose, ein weißes Hemd und ein grüner Schlips. = Our uniform is a red jumper, grey trousers, a white shirt and a green tie.

For more on clothes and colours, see pages 67-68.
For more on adjective endings see page 170.

Talk about your extracurricular activities

Hast du Aktivitäten außerhalb des Stundenplans?

= Do you have extracurricular activities?

For more on hobbies, see pages 49-51.

I'm a member of a theatre group:	bin ich Mitglied einer Theatergruppe
I play in a band:	spiele ich in einer Band
I'm a member of a football team:	bin ich Mitglied einer Fußballmannschaft

Außerhalb des Stundenplans treibe ich Sport.

= I do sport as an extracurricular activity.

Fascinating fact: German pupils don't wear school uniform

OK, so fascinating might have been pushing it a bit — but it's that kind of insider knowledge of Germany that will really impress someone reading a writing assessment of yours, say.

Talking About School

Lots of vocab on this page, but nothing too difficult grammar-wise. It's just a matter of learning it.

In deiner Schultasche... — In your school bag...

Learn this list of stuff you might find in your school bag:

Remember, plurals are always 'die'.

ballpoint pen:	der Kugelschreiber (-) /der Kuli (-s)	*felt-tip pen:*	der Filzstift (-e)
		scissors:	die Schere (-n)
pencil:	der Bleistift (-e)	*exercise book:*	das Heft (-e)
sharpener:	der Anspitzer (-)	*writing pad:*	der Schreibblock (-s / die Schreibblöcke)
rubber:	der Radiergummi (-s)	*calculator:*	der Taschenrechner (-)
ruler:	das Lineal (-e)	*school book:*	das Schulbuch (die Schulbücher)
fountain pen:	der Füller (-)	*chalk:*	die Kreide (-n)

Wo ist die Bibliothek? — Where is the library?

You might need to describe your school, or listen to somebody talking about theirs.

Wo ist die Turnhalle ? = Where is the gym?

For more on asking where something is see page 88.

In meiner Schule gibt es eine Bibliothek , eine Kantine , einen großen Sportplatz und viele Klassenzimmer .

These are accusative endings. See page 168 and 170 for more info.

= In my school there is a library, a canteen, a large sports field and many classrooms.

You can put any of these 'Places in School' in the red and green boxes in the sentences above:

Places in School

assembly hall:	die Aula	*corridor:*	der Korridor (-e)
library:	die Bibliothek	*staff room:*	das Lehrerzimmer
canteen:	die Kantine	*gymnasium:*	die Turnhalle (-n)
classroom:	das Klassenzimmer (-)	*sports hall:*	die Sporthalle (-n)
laboratory:	das Labor (-s/-e)	*sports field:*	der Sportplatz (die Sportplätze)
language lab:	das Sprachlabor (-s/-e)	*school yard:*	der Schulhof

Don't forget to learn those plurals

There's a lot of vocab in this section — make sure you learn it. The more you can reel off about your school, the better — close the book and see how much you can remember.

Classroom Language

This stuff is really important if you're not always word-perfect at understanding German.
It's really useful to be able to ask someone to repeat something, or spell out a word you're not sure about.

Ich verstehe nicht — I don't understand

These phases can be vital in your speaking assessment. Even if the worst happens, it's far better to say 'I don't understand' in German than to shrug, give a cheesy smile and mumble something in English.

Verstehst du? = Do you understand?

Ich verstehe (nicht). = I (don't) understand.

Wie spricht man das aus? = How do you pronounce that?

Wie sagt man das auf Deutsch? = How do you say that in German?

Wie buchstabiert man das? = How do you spell that?

Was bedeutet das, bitte? = What does that mean, please?

Kannst du dieses Wort erklären? = Can you (informal) explain this word?

Können Sie das bitte wiederholen? = Can you (formal) repeat that, please?

Ist das richtig? = Is that right?

Das ist falsch. = That's wrong.

Setzt euch! — Sit down!

Learn these three short phrases to avoid the wrath of a scary teacher.

Steht auf! = Stand up!

Setzt euch! = Sit down!

Seid ruhig! = Be quiet!

These phrases are all in the imperative.
For more info see page 198.

Learn these stress-reducing phrases

Even if you haven't a clue what your teacher just said, you'll get credit for asking them to repeat something — and you'll save yourself from an embarrassing silence at the same time.

More School Stuff

You can't do a German GCSE without learning a bit about German schools and the like...

Wie lange...? — How long...?

Wie lange lernst du schon Deutsch? = How long have you been learning German?

Be careful to use the present tense — you don't say 'I have been' as in English.

Ich lerne seit drei Jahren Deutsch. = I've been learning German for three years.

The word 'seit' is really useful. It means 'since' — this sentence literally translates as 'I am learning German since three years'. You use 'seit' and the present tense to say how long you've been doing anything — and you have to follow it with the dative case (see pages 157 and 179).

Meine Noten sind sehr gut — My grades are very good...

The German marking system works a bit differently to ours. Instead of A, B, C etc., they have the numbers 1-6. It's pretty simple — just make sure you're familiar with it...

German Grades

1 = very good:	1 = sehr gut
2 = good:	2 = gut
3 = satisfactory:	3 = befriedigend
4 = adequate:	4 = ausreichend
5 = (fail) inadequate	5 = mangelhaft
6 = (fail) unsatisfactory	6 = ungenügend

Deutsche Schulen — German Schools...

At first glance, the German school system seems mind-bogglingly complicated. Don't panic — again, just make sure you're familiar with the different terms.

For Little Ones

der Kindergarten — voluntary nursery school for 3-6 year olds
die Grundschule — primary school

Secondary Schools

das Gymnasium — takes the most academic pupils and prepares them for das Abitur ('A-levels') and university
die Hauptschule — focuses on vocational and practical training
die Realschule — somewhere between a Gymnasium and a Hauptschule, covers a broader range of subjects
die Gesamtschule — combines all three of the schools above in one (like a comprehensive school in the UK)
die Oberstufe — sixth form, usually part of a Gymnasium

Remember: 'seit' = 'since'

'Seit' is really such a handy little word. If you want to use it to say how long you've been doing something (like horse riding or living in London), don't forget you need the present tense.

Problems at School

OK, it's time to get it all off your chest — in German of course.

Wie geht es in der Schule? — How are things at school?

Es geht gut in der Schule, danke. = It's going well at school, thank you.

Eigentlich geht es nicht so gut. Ich habe einige Probleme... = Actually it's not going so well. I have a few problems...

Schule kann sehr stressig sein. = School can be very stressful.

Was für Probleme gibt es in der Schule? — What sort of problems are there at school?

Ich habe ein bisschen Angst vor meinen Prüfungen. = I'm a bit worried about my exams.

grades: Noten
results: Resultaten

Es gibt einen Leistungsdruck. = There's a pressure to do well.

Ich will nicht durchfallen. = I don't want to fail.

Manchmal finde ich die Arbeit ganz schwierig. = Sometimes I find the work quite difficult.

lessons: den Unterricht

'Weil' sends the verb to the end of the sentence. See pages 14 and 166.

Ich kann nicht mit meinen Freunden ausgehen, weil ich zu viel Hausaufgaben habe. = I can't go out with my friends because I have too much homework.

For more on issues that could affect you at school (like bullying and racism) see page 38.

Ich arbeite schwer, aber es ist nicht genug für meine Eltern. = I work hard, but it is not enough for my parents.

Meine Eltern sind sehr streng. Ich muss schwer studieren. = My parents are very strict. I must study hard.

Cover up this page and see how much you can remember

Those exam boards do like to get you talking through your troubles, don't they? Hey, just think of it as free therapy. You could also encounter other people talking about this little lot too.

Quick Questions

Have a go at these lovely Quick Questions I've done for you...

Quick Questions

1) How would you say the following in German?
   a) I like English.
   b) I like science.
   c) I prefer geography.
   d) I hate ICT.
   e) French is my favourite subject.

2) Translate the following sentences into German:
   a) I go to school on foot.
   b) I go to school by bus.
   c) I go to school by bike.

3) Translate these sentences into German, filling in the gaps with the right times and numbers for your school.
   a) School begins at .... .
   b) School ends at .... .
   c) We have lunch at .... .
   d) We have .... lessons per day.
   e) Each lesson lasts .... .
   f) We have .... weeks' holiday in the summer.

4) Finish off this sentence in German with an extracurricular activity you take part in: 'Außerhalb des Stundenplans ....'

5) Give the English for the following school bag items:
   a) der Bleistift
   b) der Anspitzer
   c) der Kuli
   d) der Füller
   e) das Heft

6) Give the German for the following places in school:
   a) assembly hall
   b) classroom
   c) laboratory
   d) canteen
   e) sports hall

7) How would you say the following in German?
   a) I don't understand.
   b) Can you (formal) repeat that, please?
   c) How do you spell that?

8) Write a sentence, in German, saying how long you've been learning German for.

9) Your German pen friend has just been given a grade of '1' for his English. What does this mean?

10) Translate the following sentences into English:
   a) Ich habe ein bisschen Angst vor meinen Noten.
   b) In meiner Klasse gibt es einen Leistungsdruck.
   c) Ich will nicht durchfallen.
   d) Manchmal finde ich den Unterricht ganz schwierig.
   e) Schule ist stressig, weil ich so viel Hausaufgaben habe.

Work Experience

The next few pages encourage you to think about your future in even more detail. If you can't quite manage to see your future without the aid of a crystal ball then get exercising your imagination.

Wo hast du das Betriebspraktikum gemacht? — Where did you do your work experience?

Work experience is quite simply joyous — I remember my week spent bored to death in a certain high street bank. At least it helped me decide there was no way on this Earth that banking was for me.

Put the place you worked in here.

Ich habe das Betriebspraktikum bei Siemens gemacht.

work experience: das Arbeitspraktikum
die Arbeitserfahrung

= I did my work experience at Siemens.

Ich habe anderthalb Wochen dort gearbeitet.

= I worked there for a week and a half.

two weeks: zwei Wochen

Hat dir die Arbeit gefallen? — Did you like the work?

More opinions wanted — own up, did you or did you not like it..?

Die Arbeit hat Spaß gemacht . = The work was fun.

was stressful: war stressig
was interesting: war interessant

comfortable: wohl
at home: zu Hause

Ich fühlte mich einsam . = I felt lonely.

Meine Mitarbeiter waren ganz unfreundlich .

= My work colleagues were quite unfriendly.

very friendly: sehr freundlich
interesting: interessant

You'll need to get the past tense right for this

If you haven't done any work experience then you'd better learn how to say that in German in case you're asked — it's just 'ich habe kein Betriebspraktikum gemacht', in case you're interested.

Plans for the Future

If you know what you're doing after school, great — if you haven't got a clue, make it up. Job's a good 'un.

Was hast du vor, in der Zukunft zu machen? — What do you intend to do in the future?

Ich möchte einen Beruf haben, wo ich Probleme löse .

= I'd like a job where I solve problems.

meet new people:	neue Leute treffe
work with numbers:	mit Nummern arbeite
travel abroad:	ins Ausland fahre

See page 139 for more types of jobs, or look one up in a dictionary.

Ich hoffe in der Zukunft Polizistin zu werden.

= I hope to become a policewoman in the future.

policeman: Polizist

Was möchtest du nach der Schule machen? — What would you like to do after school?

This stuff could easily come up — so you'd be daft not to learn it, really.

Abitur is the German equivalent of A-levels — except that they do more subjects than we do.

Ich möchte das Abitur machen. = I would like to do 'A-levels'.

Ich möchte auf die Universität gehen. = I would like to go to university.

Ich möchte Geografie studieren. = I would like to study geography.

Ich möchte ein Jahr freinehmen. = I would like to take a year out.

Ich möchte Lehrer werden. = I would like to become a teacher.

For more jobs, see page 139. If you're a girl, you'll need to use the feminine form.

'Ich möchte' = 'I would like ...' — learn it

The sentence structures on this page are pretty straightforward — use 'ich möchte' and the infinitive of another verb to say what you would like to do. For more on this, see page 206 .

Plans for the Future

One thing to remember about GCSE German — you can very rarely say anything without giving a reason.

Give short, sharp reasons for your answers

So you've said what you want to do in the future, now you need to say why. Keep your explanations short, clear and simple. For example, 'I want to take a year out so that I can travel' — nice and concise.

And if you don't know how to use 'weil' ('because'), look it up on page 162.

Ich möchte das Abitur machen, weil ich später Biologie studieren will. = I would like to do 'A-levels', because I want to study biology afterwards.

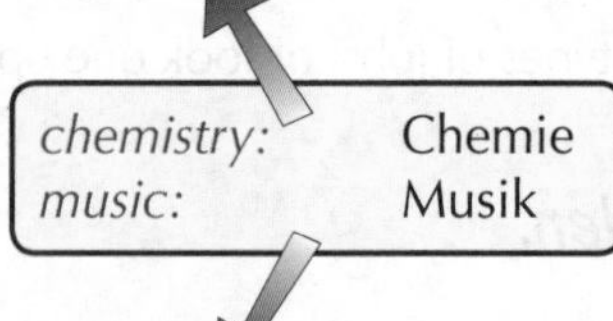

a pharmacist: Apotheker(in)
a musician: Musiker(in)

Ich möchte Englisch studieren, weil ich später Journalist werden will.

= I would like to study English, because I want to be a journalist afterwards.

For all the different school subjects see page 128.

Use 'werden' (to become) to say what job you'd like to do.

easy: einfach
difficult: schwierig

For more on 'wäre' ('would be') see page 207.

Ich möchte Arzt werden, weil der Job interessant wäre.

= I would like to become a doctor because the job would be interesting.

For other jobs, see page 139.

Ich möchte einen Beruf, der kreativer ist. = I'd like a job that's more creative.

more interesting: interessanter
not so stressful: nicht so stressig

Get these sentence structures right and you'll sound dead impressive

Things like the stuff on this page come up year after year — so if you've learnt it all, you'll be laughing. Use words like 'weil' for extra marks. Being able to explain why is dead impressive.

Types of Job

There are more jobs here than you can shake a stick at — and you do need to be able to recognise all of them because any of the little blighters could pop up in your listening and reading exams.

You usually add an '-in' to make a job feminine

1. For most jobs, you add '-in' to the end to make it feminine.
2. If the job ends in '-mann', change that to '-frau' for a woman.
3. Watch out for exceptions like 'Friseur/Friseuse', and for places where you have to add an umlaut as well as the feminine ending.

Architekt (m) *Architektin (f)* = architect

Kaufmann (m) *Kauffrau (f)* = businessman/woman

Arzt (m) *Ärztin (f)* = doctor

As you'd expect, the gender of the job is always masculine for a man and feminine for a woman.

Grey-suit-type jobs

businessman/woman:	Geschäftsmann/-frau Kaufmann/-frau
secretary:	Sekretär(in)
manager:	Manager(in)
programmer:	Programmierer(in)
civil servant:	Beamter/Beamtin
lawyer:	Rechtsanwalt/ Rechtsanwältin
interpreter:	Dolmetscher(in)

Arty jobs

actor/actress:	Schauspieler(in)
musician:	Musiker(in)
writer:	Schriftsteller(in)
painter:	Maler(in)
TV presenter:	Moderator(in)
singer:	Sänger(in)

Get-your-hands-dirty jobs

mechanic:	Mechaniker(in)
electrician:	Elektriker(in)
plumber:	Klempner(in)
chef:	Koch/Köchin
butcher:	Metzger(in)
baker:	Bäcker(in)
farmer:	Bauer/Bäuerin
builder:	Bauarbeiter(in)

A load more jobs

engineer:	Ingenieur(in)
architect:	Architekt(in)
salesperson:	Verkäufer(in)
journalist:	Journalist(in)
teacher:	Lehrer(in)
head teacher:	Direktor(in)
librarian:	Bibliothekar(in)
computer scientist:	Informatiker(in)
hairdresser:	Friseur/Friseuse
policeman/woman:	Polizist(in)
firefighter:	Feuerwehrmann/-frau
postman/woman:	Briefträger(in)
air steward(ess):	Steward(ess)
soldier:	Soldat(in)

Medical jobs

dentist:	Zahnarzt/Zahnärztin
pharmacist:	Apotheker(in)
nurse:	Krankenschwester (f), Krankenpfleger (m)
doctor:	Arzt/Ärztin
vet:	Tierarzt/Tierärztin

Other job situations

student:	Student(in)
work experience:	das Praktikum
weekend job:	der Wochenendjob
part-time worker:	Teilzeitarbeiter(in)
housewife/husband:	Hausfrau/-mann

Learn the female versions too

Don't be put off by the long lists. Start off with the jobs you find easiest, and remember that you'll probably only need to say the ones people in your family do — but you should understand the rest.

Jobs: Advantages and Disadvantages

Pretty self-explanatory this, really. You have to be able to talk about the pros and cons of different jobs.

Was für Beruf möchtest du? — What sort of job would you like?

Ich will im Freien arbeiten. = I want to work outdoors.

with animals:	mit Tieren
with the public:	mit der Öffentlichkeit
in a hospital:	in einem Krankenhaus

Ich möchte selbständig sein. = I'd like to be self-employed.

Ich will nicht in einem Büro arbeiten. = I don't want to work in an office.

with children: mit Kindern

Ich möchte nicht gern... — I wouldn't like...

OK, so what don't you want to do?

a soldier: Soldat *a policeman:* Polizist

Ich möchte nicht gern Rechtsanwalt sein... = I wouldn't like to be a lawyer...

...obwohl das Gehalt ganz gut ist. = ... although the pay is quite good.

'Obwohl' affects word order — see page 166 for more info.

For more on 'wäre' ('would be') see page 207.

Die Arbeit wäre zu schwierig. = The work would be too hard.

stressful: stressig *boring:* langweilig

Die Arbeitszeit wäre zu lang. = The working hours would be too long.

Ich bin lieber... — I'd prefer to be...

Ich bin lieber Architekt. = I'd prefer to be an architect.

a doctor:	Arzt
a musician:	Musiker

For more jobs, see page 139. If you're a girl, you'll need to use the feminine form.

Think about what you'd like to do in the future

This page kinda relies on you having an opinion. The more interesting things you can think of to say, the more marks you'll get. Which is really the whole point after all. So get your thinking-cap on...

Working Abroad

Working abroad is the perfect opportunity to put all your finely-honed German skills to use. First up, a mite of work experience...

Arbeiten im Ausland... — Working abroad...

Nächstes Jahr, möchte ich ein Betriebspraktikum in Deutschland machen.

= Next year, I would like to do a work experience placement in Germany.

Ich würde gern mein Deutsch verbessern. = I would like to improve my German.

Ich werde in einer Tierarztpraxis arbeiten.
Ich interessiere mich für Tiere.

= I will work at a veterinary practice.
I'm interested in animals.

For more about work experience, see page 136.

Möchtest du im Ausland arbeiten? — Would you like to work abroad?

Me? Work abroad? With all that sun, sand and sea? No thank you.
But just in case that appeals to you, here's how to tell people all about your plans...

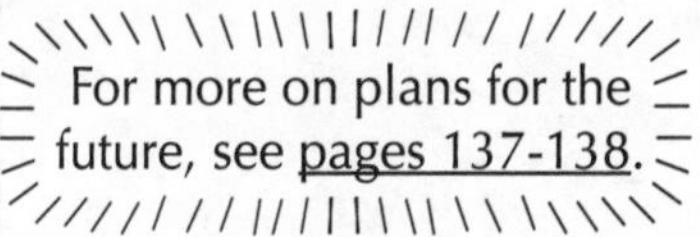
For more on plans for the future, see pages 137-138.

Austria:	nach Österreich
Switzerland:	in die Schweiz

Nach meinem Abitur werde ich nach Deutschland fahren.

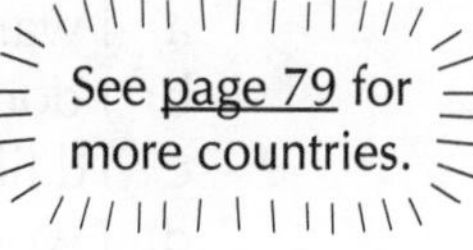
See page 79 for more countries.

= After my 'A-levels', I will go to Germany.

Ich möchte ...

= I would like ...

... to work in a ski resort:	in einem Skiurlaubsort arbeiten
... to work in a hotel:	in einem Hotel arbeiten
... to be an au pair:	Au-pair sein
... to travel and meet people:	reisen und Leute kennen lernen

Ich möchte ein Jahr freinehmen, um ein Jahr in Europa zu verbringen. = I would like to take a gap year in order to spend a year in Europe.

Es wird ein tolles Erlebnis sein. = It will be a great experience.

There's more on the future tense in the grammar section

You need to know what to say if someone asks you whether you'd like to work abroad, but this sort of thing also crops up in exams, so you might get to hear or read about other people's opinions too.

Quick Questions

Hmm, <u>about time</u> for another lot of Quick Questions I think.
Don't worry, they won't take you long...

Quick Questions

1) Jacob has written this short piece about his work experience.
Translate it into English.

> Ich habe das Arbeitspraktikum bei Volkswagen gemacht. Ich habe zwei Wochen dort gearbeitet. Die Arbeit war wirklich interessant und meine Mitarbeiter waren sehr freundlich. Ich fühlte mich zu Hause. Ich hoffe in der Zukunft Ingenieur zu werden.

2) Write a couple of sentences (in German) about what you'd like to do after school.
Include at least one reason <u>why</u>.

3) Give the names of the following jobs in German:
   a) doctor (male)
   b) teacher (female)
   c) lawyer (male)
   d) police woman
   e) actor (male)

4) Give the English names of the following jobs (and say whether they're male or female):
   a) Direktor
   b) Friseuse
   c) Architektin
   d) Klempner
   e) Krankenpfleger
   f) Dolmetscher

5) Translate these sentences into German:
   a) I want to work with animals.
   b) I don't want to work with children.
   c) I'd like to be self-employed.
   d) I wouldn't like to be a doctor, although the pay is quite good.
   e) The working hours would be too long.
   f) I'd prefer to be a builder.

6) Claudia and Max are talking about working abroad next year.
Translate what they are saying into English.

Max:	Was wirst du nach dem Abitur machen, Claudia?
Claudia:	Also, im Juli werde ich nach Italien fahren. Ich möchte Au-pair sein. Und du? Möchtest du im Ausland arbeiten?
Max:	Ja, hoffentlich werde ich nach England fahren. Ich möchte reisen und Leute kennen lernen und dann in einem Hotel arbeiten.
Claudia:	Prima! Das wird dein Englisch bestimmt verbessern.

Getting a Job

Everybody needs a job. This page is all about how to nab yourself one.
Don't say you never learn anything useful...

Die Stellenangebote... — Job vacancies...

You might see (and be asked questions about) adverts like these in the reading exam...

Stellenangebot:
Wir suchen Kellner/Kellnerin.
Samstag und Sonntag Abende
19.00-22.00

= Job offer:
We're looking for a waiter/waitress.
Saturday and Sunday evenings
7-10 pm

Sind Sie kreativ?
Möchten Sie mit Kindern arbeiten?
Wir brauchen Sie!
Telefonieren: 01 23 45

= Are you creative?
Would you like to work with children?
We need you!
Telephone: 01 23 45

Wir suchen einen(e)Verkäufer/Verkäuferin.
Fünf Stunden pro Woche.
Sie müssen verantwortlich und fleißig sein.
Näheres erfahren Sie unter Telefonnummer:
54 32 10

= We are looking for a shop assistant.
5 hours a week.
You must be responsible and hard-working.
For further details, call this number:
54 32 10

Mein Lebenslauf... — My CV ...

Well you can't apply for that dream job without one...

LEBENSLAUF

Persönliche Daten:	Marie Dalton 12 Pemberton Way, Loxley, Barnshire, BA22 3PM Tel: 01234 567 765 E-mail: m.dalton@wahooworld.co.uk
Ausbildung:	
2007:	Hochschulabschluss in Philosophie (erste Klasse)
2004:	A-Levels: Philosophie (A), Mathe (B), Deutsch (B)
Berufstätigkeit:	
Seit 2007:	Einkaufsassistentin für Loxley Leisure
2004-2007:	Studentin
Sonstige Kenntnisse:	Erste-Hilfe-Qualifikation Führerschein Ich spreche Englisch, Deutsch und Italienisch

CURRICULUM VITAE

Personal Details:	Marie Dalton 12 Pemberton Way, Loxley, Barnshire, BA22 3PM Tel: 01234 567 765 E-mail: m.dalton@wahooworld.co.uk
Education:	
2007:	Degree in Philosophy (first class)
2004:	A-Levels: Philosophy (A), Maths (B), German (B)
Work Experience:	
Since 2007:	Purchasing assistant for Loxley Leisure
2004-2007:	Student
Other Skills:	First aid qualification Driving licence I speak English, German and Italian

This page covers the basics

This page is pretty darn important, so make sure you're familiar with it. You could get given this sort of thing in the reading exam, or you might have to write something similar yourself.

Getting a Job

OK, so you've seen the adverts, now it's time to write that letter of application...

Die Stellenbewerbung... — Job application...

You'll need a covering letter to go with that CV of yours, so here's a nice little example for you. For more on writing formal letters, see page 16.

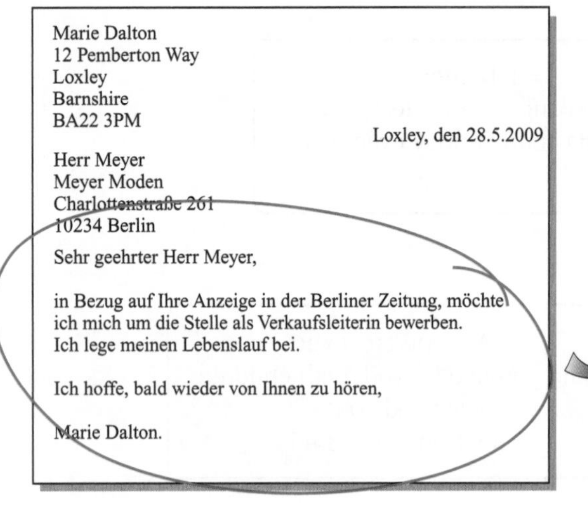

Marie Dalton
12 Pemberton Way
Loxley
Barnshire
BA22 3PM

Loxley, den 28.5.2009

Herr Meyer
Meyer Moden
Charlottenstraße 261
10234 Berlin

Sehr geehrter Herr Meyer,

in Bezug auf Ihre Anzeige in der Berliner Zeitung, möchte ich mich um die Stelle als Verkaufsleiterin bewerben. Ich lege meinen Lebenslauf bei.

Ich hoffe, bald wieder von Ihnen zu hören,

Marie Dalton.

Dear Mr Meyer,

With regard to your advert in the Berliner Zeitung, I would like to apply for the position of sales manager. I enclose my CV.

I hope to hear from you soon,

Marie Dalton.

Vielen Dank für Ihre Berwerbung... — Many thanks for your application...

A lot of the stuff in your GCSEs will be addressed to you informally, i.e. you'll be called 'du' and not 'Sie'. In an interview you would always be 'Sie'. Better get used to it.

Wir laden Sie am Montag, den dritten Juli, zu einem Vorstellungsgespräch ein.

= We invite you to come for an interview on Monday the 3rd of July.

Bringen Sie bitte Ihren Lebenslauf mit. = Please bring your CV.

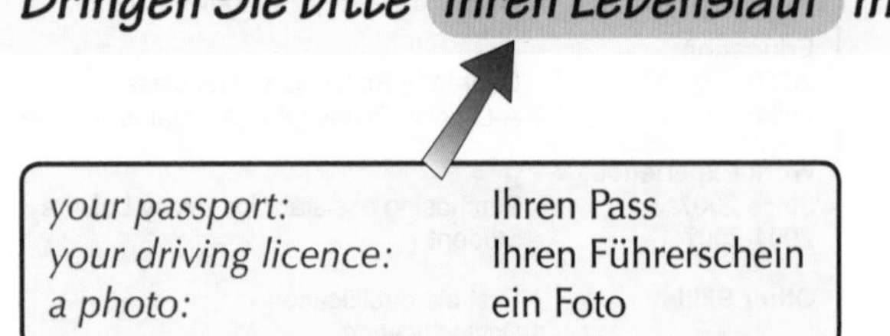

your passport:	Ihren Pass
your driving licence:	Ihren Führerschein
a photo:	ein Foto

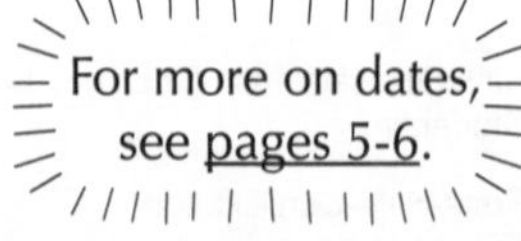

For more on dates, see pages 5-6.

Learn these stock phrases, then add some extra bits of your own

Obviously if you have to write a letter of application at any point, you're going to want to go into a bit more detail than the letter above. You could even include some of the bits on the next page...

Getting a Job

So you've been offered an interview. What on earth are you going to say when you get there? This page will give you a few clues, but remember — if you end up answering questions like these in a speaking assessment, you'll need to come up with some original ideas of your own.

Vorstellungsgespräch Fragen — Interview Questions

Für welche Stelle interessieren Sie sich? = Which position are you interested in?

Warum möchten Sie diese Stelle? = Why do you want this job?

Was haben Sie in der Schule gemacht? = What did you do at school?

Vorstellungsgespräch Antworten — Interview Answers

Ich möchte gern als Helfer bei der Touristeninformation in Münster arbeiten.

= I'd like to work as an assistant in the tourist information office in Münster.

Ich möchte gern mein Deutsch verbessern. = I'd like to improve my German.

Ich interessiere mich für Tourismus. = I'm interested in tourism.

qualifications: Qualifikationen

responsible: verantwortlich
hard-working: fleißig

For more personality traits, see page 33.

Ich habe die nötige Erfahrung. Ich bin flexibel und vernünftig.

= I have the necessary experience. I'm flexible and sensible.

Ich habe eine Gesamtschule in Fareham besucht.

= I went to a comprehensive in Fareham.

In der Schule waren Deutsch und Französisch meine Lieblingsfächer.

= German and French were my favourite subjects at school.

You could get a job interview as a role play in a speaking assessment

Most of this stuff isn't new, but get used to dealing with it in this context. There's loads of clever stuff to say here and you can use a lot of it when you're writing job applications too (see page 144).

Telephones

Phone calls come up all the time. So make sure you learn this page. You need to know what to say when you call someone, how to answer the phone, and about passing a message on.

Telefonieren — Telephoning

Was ist deine Telefonnummer? = What is your telephone number?

Use 'deine' for someone you know well. If you need to be more formal, use 'Ihre'.

Meine Telefonnummer ist achtundzwanzig, neunzehn, zwoundfünfzig.

= My telephone number is 281952.

German phone numbers are usually given in pairs like this. The number 2, 'zwei', is sometimes said as 'zwo' on the phone. See page 2 for more numbers.

Please call me (informal): Rufst du mich an, bitte.

Rufen Sie mich an, bitte. = Please call me (formal).

Hallo, ist Lisa da? — Hello, is Lisa there?

Say this when you answer the phone:

Hallo! Reginald am Apparat. = Hello! Reginald speaking.

These are for when you phone someone:

Hallo! Hier spricht Andreas. = Hello! Andreas speaking.

Kann ich mit Lisa sprechen? = Can I speak to Lisa?

Der Anrufbeantworter — The answering machine

You have to understand phone messages, and be able to leave one. This is your bog-standard message:

Hallo, hier spricht Gabriele. Meine Telefonnummer ist neunundfünfzig, neunzehn, sechsundfünfzig. Kann Bob mich um 20 Uhr zurückrufen? Danke. Auf Wiederhören.

You say 'Auf Wiederhören' not 'Auf Wiedersehen' when you're on the phone.

= Hello, Gabriele speaking. My phone number is 59 19 56.
Can Bob call me back at 8pm? Thanks, bye.

It helps to know your numbers for this

Whether you end up having to talk on the phone in a speaking assessment, or listen to a phone conversation in your listening exam, this stuff is pretty crucial. Get learning those set phrases.

Telephones

More telephone-related phrases for you to cast your eyes over...

Ich höre zu... — I'm listening...

More stuff you might hear on the phone...

Warten Sie einen Moment, ich verbinde Sie. = Wait a moment, I'll put you through.

Augenblick, ich bin gleich wieder da. = Just a moment, I'll be right back.

Darf ich etwas ausrichten? = May I take a message?

Sie haben die falsche Nummer. = You've got the wrong number.

Sorry, wrong number.:
Es tut mir leid, falsch verbunden.

Können Sie mir helfen, bitte? — Can you help me please?

Here's how to ask for information:

a hairdresser:	einen Friseur
a dentist:	einen Zahnarzt
a chemist:	einen Drogist

Entschuldigung, wo kann ich einen Klempner finden?

= Excuse me, where can I find a plumber?

Sie sollten im Telefonbuch suchen. = You should look in the phone book.

on the internet:	im Internet
in the post office:	in der Post
in the tourist information office:	im Verkehrsamt

Phone calls are a listening exam favourite

There's not too much extra to learn on this page really — which is excellent news, I'm sure you'll agree. Not long to go now till the end of the section... and some lovely Exam Practice.

The Business World

This page covers those little consumer-y type problems you might find yourself with. Which is nice.

Es gibt ein Problem mit meiner Bestellung... — There's a problem with my order...

Here's an example of a phone conversation between a vendor and a customer:

Verkäuferin:

'Hallo, ComputerWelt. Erika am Apparat.'
Hello, ComputerWelt. Erika speaking.

'Also, kann ich Ihren Namen haben, bitte?'
OK, can I have your name please?

'Danke schön. Ich habe Ihre Bestellung gefunden. Was für ein Problem gibt es?'
Thank you. I've found your order. What's the problem?

'Es tut mir leid, mein Herr. Morgen früh werden wir Ihnen die Tastatur schicken.'
I'm sorry sir. We'll send the keyboard to you tomorrow morning.

'Bitte schön. Sonst noch etwas?'
You're welcome. Will there be anything else?

'Auf Wiederhören.'
Goodbye.

Kunde:

'Hallo. Letzte Woche habe ich einen Computer bestellt, aber es gibt ein Problem mit der Bestellung.'
Hello. I ordered a computer last week, but there's a problem with the order.

'Ja. Mein Name ist Hans Klaus.'
Yes. My name is Hans Klaus.

'Sie haben den Computer und den Bildschirm geschickt, aber die Tastatur ist noch nicht angekommen.'
You've sent the computer and the monitor, but the keyboard hasn't arrived yet.

'Das ist toll. Danke schön.'
That's great. Thank you.

'Nein danke, das ist alles. Auf Wiederhören.'
No thanks, that's everything. Goodbye.

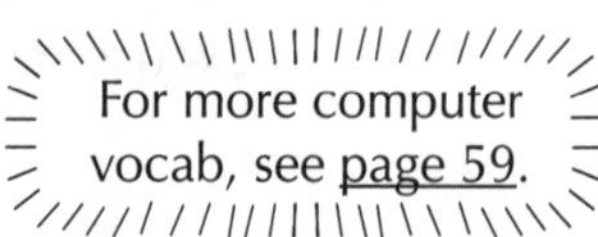
For more computer vocab, see page 59.

You could get a conversation like this in a listening exam

Obviously there are loads of different possible scenarios, but they'll all use vocab you should already be familiar with. The important thing is not to get thrown by hearing it in a different context.

Quick Questions

Here we go: your last set of Quick Questions before Exam Practice and the end of Section Six. Take your time and try to answer them without looking back at the page.

Quick Questions

1) You're job hunting in Germany. Here are some extracts from advertisements you see in the local paper. What do they say in English?
   a) Stellenangebot: Wir suchen Koch/Köchin.
   b) Möchten Sie mit Tieren arbeiten?
   c) Sie müssen verantwortlich sein.
   d) Sie müssen einen Führerschein haben.
   e) Näheres erfahren Sie unter Telefonnummer: 02 34 61.
   f) Wir brauchen einen(e) Teilzeitarbeiter(in). Sechs Stunden pro Woche.

2) Give the German for:
   a) job vacancies
   b) job application
   c) my CV

3) What's the German for:
   a) the manager?
   b) the manageress?

4) You receive a letter from one of the firms you apply to saying: "Wir laden Sie am Dienstag, den achten März, zu einem Vorstellungsgespräch ein". What does this mean?

5) You're applying to work as a waiter/waitress in a hotel in Stuttgart for the summer. You get asked the following questions in the interview. For each one, write out what your answer might be in German (use your imagination).
   a) Für welche Stelle interessieren Sie sich?
   b) Warum möchten Sie diese Stelle?
   c) Was haben Sie in der Schule gemacht?
   d) Haben Sie ein Arbeitspraktikum gemacht?

6) Sarah is ringing her German exchange partner, Katja, to arrange details of her trip, but when she calls no one answers. She has to leave the following message. How would she say it in German?

   Hello, Sarah speaking. My phone number is 37 89 65.
   Can Katja call me back at 7 pm? Thanks. Bye.

7) You're working for a German call centre. How would you say the following phrases?
   a) (When you answer the phone) Hello! Chris speaking.
   b) Wait a moment, I'll put you through.
   c) May I take a message?
   d) Sorry, wrong number.
   e) Can I have your name please?
   f) You should look on the internet.

Listening Questions

1 Bernd is telling you what school subjects he likes and dislikes.

a) His favourite subject is:

A  B  C 

Write the correct letter in the box. ☐

b) He likes science because:

A His teacher is funny.

B He thinks science is easy.

C Science is really useful.

Write the correct letter in the box. ☐

Track 13

2 Boris and Katja are talking about their future plans.

a) What does Katja say she wants to do after the exams?

A go to university B take a gap year C learn to paint

Write the correct letter in the box. ☐

b) What job does Boris say he wants to do after university?

A teacher B dentist C vet

Write the correct letter in the box. ☐

Reading Question

As far as I'm concerned, practice makes perfect — and the more you get, the better. Which is why I've kindly decided to give you two reading questions in this section instead of one. I know. You can thank me later.

1 This German student is writing about his problems in school.

> Die Schule ist zurzeit für mich nicht so gut. Ich habe viel Angst vor meinen Prüfungen, weil ich nicht durchfallen will. Meine Eltern sind sehr streng und erlauben mir gar nicht mit meinen Freunden auszugehen. Sie beklagen sich immer über meine Noten. Ich habe in der letzten Klassenarbeit nur eine Vier in Mathe bekommen. Ich habe jeden Tag zwei oder drei Stunden Hausaufgaben zu tun. Es gibt hier so einen Leistungsdruck. Ich finde den Unterricht ab und zu ganz schwierig, aber die Lehrer haben keine Zeit, mir zu helfen. Ich muss auch eine Brille tragen und die anderen Schüler sind mir manchmal gemein. Das ist so unfair! Schule ist viel zu viel stressig und macht nicht mehr Spaß. Ich möchte mich sofort einen Job finden und die Schule verlassen.
>
> Markus

For each of the statements below, write **T** (true) or **F** (false) in the box.

a) Markus's parents let him go out when he wants. ☐

b) He has two to three hours homework every day. ☐

c) The teachers don't have time to help him. ☐

d) He has to wear glasses. ☐

e) He wants to stay on at school. ☐

Reading Question

2 Some people are talking about their jobs.
Choose the correct word to fill in the gaps in the text.
Write the correct letter in the box.

a) Ich arbeite in einem Büro. Die Arbeitszeit ist nicht zu lang, aber ich finde die Arbeit manchmal stressig. Das Gehalt ist ziemlich gut, jedoch suche ich im Moment einen .... , der kreativer ist.

A Beruf

B schwierig

C Lehrer ☐

It's always best to read the whole text and the question through before answering.

b) Ich arbeite mit der Öffentlichkeit in einem .... Ich bin eigentlich Empfangsdame und muss mit den Patienten Formularen immer ausfüllen und den Weg zu den Kliniken ganz genau beschreiben. Es kann ein bisschen langweilig sein.

A Büro

B Fabrik

C Krankenhaus ☐

c) Ich bin Informatiker bei einer großen Firma in Berlin. Ich arbeite hier seit zehn Jahren und obwohl ich nur fünfunddreißig bin, habe ich Lust .... zu arbeiten. Ich bleibe lieber zu Hause und vielleicht später werde ich selbständig sein.

A teilzeitig

B England

C Student ☐

Speaking Question

Depending on your exam board, you could find yourself having to do an unscripted role play as part of your speaking assessment — the humble job interview is a great example.

Task: Job interview
You are being interviewed for a holiday job as a waiter / waitress in a German restaurant. Your teacher will play the part of the restaurant manager.

You should cover the following points, but you will also have to answer unexpected questions. The following points are suggestions of the information you can include:

- Explain why you want this job
- Give some information about your school subjects
- Describe any work experience you have done
- Give some information about a part-time job you have
- Describe what qualities you have that would make you a good waiter / waitress
- Ask what the working hours will be

The whole conversation should last about five minutes.

Notes for Teachers
You need to ask the student the following questions:

- Warum möchten Sie diese Stelle?
- Was sind Ihre Lieblingsfächer?
- Haben Sie ein Betriebspraktikum gemacht?
- Haben Sie einen Teilzeitjob?
- Was für Charaktereigenschaften haben Sie, um Sie für diesen Job gut geeignet zu machen?
- Haben Sie irgendwelche Fragen?

Examples of unpredictable questions:
- Haben Sie Aktivitäten außerhalb des Stundenplans?
- Essen Sie oft in Restaurants?
- Was für einen Beruf wollen Sie in der Zukunft machen?

If the student asks about working hours, tell them:
'Ungefähr neun Stunden pro Woche. Sie werden Freitag und Samstag Abende von sechs Uhr bis halb elf arbeiten.'

Writing Questions

A couple more writing tasks for you to turn your hand to here. Let your imagination run riot.

Task 1: You have just completed your work experience in Germany and you have been asked to write about your experiences for your twin town newsletter.

You could write about the following:

- Where you went
- What you did
- How you coped with the work
- What you thought of your colleagues
- A particular event / incident / memorable occasion when you were there
- Your overall impressions

Remember: to score the highest marks you need to answer the task fully (for grades C and above you will need to write 200-300 words).

Task 2: Your partner school wants to know about your school from a pupil's point of view. Write an article describing your school.

You could write about the following:

- Name of school, type of school, location
- How long you've been there for
- Details of the building
- Pupils (ages / how many); teachers (how many / opinions)
- School routine
- Your ideal school

To get the best marks, you need to write in more than one tense — so think about how you could include different tenses.

This could be a school of the future (squeezing another tense in).

Remember: to score the highest marks you need to answer the task fully (for grades C and above you will need to write 200-300 words).

Revision Summary

You really need to <u>know</u> this stuff. Go through these questions — if you can answer them all without looking anything up, then give yourself a pat on the back and <u>smile widely</u>. If there are some you can't do, <u>look them up</u>. Then try again. And again. Keep going till you can do 'em all.

1) Say what all your GCSE subjects are in German (or as many as possible).
I guess one of them will be Deutsch...

2) Roland goes to school by bike, but Sonia goes by car.
How would each of them tell the other in German how they get to school?

3) How would you say in German that your lunch break begins at 12:45 pm and lasts one hour?

4) Marie wants to know what your school is like.
Tell her in German there's an assembly hall, a canteen, a library and a large sports field.

5) Your teacher has just said a long sentence in German and you don't understand.
How would you ask her to repeat it?

6) How do you say in German that you've been learning French for five years and German for four years?

7) Your German friend Michael is looking a bit down. You ask him if he has any problems at school and he tells you that he sometimes finds the work a bit difficult and he's worried about his exams. Write down what he's told you in German.

8) Write a full German sentence explaining where you did your work experience.
If you haven't done work experience then write that down.

9) Write the German for whether you liked your work experience and why,
or say whether you would like to do work experience and where.

10) Monika wants to study physics.
How does she say that she wants to do the Abitur so that she can go to university?
How does she say her favourite subjects are maths, physics and chemistry?

11) Write down the German names of four occupations that you might possibly do in the future and four that you would never ever want to do. Say why you wouldn't want to do one of the jobs.

12) You have two German pen friends, Nadja and Karl. Nadja wants to have a job where she works with animals and Karl wants to take a gap year in Europe. How would each of them say that?

13) How would you write a reply in German to a job advert for an assistant in a bookshop?
Explain why you want the job and why you think you're suitable.

14) A friend of your brother's calls.
Write down a message in German for your brother, saying his friend can't go out tonight.

Cases: Nominative and Accusative

Cases are a pain in the neck. They can seem pretty nasty, but if you get the four cases clear in your head, it'll make the rest of this grammar stuff a lot easier. And that could make a real difference to your marks.

'Cases' mean you have to change words to fit

The only reason you need to know about cases is that some words have to be spelt differently depending on what case they're in.

EXAMPLE: ***Der rote Hund* folgt *dem roten Hund*.** = The red dog follows the red dog.

Both these bits mean the same thing ('the red dog') but some of the letters in the words have changed, because the second bit is in a different case from the first bit.

This page and the next page are about when you use the different cases.
How you change the words to fit the case is on page 159, pages 167-171 and pages 177-182.

The most often-used cases are the nominative and the accusative

What case a bit of the sentence is depends on what the words are doing in the sentence:

Hermann isst Eis. = Hermann eats ice cream.

...this bit of the sentence is who is doing it... (Hermann — or Harold, or Henry or the Queen of Sheba or whoever — is eating ice cream.)

= Nominative Case

This is kind of the normal common-or-garden case. If you look up a word in the dictionary, it'll tell you what it is in the nominative case.

This bit of the sentence is what is going on... it's the verb. (Hermann is eating ice cream, or buying it, or drinking it or whatever.)

...and this bit of the sentence is who or what it is done to. (Hermann is eating ice cream, or biscuits, or toast or whatever.)

= Accusative Case

That's the secret of all this mysterious-sounding 'nominative' and 'accusative' cases business.
Or, in two lines...

The Golden Rules

NOMINATIVE = who (or what) is DOING it

ACCUSATIVE = who (or what) it's DONE TO

For grammar fans — the subject of the verb is in the nominative case. The object of the verb is in the accusative case.

Memorise those Golden Rules

Cases are one of the trickiest things about GCSE German, so get this stuff learnt and you're well on your way to success. The nominative and accusative cases are an absolute must — you need to know them.

Cases: Genitive and Dative

Top Tip Number 1 in a series of 1 — read page 156 before you tackle this page.
The genitive and the dative cases sound hard, but they're just as easy as the accusative.

The **genitive** case — things like **Bob's**, **Sue's**...

When you want to say things like Bob's, the milkman's, my mum's... you use the genitive case.

Der Wagen meines Vaters. = My father's car. (The car of my father.)

GENITIVE CASE

Hermann isst das Eis des Mädchens. = Hermann eats the girl's ice cream. (Hermann eats the ice cream of the girl.)

NB: Stuff like 'my dad's a doctor' isn't in the genitive — it's short for 'my dad is a doctor', which has got nothing to do with a doctor belonging to your dad.

The **dative** case — to Bob, from Bob...

Make sure you totally understand the accusative case (see page 156), then look at these sentences:

Hermann schreibt einen Brief. = Hermann writes a letter.

ACCUSATIVE CASE

Hermann schreibt einem Freund. = Hermann writes to a friend.

DATIVE CASE

1. These sentences are different. The friend is not being written — he's being written to. So the letter is more directly involved in the action than the friend is. That's why they're in different cases.
2. Usually when you've got a word like 'on', 'at', 'from', 'of', 'for', 'in', 'by', 'with', 'to'... in the English translation, that's when you need to use the dative in the German. (Sometimes you need to use the accusative with words like this though — see page 179.)
3. There are a few sneaky exceptions that don't have one of those words, but are in the dative case anyway — see page 181.

For grammar fans — the indirect object of the verb is in the dative case.

Use the genitive and dative cases correctly to really show off

Not my idea of fun, but you need to learn about the genitive and dative cases so you know when to change the endings on things like nouns and adjectives.

Nouns

Scary — it looks like there's a lot on this page, but it's all pretty simple stuff about words for people and objects — nouns. Just about every sentence has a noun in it, so this is dead important.

Every German noun starts with a capital letter

In English, words like Richard, London and January always have capital letters.
In German absolutely every noun (object, person or place) has a capital letter.

EXAMPLE: *apple:* der Apfel *elephant:* der Elefant *cow:* die Kuh *baby:* das Baby

Every German noun is masculine, feminine or neuter

It's no good just knowing the German words for things — you have to know whether each one's masculine, feminine or neuter too.

DER, DIE AND DAS

A DER in front means it's masculine
(in the nominative case).
DIE in front = feminine
(or a plural).
DAS in front = neuter.

The Golden Rule

Each time you learn a word, remember a der, die or das to go with it — don't think 'cow = Kuh', think 'cow = die Kuh'.

Whether a word is masculine, feminine or neuter affects loads of stuff. You have to use different words for 'the' and 'a', and you have to change adjectives (like big, red, shiny) to fit the word.

EXAMPLE: *a big apple:* ein großer Apfel (masculine)
a big cow: eine große Kuh (feminine)

See pages 167-170 for more on this.

These rules help you guess what a word is

If you have to guess if a word is masculine, feminine or neuter, these are good rules of thumb:

Rules of Thumb for Masculine, Feminine and Neuter Nouns

MASCULINE NOUNS:	FEMININE NOUNS:	NEUTER NOUNS:
nouns that end:	nouns that end:	nouns that end:
-el -us -ling	-ie -heit -tion	-chen -um -lein -ment
-er -ismus	-ei -keit -sion	
	-ung -tät -schaft	also: infinitives of verbs used as nouns, e.g. das Turnen (gymnastics)
also: male people, days, months, seasons	also: most female people	

To get your writing right, you need to know your genders

Make sure you remember that Golden Rule — every time you learn a noun in German, you have to learn whether it's der, die or das. If you get them wrong all the time, you'll sound really sloppy.

Nouns

There are a few more things you need to know about nouns...

Nouns get these endings to fit the case

Nouns sometimes have to change, depending on what case they're in.
You change them by adding on the right ending from this table.
You don't have to change them very often — that's why the table is mostly blank.

Endings for nouns in different cases

	Masculine	Feminine	Neuter	Plural
Nominative	-	-	-	-
Accusative	-	-	-	-
Genitive	-s	-	-s	-
Dative	-	-	-	-n

There are quite a few words where you have to add '-es' rather than '-s' in the genitive — they tend to end in '-s', '-ß', '-x' or '-z'.

EXAMPLE: Normally, 'apples' = 'Äpfel', but in the dative plural it's 'Äpfeln'.

Ich singe den Äpfeln. = I sing to the apples.

**NB: If it already ends in 'n', you don't add an extra 'n'.
For example, streets = Straßen, and in the plural dative it's still Straßen.**

Watch out though. Some words don't follow this pattern — if you've learnt some different endings for a word, then make sure you use those instead.

Weak nouns have weird endings

Some masculine nouns take different endings to the ones above.
They're called weak nouns and most of them are words for people or animals.
As long as you learn which nouns they are, it's not too tricky — the endings are actually dead simple.

1) There's no ending to add for the nominative singular case.
2) For most weak nouns, the ending in all other cases is '-n' (if the noun ends in '-e') or '-en' (for all others). E.g. 'der Junge' → 'den Jungen' in the accusative, 'der Mensch' → 'dem Menschen' in the dative.
3) There are just a couple of sneaky exceptions — a few weak nouns take the ending '-ns' in the genitive singular instead of '-n'. The only ones like this that you're likely to meet at GCSE are 'der Name' (name), 'der Buchstabe' (letter), 'der Glaube' (belief) and 'der Gedanke' (thought).
4) Oh, and 'der Herr' is a bit of a rascal too — it's got the ending '-n' instead of '-en' in the singular accusative, dative and genitive.

For common nouns, learn which endings to add and when

Nouns. They're not there to make your life any easier. But if you learn these rules you should be able to keep them all under control — and produce some beautiful pieces of German prose.

Nouns

The stuff on page 158 is fine if you've only got one of something. But if you've got more than one then it's not going to be much help to you. That's why you also need to know about plurals...

When you learn a German word, learn the **plural** too

In English you generally add an 's' to make things plural, e.g. boy + s = boys.
German is much trickier — there are nine main ways to make something plural. Yuck.

Nine Ways to Make Something Plural

No change,	*der Metzger → die Metzger (butchers).*
Add an umlaut to the stressed syllable,	*der Apfel → die Äpfel (apples).*
Add an 'e' on the end,	*der Tag → die Tage (days).*
Add an umlaut and an 'e' on the end,	*die Hand → die Hände (hands).*
Add an 'er' on the end,	*das Lied → die Lieder (songs).*
Add an umlaut and an 'er' on the end,	*das Haus → die Häuser (houses).*
Add an 's' on the end,	*das Sofa → die Sofas (sofas).*
Add an 'n' on the end,	*die Straße → die Straßen (streets).*
Add an 'en' on the end,	*das Bett → die Betten (beds).*

Most feminine nouns do one of these two things.

Whatever gender a noun is, its plural is always a 'die' word (in the nominative and accusative cases).

1. When you look them up in a dictionary, you get the plural in brackets like this: 'Bett (-en)', which means 'Betten', or 'Hand (¨e)', which means 'Hände'.

2. A compound noun is a noun made up of two or more words stuck together. When you add an umlaut, it goes on the stressed syllable of the 'root word' (the last bit of the compound noun). E.g. the plural of 'die Bratwurst' is 'die Bratwürste', not 'die Brätwurste'.

Some **adjectives** can be used as **nouns**

In English you can use some adjectives (see pages 169-171) as nouns (e.g. the good, the bad and the ugly). Well, it's the same in German — but you can do it with pretty much any adjective.

***Der Deutsche* ist sehr freundlich.** = The German (man) is very friendly.

The old man: Der Alte *The pretty girl:* Die Hübsche

Because the adjective is now a noun, it has to have a capital letter.

You don't always have to say whether you're talking about a man or a woman in German, because it's clear from whether you use der (for a man) or die (for a woman).

The noun has the same ending that it would have if it was still an adjective (see pages 169-170 for the tables of endings).

Each time you learn a word, learn how to make the plural too

Nouns, nouns, nouns — you just can't move for them, they're absolutely everywhere. It's a pain, but if you can get your head round them now then you're on to a winner. You know what to do...

Word Order

You need to write proper sentences — so I'm going to tell you where to stick your words...

The **five commandments** for German word order

There are five important rules about German word order that you absolutely have to know. Here are the first three (the others are on the next page):

1 Put the verb second

The verb (the action word) almost always goes second in a German sentence.

E.g. ***Ich spiele Fußball.*** = I play football.

The word order in simple sentences like this is the same as in English. The person or thing doing the action goes first, and the verb comes second.

The word order for questions and instructions is different. See pages 7 and 198 for more details.

2 Keep the verb second

As long as you keep the verb second, you can be fairly flexible with the word order in German.

E.g. If you want to say 'I play football at the weekend', you can say...

Ich spiele am Wochenende Fußball. = (I play at the weekend football.)

OR

Am Wochenende spiele ich Fußball. = (At the weekend play I football.)

Swap the verb and the person doing the action around, so that the verb is still the second 'bit' in the sentence (although in this case, not the second word).

3 If there are two verbs, send one to the end

If you've got two verbs, treat the first one as normal and send the second one to the end of the sentence.

E.g. ***Ich werde nach Deutschland fahren.*** = (I will to Germany go.)

The verb comes second (usually)

This word order malarkey might seem mightily confusing at first glance, but trust me — if you follow these rules (and the ones on the next page) you won't go far wrong.

Word Order

Here's the rest of what you need to know about word order.

The **five commandments** for German word order

Here are the last two of those five commandments...

Remember — WHEN, HOW, WHERE

At school, you might have heard the phrase 'Time, Manner, Place' — it just means that if you want to describe WHEN, HOW and WHERE you do something, that's exactly the order you have to say it in.

E.g. ***Ich gehe heute Abend mit meinen Freunden ins Kino .***

heute Abend	mit meinen Freunden	ins Kino
WHEN (Time)	HOW (Manner)	WHERE (Place)

= (I go this evening with my friends to the cinema.)

5 Watch out for 'joining words' — they can change word order

Some conjunctions (joining words) can mess up the word order by sending the verb to the end of the sentence. Watch out though — they don't all do this. See pages 165-166 for more info.

E.g. ***Ich schwimme, weil ich sportlich bin .*** = (I swim because I sporty am.)

'Weil' ('because') is a joining word which sends the verb ('bin') to the end of the sentence.

If you wanted to really, really show off, you could swap the word order around even further so that the bit with 'weil' in goes first:

Weil ich sportlich bin, schwimme ich .

Keep this bit of the sentence exactly the same.

Swap this bit around so that the main verb still comes second.

Honestly, it's not as complicated as it looks

When you're writing anything in German, always keep this lot in mind — and give your work a quick squiz afterwards to check you've got it all right. Phew. Thank a deity of your choice that lot's over.

Quick Questions

Everyone loves a bit of grammar, so I know you'll be thrilled to learn that after each few pages of the grammar section, you'll be rewarded with not one, but two fabulous pages of Quick Questions to make sure you know your stuff. Turn the page if you don't believe me...

Quick Questions

1) Write down which case the underlined part of each of these sentences is in:
   a) Ich esse deine Apfelsine.
   b) Ich lerne gern Deutsch.
   c) Du isst meine Ananas.
   d) Sie lernt nicht gern Erdkunde.
   e) Er wirft es seinem Hund.
   f) Das ist die Kartoffel meiner Mutter.
   g) Ich sehe die Kuh.
   h) Ich sehe die Kuh.
   i) Die Kuh sieht mich.
   j) Die Kuh sieht mich.
   k) Ich trinke die Milch der Kuh.
   l) Ich trinke die Milch der Kuh.
   m) Ich trinke die Milch der Kuh.
   n) Ich gebe die Kuh meinen Schwestern.
   o) Ich gebe die Kuh meinen Schwestern.
   p) Ich gebe die Kuh meinen Schwestern.

2) Write down whether each of these German words is masculine, feminine or neuter:
   a) Donnerstag
   b) Hähnchen
   c) Gesellschaft
   d) Meinung
   e) Himmel
   f) Tourismus
   g) Zeitung
   h) Februar
   i) Fräulein
   j) Gymnasium
   k) Bücherei
   l) Radfahren
   m) Zucker
   n) Medikament
   o) Herbst

3) Look up the German for these words and write down whether they are masculine, feminine or neuter:
   a) motorway
   b) art
   c) bread roll
   d) stadium
   e) forest
   f) bacon
   g) peach
   h) waterskiing
   i) chess
   j) physics
   k) church
   l) hare

4) Complete these sentences using the correct underlined word.
   Hint: they're all weak nouns.
   a) Der Junge/Jungen war groß.
   b) Ich habe den großen Junge/Jungen gesehen.
   c) Das Mädchen mag den Studenten/Student.
   d) Das Mädchen gibt dem Student/Studenten ein Geschenk.
   e) Der Herr singt den Löwe/Löwen ein schönes Lied.
   f) Der Löwe isst den Herrn/Herren.

5) Turn these words from the singular to plural.
   If you don't know how to do that for any of them, look the word up.
   a) die Flasche
   b) der Vogel
   c) die Erbse
   d) das Bier
   e) der Zoo
   f) der Salat
   g) die Regel
   h) das Meerschweinchen
   i) der Rock
   j) die Bäuerin
   k) der Reisebus
   l) das Feld
   m) das Tuch
   n) die Fabrik
   o) das Museum

6) Now try turning these words from plurals to singular.
   Don't forget to include 'der', 'die' or 'das' in your answers.
   a) die Landkarten
   b) die Romane
   c) die Hüte
   d) die Kekse
   e) die Freibäder
   f) die Einkaufszentren
   g) die Kleider
   h) die Kulis
   i) die Käse
   j) die Löcher
   k) die Rechnungen
   l) die Sehenswürdigkeiten

Quick Questions

Quick Questions

7) Translate these sentences into English:
   a) Der Glückliche singt ein Lied.
   b) Die Lustige trägt einen Hut.
   c) Kennst du den Ängstlichen?
   d) Die Hungrigen kaufen sechzehn Birnen.
   e) Das Auto des Stolzen ist blau.
   f) Der Hilfreiche findet die Wichtige.
   g) Die Blöde schreibt dem Ernsten eine Postkarte.

8) For each of the following sentences, write down whether or not the word order is correct. If it's wrong, say why and rewrite the sentence so the word order is correct (there might be more than one way to do this for some of them).
   a) Ich nach Spanien fahre.
   b) Du kaufst Brot in der Bäckerei.
   c) Dienstags gehe ich ins Schwimmbad.
   d) Nächste Woche gehe ich ins Kino.
   e) Er ein neues Auto hat.
   f) Heute ich spiele Fußball.
   g) Ich fahre in die Schule mit dem Rad jeden Tag.
   h) Morgen kaufe ich eine neue Jacke.
   i) Sie geht ins Stadion mit ihren Freunden.
   j) Später spiele ich Tennis mit meiner Freundin im Park.

9) Rewrite each of the following sentences so that the word order is correct (there might be more than one way to do this for some of them).
   a) jeden Tag im Hallenbad ich schwimme
   b) sie Klavier spielt abends
   c) gehen morgen wir ins Restaurant
   d) Zug fahre ich mit dem nach oft London
   e) ich spielen Tennis kann
   f) werde Jahr nächstes fahren Frankreich nach ich
   g) meine Großmutter werde besuchen ich Samstag
   h) muss ich meiner Mutter mit die Stadt in heute gehen

10) Translate these sentences into German:
   a) He runs every day.
   b) I'm meeting my friends at two o'clock.
   c) They are playing tennis in the park tomorrow.
   d) We're not going to the beach, because the weather is bad.
   e) You ('du') must go to school on Monday.
   f) I travel to school by train every day.

11) Use 'weil' to join the sentences on the left with the ones on the right. Remember to change the word order of the sentence on the right.

a) Ich mag meinen Bruder.	Er ist lustig.
b) Ich bin traurig.	Mein Goldfisch ist krank.
c) Er arbeitet beim Zoo.	Tieren gefallen ihm.
d) Ich gehe aus.	Es ist sonnig und warm.

Conjunctions

These words help you to join phrases together to make more interesting sentences.

Und = And

Ich spiele gern Fußball. AND *Ich spiele gern Rugby.*

= I like playing football. = I like playing rugby.

→ *Ich spiele gern Fußball und Rugby.* = I like playing football and rugby.

ANOTHER EXAMPLE:

Ich habe einen Bruder und eine Schwester. = I have a brother and a sister.

Oder = Or

Er spielt jeden Tag Fußball. OR *Er spielt jeden Tag Rugby.*

= He plays football every day. = He plays rugby every day.

→ *Er spielt jeden Tag Fußball oder Rugby.* = He plays football or rugby every day.

ANOTHER EXAMPLE: *Ich möchte Ärztin oder Polizistin werden.*

= I would like to become a doctor or a policewoman.

Aber = But

Ich spiele gern Fußball. BUT *Ich spiele nicht gern Rugby.*

= I like playing football. = I don't like playing rugby.

→ *Ich spiele gern Fußball, aber ich spiele nicht gern Rugby.*

= I like playing football but I don't like playing rugby.

ANOTHER EXAMPLE:

Ich will Tennis spielen, aber es regnet. = I want to play tennis, but it's raining.

The examiners will be looking for joining words like these

At last, a fairly easy page. You use 'and', 'or' and 'but' all the time when you're speaking English — if you don't use them when you speak German, you'll sound a bit weird. Which no one wants.

Conjunctions

Examiners really do love it if you use joining words in your work.
Show them just how clever you are by using ones that affect word order.

These joining words affect the **word order**

The words below work in the same way as the stuff on page 165, but with one difference — if there's a verb (see page 187) after them, then that verb gets sent to the end of the sentence.

weil = because

Bob geht ins Kino, weil Hermann ~~geht~~ ins Kino geht.

= Bob is going to the cinema, because Hermann is going to the cinema.

während = while

Es regnet, während ich ~~spiele~~ Hockey spiele. = It rains while I play hockey.

More joining words

if/when:	wenn
after:	nachdem
so that:	damit
before:	bevor
until:	bis
when:	als
whether:	ob
although:	obwohl
that:	dass
because:	denn

This one doesn't send the verb to the end.

All these joining words (and 'aber' on the last page) need a comma before them in a sentence.

Here are a couple of other examples that you might come across a fair bit:

Ich denke, dass Deutsch total fabelhaft ist. = I think that German is totally fabulous.

The verb gets sent to the end.

Es ist prima, wenn man Deutsch spricht. = It's great, if you speak German.

'Weil' sends the verb to the end of the sentence...

...very important one to remember, that. If you can get the hang of using 'weil' properly, then it doesn't take much to get your sentence structure right when you're using words like 'dass' or 'obwohl'.

Articles

'The' and 'a' are really important words — you use them all the time.
They're tricky in German, because there are different ones for masculine, feminine or neuter words (see page 158), and for different cases (nominative, accusative or whatever — see pages 156-157).

'The' — start by learning der, die, das, die

1) In English there's just one word for 'the' — simple.
2) In German, you need to know whether you want the masculine, feminine or neuter, and what case you want (nominative, accusative, genitive or dative).
3) Start by learning the first line — der, die, das, die.
You absolutely have to know those ones.

Table of the German words for 'THE'

	Masculine	Feminine	Neuter	Plural
Nominative	der	die	das	die
Accusative	den	die	das	die
Genitive	des	der	des	der
Dative	dem	der	dem	den

This table is pretty scary, but you have to know it all to get everything right in your writing tasks. Cover the page, and write the table out. When you can get it right every time, you'll know which word to use when you're writing or speaking in German.

Examples

Masculine, nominative:

Der Apfel ist rot. = The apple is red.

Plural, nominative:

Die Äpfel sind rot. = The apples are red.

Masculine, dative:

Ich singe dem Apfel ein Lied. = I sing a song to the apple.

Plural, dative:

Ich singe den Äpfeln ein Lied. = I sing a song to the apples.

For why the last one is Äpfeln instead of Äpfel, see page 159.

Learn the different words for 'the'

There's no getting round it, you need all this stuff to be able to write in German. You have to be able to cover up the page and write out the table — keep on practising till you can.

Articles

Yep, you've guessed it — there are a fair few different words for 'a' in German too...

'A' — start by learning **ein, eine, ein**

1) Like the German for 'the', the word for 'a' is different for masculine, feminine or neuter, and for different cases (nominative, accusative, genitive or dative).
2) Start by learning the first line — ein, eine, ein. When you've got that sorted, move on to the other ones.

Table of the German words for 'A'

	Masculine	Feminine	Neuter
Nominative	ein	eine	ein
Accusative	einen	eine	ein
Genitive	eines	einer	eines
Dative	einem	einer	einem

Examples

Masculine, nominative:

Ein Hund. = A dog.

Masculine, accusative:

Ich habe einen Hund. = I have a dog.

Feminine, nominative:

Eine Katze. = A cat.

Feminine, accusative:

Ich habe eine Katze. = I have a cat.

Trickier examples

Masculine, genitive:

For more on why there's an 's' on the end of 'Vogel', see page 159.

Wegen eines Vogels... = Because of a bird...

Feminine, dative:

Ich schreibe einer Freundin. = I write to a (female) friend.

You need to know these words for 'a' too

It's stuff like this that makes me glad I speak English — just one word for 'the', and one word for 'a'... (Well two words actually, let's not forget about 'an'.) It's important you learn this lot though.

Adjectives

Make your sentences a lot more interesting (which means more marks) with some adjectives (describing words). Here are 21 of them to whet your appetite:

21 top adjectives

big/tall:	groß	*easy:*	einfach	*ugly:*	hässlich	*interesting:*	interessant
small/short:	klein	*difficult:*	schwierig	*old:*	alt	*boring:*	langweilig
long:	lang	*good:*	gut	*young:*	jung	*strange:*	seltsam
wide:	breit	*bad:*	schlecht (or schlimm)	*new:*	neu	*normal:*	normal
happy:	glücklich			*fast:*	schnell		
sad:	traurig	*beautiful:*	schön	*slow:*	langsam		

See page 68 for colours.

Adjectives that go **after** the noun **don't change**

When the describing word (the adjective — e.g. red) is somewhere after the word it's describing (e.g. apple), it doesn't change at all.

Der Apfel ist rot. = The apple is red.

Das Haus ist rot. = The house is red.

Die Lampe ist rot. = The lamp is red.

For how to add things like 'very' and 'almost', see page 172.

You just use the basic describing word, without any endings.

Endings for when the adjective comes **before** the **noun**

In the sentences below, red comes before apples, so you have to give it the right ending from this table:

Endings for adjectives before the noun

	Masculine	Feminine	Neuter	Plural
Nominative	roter	rote	rotes	rote
Accusative	roten	rote	rotes	rote
Genitive	roten	roter	roten	roter
Dative	rotem	roter	rotem	roten

You almost never need to use the ones shaded in grey.

Plural, accusative: ***Ich habe rote Äpfel.*** = I have red apples.

You also have to use these endings if the describing word comes after a number bigger than one, or after viele (many), wenige (few), einige (some), etwas (something) or nichts (nothing).

Plural, nominative: ***Zwei rote Äpfel.*** = Two red apples.

Ich habe viele große Äpfel. = I have many big apples.

If you love grammar — these endings are for when there's no article before the adjective.

To get top marks you need to get your endings right

I love a good adjective. They make life just that bit more interesting. Examiners love a good adjective too — so use them and use them well. There are more adjective endings on the next couple of pages.

Adjectives

Here are a few more adjective endings for you to learn — well, I do know how you love those tables.

There are special endings **after 'the'**

You've got to add these endings if the describing word comes after 'the' (der, die, das etc.), 'dieser' (this), 'jeder' (each/every), 'beide' (both), 'welcher' (which) and alle (all).

Endings for adjectives after definite articles

	Masculine	Feminine	Neuter	Plural
Nominative	rote	rote	rote	roten
Accusative	roten	rote	rote	roten
Genitive	roten	roten	roten	roten
Dative	roten	roten	roten	roten

Masculine, nominative:

Der rote Apfel. = The red apple.

Dieser kleine Apfel ist gut. = This small apple is good.

If you love grammar — these endings are for when it's after a definite article or a demonstrative adjective.

There are special endings **after 'a'** and **belonging words**

You need these endings when the describing word comes after ein (a, or one) or kein (no, or none), or after belonging words like mein, dein, sein, ihr...

Endings for adjectives after indefinite articles

	Masculine	Feminine	Neuter	Plural
Nominative	roter	rote	rotes	roten
Accusative	roten	rote	rotes	roten
Genitive	roten	roten	roten	roten
Dative	roten	roten	roten	roten

Masculine, nominative:

Der rote Apfel. = The red apple.

Mein roter Apfel ist gut. = My red apple is good.

If you love grammar — these endings are for when it's after an indefinite article or a possessive adjective.

Nothing too tricky here, just follow the rules

Once you know this stuff, you know it. And lots of the words end in '-en', which makes it easier. Learn the nominative and accusative part of each table first — they're the ones you'll need most often.

Adjectives

Now for some slightly different types of adjective...

My, your, our — words for who it belongs to

You have to be able to use and understand these words to say that something belongs to someone:

The possessive adjectives

mein:	*my*	unser:	*our*
dein:	*your (informal singular)*	euer:	*your (informal plural)*
sein:	*his*	Ihr:	*your (formal singular & plural)*
ihr:	*her*		
sein:	*its*	ihr:	*their*

But watch out — they need the right ending to go with the object you're talking about (they're the same as the ein/eine/ein table — see page 170 — except there's an extra 'plurals' column):

Table of endings for 'mein'

	Masculine	Feminine	Neuter	Plural
Nominative	mein	meine	mein	meine
Accusative	meinen	meine	mein	meine
Genitive	meines	meiner	meines	meiner
Dative	meinem	meiner	meinem	meinen

Here's an example sentence for each case, using the right ending for 'mein'.

Meine Tasche ist blau. = My bag is blue.

Ich mag mein Fahrrad. = I like my bike.

Das Auto meines Vaters ist rot. = My father's car is red. (The car of my father is red.)

Ich schreibe meinen Eltern. = I write to my parents.

This is the neat bit — all of them use the same endings as 'mein' does.

E.g. ***Deine Tasche ist blau.*** = Your bag is blue.

Seine Tasche ist blau. = His bag is blue.

Unsere Tasche ist blau. = Our bag is blue.

Welcher, dieser and jeder — Which, this and every

Three dead handy words that you need to be able to use.

Welche Schokolade schmeckt besser? = Which chocolate tastes better?

Which apple: Welcher Apfel
Which bread: Welches Brot

The endings follow the same pattern as 'der' — look at the last letter for each word in the table on page 167, e.g. the last line would be diesem, dieser, diesem, diesen.

Diese Katze gehört Camilla. = This cat belongs to Camilla.

Jeder Lehrer ist blau. = Every teacher is blue.

For grammar fanatics: 'Welcher' is an interrogative adjective, and 'dieser' and 'jeder' are demonstrative adjectives.

Those possessive adjectives are really useful

You need words like 'my' all the time — for talking about your family and friends, describing yourself... And remember, 'welcher' = which, 'dieser' = this and 'jeder' = each or every.

Adverbs

This page is about describing things you do, e.g. 'I speak German perfectly', and about adding more info, e.g. 'I speak German almost perfectly'.

Make your sentences **better** by saying **how** you do things

In English, you don't say 'We speak strange' — you add an 'ly' onto the end to say 'We speak strangely'. In German, you don't have to do anything — you just stick the describing word in as it is.

EXAMPLE: ***Ich fahre langsam.*** = I drive slowly (slow).

badly (bad):	schlecht
quickly (fast):	schnell

'Langsam' is just the German word for 'slow' — you can use any other suitable describing word here.

Ich singe. = I sing.

Ich singe laut. = I sing loudly.

Ich singe schlecht. = I sing badly.

Use one of these words to give **even more detail**

Stick one of these words in front of the describing word in a sentence to add detail and impress your teacher:

You can use them for sentences saying how something is done...

Ich fahre sehr langsam.

= I drive very slowly.

quite:	ganz/ziemlich
slightly:	etwas/ein wenig
a bit:	ein bisschen
almost:	fast
too:	zu

...and for sentences about what something is like.

Bob ist ganz glücklich.

= Bob is quite happy.

These words give **extra detail** about **time** and **place**

You'll get even more marks if you can add information about when you do something...

now and then:	ab und zu
now and then:	dann und wann
as soon as possible:	so bald wie möglich
last week:	letzte Woche
next weekend:	nächstes Wochenende

Ich gehe oft ins Kino. = I often go to the cinema.

The word order changes because the verb has to come second. See page 161.

Manchmal isst sie Birnen. = Sometimes she eats pears.

...and where it is: ***Ich wohne hier.*** = I live here.

Ich wohne nicht gern dort. = I don't like living there.

Using adverbs in German is really simple

To say how you do something, you just stick in a describing word — no endings, no faffing, brilliant.

Quick Questions

These Quick Questions aren't just here because I like writing 'em (trust me). They're here to help you find out what you know and practise using what you've learnt. So give them a go. Please.

Quick Questions

1) Use the German word for 'and' to join the sentences on the left with those on the right. Then translate the sentences into English.
   a) Ich kaufe Äpfel. — Ich kaufe Eier.
   b) Ich habe zwei Katzen. — Ich habe einen Hund.
   c) Ich möchte einen Apfelstrudel. — Ich möchte einen Kaffee.

2) Use the German word for 'or' to join the sentences on the left with those on the right. Then translate the sentences into English.
   a) Jeden Tag schwimme ich. — Jeden Tag jogge ich.
   b) Samstags gehe ich in die Stadt. — Samstags gehe ich ins Sportzentrum.
   c) Ich möchte Dolmetscher werden. — Ich möchte Journalist werden.

3) Use the German word for 'but' to join the sentences on the left with those on the right. Then translate the sentences into English.
   a) Ich mag Englisch. — Ich mag nicht Mathematik.
   b) Ich möchte ins Kino gehen. — Ich habe kein Geld.
   c) Ich muss meine Hausaufgaben machen. — Ich will Fußball spielen.

4) Name ten German joining words that affect word order.

5) Join the phrases on the left with those on the right using the word in brackets. You'll need to change the word order of the second sentence.
   a) Ich meine... *(dass)* Dein Kleid ist fürchterlich.
   b) Ich denke... *(dass)* Du bist sehr unhöflich.
   c) Heute werde ich spazieren gehen... *(wenn)* Das Wetter ist schön.
   d) Ich spreche gern Deutsch. *(obwohl)* Es ist manchmal ganz schwer.
   e) Er wäscht ab. *(während)* Ich sauge Staub.

6) Complete the sentences below by choosing the correct underlined word. If you don't know the gender of a word, look it up in the dictionary.
   a) Ich habe ein/einen Film gesehen.
   b) Der/Den Film war mies.
   c) Das Auto des/der Frau war sehr alt.
   d) Die Führerin des/der Autos war sehr jung.
   e) Ich esse ein/eines Eis.
   f) Der Affe isst einen/eine Banane.
   g) Ich singe die/der Hübschen.
   h) Die/Der Katze ist sehr glücklich.
   i) Wir singen die/den Kindern.
   j) Die/Den Kinder sind wirklich undankbar.
   k) Ich schreibe dem/das Hotel.
   l) Ich habe einen/einem neuen Hund gekauft.
   m) In der Stadt gibt es eine/einer Bibliothek.

7) Translate these sentences into German:
   a) The banana is yellow.
   b) The milk is cold.
   c) The boy is boring.
   d) The song is terrible.

Quick Questions

Quick Questions

8) Give the correct endings for each of the adjectives.
If you're not sure about genders, use a dictionary to check them.
   a) Heiß... Kaffee.
   b) Schön... Auto.
   c) Gut... Geschichte.
   d) Ich habe gelb... Bananen.
   e) Drei seltsam... Kinder sind mir gefolgt.
   f) Ich habe einige klein... Geschenke gekauft.
   g) Es gibt viele modern... Geschäfte.

9) What are the correct endings for the adjectives in these sentences?
If you're not sure about genders, use a dictionary to check them.
   a) Ich habe ein toll... Buch gelesen.
   b) Der jung... Mann war in der Bibliothek.
   c) Das Fahrrad des jung... Manns war rot.
   d) Ich habe einen schön... Schmetterling gefunden.
   e) Das schnell... Auto hat eine Panne gehabt.
   f) Das Kaninchen gehört meiner klein... Schwester.
   g) Ich schreibe meinem interessant... Lehrer.
   h) Das Haus der seltsam... Frau war hässlich.

10) Complete the sentences below by choosing the right underlined word.
If you're not sure about genders, use a dictionary to check them.
   a) <u>Mein/Meinen</u> Kuli funktioniert nicht.
   b) <u>Ihre/Ihr</u> Auto ist blau.
   c) Das Kleid <u>meiner/meine</u> Schwester ist lila.
   d) <u>Dein/Deines</u> Mittagessen ist fertig.
   e) Ich schreibe <u>meiner/meinem</u> Freundin.
   f) Er spielt <u>seine/sein</u> Musik sehr laut.
   g) Leider ist sie <u>unsere/unserer</u> Tochter.
   h) Morgen werdet ihr <u>euer/euere</u> Tante besuchen.
   i) Wir haben <u>Ihre/Ihrer</u> Bank geschrieben.

11) Again, complete these sentences by choosing the correct underlined word.
If you're not sure about genders, use a dictionary to check them.
   a) <u>Welcher/Welchen</u> Kuchen möchtest du?
   b) <u>Welches/Welche</u> Kaninchen schmeckt besser?
   c) <u>Jeder/Jedes</u> Kaninchen schmeckt gut.
   d) Ich esse <u>dieser/diesen</u> Apfel.
   e) Ich singe <u>diesen/diesem</u> Apfel.

12) Translate these sentences into English. Hint: they all contain adverbs.
   a) Ich laufe langsam.
   b) Ich laufe schlecht.
   c) Er spricht sehr laut.
   d) Du spielst ganz gut.
   e) Sie fährt zu schnell.
   f) Wir sprechen ein bisschen seltsam.

13) Translate these sentences into English:
   a) Ich gehe manchmal ins Kino.
   b) Ich schwimme oft.
   c) Zahlen Sie bitte, so bald wie möglich.
   d) Nächstes Wochenende gehen wir aus.
   e) Ab und zu esse ich Schokolade.

Comparatives and Superlatives

A lot of the time you don't just want to say that something is big, or red or whatever, you want to say that it's the biggest, or bigger than someone else's...

How to say smaller, smallest

In English you say small, smaller, smallest. It's almost the same in German:

Anna ist klein.

= Anna is small.

Stem	*old:* alt	*interesting:* interessant

Hermann ist kleiner.

= Hermann is smaller.

Stem + '-er'	*older:* älter	*more interesting:* interessanter

Sina ist der Kleinste.

= Sina is the smallest.

Stem + 'der', 'die' or 'das' and '-(e)ste'	*oldest:* der/die/das Älteste	*most interesting:* der/die/das Interessanteste

So here the adjective acts as a noun, just like in English — and of course all German nouns get a capital letter.

For most words, '-ste' is added, but sometimes it's '-este', to make it easier to pronounce. (You can't miss out the der, die or das — you CAN'T say 'Ethel ist Interessanteste'.)

You can do this with almost any describing word. A lot of short ones get an added umlaut like 'alt' does. Check out the top of page 169 for more describing words.

Just like in English, there are odd ones out — for example, you don't say good, gooder, goodest...

good: gut	*better:* besser	*the best:* der/die/das Beste
big (or tall): groß	*bigger:* größer	*the biggest:* der/die/das Größte
high: hoch	*higher:* höher	*the highest:* der/die/das Höchste
much/a lot: viel	*more:* mehr	*the most:* der/die/das Meiste
near: nah	*nearer:* näher	*the nearest:* der/die/das Nächste

Liz ist die Größte.

= Liz is the tallest.

You don't need to use a capital if the adjective goes before a noun e.g. 'the tallest tree' would be 'der größte Baum'.

Describing words that end in '-er' (like 'älter') are comparative adjectives. If you use them before a noun, they need adjective endings, like on pages 169-170.

Remember: 'klein', 'kleiner', 'kleinste'

I don't know about you, but I'm always comparing things — my biscuit's bigger than your biscuit, my bike's shinier than your bike, etc. You can use these rules to say 'my younger sister / older brother' too.

Comparatives and Superlatives

There are many more ways of comparing things, trust me...

Learn these four great ways of comparing things

Jo ist älter als Ed.

= Jo is older than Ed.

Jo ist weniger alt als Ed.

= Jo is less old than Ed.

Jo ist so alt wie Ed.

= Jo is as old as Ed.

Jo ist ebenso alt wie Ed.

= Jo is just as old as Ed.

You can compare how people do things

If you're talking about how someone does something, it's almost the same as the stuff on the last page:

Einstein fährt schnell. = Einstein drives quickly.

Bob fährt schneller. = Bob drives more quickly.

Ethel fährt am schnellsten. = Ethel drives the quickest.

The bit that's different is the last one. You add 'am' and '-(e)sten'. (Instead of 'der', 'die' or 'das', and '-(e)ste'.)

Here's one more odd one out you need to know:

Ich spreche gern Deutsch. = I like speaking German.

Ich spreche lieber Deutsch. = I prefer speaking German.

Ich spreche am liebsten Deutsch. = I like speaking German best of all.

'Best' is also slightly different: To say someone does something best, it's 'am besten'.

As always, learn the rules and the important exceptions

'Gern', 'lieber' and 'am liebsten' are all really useful words when it comes to giving your opinion on something — so if I were you, I'd definitely learn how to use them in sentences.

Prepositions

This stuff looks horrendous, but you've got to learn it if you want good marks.

TO — zu or nach

Where we use 'to', German speakers often use 'zu':

Komm zu mir. = Come to me.

zum Bahnhof gehen = to go to the station

(zum = zu dem — see page 179)

For things like to go, to do, use the infinitive — see page 187. E.g. gehen = to go, machen = to make.

For 'the train to London' (and other towns), it's 'nach':

der Zug nach London = the train to London

They sometimes use 'an', 'auf' or 'in' too.

AT — an, bei, um or zu

Where we use 'at', in German it's usually 'an': ***an der Universität*** = at university

Sometimes 'bei' is used: ***bei einer Party*** = at a party

For 'at home', it's 'zu': ***zu Hause*** = at home

For times it's 'um': ***um acht Uhr*** = at 8 o'clock

ON — an or auf

Where we use 'on', in German it tends to be 'an': ***an der Wand*** = on the wall

am = an dem — see page 179. ***am Montag*** = on Monday

For 'on foot', it's 'zu': ***zu Fuß*** = on foot

For 'on the bus' (as in 'I travel on the bus'), it's 'mit': ***mit dem Bus*** = on the bus

For on top of something, it's 'auf': ***Das Buch ist auf dem Tisch.*** = The book is on the table.

You don't always use the same preposition in German as in English

It may seem like a pain in the neck having to remember where and when to use all these little words, but trust me — if you get it right, it'll bag you loads of lovely marks in your writing assessment.

Prepositions

Yep, more sneaky wee words (or prepositions as they're known by grammar fanatics). Make sure you learn which words to use and where — it's not always obvious from the English.

IN — in or an

Where we use 'in', German speakers also tend to use 'in':

in Deutschland = in Germany ***im Bett*** = in bed (im = in dem — see page 179)

For in the morning/evening, it's 'an': ***am Morgen*** = in the morning (am = an dem — see page 179)

FROM — von or aus

When we use 'from' in English, they usually use 'von' in German, including for where someone/thing has come from recently:

For 'made from' see 'made of'.

Der Zug ist von London gekommen. = The train has come from London.

For where someone/thing is from originally, it's 'aus': ***Ich komme aus England.***

= I come from England.

OF — 'von', 'aus' or left out

Where we use 'of', the German is usually 'von': ***ein Freund von mir*** = a friend of mine

For 'made of', it's 'aus': ***aus Wolle*** = made of wool

You leave it out of dates: ***der erste März*** = the first of March

See page 6 for more on dates.

It's often left out in genitive sentences too: ***einer der Besten*** = one of the best

FOR — für or seit

Where we use 'for', German speakers usually use 'für': ***ein Geschenk für mich*** = a present for me

For time amounts in the past, it's 'seit': ***Ich habe sie seit zwei Jahren nicht gesehen.***

= I haven't seen her for two years.

You need to know which preposition to use and where

You absolutely must learn all these prepositions — and when to use them. For common phrases especially, you need to know when the preposition you use is different to the English one.

Prepositions

So, you've learnt all those sneaky wee words and you know when to use them — so far, so good. Now you've just got to get to grips with those pesky 'short forms' — oh, and learn how prepositions affect case.

An dem → am — short forms

Some of the words on the previous two pages get shortened when they go with dem, das or der. For example:

an dem ersten Januar  *am ersten Januar*

= on the first of January

Short forms

an dem = am	*bei dem* = beim
an das = ans	*von dem* = vom
in dem = im	*zu der* = zur
in das = ins	*zu dem* = zum

To be 100% right, you have to use the right case

When they're in a sentence, these words change the case (pages 156-157) of the stuff that comes after them. To be sure what case to use, you have to learn these lists.

Accusative
bis = *till, by*
durch = *through*
für = *for*
gegen = *against, about*
ohne = *without*
um = *round, around, at*

Dative
aus = *from, out of, made of*
bei = *at, near*
gegenüber = *opposite, facing*
mit = *with*
nach = *to, after*
seit = *since, for*
von = *from, of*
zu = *to, at*

Dative or Accusative
an = *to, on, in, at*
auf = *on, to, at*
entlang = *along*
hinter = *after, behind*
in = *in, to*
neben = *next to, beside*
über = *via, above, over*
unter = *under, among*
vor = *before, ago, in front of*
zwischen = *between*

Genitive
außerhalb = *outside of*
statt = *instead of*
trotz = *despite*
während = *during, while*
wegen = *because of*

For prepositions which use either the dative or accusative case, use the accusative when what you're talking about is moving and the dative if there's no movement.

Die Katze schläft hinter dem Sofa. = The cat sleeps behind the (dative) sofa.

The cat isn't moving.

Die Katze läuft hinter das Sofa. = The cat runs behind the (accusative) sofa.

The cat is moving.

Watch out for prepositions that can go with more than one case

The take-home message here: to get the most marks, you have to use the right case. If you're not sure about cases, go and look them up (on pages 156-157) — they're pretty darned important.

Pronouns

Dead handy page, this. Pronouns are everywhere, and they can make your German sound much more natural.

Pronouns **replace** nouns

Pronouns are words like 'you', 'she' or 'them'.

'He' is a pronoun. It means you don't have to say 'Dave' again.

Dave has a new job at the poodle parlour. He likes shaving poodles.

You use different sets of pronouns for different cases.
If you're not sure about this case stuff, look at pages 156-157.

You use **ich** (I) in the **nominative** case

You need 'I', 'you', 'he', etc. the most often — for the main person/thing in a sentence (the subject). Learn them all, or you'll be totally scuppered in the exams.

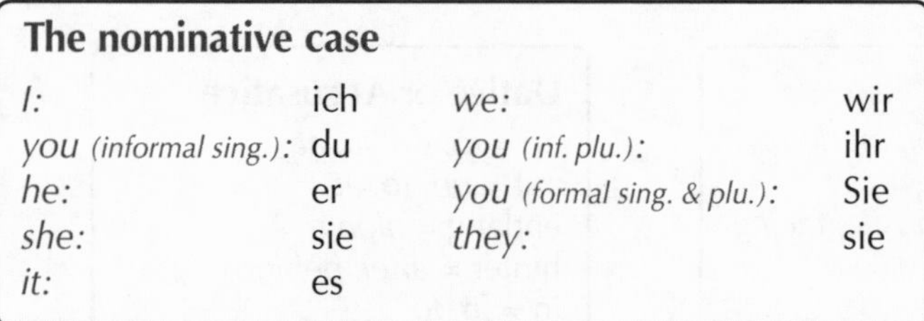

The nominative case

I:	ich	*we:*	wir
you (informal sing.):	du	*you (inf. plu.):*	ihr
he:	er	*you (formal sing. & plu.):*	Sie
she:	sie	*they:*	sie
it:	es		

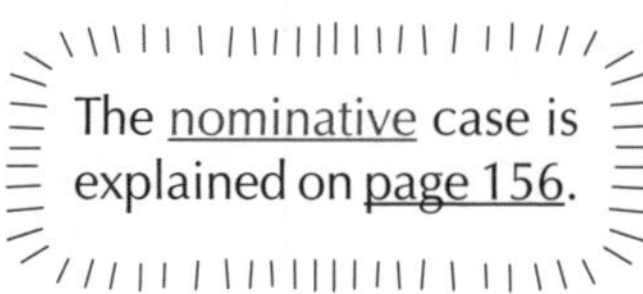

The nominative case is
explained on page 156.

Der Hund beißt den Kamm. = The dog bites the comb.

Er beißt den Kamm. = He bites the comb.

Remember — in English there's only one word for 'you', but in German there are loads.
The nominative words for you are:

du = you (informal singular)
for talking to one person you know well, or another young person

ihr = you (informal plural)
the same as 'du' but for talking to more than one person

Sie = you (formal singular and plural)
for talking to one or more older people who you don't know well or who you should be polite to

Pronouns are words like 'I', 'you', 'he', 'she', etc.

You use pronouns all the time in English, so you've got to be able to use them in German too. This page is really straightfoward — you probably know a lot of it already (so it'll be dead easy to learn).

Pronouns

It should come as no surprise to you by now that you use different pronouns in different cases...

You use **mich** (me) in the **accusative** case

These are for the person/thing in a sentence that's having the action done to it (the direct object). This is the accusative case.

Dave kitzelt den Hund. = Dave tickles the dog.

Dave kitzelt ihn. = Dave tickles him.

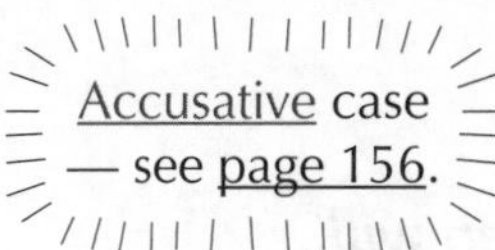
Accusative case — see page 156.

The accusative case

me:	mich	*us:*	uns
you (informal sing.):	dich	*you (inf. plu.):*	euch
him:	ihn	*you (frml sing. & plu.):*	Sie
her:	sie	*them:*	sie
it:	es		

There are special words for **to me**, **to her**, **to them**

For things that need 'to', 'by', 'with' or 'from' — like writing to someone — you use the dative case.

Der Hund gibt Dave den Kamm. = The dog gives the comb to Dave.

Der Hund gibt ihm den Kamm. = The dog gives the comb to him.

The dative case

to me:	mir	*to us:*	uns
to you (inf. sing.):	dir	*to you (inf. plu.):*	euch
to him:	ihm	*to you (frml sing. & plu.):*	Ihnen
to her:	ihr	*to them:*	ihnen
to it:	ihm		

Grammar spotters call these indirect object pronouns.

See page 157 for more on the dative case.

Remember: use mich in the accusative and mir in the dative

OK, so learning German grammar isn't exactly a laugh a minute. But it's your GCSE and if you want to get through it, then you really need to understand this stuff. You've just got to knuckle down and do it.

Pronouns

You need to know things like 'one' or 'someone' and ask questions like 'who?' or 'what?'.

The German word 'man' means 'one', not 'man'

Get this in your skull now — 'man' means 'one'. It doesn't mean the English word 'man'.
The Germans use 'man' more than we use 'one' in English — it isn't posh at all.

Wie sagt man das auf Deutsch? = How does one say that in German? (How do you say that in German?)

In English, we usually say 'you' instead of 'one' in everyday conversation.

Someone, no one — jemand, niemand

The word for 'someone' is the same as for 'anyone' — 'jemand'.

Kann jemand helfen? = Can someone help?

... wenn jemand mitmachen will... = ... if anyone wants to join in...

'Niemand' means 'no one'. It's a bit like 'jemand', so don't get them mixed up.
Remember — 'niemand' begins with an 'n' for no one.

Warum ist niemand gekommen? = Why has no one come?

Wer? — Who? / Was? — What? / Was für? — What sort of?

Get learning these useful question words...

Wer sitzt auf der Katze? = Who is sitting on the cat?

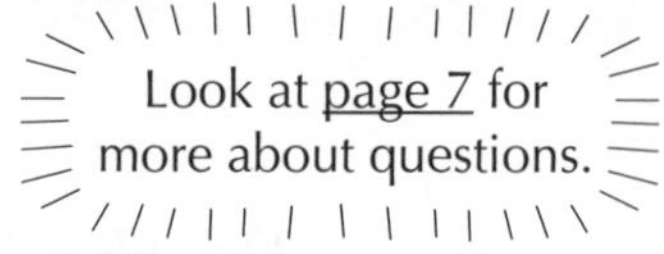
Look at page 7 for more about questions.

Was kratzt dich, Albert? = What is scratching you, Albert?

Was für eine Katze ist es? = What sort of cat is it?

'Who' changes for the different cases — 'wer' is just the one you'll see the most.

'Who' in the different cases		
Nominative	who	wer
Accusative	whom	wen
Dative	to whom	wem

Wer ist das? = Who is that?

Wen liebst du? = Whom do you love?

Zu wem höre ich? = To whom am I listening?

It's important to know these question words

Shut the book and scribble down the words for 'one', 'someone'/ 'anyone', 'no one', 'who' and 'what'. Keep going till you know them all. All that wer/wen/wem malarkey is top level, impressive stuff.

Relative Pronouns

Tricky stuff this, but learn it and you'll nab yourself loads of juicy marks.

Relative pronouns — 'that', 'which', 'whom', 'whose'

You need to understand all these words — and if you're after top marks, you need to be able to use them yourself. Words like 'that', 'which', 'whom' and 'whose' are relative pronouns — they relate back to the thing you're talking about. This is the kind of thing I mean:

The dog, which had dug up my sprouts, looked guilty.

The 'which' refers back to the dog.

In German the relative clause (the bit with the relative pronoun in) is separated from the rest of the sentence by commas.

Relative pronouns change the word order. They send the verb to the end of the relative clause (the bit inside the commas).

The pronoun refers to 'der Mann'.

The verb goes to the end of the clause.

Der Mann, der in der Ecke sitzt, ist ganz klein.

= The man who sits in the corner is quite small.

'Was' can be used as a relative pronoun

'Was' can be used as a relative pronoun — for example, you use it after 'alles', 'nichts', 'etwas' 'vieles' and 'weniges'.

E.g. ***Alles, was der Lehrer sagte, war interessant.***

= Everything that the teacher said was interesting.

Nichts, was ich gegessen habe, hat gut geschmeckt.

= Nothing that I ate tasted good.

Relative pronouns affect word order

These relative pronouns might be confusing at first, but you really do need to be able to understand and use them. The next page tells you which pronouns to use and where — there's even a handy little table.

Relative Pronouns

OK, so you need to know what the German relative pronouns are and when to use each one. This page'll point you in the right direction.

You've got to use the right one...

It's a bit tricky working out which pronoun you need, but as you'd probably expect, it just depends on the noun (page 158) and its case (pages 156-157). I've explained how to use this table in the subsection below, but here's a few examples to start with:

Table of relative pronouns

	Masculine	Feminine	Neuter	Plural
Nominative	der	die	das	die
Accusative	den	die	das	die
Genitive	dessen	deren	dessen	deren
Dative	dem	der	dem	denen

Die Katze, die mich gebissen hat, war schwarz. = The cat that bit me was black.

Der Mann, den ich gesehen habe, war witzig. = The man whom I saw was funny.

Das Pferd, dessen Bein gebrochen ist, ist traurig. = The horse whose leg is broken is sad.

Die Jungen, denen er eine Frage stellt, verstehen nicht. = The boys (to) whom he asks a question don't understand.

How to use the table...

1) Translate the sentence, leaving out the pronoun.
2) Is the noun it refers to masculine, feminine or neuter, or is it plural? Look down the relevant column.
3) Which case do you need? (Use the examples next to the table to help.) Look across the row you need.

E.g. Say you want to translate: The chair that is broken is mine.

1) Translate without the pronoun: *Der Stuhl, ... gebrochen ist, ist meiner.*
2) 'The chair' ('der Stuhl') is masculine.
3) 'That' refers to 'the chair', which is the subject, so you use the nominative case (see page 156).

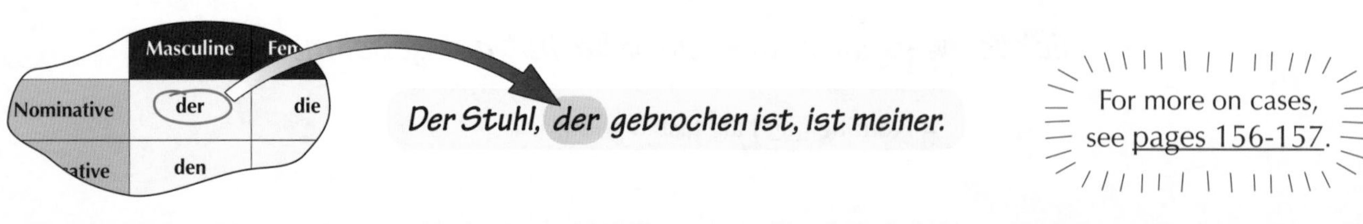
Masculine
Nominative
der
die
den
Der Stuhl, der gebrochen ist, ist meiner.
For more on cases, see pages 156-157.

To get the best marks, you need to understand this table

This is really top level, as-good-as-it-gets stuff. If you can use relative pronouns correctly — especially in the accusative, genitive or dative cases — anyone marking your work will be totally bowled over.

Quick Questions

It's time to test your extensive knowledge of German grammar with a few Quick Questions...

Quick Questions

1) 'Alex ist schnell' means 'Alex is fast' in German.
How would you say the following in German?
a) Hannah is faster. b) Lena is the fastest.

2) 'Ich bin alt' means 'I am old' in German.
How would you say the following in German?
a) You ('du') are older. b) He is the oldest.

3) Finish these sentences off in German, by translating the English word in brackets:
a) Der Hund war... *(big)* b) Das Pferd war... *(bigger)* c) Der Elefant war... *(the biggest)*
d) Äpfel sind... *(good)* e) Kekse sind... *(better)* f) Kuchen sind... *(the best)*
g) Der Zoo ist... *(near)* h) Das Freibad ist... *(nearer)* i) Das Kino ist... *(the nearest)*

4) Julia tells you 'Ich bin größer als Erik'. How would you tell her the following in German?
a) Mia is less tall than Erik.
b) Jakob is as tall as Mia.
c) Nina is just as tall as Jakob.

5) Felix tells you 'Ich singe laut'. Tell him (in German) that:
a) Maria sings more loudly. b) Michael sings the loudest.

6) 'Ich spiele gern Hockey' means 'I like playing Hockey' in German.
How would you say the following in German?
a) I prefer playing tennis. b) I like playing football best of all.

7) 'Ich tanze gut' means 'I dance well' in German.
How would you say the following in German?
a) I dance better. b) I dance best of all.

8) Complete these German sentences by picking the correct underlined word.
I've given you the English translation on the right to help you out.
a) Ich gehe zu/nach der Post. = *I go to the post office.*
b) Der Zug zu/nach Chester ist angekommen. = *The train to Chester has arrived.*
c) Ich bin auf/an der Bank. = *I am at the bank.*
d) Ich bin zu/an Hause. = *I am at home.*
e) Mein Geburtstag ist am/um Dienstag. = *My birthday is on Tuesday.*
f) Die Katze schläft auf/an dem Tisch. = *The cat sleeps on the table.*
g) Am/Im Morgen gehe ich aus. = *In the morning I go out.*
h) Der Hund ist im/am Bett. = *The dog is in bed.*
i) Sie kommt aus/von Frankreich. = *She comes from France.*
j) Das Schiff ist aus/von Amerika gekommen. = *The ship has come from America.*
k) Meine Bluse besteht aus/auf Seide. = *My blouse is made of silk.*
l) Das ist sehr nett von/aus dir. = *That is very nice of you.*
m) Ich habe seit/für drei Jahren nicht gespielt. = *I haven't played for three years.*

9) The following are all 'short forms' of German words.
Write out in full the words each one is short for.
a) am b) im c) ins d) zum
e) zur f) beim g) vom h) ans

Quick Questions

Quick Questions

10) Name the case used with each preposition in the following sentences. I've underlined the prepositions for you.
   a) Ich spreche mit meiner Freundin.
   b) Ich gehe in die Schule.
   c) Ich bin in der Stadt.
   d) Trotz des Wetters gehen wir aus.
   e) Du musst durch den Tunnel fahren.
   f) Die Kirche ist gegenüber dem Sportzentrum.
   g) Ich habe sie seit dem zweiten Dezember nicht gesehen.
   h) Es hat während des Sturms gebrochen.

11) For each of these sentences, replace the underlined subject with the right pronoun:
   a) Anna ist eine sehr gute Lehrerin.
   b) Thomas arbeitet hart.
   c) Das Pferd isst das Erdbeereis.
   d) Die Jungen spielen Fußball im Park.

12) What word for 'you' would you use if you had to talk to the following people in German?
   a) your friend
   b) a policeman
   c) a group of your classmates
   d) two strangers asking you for directions

13) How would you say 'I love you' in German?

14) How would you say 'he loves me' in German?

15) How would you say 'I love him' in German?

16) For each of these sentences, replace the underlined indirect object with the right pronoun. Hint: these pronouns are all in the dative case.
   a) Ich spiele Federball mit Markus.
   b) Ich gebe Charlotte das Geschenk.
   c) Sie wohnt mit Alex und Paul.

17) How would you say 'How does one say that in German?' in German?

18) 'Ich wohne da' means 'I live there' in German. How would you say 'no one lives there' in German?

19) How would you say 'who lives there?' in German?

20) How would you say 'what lives there?' in German?

21) How would you say 'with whom do you live?' in German?

22) For each of the following sentences fill in the gaps with the correct relative pronoun:
   a) Die Katze, ... sehr gut Tennis spielt, ist schwarz.
   b) Das Mädchen, ... Süßigkeiten ich gestohlen habe, ist böse.
   c) Die Frau, ... ich schreibe, ist wirklich alt.
   d) Der Junge, ... ich das Essen gebe, ist dankbar.
   e) Der Löwe, ... ich im Zoo gesehen habe, war sehr intelligent.

Verbs, Tenses and the Infinitive

Verbs are pretty darn important. Make sure you know all this stuff — it'll make your life a whole lot easier over the next few pages.

Verbs are action words — they tell you what's going on

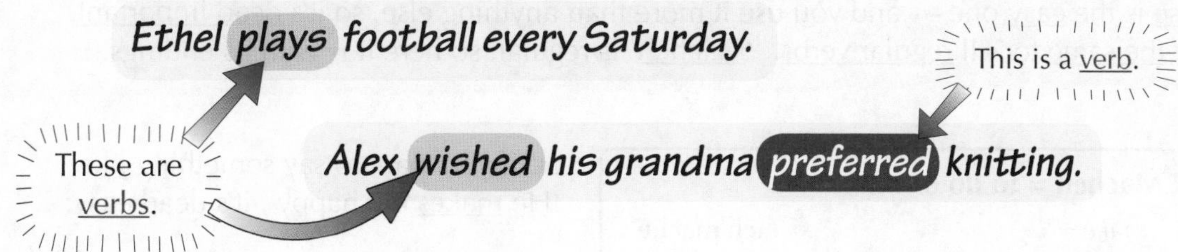

Ethel plays football every Saturday.
This is a verb.
These are verbs.
Alex wished his grandma preferred knitting.

There's a load of stuff you need to know about verbs, but it all boils down to these next two points:

1 You have different words for **different times**

You say things differently if they happened last week, or aren't going to happen till tomorrow.

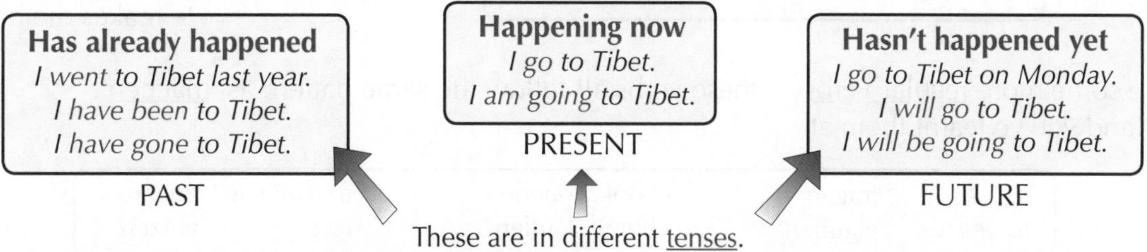

Has already happened
I went to Tibet last year.
I have been to Tibet.
I have gone to Tibet.
PAST
Happening now
I go to Tibet.
I am going to Tibet.
PRESENT
Hasn't happened yet
I go to Tibet on Monday.
I will go to Tibet.
I will be going to Tibet.
FUTURE
These are in different tenses.

2 You have different words for **different people**

You don't say 'I plays football' — it'd be daft. You change the verb to fit the person.

Happening to ME	**Happening to YOU**	**Happening to HER**
I am miserable.	*You are miserable.*	*She is miserable.*

OK, you get the picture — verbs are dead important. You use them all the time, so you need to learn all this stuff. That's why I go on about them so much.

The word you look up in the dictionary means 'to...'

When you want to say 'I dance' in German, you start by looking up 'dance' in the dictionary. But you can't just use the first word you find — there's more to it than that...

When you look up a verb in the dictionary, this is what you get:

to go:	gehen
to dance:	tanzen

For grammar fans, this is the infinitive.

You're not supposed to just use the verb in its raw state — you have to change it so it's right for the person and time you're talking about. The different verb forms are covered on the next few pages.

Read this page before you carry on

This is mega-important stuff. Over the next few pages I've told you loads about verbs because there's loads you need to know. And if you haven't understood this page first, the next ones'll be dead tricky.

Present Tense

If you want loads of marks, you've got to make your German sound natural. One sure-fire way to lose marks is to say something daft like 'I likes to gone swimming.' Here's how you can avoid it...

The **present** tense is **what's happening now**

The present tense is the easy one — and you use it more than anything else, so it's dead important. The endings are the same for all regular verbs. 'Machen' is regular, so here it is with its endings...

The first bit ('mach') doesn't change.

Machen = to do or make	
I make =	ich mach**e**
you (inf. sing.) make =	du mach**st**
he makes =	er mach**t**
she makes =	sie mach**t**
it makes =	es mach**t**
we make =	wir mach**en**
you (inf. plu.) make =	ihr mach**t**
you (frml. sing. & plu.) make =	Sie mach**en**
they make =	sie mach**en**

inf. = informal
frml. = formal
sing. = singular
plu. = plural

So if you want to say something like 'He makes me happy', it's dead easy:

1) Start by knocking off the '-en': machen
2) Then add on the new ending: macht
3) And — ta da...

Er macht mich glücklich.

= He makes me happy.

Here are some more regular verbs — these verbs all follow the same pattern as 'machen'. Learn it and you've learnt them all.

to ask:	fragen	*to book:*	buchen	*to explain:*	erklären
to believe:	glauben	*to buy:*	kaufen	*to dance:*	tanzen

Watch out — There's **a catch...**

Some regular verbs don't end in '-en' — they end in '-rn' or '-ln'.
Still, it's no problem — they follow nearly the same rules. Just watch out for missing '-e's.

'-rn' verbs:

You miss out the '-e' before the '-r' for ich.

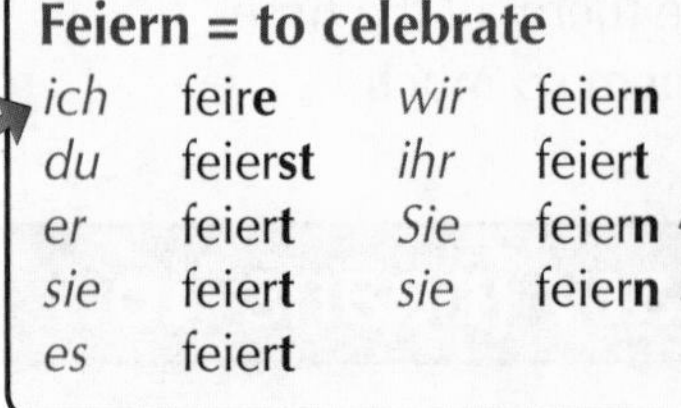

Feiern = to celebrate			
ich	feir**e**	*wir*	feier**n**
du	feier**st**	*ihr*	feier**t**
er	feier**t**	*Sie*	feier**n**
sie	feier**t**	*sie*	feier**n**
es	feier**t**		

You only add '-n' instead of '-en' for wir, Sie and sie.

'-ln' verbs:

Lose the '-e' before the 'l' for ich.

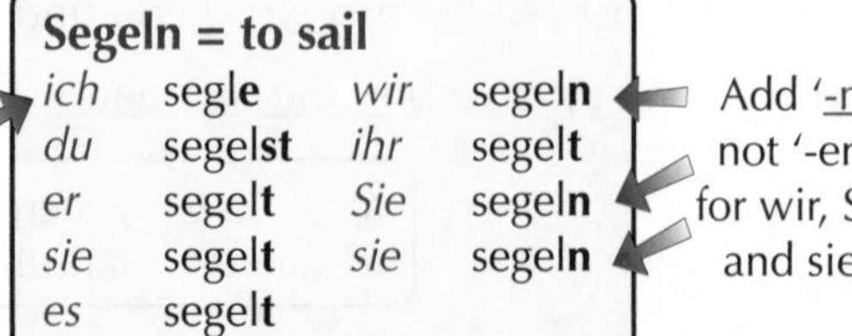

Segeln = to sail			
ich	segl**e**	*wir*	segel**n**
du	segel**st**	*ihr*	segel**t**
er	segel**t**	*Sie*	segel**n**
sie	segel**t**	*sie*	segel**n**
es	segel**t**		

Add '-n' not '-en' for wir, Sie and sie.

Just learn one of these types, and you can use the same rules for the other. Great stuff.

Learn the endings for regular '-en' verbs

OK, this is pretty easy stuff. Make sure you learn all those endings for regular verbs — it'll make your life a whole lot easier, trust me. Remember the endings go a bit weird in places for '-rn' and '-ln' verbs.

Present Tense

You could be conned into thinking nearly all verbs are regular (see page 188). But in fact, loads aren't.

Sein, haben, fahren and essen are irregular

Verbs that don't follow the same pattern as regular verbs are called 'irregular verbs' (how original). Most of the really useful verbs are irregular — d'oh. Anyway, here are four that you'll need a lot...

'Sein' means 'to be' — it's probably the most important verb in the world... ever. So learn it.

Sein = to be

I am =	ich	bin	wir	sind	*= we are*
you (inf. sing.) are =	du	bist	ihr	seid	*= you (inf. plu.) are*
he is =	er	ist	Sie	sind	*= you (frml. sing. & plu.) are*
she is =	sie	ist	sie	sind	*= they are*
it is =	es	ist			

inf. = informal
frml. = formal
sing. = singular
plu. = plural

2

You'll need this verb loads — 'haben' ('to have'). It's easy to learn, so there's no excuse.

Haben = to have

I have =	ich	habe	wir	haben	*= we have*
you (inf. sing.) have =	du	hast	ihr	habt	*= you (inf. plu.) have*
he has =	er	hat	Sie	haben	*= you (frml. sing. & plu.) have*
she has =	sie	hat	sie	haben	*= they have*
it has =	es	hat			

3

Fahren = to go, to drive

I go =	ich	fahre	wir	fahren	*= we go*
you (inf. sing.) go =	du	fährst	ihr	fahrt	*= you (inf. plu.) go*
he goes =	er	fährt	Sie	fahren	*= you (frml. sing. & plu.) go*
she goes =	sie	fährt	sie	fahren	*= they go*
it goes =	es	fährt			

'Fahren' means 'to go or drive'. You need it loads for travel and holidays (Section Four).

4

'Essen' ('to eat') nearly follows the rules. But not quite...

Essen = to eat

I eat =	ich	esse	wir	essen	*= we eat*
you (inf. sing.) eat =	du	isst	ihr	esst	*= you (inf. plu.) eat*
he eats =	er	isst	Sie	essen	*= you (frml. sing. & plu.) eat*
she eats =	sie	isst	sie	essen	*= they eat*
it eats =	es	isst			

These are the weird bits.

All these verbs are irregular too, so watch out for them:

to be called (he is called):	heißen (er heißt)	*to wear, carry (he wears, carries):*	tragen (er trägt)
to know (he knows):	wissen (er weiß)	*to ought to (he should):*	sollen (er soll)
to give (he gives):	geben (er gibt)	*to see (he sees):*	sehen (er sieht)

Learn these irregular verbs — you'll use them a lot

People talk about German being easy, because it's got loads of rules to follow. But it's a right pain that loads of words don't follow the rules. And of course it's all the really important stuff that doesn't.

Present Tense

Here are some more things you need to know about verbs in the present tense.

Some verbs make you use the dative case

You normally only need the dative case when you're saying 'to something or someone'.

Diese Zähne gehören ***mir****, nicht* ***dir****.* = These teeth belong to me, not to you.

But some German verbs always need the dative case.
You'd think 'I help the elephants' would be 'ich helfe die Elefanten' — but it isn't.
'Helfen' ('to help') is one of the awkward verbs that need the dative case, so you say:

Ich helfe den Elefanten.
= I help the elephants.
You use 'den' because 'Elefanten' is plural and 'helfen' needs the dative.

These verbs all need the dative case — make sure you know which they are.

to thank:	danken	*to hurt:*	wehtun	*to believe:*	glauben
to follow:	folgen	*to write to:*	schreiben	*to congratulate:*	gratulieren
to answer:	antworten	*to belong to:*	gehören		

Instead of 'I go swimming', say 'I go to swim'

You sometimes need to say 'I go swimming' rather than just 'I swim' — so you need two verbs. For the first verb, you need to put it in the right form for the person, but for the second, you just need the infinitive.

bowling:	kegeln	*dancing:*	tanzen
hiking:	wandern	*fishing:*	angeln
jogging:	joggen	*camping:*	zelten
running:	laufen	*skiing:*	Ski fahren / Ski laufen

Remember which verbs take the dative case

Make sure you understand the 'I go swimming' bit too — the 'go' works like normal, the 'swimming' part needs to be in the infinitive (that's what you look up in the dictionary). There you go. All sorted.

Future Tense

You'll need to talk about things that are going to happen at some point in the future.

1) You can use the **present tense** to talk about the **future**

To say something is going to happen in the future, you can just say that it does happen and then say when it's going to happen.

HAPPENING NOW  ***Ich fahre nach Wales.*** = I am going to Wales.

See pages 188-190 for all the stuff on the present tense.

next week:	nächste Woche	*on Monday:*	am Montag
tomorrow:	morgen	*this summer:*	diesen Sommer

GOING TO HAPPEN  ***Ich fahre nächstes Jahr nach Wales.***

This tells you when it's going to happen. = I am going to Wales next year.

WATCH OUT though: this isn't the proper future tense.
If you want to get top marks, you'll have to use 'werden'...

2) You can use **'werden'** — 'to be going to do...'

This part's slightly trickier, but you'll get more marks for using it properly. 'Ich werde' means 'I will'. You put the right form of 'werden' for the person, and the infinitive of the other verb at the end.

Ich werde nächstes Jahr nach Wales fahren. = I will go to Wales next year.

Look at page 187 to find out about the infinitive.

Werden = to be going to do

I will =	ich	werde	wir	werden	= *we will*
you (inf. sing.) will =	du	wirst	ihr	werdet	= *you (inf. plu.) will*
he will =	er	wird	Sie	werden	= *you (frml. sing. & plu.) will*
she will =	sie	wird	sie	werden	= *they will*
it will =	es	wird			

inf. = informal
frml. = formal
sing. = singular
plu. = plural

'Werden' is an irregular verb. That's why the endings are all a bit weird.

Another example:

Eines Tages wirst du in die Schule gehen. = One day you will go to school.

The best way to talk about the future is to use 'werden'

You can use time phrases like 'nächste Woche' in both forms of the future and you can stick 'em pretty much anywhere in the sentence — as long as you don't break the rules of word order (see page 161).

Perfect Tense

Sometimes they'll want you to talk about stuff that's already happened — so you need to say 'I have done...' or 'I did...', instead of 'I do...'. (It's the perfect tense, if you're interested.)

Was hast du gemacht? — What have you done?

The past tense looks a bit fiddly, I agree, but it's easy once you've learnt the basics.

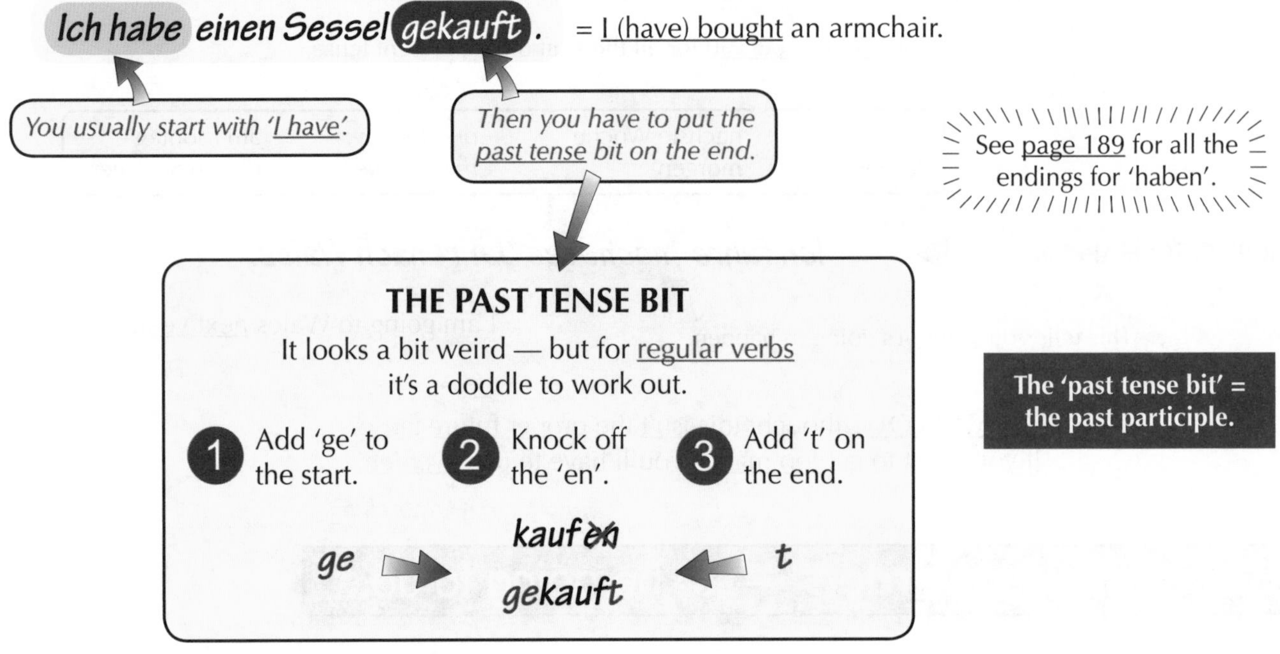

Ich habe einen Sessel gekauft. = I (have) bought an armchair.
You usually start with 'I have'.
Then you have to put the past tense bit on the end.
See page 189 for all the endings for 'haben'.
THE PAST TENSE BIT
It looks a bit weird — but for regular verbs it's a doddle to work out.
1 Add 'ge' to the start.
2 Knock off the 'en'.
3 Add 't' on the end.
ge
kaufen
gekauft
t
The 'past tense bit' = the past participle.

Here are some more examples — they all work the same way.

to do, make:	machen ⇒	gemacht:	*done, made*
to ask:	fragen ⇒	gefragt:	*asked*
to book:	buchen ⇒	gebucht:	*booked*
to clean:	putzen ⇒	geputzt:	*cleaned*

Er hat mich nichts gefragt. = He has asked me nothing.

Sie haben in den Ferien viel gemacht. = They did lots in the holidays.

You really need to know the different forms of 'haben' for this

If you find yourself using a regular verb in the past tense, just get the right form of 'haben' for the person you're talking about, then follow the three easy steps for finding the past participle. Lovely.

Perfect Tense

As always, there are some irregular verbs out there that you need to know.
Not all verbs take 'haben' in the perfect tense either.

Irregular verbs **don't** follow the **pattern**

OK, great — that's easy... then you get to the ones that don't follow the pattern (irregular verbs). Marvellous. Still, no way round it — you've just got to drum these into that brain of yours.

to sleep:	schlafen ⇒	geschlafen	*to see:*	sehen ⇒	gesehen
to take:	nehmen ⇒	genommen	*to sing:*	singen ⇒	gesungen
to eat:	essen ⇒	gegessen	*to break:*	brechen ⇒	gebrochen
to drink:	trinken ⇒	getrunken	*to receive:*	bekommen ⇒	bekommen
to give:	geben ⇒	gegeben	*to forget:*	vergessen ⇒	vergessen
to bring:	bringen ⇒	gebracht	*to understand:*	verstehen ⇒	verstanden

Watch out — no 'ge' on the front.

For grammar fans — these are past participles.

Ist sie gegangen — Has she gone?

Some verbs need 'I am' instead of 'I have' to make them past tense.
It's kind of like you're saying 'I am gone' instead of 'I have gone'.

She is:	Sie ist
They are:	Sie sind

⇒ ***Ich bin gegangen.*** = I have gone / I went.

It's mostly movement verbs that need 'I am'. Here's a list of some common ones that do — you have to remember which they are and learn the past tense bits, because most of them are irregular.

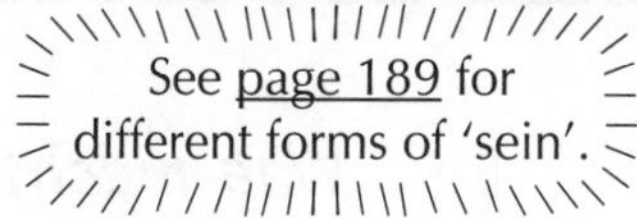
See page 189 for different forms of 'sein'.

to go, drive:	fahren ⇒	gefahren	*to stay:*	bleiben ⇒	geblieben
to run:	laufen ⇒	gelaufen	*to be:*	sein ⇒	gewesen
to climb:	steigen ⇒	gestiegen	*to happen:*	geschehen ⇒	geschehen
to follow:	folgen ⇒	gefolgt	*to happen:*	passieren ⇒	passiert
to come:	kommen ⇒	gekommen			

'Movement' verbs take 'sein'

OK, this page ain't easy — no sirreee. But it's dead important — at some point you'll definitely need to talk or write about something that's happened in the past. Make sure you get to grips with it.

Imperfect Tense

Fed up of the past tense yet? Yep, me too. But this stuff is <u>really handy</u>, so it's worth the pain.

Ich hatte — I had / Ich war — I was

These little words are absolute <u>gold dust</u> — you'll soon find yourself using them all the time.

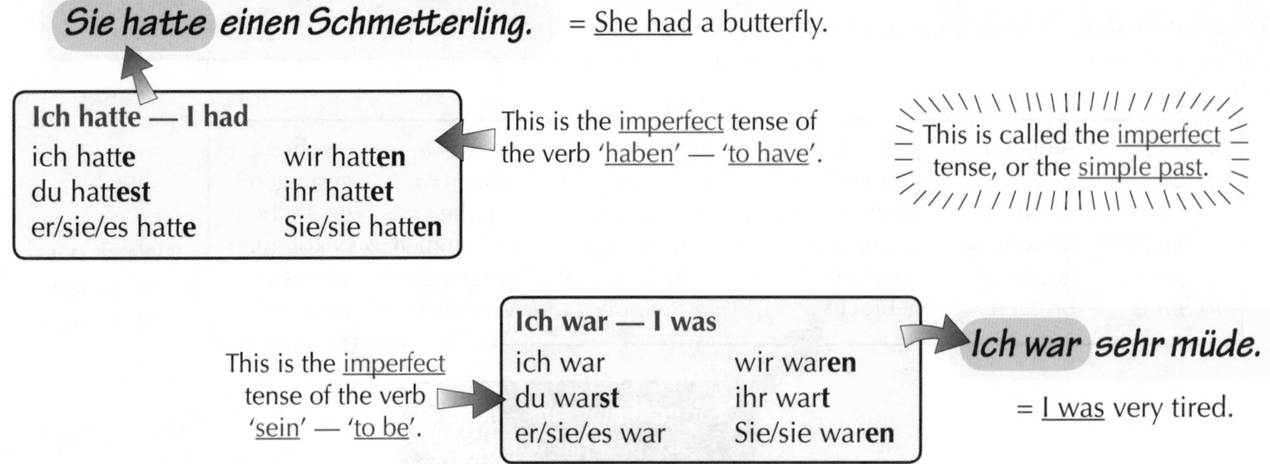

Sie hatte einen Schmetterling. = <u>She had</u> a butterfly.

Ich hatte — I had

ich hatt**e**	wir hatt**en**
du hatt**est**	ihr hatt**et**
er/sie/es hatt**e**	Sie/sie hatt**en**

This is the <u>imperfect</u> tense of the verb '<u>haben</u>' — '<u>to have</u>'.

This is called the <u>imperfect</u> tense, or the <u>simple past</u>.

Ich war — I was

ich war	wir war**en**
du war**st**	ihr war**t**
er/sie/es war	Sie/sie war**en**

This is the <u>imperfect</u> tense of the verb '<u>sein</u>' — '<u>to be</u>'.

Ich war sehr müde. = <u>I was</u> very tired.

More verbs in the imperfect tense

You use this when you're talking about things that happened in the past, without using '<u>haben</u>' or '<u>sein</u>' (that would be the perfect tense, see <u>page 192</u>). So, you use it to say things like '<u>I drank</u>' or '<u>they jumped</u>'.

All <u>regular</u> verbs take these endings (in bold):

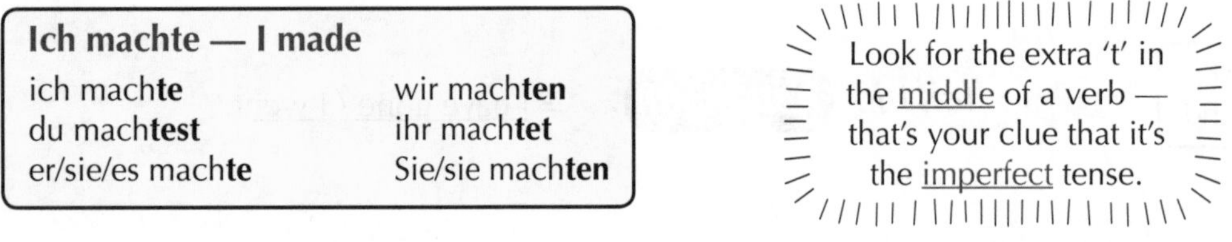

Ich machte — I made

ich mach**te**	wir mach**ten**
du mach**test**	ihr mach**tet**
er/sie/es mach**te**	Sie/sie mach**ten**

Look for the extra 't' in the <u>middle</u> of a verb — that's your clue that it's the <u>imperfect</u> tense.

E.g. ***Was machtest du?*** = What <u>did</u> you <u>do</u>?

These are the <u>most common</u> irregular verbs. They use the <u>same endings</u> as '<u>war</u>' in the box above. It looks really good if you can use them in your writing assessment.

Verb	Imperfect	English						
kommen	ich kam	*I came*	*essen*	ich aß	*I ate*	*laufen*	ich lief	*I ran*
denken	ich dachte	*I thought*	*trinken*	ich trank	*I drank*	*springen*	ich sprang	*I jumped*
fahren	ich fuhr	*I drove*	*sehen*	ich sah	*I saw*	*ziehen*	ich zog	*I pulled*
gehen	ich ging	*I went*	*werden*	ich wurde	*I became*	*sein*	ich war	*I was*
helfen	ich half	*I helped*	*bringen*	ich brachte	*I brought*	*haben*	ich hatte	*I had*
schreiben	ich schr<u>ie</u>b	*I wrote*	*nehmen*	ich nahm	*I took*	*geben*	ich gab	*I gave*
			singen	ich sang	*I sang*	*gewinnen*	ich gewann	*I won*

'Ich war' und 'ich hatte' — very important

I'm not telling you about this because of some <u>strange whim</u> of mine — if you don't know this stuff, you won't be able to say things like '<u>I won the lottery</u>' or '<u>I had eaten lots</u>'. And that'd be a terrible shame.

The Imperfect and Pluperfect Tenses

Just a bit more past tense to go, then you can move on to the Quick Questions. Much more fun.

'Seit' and the imperfect tense...

You can use the imperfect tense with 'seit' to talk about things that started in the past, and carried on until more recently. Sounds confusing, but it's quite simple really...

Ich sang seit fünf Jahren. = I had been singing for five years.

I had bought / gone etc...

This is when you use two past tense verbs together. For example, instead of saying 'I have bought a book' — 'Ich habe ein Buch gekauft' (see page 192), you say this:

Ich hatte ein Buch gekauft. = I had bought a book.

Use the imperfect tense of the verb 'haben' — 'to have' (page 194).

Use the perfect tense of the other verb (see page 192).

Grammar fiends call this the pluperfect tense.

Ich hatte gekauft — I had bought

ich hatte gekauft	*wir hatten gekauft*
du hattest gekauft	*ihr hattet gekauft*
er/sie/es hatte gekauft	*Sie/sie hatten gekauft*

Just like with the perfect tense, with some verbs you have to use 'sein' instead of 'haben'. For example, instead of saying 'ich bin gegangen' ('sein' verbs — see page 193), you say this:

Ich war gegangen. = I had gone.

Tip: the same verbs take 'sein' in both tenses.

Ich war gegangen — I had gone

ich war gegangen	*wir waren gegangen*
du warst gegangen	*ihr wart gegangen*
er/sie/es war gegangen	*Sie/sie waren gegangen*

Getting the pluperfect right looks really impressive

And while we're at it, so does using 'seit' properly with the imperfect tense. It's a fairly tricky page this, but being able to do the tricky stuff is what gets you top marks. Keep going over it till you get it right.

Quick Questions

There's an awful lot to remember about verbs and tenses — but you do need to know it all. To get the best marks in your coursework assessments, you will have to speak or write in more than one tense. Make sure you know your stuff, with these questions.

Quick Questions

1) 'Ich kaufe Äpfel' means 'I buy apples' in German. 'Kaufen', 'to buy', is a regular verb. How would you say the following in German?
a) You ('du') buy apples. b) He buys apples.
c) She buys apples. d) We buy apples.
e) You ('Sie') buy apples. f) You ('ihr') buy apples.

2) 'Segeln' means 'to sail'. How would you say the following in German?
a) I sail b) you ('du') sail c) she sails
d) we sail e) they sail f) you ('ihr') sail

3) Match the people on the left with the correct form of the verb 'sein' on the right:
a) ich bist
b) du seid
c) er ist
d) wir bin
e) ihr sind
f) sie sind

4) Match the people on the left with the correct form of the verb 'haben' on the right:
a) ich haben
b) du hat
c) er hast
d) wir habt
e) ihr haben
f) sie habe

5) How would you say the following in German?
a) he drives b) they drive c) you ('du') eat d) you ('ihr') eat
e) he knows f) he is called g) she wears

6) Name three German verbs that take the dative case.
Write three sentences, each containing one of the verbs you've picked.

7) Translate the following sentences into German:
a) I go swimming. b) He goes bowling. c) She goes jogging.
d) We go dancing. e) They go camping. d) You ('du') go shopping.

8) Change these sentences into the future tense by using the right form of 'werden' and the infinitive of the underlined verb:
a) Ich mache meine Hausaufgaben.
b) Er fährt nach London.
c) Sie ist wirklich glücklich.
d) Du spielst Rugby am Wochenende.
e) Sie feiert ihren Geburtstag nächste Woche.
f) Morgen gehen wir ins Kino.
g) Ihr esst am Freitag im Restaurant.
h) Diesen Sommer fliegen Sie nach Spanien.

Quick Questions

Quick Questions

9) Change all these present tense sentences into the perfect tense.
Hint: all the verbs use 'haben' — the last few are irregular.
a) Er kocht mein Lieblingsessen.
b) Ich buche das Hotel.
c) Du spielst mit der Katze.
d) Ihr arbeitet bei uns.
e) Sie putzen das Wohnzimmer.
f) Du siehst einen guten Film.
g) Ich bekomme ein interessantes Paket.
h) Wir trinken kalte Limonade.
i) Sie vergessen ihre Turnschuhe.
j) Er versteht sie nicht.

10) The verbs in these sentences all use 'sein' in the perfect tense.
Change the sentences into the perfect tense.
a) Ich gehe in die Schule.
b) Ihr fahrt nach Österreich.
c) Er läuft im Park.
d) Du folgst mir durch die Stadt.
e) Wir kommen am Abend.
f) Sie bleiben zum Mittagessen.
g) Ich bin sehr glücklich.
h) Es passiert sehr schnell.

11) Match the people on the left with the correct imperfect form of 'sein' on the right:

a) ich	war
b) du	waren
c) er	warst
d) wir	wart
e) ihr	war
f) sie (they)	waren

12) What do the following mean in English? Hint: they're all in the imperfect tense.

a) ich machte	b) er kam	c) sie fuhren
d) sie half	e) du trankst	f) er aß
g) ich sah	h) Sie brachten	i) wir zogen
j) es gab	k) ihr schriebt	l) sie lief

13) Translate these sentences into English:
a) Ich spielte seit drei Jahren Tischtennis.
b) Er fuhr seit fünf Jahren mit dem Bus in die Schule.
c) Wir liefen seit sechs Monaten am Strand.
d) Du wohntest seit drei Wochen im Hotel.

14) Change these perfect tense sentences into the pluperfect tense.
Then translate the pluperfect sentences into English.
a) Sie hat ein schönes Kleid gekauft.
b) Ich bin nach Schottland gefahren.
c) Wir haben unseres Frühstück gegessen.
d) Sie sind uns gefolgt.
e) Du hast meinen Geburtstag vergessen.

Imperatives

This page is all about telling people what to do. So learn it.

Komm herein! — Come in! Setz dich hin! — Sit down!

This is known as the imperative. It's used to give instructions and is really useful when you're bossing people about.

Here's how to turn a verb into an imperative:

Example — telling people to go:

Verb	Imperative	English
du gehst	*Geh!*	Go! (informal, singular)
ihr geht	*Geht!*	Go! (informal, plural)
Sie gehen	*Gehen Sie!*	Go! (formal, sing. & plu.)
wir gehen	*Gehen wir!*	Let's go!

You can use these endings for most verbs.

Luckily, the only form that ends differently from the normal present tense is the 'du' form. It loses its ending (the '-st').

Some verbs lose the '-st' in the 'du' form, but gain an '-e'.

The 2nd column shows what you turn the verb into to get the imperative.

Make sure you learn these:

Komm herein! = Come in!

Hilf mir! = Help me!

Bring den Hund mit! = Bring the dog along.

Nimm das Buch! = Take the book.

Setz dich hin! = Sit down.

Frag den Mann da! = Ask the man there.

You'd normally end an imperative sentence in German with an exclamation mark — even if you wouldn't for the same sentence in English.

Revise!

You need to know this stuff because they'll expect you to understand things like signs and instructions — these'll generally be in the 'du' (like the examples at the bottom of the page) or 'Sie' forms.

Reflexive Verbs

This page tells you how to say 'myself', 'yourself', 'themselves', etc. It's dead important that you learn all this stuff, because some verbs just don't make sense without them.

Talking about yourself — 'sich'

'Sich' means 'oneself'. All the different ways to say 'self' are in the box below.

You can tell which verbs need 'self' by checking in the dictionary.
If you look up 'to wash oneself', it'll say 'sich waschen'.

Sich = oneself

myself:	mich	*ourselves:*	uns
yourself (informal):	dich	*yourselves (informal plural):*	euch
himself:	sich	*yourself, yourselves (formal):*	sich
herself:	sich	*themselves, each other:*	sich
itself:	sich		

Ich wasche mich — I wash myself

You need to talk about your 'daily routine'. So if you don't know how to say 'I wash myself', everyone'll think you smell.

Remember — these verbs don't make sense without the 'sich' bit.

Sich waschen = to wash oneself

I wash myself =	ich wasche mich		
you wash yourself (informal) =	du wäschst dich	wir waschen uns =	*we wash ourselves*
he washes himself =	er wäscht sich	ihr wascht euch =	*you wash yourselves (informal)*
she washes herself =	sie wäscht sich	Sie waschen sich =	*you wash yourself, yourselves (formal)*
it washes itself =	es wäscht sich	sie waschen sich =	*they wash themselves*

There are lots of these verbs, but here are a few of the most useful ones. Learn these:

to dress oneself:	sich anziehen	*to excuse oneself:*	sich entschuldigen
to feel:	sich fühlen	*to sit oneself down:*	sich setzen
to get changed:	sich umziehen	*to sun oneself:*	sich sonnen

The separable bits of verbs are highlighted in green.

... and learn how they work:

Ich fühle mich schlecht. = I feel bad (ill).

The 'mich' goes straight after the verb.

Ich ziehe mich an. = I dress myself.

With separable verbs (page 201), 'mich' goes straight after the main verb.

When you've got the hang of one, you've got the hang of them all

Remember: if you look up a reflexive verb in the dictionary, it'll have the word 'sich' alongside it. When you use the verb, you have to use the right form of 'sich' for the person you're talking about.

Reflexive Verbs

Reflexive verbs do get a teeny-weeny bit more complicated, but you can handle it. I promise.

Ich putze mir die Zähne — I clean my teeth

Some verbs need you to use 'to myself' or 'to yourself'. This is the dative case.

These are the three most important ones:

to clean one's teeth:	sich die Zähne putzen
to want/wish for ... :	sich ... wünschen
to imagine ... :	sich ... vorstellen

'Vorstellen' is a separable verb. See page 201.

This is how you put them in a sentence...

Ich wünsche mir ein Pferd. = I want a horse.

These are the bits you change for each person.

Mir = to myself

to myself:	mir	*to ourselves:*	uns
to yourself (inf.):	dir	*to yourselves (informal):*	euch
to him/her/itself:	sich	*to yourself, yourselves (frml.):*	sich
		to themselves:	sich

Ich habe mich gewaschen — I have washed myself

The perfect tense of these verbs is pretty much the same as normal (see page 192) except they all go with 'haben', not 'sein'.

Sie hat sich schlecht gefühlt. = She felt bad (ill).

Put the 'sich' straight after 'haben'.

Learn the different forms of 'mir'

There now, that wasn't too bad. It's really just a case of learning all that 'mir', 'dir' business and which verbs use the dative case. The perfect tense stuff is pretty straightforward too.

Separable Verbs

Just when you thought verbs couldn't get any worse — it's time to get to grips with separable ones. Actually, they're surprisingly straightfoward. Which is nice.

Separable verbs are made up of **two bits**

Some verbs are made up of two bits: the main verb and a bit stuck on the front, that can split off.

abfahren = to depart

Ignore 'ab' for now and use 'fahren' as a normal verb — then send 'ab' to the end of the sentence:

Ich fahre um neun Uhr ab. = I depart at 9 o'clock.

Treat the two bits as **separate words**

When you come across one of these verbs, think of it as two separate words. It's much easier.

Sie nimmt ihre Katze ins Kino mit. = She takes her cat into the cinema with her.

Wir gehen am zwanzigsten August weg. = We go away on the 20th of August.

Here are some separable verbs you might come across quite a bit — I've underlined the bits that split off.

to wash up:	abwaschen	*to take with you:*	mitnehmen
to arrive:	ankommen	*to check:*	nachsehen
to stop:	aufhören	*to happen:*	vorkommen
to go out:	ausgehen	*to go out/away:*	weggehen
to show:	darstellen	*to look at:*	zuschauen
to enter:	eintreten	*to give back:*	zurückgeben

Sometimes you get two bits added on — like 'herauskommen' ('to come out'). The two added bits stay together as if they were just one bit.

E.g. ***Schließlich kommen sie heraus.*** = Finally they come out.

'I arrive at 9.00' = 'Ich komme um neun Uhr an'

The best way to remember this is that a separable verb is really just two separate words. They're usually split up in the present tense, and you only make them into one word if they're right next to each other.

Separable Verbs

You're going to have to use separable verbs in different tenses too, but don't panic — things are still pretty straightforward, I promise.

The **past tense** is a bit **weird** with these verbs

To make the past (perfect) tense of a separable verb, you split it up then put it back together. You leave the front bit as it is, then turn the main bit into the past tense.

aufhören = to stop → ***aufgehört*** = stopped

So you end up with the 'ge' in the middle of the word.

You put the 'haben' (or 'sein') bit in the normal place, then shove the past tense bit at the end.

Here's an example: ***Er hat endlich aufgehört.*** = He has finally stopped.

Here's **how to spot separable verbs** anywhere

In your reading or listening paper, you've got to be able to spot these verbs, so you know what's going on. Check each sentence to see if there are two bits of a separable verb hiding in there. Watch out though — they could be the wrong way round.

Here are a few examples with 'zurückfahren' ('to go back'):

Er will zurückfahren. = He wants to go back.

Wenn er zurückfährt, werde ich weinen. = If he goes back, I will cry.

Sie fuhr nach Berlin zurück. = She went back to Berlin. ← This is the imperfect tense of 'fahren'. There's more about this on page 194.

Morgen fahre ich zurück. = Tomorrow, I go back.

Ich werde morgen zurückfahren. = I will go back tomorrow.

These are talking about the future — see page 191.

You need to be able to recognise separable verbs in different forms

Get to grips with spotting those separable verbs — it'll make reading and listening much easier. After 'werden' or a modal verb, the separable verb gets sent to the end of the sentence and is all one word.

Negatives

This is one of those bits where if you learn just a couple of things, you can say loads more.

Nicht — Not

Der Vogel wollte nicht singen. = The bird did not want to sing.

Ich lese nie Bücher. = I never read books.

Das mache ich nicht mehr. = I don't do that any more.

Negative words:

not:	nicht
no longer:	nicht mehr
not even:	nicht einmal
never:	nie
not yet:	noch nicht
nowhere:	nirgendwo

If you want to say a joke is neither clever nor funny, then it's a bit different:

neither ... nor: weder ... noch

Ihre Haare sind weder blond noch braun. = Her hair is neither blonde nor brown.

Ich habe keine Bratkartoffeln — I have no roast potatoes

'Kein' means 'no' — as in 'I have no potatoes'. 'Kein' has different forms for different cases — in fact it takes exactly the same endings as 'mein' — see page 171.

Ich habe keinen Kartoffelsalat. = I have no potato salad.

Keine Hunde sind grün. = No dogs are green.

Niemand — Nobody...

You need to be able to say 'nobody' and 'nothing'. It's not much to learn, so there's no excuse.

Ich habe niemand gesehen. = I've seen nobody.

nothing: nichts

Some handy variations:

nothing yet:	noch nichts
nothing left/nothing more:	nichts mehr
nobody yet:	noch niemand
nobody else/nobody any more:	niemand mehr

Ich sehe gar nichts. = I see nothing at all.

You can put 'gar' in front of 'nicht' or 'nichts' to emphasise it — like saying 'nothing at all'.

You need to be able to say 'nothing'...

'Nicht', 'nichts', 'niemand' and 'kein' are really basic essential words, but if you want a decent mark, learn the others too. Cover the page, scribble them down, and see what you know.

Modal Verbs

Geesh — there's loads of this grammar stuff. Still, the quicker you learn it, the quicker you can put this book down and get on with the rest of your life. Here's a nice bit about modal verbs...

Ich muss diese Verben lernen... I must learn these verbs...

Instead of saying 'I learn judo', you might want to say 'I should learn judo' or 'I want to learn judo'. Here are six really handy verbs you can use to give your opinions about doing something.

1 Wollen = to want

ich	*will*	*wir*	*wollen*
du	*willst*	*ihr*	*wollt*
er	*will*	*Sie*	*wollen*
sie	*will*	*sie*	*wollen*
es	*will*		

2 Mögen = to like

ich	*mag*	*wir*	*mögen*
du	*magst*	*ihr*	*mögt*
er	*mag*	*Sie*	*mögen*
sie	*mag*	*sie*	*mögen*
es	*mag*		

(For 'I would like' — 'ich möchte', see page 206.)

3 Dürfen = may

ich	*darf*	*wir*	*dürfen*
du	*darfst*	*ihr*	*dürft*
er	*darf*	*Sie*	*dürfen*
sie	*darf*	*sie*	*dürfen*
es	*darf*		

4 Können = can

ich	*kann*	*wir*	*können*
du	*kannst*	*ihr*	*könnt*
er	*kann*	*Sie*	*können*
sie	*kann*	*sie*	*können*
es	*kann*		

5 Sollen = to be supposed to

ich	*soll*	*wir*	*sollen*
du	*sollst*	*ihr*	*sollt*
er	*soll*	*Sie*	*sollen*
sie	*soll*	*sie*	*sollen*
es	*soll*		

6 Müssen = must

ich	*muss*	*wir*	*müssen*
du	*musst*	*ihr*	*müsst*
er	*muss*	*Sie*	*müssen*
sie	*muss*	*sie*	*müssen*
es	*muss*		

This is how you use them:

Ich muss einen Brief schreiben. = I must write a letter.

You need the right form of the modal verb ('I want' or 'he wants') because that's the main verb...

...and you need the infinitive of the other verb (see page 187 if you're not sure what that is). You stick this at the end of the sentence.

Du sollst deine Hausaufgaben machen. = You are supposed to do your homework.

Sie können sehr gut singen. = They can sing very well.

Modal verbs crop up everywhere — learn them now

A lot to learn here, but these modal verbs are absolutely crucial. The main things to remember are that the other verb has to be in the infinitive, and it has to go to the end of the sentence.

Modal Verbs

As with all verbs, you have to be able to use modal verbs in the past tense. Here's how.

You can use **modal verbs** in the **past tense** too

If you want to say something like 'I wanted to wash the car', then you have to use the past tense of the modal verb.

Here's what happens with 'können':

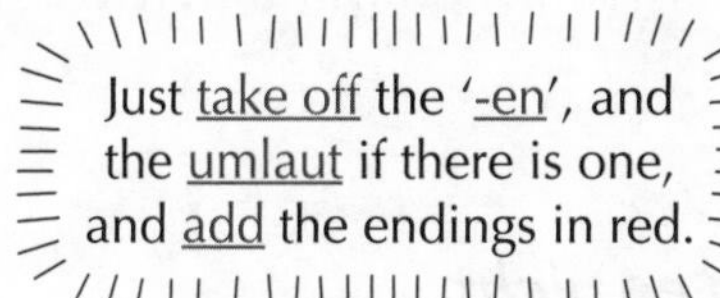

Just take off the '-en', and
the umlaut if there is one,
and add the endings in red.

Können = can

ich	*konnte*	*wir*	*konnten*
du	*konntest*	*ihr*	*konntet*
er	*konnte*	*Sie*	*konnten*
sie	*konnte*	*sie*	*konnten*
es	*konnte*		

Follow this pattern for 'wollen', 'dürfen', 'müssen' and 'sollen' too.

Wollen = to want

ich	*wollte*	*wir*	*wollten*
du	*wolltest*	*ihr*	*wolltet*
er	*wollte*	*Sie*	*wollten*
sie	*wollte*	*sie*	*wollten*
es	*wollte*		

Dürfen = to be allowed to

ich	*durfte*	*wir*	*durften*
du	*durftest*	*ihr*	*durftet*
er	*durfte*	*Sie*	*durften*
sie	*durfte*	*sie*	*durften*
es	*durfte*		

Müssen = to have to

ich	*musste*	*wir*	*mussten*
du	*musstest*	*ihr*	*musstet*
er	*musste*	*Sie*	*mussten*
sie	*musste*	*sie*	*mussten*
es	*musste*		

Sollen = to be supposed to

ich	*sollte*	*wir*	*sollten*
du	*solltest*	*ihr*	*solltet*
er	*sollte*	*Sie*	*sollten*
sie	*sollte*	*sie*	*sollten*
es	*sollte*		

WATCH OUT
'Mögen' is a bit different. It changes to 'mochten' in the past tense. It takes the same endings as all the others though.

Mögen = to like

ich	*mochte*	*wir*	*mochten*
du	*mochtest*	*ihr*	*mochtet*
er	*mochte*	*Sie*	*mochten*
sie	*mochte*	*sie*	*mochten*
es	*mochte*		

Use them as you would in the present tense (see page 204). Here are a couple of examples:

Ich musste einen Apfel kaufen. = I had to buy an apple.

Ich wollte den Kuchen essen. = I wanted to eat the cake.

You should have learnt these verbs

Learning how to use modal verbs in the past tense is dead important. How else would you say: 'I wanted to do my homework, but I wasn't able to'? Exactly. Flipping useful things, modal verbs.

Conditional and Imperfect Subjunctive

OK, I'll admit it. This is tricky. But it is important, so if you want top marks you need to learn it.

Ich würde — I would

The word for 'would' in German is 'würden'.

Ich würde — I would:

ich würde	*wir würden*
du würdest	*ihr würdet*
er/sie/es würde	*Sie/sie würden*

This is the conditional. You use it to talk about something that hasn't happened.

Ich würde Chinesisch lernen, aber ich kann es nicht.

= I would learn Chinese, but I can't.

'Würden' works like a modal verb (page 204), so the other verb has to be in the infinitive, and go at the end.

Ich möchte — I would like

Dead useful verb, this, so get it learnt.

Ich möchte fünfzig Tassen Tee, bitte. = I would like fifty cups of tea, please.

Ich möchte — I would like

ich möchte	*wir möchten*
du möchtest	*ihr möchtet*
er/sie/es möchte	*Sie/sie möchten*

For grammatical types, this is the imperfect subjunctive of 'mögen' — 'to like' (page 204).

Ich möchte Chinesisch lernen. = I would like to learn Chinese.

The other verb has to be in the infinitive, and go at the end.

I know this is pretty complicated grammar, but you should already be familiar with 'möchten' — it's part of the basic shopping vocab (see page 64).

You probably already know all this 'ich möchte' business

Which means you've got more time to learn all about 'würden'. Excellent. And if you don't already know them, you'll need to learn the different forms of 'möchten' for 'du', 'er', 'wir', 'Sie', etc., etc.

Conditional and Imperfect Subjunctive

More key stuff for you to learn here...

Ich könnte — I could   Ich sollte — I should

You need to know 'could' (könnten) and 'should' (sollten), too.

Ich könnte — I could:	
ich könnte	*wir könnten*
du könntest	*ihr könntet*
er/sie/es könnte	*Sie/sie könnten*

Ich sollte — I should:	
ich sollte	*wir sollten*
du solltest	*ihr solltet*
er/sie/es sollte	*Sie/sie sollten*

'Ich könnte' means 'I could' as in 'I would be able' — as opposed to 'ich konnte', which means 'I was able' (see page 205).

Ich sollte essen. = I should eat.

Ich wäre — I would be   Ich hätte — I would have

Wenn ich fünf Million Euro hätte, wäre ich sehr reich.

= If I had 5 million euros, I would be very rich.

Here's how you say 'would be' and 'would have' for all the different people:

Ich wäre = I would be			
ich	*wäre*	*wir*	*wären*
du	*wärest*	*ihr*	*wäret*
er	*wäre*	*Sie*	*wären*
sie	*wäre*	*sie*	*wären*
es	*wäre*		

Ich hätte = I would have			
ich	*hätte*	*wir*	*hätten*
du	*hättest*	*ihr*	*hättet*
er	*hätte*	*Sie*	*hätten*
sie	*hätte*	*sie*	*hätten*
es	*hätte*		

This is also the imperfect subjunctive, but you use it to talk about something unreal that's unlikely to happen.

Tricky stuff — but dead impressive if you get it right

Get all this stuff right in your writing assessments and you'll be in Marksville, Arizona. Same goes for the speaking assessments actually.

Impersonal Verbs

With some verbs you have to stick an 'es' (which means 'it') in.
1) Whatever is doing the action becomes something that's having something done to it.
2) So instead of saying something like 'I don't feel good' you'd say: 'It feels to me not good'.

Wie geht es dir? — How are you?

It looks strange, but you have to learn it — and never say 'ich bin gut' for 'I'm fine'.

Mir geht's gut. = I'm fine.

This is just short for 'geht es'.

Es geht mir nicht so gut. = I don't feel so good.

Other useful phrases that use 'es'

Here are some more of these awkward phrases. They're easy once you've learnt them properly.

But: say 'Mir ist warm' for 'I'm warm' (i.e. not 'Es ist mir warm').

Ist es dir zu warm? = Is it too warm for you?

Es tut weh. = It hurts.

Es regnet. = It's raining.

This'll come in handy for talking about the weather — see pages 98-99.

Es gibt viel zu tun. = There is lots to do.

(more literally, 'it gives lots to do')

(literal translation: 'it pleases to me')

Es gefällt mir in München. = I like it in Munich.

Es tut mir leid, aber heute bin ich nicht frei. = I'm sorry, but I'm not free today.

(literally, 'it does sorrow to me')

You'll use these phrases all the time

This might seem like some overly complicated grammar, but the trick is to just learn these phrases. Believe me, you'll be surprised at just how often you end up using them. So get to it.

Infinitive Constructions

Here are a few more miscellaneous things that you really need to know...

Um... zu — in order to, ohne... zu — without

Here are some handy ways of saying 'in order to' and 'without'.

***Um** diesen Satz **zu verstehen**, muss man Deutsch sprechen können.*

= In order to understand this sentence, you must be able to speak German.

*Sie kann nicht verlassen **ohne** ihn **zu küssen**.* = She can't leave without kissing him.

The verb that's in the infinitive comes after the 'zu'.

Ignore 'zu' before a verb if there's no 'um'

When verbs link with an infinitive in the sentence, you sometimes find 'zu' before the infinitive. Basically, if the first verb is a modal verb (see page 204), you don't need the 'zu' — if not, you do.

*Ich **versuche** den besten Satz in der Welt **zu schreiben**.*

= I'm trying to write the best sentence in the world.

*Die Stunde **beginnt** langweilig **zu werden**.*

= The lesson is beginning to get boring.

Learn 'um... zu...' — it's really useful

This grammar stuff can be seriously scary. But if you learn all the phrases on these pages, it becomes a lot easier. And don't worry too much about all the weirdy grammar names. Sorted.

Quick Questions

You'll be pleased to know that this is your last set of Quick Questions for the entire book. Hurrah!

Quick Questions

1) What do the following mean in English?
a) Geh weg! b) Nimm das Baby! c) Gib mir das Buch! d) Warte hier, bitte!

2) Turn the following into imperative instructions:
a) Du gehst um die Ecke. b) Ihr kommt herein.
c) Sie singen lauter. d) Du isst dein Essen.
e) Du spielst besser. f) Sie antworten mir.
g) Ihr folgt mir. h) Du liest diesen Artikel.

3) Write the correct form of 'sich' for the people sitting down below:
a) ich setze .... b) du setzt ....
c) er setzt .... d) sie setzt ....
e) wir setzen .... f) ihr setzt ....
g) Sie setzen .... h) sie setzen ....

4) You're on a beach holiday in Northern Germany. How would you say 'I sun myself' to the nice German man on the neighbouring sunlounger?

5) How would you say 'he feels ill' in German?

6) Write the correct form of 'mir' for the people cleaning their teeth below:
a) Ich putze .... die Zähne. b) Du putzt .... die Zähne.
c) Er putzt .... die Zähne. d) Wir putzen .... die Zähne.
e) Ihr putzt .... die Zähne. f) Sie putzen .... die Zähne.

7) You stumble across a magic lamp whilst in Munich.
How would you say 'I wish for a dog' in German?

8) How would you say 'I imagine a brown dog' in German?

9) How would you say 'we felt bad' in the German perfect tense?

10) How would you say 'I wished for a dog' in the German perfect tense?
Hint: 'wünschen' is a regular verb.

11) Translate the following sentences into English:
a) Ich komme um zwölf Uhr an.
b) Schließlich hört die Musik auf.
c) Wir sollen abwaschen.
d) Er nahm seine Bücher mit.
e) Letzten Abend ist sie ins Kino ausgegangen.
f) Ich bin traurig, weil ich den braunen Hund zurückgegeben habe.

12) 'Der Zug fährt um zehn Uhr ab' means 'the train departs at 10 o'clock'.
Translate the following sentences into German.
a) The train must depart at 10 o'clock.
b) Yesterday, the train departed at 9 o'clock. (perfect tense)
c) Yesterday, the train departed at 9 o'clock. (imperfect tense)
d) Tomorrow, the train will depart at 11 o'clock.

13) Turn these sentences from positive to negative, then translate them into English.
You can use any negative words you like, as long as the sentence makes sense.
a) Ich höre Rapmusik. b) Ich sehe am Wochenende fern.
c) Wir schwimmen im Meer. d) Du spielst Klavier gut.
e) Sie müssen das Abendessen kochen.

Quick Questions

Quick Questions

14) How would you say the following in German? For some of these sentences, you might need to look up words in the dictionary or check the endings for 'kein'.
a) I don't have a pen. b) I have no apples.
c) He never plays sport. d) Her eyes are neither blue nor green.
e) That is no longer true. f) You've eaten no peas.
g) I've seen nobody yet. h) You will say nothing more.

15) Translate these sentences into English:
a) Wir müssen Bockwürste und Käse kaufen.
b) Ich kann meinen Hut nicht finden.
c) Ihr sollt die erste Straße links nehmen.
d) Sie können hier in der Ecke sitzen.
e) Er will als Tierarzt arbeiten.
f) Magst du Rad fahren?
g) Darf ich die Toilette benutzen?
h) Wir wollen nach Köln fahren.

16) Now put the German sentences from the question above into the past tense.

17) Mia says to you, 'Ich würde ins Kino gehen, aber ich muss meine Hausaufgaben machen'. What does this mean in English?

18) How would you tell your friend 'Mia would go to the cinema, but she must do her homework' in German?

19) 'Kopfschmerzen' means 'headache' in German. How would you say: 'I would play Tennis, but I have a headache' in German?

20) How would you say the following in German?
a) I would like a cup of tea.
b) We would like a cup of tea.
c) Would you ('du') like a cup of tea?

21) Translate the following into German:
a) I could play tennis, but I don't want to.
b) I should play tennis, but I don't want to.

22) What does this mean in English?
'Wenn du einen braunen Hund hättest, wärest du sehr glücklich.'

23) How would you say these common phrases in German?
a) I don't feel so good. b) I'm fine. c) It hurts.
d) It's raining. e) There's lots to do. f) I'm sorry.

24) Complete the German sentences on the left by translating the bits in English on the right:
a) Sie können das Museum nicht betreten... ... *without buying an entrance ticket.*
b) Man muss sehr hart arbeiten... ... *in order to learn German.*
c) Ich fahre mit dem Zug nach London... ... *in order to visit my friends.*
d) Dreimal pro Woche geht er joggen... ... *in order to stay fit.*
e) Man kann Berlin nicht verlassen... ... *without visiting the zoo.*

Revision Summary

The stuff in this section really helps you to put words together to say what you want. The way to make sure you've learnt it is to check you can do all these questions. Try them all, and look up any you can't do. Then try them all again. And keep doing that until you can answer every single one.

1) In the sentence 'Lucas isst ein Eis' — Lucas eats an ice cream, is 'Lucas' in:
   a) the nominative b) the accusative?
2) When do you use the genitive case?
3) Which part of the following sentence is in the dative case?
   'Ich spreche zu meiner Schwester' — I speak to my sister
4) How do you say 'It is sunny (sonnig) but not warm (warm)' in German?
5) Rearrange the order of this sentence so it's correct:
   'Ich bin müde, weil ich hatte keinen Schlaf' — I am tired because I haven't had any sleep.
6) What are the words for 'the' and 'a' that go with each of these words in the nominative case?
   a) Käse (masculine) b) Baumwolle (feminine) c) Messer (neuter)
7) What are the words for 'the' and 'a' that go with the words in Q6 in the accusative case?
8) How do you say this sentence in German: 'I have an ugly (hässlich) cat (Katze)'?
9) What are the German words for: a) my b) his c) your (informal plural)?
   For each answer, give the nominative for each gender.
10) How do you say 'Now and then I am very funny (lustig)' in German?
11) How do you say 'I am nearer than Lotte' in German? How do you say 'I am the nearest'?
12) What do these words mean in English? a) nach b) bei c) seit
13) Which case do these prepositions take? a) für b) mit c) wegen
14) What are the German words for 'I', 'you' (informal singular), 'he', 'she', 'it', 'we', 'you' (formal) and 'they' in: a) the nominative b) the accusative c) the dative?
15) How do you say 'who' in German? What about 'whom' and 'to whom'?
16) Translate this sentence and pick out the relative clause:
    'Der Mann, der sehr dick ist, isst einen Kuchen.'
17) How do you say each of these in German?
    a) he is b) they are c) you (informal singular) have d) I drive e) you (informal plural) eat
18) How do you say 'I will go to the shops' in German?
19) How do you say these sentences in German? Use the perfect tense.
    a) They made a cake. b) He booked a room. c) We drank coffee. d) They ran quickly.
20) How do you say these sentences in German? Use the imperfect tense.
    a) She had four dogs. b) They were friends. c) I ate a banana.
21) How do you say these sentences in German? Use the pluperfect tense.
    a) I had bought a skirt. b) She had been shopping.
22) Translate these phrases into English:
    a) Geh! b) Komm herein! c) Nimm das Buch! d) Setz dich hin!
23) How do you say these phrases in German?
    a) I wash myself b) He excuses himself c) They clean their teeth d) You washed yourself
24) What do these words mean in English?
    a) nicht einmal b) kein c) niemand d) gar nichts
25) How do you say these phrases in German?
    a) I must eat vegetables b) He can c) They are supposed to go d) I wanted
26) How do you say these phrases in German?
    a) I would wash up b) I would like to drive the car c) I should watch TV d) I would be tired
27) How do you say these phrases in German?
    a) I don't feel so good b) There's lots to do
28) What does the following sentence mean in English?
    'Ich gehe in die Stadt, um meinen Freund zu sehen.'

Do Well in Your Exam

Here are some handy hints to help you in your exams. And not a smidgen of learning in sight. Ahh.

Read the questions **carefully**

Don't go losing easy marks — it'll break my heart. Make sure you definitely do the things on this list:

1. Read all the instructions properly.
2. Read the question properly.
3. Answer the question — don't waffle.

Don't give up if you don't **understand**

If you don't understand, don't panic. The key thing to remember is that you can still do well in the exam, even if you don't understand every German word that comes up. The next couple of pages will give you a few tips on how.

If you're reading or listening — look for **lookalikes**

1. Some words look or sound the same in German and English.
2. These words are great because you'll recognise them when you see or hear them.
3. Be careful though — there are some exceptions you need to watch out for. Here are just a few examples of German words that look like an English word but have a totally different meaning:

sensibel:	*sensitive*	also:	*so*	der Fotograf:	*photographer*
groß:	*big/tall*	sympathisch:	*nice*	das Rezept:	*prescription*
fast:	*almost*	die Fabrik:	*factory*	der Roman:	*novel*
bald:	*soon*	die Marmelade:	*jam*	die Wand:	*wall*
aktuell:	*current*	das Gymnasium:	*grammar school*	Ich will...:	*I want...*

Words like these are called 'falsche Freunde' — false friends.

Look for lookalikes, but beware of false friends

I can't emphasise enough how important it is to read the questions and instructions through properly. It might seem obvious now, but it's amazing how many people get caught out in the exam...

Do Well in Your Exam

More ways to improve your marks and still not a drop of learning on the horizon...
It's almost as good as free cake.

Look for the **verb**...

Here are a few tips to help you out if you're struggling with sentences in the reading exam.

1. The verb (or 'doing word') is probably going to give you the biggest clue as to what the sentence is about. Word order in German isn't always the same as it is in English, so you might have to go looking for one...

The first verb, 'have to', is the second idea in the sentence.

Nach der Schule muss ich mit meiner Mutter meine Großeltern besuchen.

= After school, I have to visit my grandparents with my mother.

The second verb, 'to visit', is sent to the end of the sentence.

2. German is full of scarily long words. Don't be put off if you don't understand one at first glance though — they're often 'compounds' made up of two or three smaller words stuck together. Try breaking a word up to get at its meaning...

A compound verb

zusammenkommen:	'*zusammen*' = together, '*kommen*' = to come:	→	to meet
der Tiefkühlschrank:	'*tief*' = deep, '*kühl*' = cool, '*der Schrank*' = cupboard:	→	freezer

A compound noun

3. Don't ignore shorter words — they can make a big difference to the meaning of a sentence...

Ich spiele gern Sport, besonders Tennis. = I like playing sport, especially Tennis.

Ich spiele gern Sport außer Tennis. = I like playing sport, except Tennis.

4. Don't panic if you don't understand absolutely everything.
Often, the important thing is to get the gist of what you're reading (or even listening to).

Don't leave blank spaces — an educated guess is better than nothing

Despite what some people might say, exams aren't meant to be easy. There are bound to be a few tricky bits, but you stand a good chance of working them out if you use your noggin.

Do Well in Your Exam

Exam tips — I've got so many of them up my sleeve, I just don't know when to stop...

Make use of the **context**

You'll likely come across the odd word that you don't know, especially in the reading exam. Often you'll be able to find some clues telling you what the text is all about.

1) The type of text, e.g. newspaper article, advertisement, website
2) The title of the text
3) Any pictures
4) The verbal context

Say you see the following in the reading exam, and don't know what any of these words mean:

"...die Kleidung aus Polyester, aus Wolle, aus Baumwolle und aus Seide."

1) Well, the fact that this is a list of things, all starting with 'aus ...' coming after the German word for 'clothes' suggests they're all things that clothes can be made out of.
2) You can guess that 'Polyester' means 'polyester', and 'Wolle' means 'wool'.
3) So it's a pretty good guess that the two words you don't know are different types of fabric. (In fact, 'Seide' means 'silk' and 'Baumwolle' means 'cotton'.)
4) Often the questions won't depend on you understanding more difficult words like these. It's important to be able to understand the gist though, and not let these words throw you.

Take **notes** in the **listening** exam

1. You'll have 5 minutes at the start of the exam to have a quick look through the paper. This'll give you a chance to see how many questions there are, and you might get a few clues from the questions about what topics they're on, so it won't be a horrible surprise when the tape starts running.

2. You'll hear each extract twice. Different people have different strategies, but it's a good idea to jot down a few details that you think might come up in the questions, especially things like:

Dates Numbers Spelt-out names

3. But... don't forget to keep listening to the gist of the recording while you're making notes.

The exam question should give you a bit of background

For example, you'll be told whether you're reading a newspaper article or someone's blog and probably whether the article's about health or holidays. That should get you thinking along the right lines...

How to Use Dictionaries

You're allowed to use a dictionary to help you in your writing task. 'Yippee!' I hear you cry — but using a dictionary isn't as easy as it seems. Finding the right word can be dead tricky, so here are some tips to help you make the most of one. And remember: if it doesn't make sense, you've got the wrong word.

Don't translate **word** for **word** — it **DOESN'T** work

Turn each word of this phrase into English, and you get rubbish:

Wie heißt du?  ***How called you?*** NO!

It's the same the other way round — turn English into German word by word, and you get gibberish — don't do it.

What are you called? 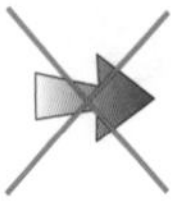 ***Was bist du geheißen?*** NO!

If it **doesn't** make **sense**, you've got it **wrong**

Some words have several meanings — don't just pick the first one you see. Look at the meanings listed and suss out which one is what you're looking for.

If you read this... ***Ich finde es sehr schwer, Deutsch zu sprechen.***

...you might look up 'schwer' and find this:

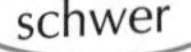

schwer

a heavy; (schwierig) difficult, hard; (schlimm) serious, bad // ad (sehr) very (much); (verletzt etc.) seriously, badly; S-arbeiter m manual labourer; S-e f weight, heaviness; (PHYS) gravity; schwerelos a weightless

So the sentence could mean:

I find it very heavy to speak German. ✘

I find it very difficult to speak German. ✔

I find it very serious to speak German. ✘

This is the only one that makes sense.

The Golden Rule is: it has to make sense

Using a dictionary means you have to use your head a bit too. 'I find it very heavy to speak German' doesn't make sense — so it can't be right. I know I'm repeating myself here, but this is very important...

How to Use Dictionaries

I love dictionaries (no, really), but there are a surprising number of ways you can go wrong with one — which is why I haven't finished telling you about them yet...

Look up **bits** of long words

Not all long German words are in all dictionaries. But you can look up parts of these words.

Say you need to know what Wetterbericht means...

1. If you tried to look up 'Wetterbericht', you might only find the word 'Wetter': weather.
2. So the whole word might be 'weather something'.
3. Look up the rest of it ('Bericht') and it turns out it means 'report'.
4. So 'Wetterbericht' means 'weather report'.

Here's another example: 'Fachsprache'.

1. If you try to look it up, you might not find it, but you do find 'Fach-' (which means technical or expert).
2. So try to find the rest of the word — look up 'Sprache' (which means language).
3. 'Fachsprache' means 'technical language'.

Use your dictionary, but **sparingly**

1) DON'T try to use the dictionary to learn a completely new, fancy way of saying something.
2) Use it to look up a particular word that you've forgotten — a word that, when you see it, you'll know it's right.
3) Use it to check genders of nouns — that's whether words are masculine, feminine or neuter.
4) Use it to check plurals too — although that's a bit trickier. In most dictionaries, you have to look up the German word to find its plural (which won't be written out in full).
5) Check any spellings you're unsure of.

Most importantly, don't use the dictionary to delve into the unknown. If you stick to what you know, you're far less likely to go wrong.

Don't go mad on the dictionary front or it'll all go wrong

Instead of writing complicated sentences where you have to look up every word, try to use the German you already know. Dictionaries can be really helpful — just make sure you can use them properly.

Hints for Writing

Here are a few general hints about how you should approach the writing tasks.

Write about what you **know**

1) You won't be asked to write about obscure German poetry.
2) You will need to cover certain specific things that the question asks you to, but there'll be plenty of scope to be imaginative.
3) Usually the writing tasks will give you some flexibility so you can base your answer on something you know about.

Examiners like to know **when** and **why**...

1) Saying when and how often you did things gets you big bonus marks. Learn times and dates carefully (see pages 4-6).
2) Make sure you write about what you've done in the past (see pages pages 192-195) or what you will do in the future (page 191).
3) Give descriptions where possible, but keep things accurate — a short description in perfect German is better than a longer paragraph of nonsense.
4) Examiners also love opinions (see pages 12-14). Try to vary them as much as possible.

...and **where** and **who** with...

The examiners really are quite nosy, and love as many details as you can give. It's a good idea to ask yourself all these 'wh-' questions, and write the bits that show your German off in the best light. Also, it doesn't matter if what you're writing isn't strictly true — as long as it's believable.

Vocab and grammar make you look **good**

1) The more correct grammar and vocab you can include, the better. But a correct simple sentence is much better than something complicated that doesn't make sense.
2) Your grammar doesn't have to be perfect — don't panic if you write something and then realise that it wasn't quite right. But if you want to get really good marks, you need to get your grammar sorted.
3) Make sure you pay attention to things like word order and adjective endings. There's a special grammar section in this book (see pages 156-212) to help you out.

When it comes to the writing task, always plan ahead

To get the best marks you'll need a plan. Think about what you're going to write first and how you're going to cover all the points in the task. Then think about how you can show off your German.

Hints for Writing

Accuracy is really important in the writing assessment. Without it, your work will look like sloppy custard.

Start with the **verb**

1. Verbs really are the cornerstone of any sentence. If you get the verb right, everything else should fall into place.

EXAMPLE: ***Last weekend, I played badminton with my friends.***

You need 'haben', 'to have', as well as the past participle of the verb 'spielen', 'to play'.

Letztes Wochenende habe ich Badminton mit meinen Freunden gespielt.

You also need to think about word order and where the verbs appear in the sentence.

2. Be careful to get the whole expression that uses the verb, not just the verb itself.

EXAMPLE: *It was fun.* ← **You don't use 'war' here. Germans literally say 'it makes fun' rather than 'it is fun'.** *Es hat Spaß gemacht.*

Check and re-check

No matter how careful you think you're being, mistakes can easily creep into your work. Go through the checklist below for every sentence straight after you've written it.

1) Are the ENDINGS of the verbs right?
Er spiele Tennis. ✗ Er spielt Tennis. ✓

2) Is the WORD ORDER right?
Heute ich gehe ins Kino. ✗ Heute gehe ich ins Kino. ✓

3) Have you got the correct GENDERS for things?
Die Kleid. ✗ Das Kleid. ✓

4) Is everything in the right CASE?
Ich esse der Apfel. ✗ Ich esse den Apfel. ✓

5) Do your adjectives AGREE?
Der groß Hund. ✗ Der große Hund. ✓

6) Have all your nouns got CAPITALS?
Ich wohne in einer stadt. ✗ Ich wohne in einer Stadt. ✓

When you've finished your work, read it through again

Grammar. It might seem boring, but you've just got to know it. The more correct vocab and grammar you include in your work, the more lovely marks will fly your way. So get learning it.

Hints for Speaking

The speaking assessment fills many a student with dread. Remember though — it's your chance to show what you can do. It won't be nearly as bad as you think it's going to be. Honest.

Be Imaginative

There are two tricky things about the speaking assessment — one is what to say, and two is how to say it. No matter how good your German is, it won't shine through if you can't think of anything to say.

Say you're asked to talk about your daily routine (or to imagine someone else's daily routine). It would be easy to give a list of things you do when you get in from school:

"Ich mache meine Hausaufgaben. Ich sehe fern. Ich esse. Ich gehe ins Bett."

= I do my homework. I watch television. I eat. I go to bed.

It makes sense, but the problem is, it's all a bit samey...

1. Try to think of when this isn't the case, and put it into a DIFFERENT TENSE:

"Morgen werde ich Fußball nach der Schule spielen."

= Tomorrow I will play football after school.

2. Don't just talk about yourself. Talk about OTHER PEOPLE — even if you have to imagine them.

"Manchmal sehe ich mit meiner Schwester fern, aber sie mag Zeichentrickfilme und ich sehe lieber die Nachrichten."

= Sometimes I watch TV with my sister, but she likes cartoons and I prefer to watch the news.

3. Give loads of OPINIONS and REASONS for your opinions.

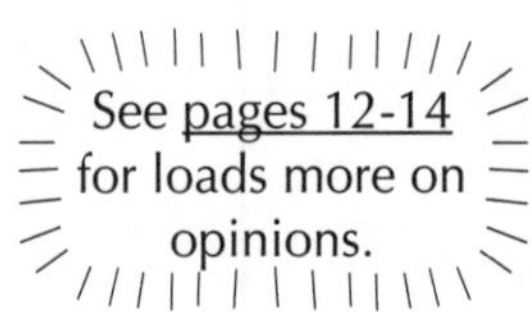
See pages 12-14 for loads more on opinions.

"Ich mache meine Hausaufgaben vor dem Abendessen. Dann kann ich mich später entspannen."

= I do my homework before dinner. Then I can relax later on.

Use your imagination

There's no need to talk about unicorns and what-not, but to get the best marks you do need to include plenty of good vocab, opinions and tenses. Remember — it's all about showing off your German.

Hints for Speaking

Even with all that careful planning, sometimes things can still go a bit wonky.
Never fear though — here's how to come out the other side smiling...

Try to find **another way** of saying it

There may be a particular word or phrase that trips you up. There's always a way round it though.

1. If you can't remember a German word, use an alternative word or try describing it instead.

2. E.g. if you can't remember that 'strawberries' are 'die Erdbeeren' and you really need to say it, then describe them as 'small red fruit', or 'kleines rotes Obst'.

3. You can fib to avoid words you can't remember — if you can't remember the word for 'dog' then just say you've got a cat instead. Make sure what you're saying makes sense though — saying you've got a pet radio isn't going to get you any marks, trust me.

4. If you can't remember the word for a cup (die Tasse) in your speaking assessment, you could say 'glass' (das Glas) instead — you'll still make yourself understood.

You may just need to **buy** yourself some **time**

If you get a bit stuck for what to say, there's always a way out.

1. If you can't think of a way around it, you can ask for help in the speaking assessment — as long as you ask for it in German.

2. If you can't remember what a chair is, ask your teacher: "Wie sagt man 'chair' auf Deutsch?" It's better than wasting time trying to think of the word.

3. If you just need some thinking time in your speaking assessment or you want to check something then you can use these useful sentences to help you out:

The added bonus of using phrases like these is that they make you sound more like a real German.

Also...	*So...*
Ach so!	*Oh, I see!*
Ja, natürlich...	*Yes, of course...*
Ich bin nicht sicher.	*I'm not sure.*
Können Sie das bitte wiederholen?	*Can you repeat that please?*
Ich verstehe nicht.	*I don't understand.*
Können Sie das erklären?	*Can you explain that?*

Take... your... time

Try not to gabble through everything you have to say at a hundred miles an hour. Instead, take a deep breath and talk at a nice, natural pace — just like you would in any other conversation. Easy.

Hints for Speaking

Just a few more handy hints and pointers to help you on your way, and then it's on to some Practice Exams and Assessments — just to see if you've taken all this on board.

A couple of 'DON'T's...

1. DON'T try to avoid a topic if you find it difficult — that'll mean you won't get any marks at all for that bit of the assessment. You'll be surprised what you can muster up if you stay calm and concentrate on what you do know how to say.

2. DON'T make up a word in the hope that it exists in German unless you're really, really stuck (and you've tried all the other tricks on these pages). If it's your last resort, it's worth a try.

Have **confidence**

1. Believe it or not, the teacher isn't trying to catch you out. He or she wants you to do well, and to be dazzled by all the excellent German you've learnt.

2. Speaking assessments can be pretty daunting. But remember it's the same for everyone.

3. Nothing horrendous is going to happen if you make a few slip-ups. Just try and focus on showing the teacher how much you've learnt.

4. Don't be afraid to make mistakes — even native German speakers make 'em. Don't let a silly error shake your concentration for the rest of the assessment.

Most importantly — DON'T PANIC

That's easy for me to say I know, but seriously, stay calm and you stand a far better chance of navigating the bumpy bits. Well, that's it for now folks — some Practice Exams await you...

Practice Exam

Once you've been through all the questions in this book, you should feel pretty confident about the exam. As final preparation, here's a **practice exam** to prepare you for the real thing. It's designed to give you the best exam practice possible for the listening exam, whichever syllabus you're following.

General Certificate of Secondary Education

CGP Practice Exam Paper GCSE German

GCSE German

Centre name					
Centre number					
Candidate number					

Listening Paper

Surname	
Other names	
Candidate signature	

Time allowed: 40 minutes approximately
+ 5 minutes reading time before the test.

Instructions
- Write in black ink or ballpoint pen.
- Before the CD is started you will be given **5** minutes during which you may read through the questions and make notes.
- Answer **all** questions in the spaces provided.
- Answer all questions in **English**.
- Give all the information you are asked for, and **write neatly**.

This is what you should do for each item:
- Before each new question, read through all the question parts and instructions carefully.
- Listen carefully to the recording. There will be a pause to allow you to re-read the question, make notes or write down your answers.
- Listen to the recording again. There will be another pause to allow you to complete or check your answers.
- You may write at any point during the exam.
- You will hear a single tone at the end of each item.
- You are **not** allowed to ask questions or interrupt during the exam.

Information
- The marks are shown by each question.
- The maximum mark for this paper is **40**.
- You are **not** allowed to use a dictionary.

Instructions for playing the CD.
- One track on the CD = one question.
- There are 12 questions, covered on the CD by tracks 14 – 25.

Question No.	1	2	3	4	5	6	7	8	9	10	11	12
CD Track No.	14	15	16	17	18	19	20	21	22	23	24	25

Answer ALL questions

Track 14

1 Alex is talking about where he lives.

Example: Where is Alex's hometown?

A West Germany

B East Germany

C North Germany

Write the correct letter in the box. **A**

a) Alex has lived in Salzkotten:

A all his life.

B since he was three.

C for three years.

Write the correct letter in the box. ☐

(1 mark)

b) He likes it because:

A there's lots to do.

B his friends live nearby.

C there's a cinema.

Write the correct letter in the box. ☐

(1 mark)

c) He says Hamburg is better because:

A there are more things for young people to do.

B there are lots more restaurants.

C you can go sailing.

Write the correct letter in the box. ☐

(1 mark)

Leave blank

Track 15

2 You phone a campsite in Germany and hear this message.
Fill in the missing details in the notes below.

Name of campsite: Campingplatz am Waldsee

Number of pitches for caravans: 10

Number of pitches for tents: ....

Extra charges: .... and TV connections.

Leisure facilities: .... and a playground.

Dogs welcome? ....

(4 marks)

Track 16

3 A group of friends are being interviewed about their opinions of different sports and hobbies. Which three of the following statements are true?

A Max thinks that skiing is fabulous.

B Karin likes swimming at the weekends in summer.

C Karin thinks that cycling is healthy and good for the environment.

D Leah loves many types of music.

E Max thinks sport is necessary, but uninteresting.

F Leah has piano lessons every week.

Write the correct letters in the boxes. ☐ ☐ ☐ *(3 marks)*

Track 17

4 Monika is describing her room.

A **B** **C** **D**

Which two of these items of furniture does Monika have in her room?

Write the correct letters in the boxes. ☐ ☐ *(2 marks)*

Track 18

5 Maria's father is talking about her recent school grades.

a) Why does Maria's father think her English grade is good?

A She did an exchange.

B She did extra English lessons.

C Her uncle visited. Write the correct letter in the box. ☐

(1 mark)

b) According to her father, what does Maria need to do to improve her maths grade?

A Do all her homework.

B Complete all her classwork.

C Ask for help. Write the correct letter in the box. ☐

(1 mark)

c) To get such a bad mark in biology, what does Maria's father think she's been doing?

A Not listening in lessons.

B Talking too much in lessons.

C Sleeping in lessons. Write the correct letter in the box. ☐

(1 mark)

Leave blank

Track 19

6 Elena is talking about a recent shopping trip.

a) Which of these did Elena buy last Saturday?

A  **B**  **C** 

Write the correct letter in the box. ☐ *(1 mark)*

b) Which of these is Elena going to buy this week?

A 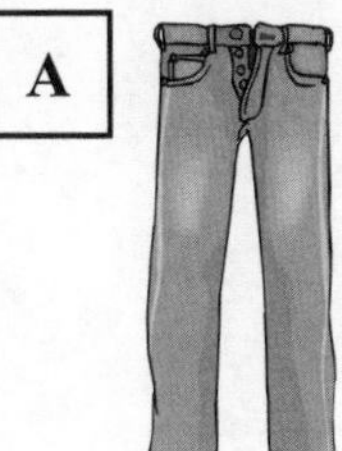 **B**  **C** 

Write the correct letter in the box. ☐ *(1 mark)*

c) Which of these did Gisela buy?

A 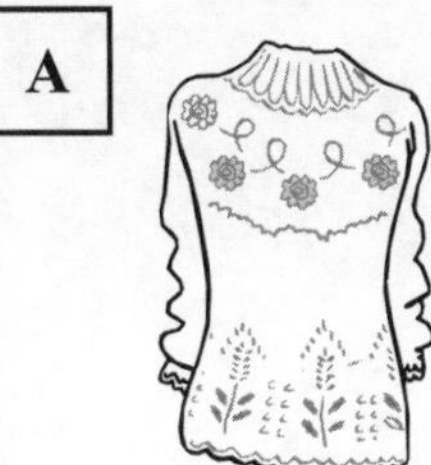 **B** 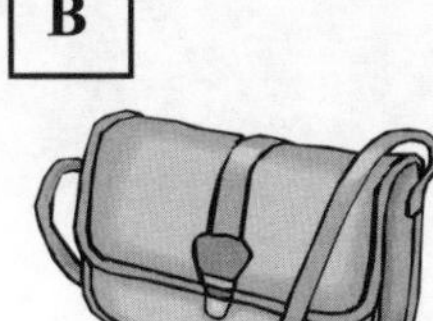 **C** 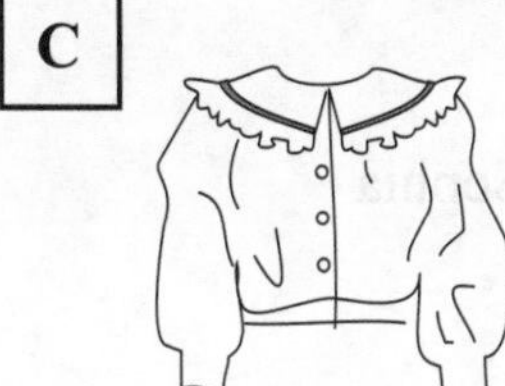

Write the correct letter in the box. ☐ *(1 mark)*

d) Why does Elena say she buys unusual clothes?

A To annoy her parents.

B To make herself stand out from other people.

C Because they are cheaper.

Write the correct letter in the box. ☐ *(1 mark)*

Track 20

7 A group of students are talking about their future plans.
Match each student with one of the statements below.

A	Is not exactly sure what they want to do.
B	Wants to be a lawyer.
C	Wants to be a doctor.
D	Wants to get married.
E	Wants to leave school straight away.
F	Wants to start their own business.
G	Has a job in mind, but their mother doesn't like it.

Write the correct letter in the box.

a) Lisa ☐ *(1 mark)*

b) Christian ☐ *(1 mark)*

c) Thomas ☐ *(1 mark)*

d) Sophia ☐ *(1 mark)*

Leave blank

Track 21

8 Two people are talking about society's problems today.

Example: What does the first speaker say is a big problem in his town?

Unemployment

a) (i) Apart from young people, who is affected by the problems in the first speaker's town?

.... *(1 mark)*

(ii) What are some of his classmates thinking of doing?

.... *(1 mark)*

b) (i) What is a bigger problem, according to the second speaker?

.... *(1 mark)*

(ii) What does she think is unfair?

.... *(1 mark)*

Track 22

9 You're working in a tourist office in Germany.
Listen to the visitors' requests and fill in the blanks in the table.

Person	Place wanted	Why?
1.		wants to visit old tower
2.	chemist's	
3.	zoo	
4.		needs to know whether to take bus or taxi there

(4 marks)

Track 23

10 You're in a restaurant.
What do these customers want?

a) A table for five with a view of:

A the sea.

B the mountains.

C the harbour. Write the correct letter in the box. ☐

(1 mark)

b) A main course suitable for:

A a vegetarian.

B a child.

C a diabetic. Write the correct letter in the box. ☐

(1 mark)

c) To:

A complain about the soup.

B congratulate the chef on the soup.

C complain about his seat. Write the correct letter in the box. ☐

(1 mark)

Track 24

11 Yannis is telling you about his holiday last year.

a) Why was this holiday a bit different from previous holidays?

.... *(1 mark)*

b) What did the campsite specialise in?

.... *(1 mark)*

c) Why did they sometimes go into the village?

.... *(1 mark)*

Leave blank

Track 25

12 Philip is talking about his grandfather.

a) What has Philip's grandfather recently completed a course in?

A How to use a mobile phone.

B How to use a digital camera.

C How to use a computer.

Write the correct letter in the box. ☐ *(1 mark)*

b) What has he done already?

A Booked a cheap flight to Canada.

B Visited his sister in Canada.

C Visited his grandchildren in Canada.

Write the correct letter in the box. ☐ *(1 mark)*

c) What does he want to do next?

A Download photos.

B Do his food shopping online.

C Write a blog for his grandchildren.

Write the correct letter in the box. ☐ *(1 mark)*

General Certificate of Secondary Education

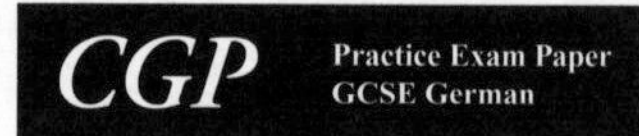

GCSE
German

Reading Paper

Centre name					
Centre number					
Candidate number					

Surname	
Other names	
Candidate signature	

Time allowed: 45 minutes

Instructions
- Write in black ink or ballpoint pen.
- Answer **all** questions in the spaces provided.
- Answer all questions in **English**.
- Give all the information you are asked for, and **write neatly**.

Information
- The marks are shown by each question.
- The maximum mark for this paper is **40**.
- You are **not** allowed to use a dictionary.

Leave blank

Answer ALL questions

1 Read this blog about teenagers' likes and dislikes.

Finn: Ich bin ziemlich sportlich. Leichtathletik gefällt mir, aber ich finde Fußball langweilig. Mein Bruder hat Computerspiele sehr gern, aber sie sind mir egal. In meiner Schule sind die meisten Lehrer nicht so schlecht, aber unseren Direktor finde ich viel zu streng.

Lena: Ich lese gern die „Bunte" Zeitschrift, weil ich mich für berühmte Leute interessiere. Zac Efron gefällt mir sehr, weil er unheimlich gutaussehend ist! Ich lerne Erdkunde am liebsten. Ich mag alles über andere Länder herausfinden.

Sofie: Ich liebe Kunst, weil ich so kreativ bin. Im Allgemeinen meine ich, dass wir viel zu viel Hausaufgaben bekommen — das ist wirklich furchtbar. In meiner Freizeit sehe ich sehr gern Theaterstücke, aber ich finde es leider viel zu teuer.

For each of the following sentences, write **T** (true), **F** (false) or **N** (not in text) in the box.

Example: Sofie loves art. **T**

a) Lena's favourite subject is history. ☐

b) Finn is a keen gymnast. ☐

c) Sofie likes the theatre, but thinks it costs too much. ☐

d) Lena is a big Zac Efron fan. ☐

e) Finn doesn't feel strongly either way about computer games. ☐

f) Finn thinks his headteacher is too relaxed. ☐

(6 marks)

2 You see this short piece about healthy living on a German website.

> Es ist sehr wichtig [**A**] zu essen, sonst wird man krank und übergewichtig. Man sollte Salat, Gemüse und frisches [ ] mindestens fünfmal pro Tag essen. Unsere Diät sollte relativ fettarm sein, das heißt nicht zu viele Pommes und andere gebratene Gerichte. Zu viel [ ] ist auch nicht gut für die Gesundheit — Kuchen und Kekse sollte man nicht jeden Tag zu sich nehmen.
>
> [ ] und Drogen sind, wie alle wissen, sehr gefährlich, weil man leicht davon abhängig werden kann.
>
> Auch ist es äußerst wichtig regelmäßig [ ] zu treiben, um fit zu [ ] .
>
> Wenn man gesund isst und trinkt und genug Bewegung kriegt, dann fühlt man sich fit und voller Energie.

Fill in the gaps using the words below. Write the correct letter in the box.

A	gesund	**E**	Zucker
B	aktiv	**F**	verbringen
C	Obst	**G**	Rauchen
D	Sport	**H**	bleiben

(5 marks)

Leave blank

3 You read this article about sports and hobbies in a German magazine.

> Warum sagen so viele junge Leute, dass sie sich langweilen, wenn es so viele verschiedene Sportarten gibt, die man treiben kann, und so viele neue Hobbys auszuprobieren? Zum Beispiel im Freien kann man Fußball, Tennis, Hockey und so weiter spielen. Man kann auch natürlich draußen schwimmen, angeln, Rad fahren, joggen, Ski fahren und es gibt noch viele andere Möglichkeiten. In einem Sportzentrum kann man unter anderem Badminton, Tischtennis und Squash machen.
>
> Und wenn man Sport nicht treibt, gibt es hunderte von anderen Hobbys wie zum Beispiel Musik hören, ins Kino oder Theater gehen, lesen und so weiter.
>
> Stundenlang vor dem Fernseher oder Computer zu sitzen ist keine gute Idee — versuch mal etwas Neues! Lern ein Musikinstrument zu spielen, werde Mitglied eines Klubs oder einer Tanzklasse! Dabei lernt man auch neue Leute kennen. Die Möglichkeiten sind grenzenlos!

Example: What three sports are named as available in a sports centre?

Badminton, table tennis and squash

a) What two water-based hobbies are named?

.... *(1 mark)*

b) Why should young people not complain that they're bored?

.... *(1 mark)*

c) What is mentioned as an advantage of taking up a new hobby?

.... *(1 mark)*

Turn over

4 Angela has written this entry on her blog.

> Spitze! Endlich kommt das Wochenende! Heute war Samstag und ich bin mit meinen Freundinnen einkaufen gegangen. Ich habe Erdbeeren, Birnen und Pfirsiche gebraucht, weil wir morgen Obstsalat zum Nachtisch essen werden. Ulrike hat keine Zahnpasta mehr gehabt — aber schließlich hat sie auch eine neue Zahnbürste, drei Flaschen Shampoo und etwas Parfüm gekauft! Anke hat ein bisschen Angst gehabt, weil es bald Winter sein wird. Sie sagte: „Ich muss dringend einen neuen Schal und neue Handschuhe finden." Marias Mutter hat sie gebeten, Rindfleisch für das Abendessen zu kaufen. Aber Renate hat die beste Idee gehabt. Sie wollte ins Kaufhaus gehen, denn es hat einen großen Schlussverkauf gegeben. Am Ende des Tages waren wir sehr ermüdet, aber wir haben einen tollen Einkaufstrip gehabt.

Example: Angela wollte...

A ...die Konditorei besuchen.

B ...den Gemüsehändler besuchen.

C ...die Apotheke besuchen.

Write the correct letter in the box. **B**

a) Ulrike kaufte viel bei...

A ...der Buchhandlung.

B ...der Schreibwarenhandlung.

C ...der Drogerie.

Write the correct letter in the box. ☐ *(1 mark)*

Leave blank

b) Anke wollte neue Kleider kaufen, ...

A ...weil sie immer modisch aussehen will.

B ...weil das Wetter bald kalt sein wird.

C ...weil sie ihren Schal verloren hat.

Write the correct letter in the box. ☐ *(1 mark)*

c) Im Kaufhaus...

A ...gab Renate ihr Geburtstaggeld aus.

B ...kaufte Angela eine Bluse.

C ...gab es Ermäßigungen.

Write the correct letter in the box. ☐ *(1 mark)*

d) Maria musste...

A ...in der Metzgerei einkaufen.

B ...im Elektrogeschäft einkaufen.

C ...im Fischladen einkaufen.

Write the correct letter in the box. ☐ *(1 mark)*

5 You receive an e-mail from your German friend Ralf, telling you about his family.

15/01/10

Grüße!

In deiner letzten E-Mail hast du über meine Familie gefragt. Also, wir sind fünf Personen, das heißt meine Eltern, mein älterer Bruder Georg, meine kleine Schwester Leonie und ich.

Ich bin ziemlich groß und schlank und ich habe lange, braune Haare und höre sehr gern Rockmusik. Ich habe auch ein Meerschweinchen namens Felix, das braun und weiß ist.

Meine Mutti heißt Silke und sie ist 48 Jahre alt. Sie ist sehr sympathisch und freundlich. Wir verstehen uns sehr gut, weil sie immer hilfsbereit ist. Sie ist klein und schlank und arbeitet als Sekretärin in einem Büro in der Stadtmitte. Vati ist 52 Jahre alt. Er heißt Wilhelm und er hat eine Glatze. Er trägt auch eine Brille. Er ist Polizist und sehr fleißig. Er geht mir ab und zu auf die Nerven, weil er so ungeduldig ist, aber meistens kommen wir gut miteinander aus.

Mein Bruder ist ein bisschen launisch, was ich schwer finde. Er ist auch faul und hilft nie im Haushalt. Er ist zwei Jahre älter als ich, also 17. Er sitzt stundenlang in seinem Schlafzimmer. Er sagt, dass er seine Hausaufgaben macht, aber ich weiß, dass er eigentlich im Internet surft! Meine kleine Schwester finde ich sehr süß. Sie heißt Leonie und sie ist 7 Jahre alt. Sie hat lockige, blonde Haare und hat tausende von Puppen!

Du kannst sie alle kennen lernen, wenn du zu Besuch kommst.
Schreib mir bitte über deine Familie und dich!

Tschüss

Dein Ralf

Leave blank

Match each of the statements below to the right person according to Ralf.
Put a cross in the correct box.

		Ralf	Silke	Wilhelm	Georg	Leonie
Example:	Is small and slim.	☐	☒	☐	☐	☐
a)	Pretends to be doing homework, but really plays on the computer.	☐	☐	☐	☐	☐
b)	Is very friendly and helpful.	☐	☐	☐	☐	☐
c)	Wears glasses.	☐	☐	☐	☐	☐
d)	Has a pet guinea pig.	☐	☐	☐	☐	☐
e)	Is very sweet.	☐	☐	☐	☐	☐
f)	Is lazy and never helps at home.	☐	☐	☐	☐	☐
g)	Likes listening to music.	☐	☐	☐	☐	☐
h)	Works very hard, but is impatient.	☐	☐	☐	☐	☐

(8 marks)

Le
bla

6 Match these statements about the environment to the English sentences below.
Write the correct letter in the box.

A Die Umwelt ist äußerst wichtig nicht nur für uns, sondern auch für unsere Kinder, Enkelkinder und so weiter. Wir müssen die Umwelt für sie schützen.

B Luftverschmutzung ist ein ernstes Problem, aber es gibt viel, was wir machen können. Wir sollten zum Beispiel mit öffentlichen Verkehrsmitteln oder mit dem Rad fahren, so dass es weniger Abgase geben würde.

C Ein sehr großes Problem besteht darin, dass zu viele Leute sich gar nicht für die Umwelt interessieren. Sie sind „zu beschäftigt", was eigentlich „zu faul" bedeutet. Viele Leute halten die Umwelt für langweilig und finden es leichter, die Gesundheit der Erde zu ignorieren.

D Es ist relativ einfach, ein bisschen umweltfreundlicher zu sein. Man könnte duschen, um Wasser zu sparen, die Lichter abschalten, um Energie zu sparen, und Plastiktüte wieder verwenden.

a) A lot of people say they are too busy to care about the environment. ☐ *(1 mark)*

b) The environment is extremely important and we must protect it for future generations. ☐ *(1 mark)*

c) There are lots of easy things you can do to be more environmentally friendly. ☐ *(1 mark)*

d) We ought to use public transport or cycle in order to cut down on air pollution. ☐ *(1 mark)*

Leave blank

7 You read these comments about people's nationalities on a German online forum.

Camille:	Ich bin Französin, aber jetzt wohne ich in den Vereinigten Staaten. Ich spreche Französisch am liebsten, aber mein Englisch verbessert sich.
Neil:	Ich bin Engländer. Ich lerne seit zwei Jahren Deutsch. Letzten Sommer bin ich nach Österreich gefahren, um meinen Brieffreund zu besuchen.
Andrea:	Ich bin Schottin und wohne in Schottland, aber meine Mutter ist Italienerin und mein Vater ist Däne. Wir sprechen viele Sprachen bei uns!
Thomas:	Ich bin Holländer, aber ich habe in vielen Ländern gewohnt. Mein Vater ist Dolmetscher und arbeitet im Augenblick bei einer australischen Firma.

Use the following words to complete the sentences below. Write the correct letter in the box.

A the USA	**B** Austria	**C** English	**D** Australia
E French	**F** Danish	**G** Scottish	**H** the Netherlands

Example: Camille lives in... **A**

a) Thomas's father works for a firm from... ☐ *(1 mark)*

b) Andrea's father is... ☐ *(1 mark)*

c) Last year Neil visited... ☐ *(1 mark)*

d) Camille is... ☐ *(1 mark)*

Le
bl

8 Sebastian has written this article about his future plans.

Immer fragt mich jedermann: „Was willst du in der Zukunft machen, Sebastian?“ Aber ich weiß nicht! Es ist sehr schwer, so eine wichtige Entscheidung zu treffen.

Meine Freundin Meike ist sehr intelligent und hofft Ärztin zu werden, also muss sie Wissenschaften studieren und dann auf die Uni gehen. Und mein Freund Karl will Rechtsanwalt werden, um eine ganze Menge Geld zu verdienen. Ich möchte auch weiter studieren, aber ich meine, dass ich nicht so klug wie sie bin.

Ich finde Fremdsprachen ziemlich leicht, also vielleicht könnte ich Dolmetscher oder Sprachlehrer werden. Oder ich könnte etwas praktischer tun, wie meine Schwester. Sie interessiert sich sehr für Autos und möchte Mechanikerin werden. Wir könnten zusammen unsere eigene Werkstatt haben — aber nein, wir streiten uns ein bisschen zu viel, meine ich.

Eigentlich meiner Meinung nach habe ich jetzt die perfekte Lösung gefunden. Ich muss ein Jahr freinehmen, damit ich mich später entscheiden kann. Kein Problem!

a) Why does Sebastian's sister want to become a mechanic?

.... *(1 mark)*

b) (i) What does Karl want to do in the future?

.... *(1 mark)*

(ii) Why?

.... *(1 mark)*

c) What does Sebastian think of foreign languages?

.... *(1 mark)*

d) Why does Sebastian want to take a gap year?

.... *(1 mark)*

e) Why does Meike have to study sciences?

.... *(1 mark)*

General Certificate of Secondary Education

GCSE German

Centre name					
Centre number					
Candidate number					

Speaking Assessment

Surname	
Other names	
Candidate signature	

- This paper contains 2 speaking tasks.

Instructions to candidates for speaking tasks
- Find a friend or teacher to read the teacher's part for you.
- You may read over the questions before you start the task.
- You may prepare a plan of up to 40 words for each task.
- Your plan cannot include full sentences.
- You may use dictionaries and other resource materials.
- There will be one unseen question for each task.

Instructions to teachers
- It is essential that you give the student every opportunity to complete their tasks.
- You may alter the target language as printed in this test. However you must remember not to provide students with any key vocabulary.
- Choose one of the suggested unseen questions for each task.

SPEAKING TASK 1

CANDIDATE'S ROLE

Task 1: Celebrity

You are discussing your favourite celebrity with a student in your German partner school. Your teacher will play the part of the student.

Your teacher will ask you the following:

- Who is your favourite celebrity at the moment?
- Why do you like this person?
- Tell me something about his / her career up until now.
- What other interests do they have?
- What are the celebrity's future plans?
- !

! Remember that the exclamation mark means you'll have to answer a question that you won't have prepared an answer to.

The whole conversation should last about five minutes.

SPEAKING TASK 1

TEACHER'S ROLE

Notes for Teachers

You need to ask the student the following questions:

- Wer ist dein Lieblingsstar im Moment?
- Warum magst du diesen Mensch?
- Erzähl mir ein bisschen über seine / ihre Karriere bis jetzt.
- Was für Interessen hat er / sie?
- Was hat er / sie vor, in der Zukunft zu tun?
- !

! The unpredictable question could be:

Ist er / sie ein gutes Vorbild für junge Leute?

SPEAKING TASK 2

CANDIDATE'S ROLE

Task 2: Celebrations

You are talking about a recent celebration with your German exchange partner. Your teacher will play the part of your exchange partner.

Your teacher will ask you the following:

- What did you celebrate recently with your family or friends?
- Who was there?
- Where was the celebration?
- What did you do?
- Did anything funny or unusual happen?
- What will you celebrate next year?
- !

! Remember that the exclamation mark means you'll have to answer a question that you won't have prepared an answer to.

The whole conversation should last about five minutes.

Leave blank

SPEAKING TASK 2

TEACHER'S ROLE

Notes for Teachers

You need to ask the student the following questions:

- Was hast du mit deiner Familie oder mit deinen Freunden neulich gefeiert?
- Wer hat an diesem Fest teilgenommen?
- Wo hat das Fest stattgefunden?
- Was habt ihr gemacht?
- Ist etwas Komisches oder Ungewöhnliches passiert?
- Was wirst du nächstes Jahr feiern?
- !

! The unpredictable question could be:

Wie würdest du feiern, wenn du viel Geld hättest?

General Certificate of Secondary Education

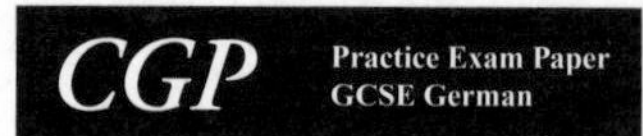

GCSE German

Writing Assessment

Centre name					
Centre number					
Candidate number					

Surname
Other names
Candidate signature

Time allowed: 60 minutes

- This paper contains 2 writing tasks.

Instructions to candidates

- Write in black ink or ballpoint pen.
- Write your name and other details in the space provided above.
- Give all the information you are asked for and write neatly.
- You may read over the questions before you start the task.
- You may prepare a plan of up to 40 words for each task.
- Your plan cannot include full sentences.
- You may use dictionaries and other resource materials.

Leave blank

Task 1: Home and Local Area

You have been asked to write an item (to be posted on your town's website) for German speakers visiting your area.

You could write about the following:

- What the area you live in is like
- What activities younger visitors might enjoy
- What activities older visitors might enjoy
- Accommodation
- Public transport
- Any special events coming up

Remember: to score the highest marks you need to answer the task fully (for grades C and above you will need to write 200-300 words).

Task 2: Future Plans

Your partner school is doing some work comparing the future plans of students in Germany with those in the UK. You volunteer to write about your plans and the plans of someone else.

You could write about the following:

- What (if any) further study you will do after your exams
- What your career plans are
- If you want to marry or have a family
- If you want to live abroad
- The future plans of another person whose ideas are different to yours

Remember: to score the highest marks you need to answer the task fully (for grades C and above you will need to write 200-300 words).

Page 11 (Quick Questions)

1) a) sieben
b) siebzehn
c) dreiundzwanzig
d) vierunddreißig
e) dreihundertsechsundneunzig
f) tausendvierhundertzweiundsiebzig
2) a) das erste
b) das dritte
c) das achte
d) das neunundzwanzigste
3) a) drei Uhr
b) halb zehn
c) Viertel vor sieben
d) zweiundzwanzig nach sechs
e) zwanzig Uhr fünfundvierzig
f) dreizehn Uhr achtundfünfzig
4) a) On Wednesdays I play football.
b) Today I'm going into town.
c) The day before yesterday I was ill.
d) He is going away in March.
e) My birthday is in spring.
f) In the year 2012.
5) a) When are you playing tennis? / When do you play tennis?
b) How many apples would you like?
c) What are you doing?
d) Where are you going (to)?
6) a) Kann Steve mitkommen?
b) Können Sie kochen?
c) Spielt Hannah Klavier?
d) Möchtest du eine Tasse Tee?
e) Gehst du aus?
7) a) Guten Abend
b) e.g. Grüß dich!
c) e.g. Es freut mich, Sie kennen zu lernen.
d) e.g. Wie geht's?
e) bitte
f) danke / danke schön
g) e.g. Ich würde gern singen.
h) e.g. Darf ich die Toilette benutzen?

Page 17 (Quick Questions)

1) a) e.g. Ich mag Sport.
b) e.g. Tennis gefällt mir.
c) e.g. Ich mag dieses Buch nicht.
d) e.g. Ich interessiere mich für Fußball.
e) e.g. Es geht.
2) **Emilie:** Hanna, what do you think of swimming?
Hanna: I think swimming is boring, but I find squash excellent.
Alex: In my opinion sport is terrible. I like the theatre.
Hanna: It's all right. What do you think about the theatre Emilie?
Emilie: I love the theatre too. It's fabulous!
3) a) e.g. Lena ist sympathisch.
b) e.g. Heike ist sehr freundlich.
c) e.g. Daniel ist mies.
d) e.g. Diese Band ist furchtbar.
e) e.g. Deutsch ist fantastisch.
4) a) Die Landschaft gefällt mir, weil sie wunderschön ist.
b) Ich mag den Film nicht, weil er langweilig ist.
c) Ich finde ihn sehr unsympathisch, weil er wirklich hässlich ist.
d) Ich mag dieses Buch, weil es sehr interessant ist.
e) Ich finde Bergsteigen toll, weil es aufregend ist.
5) e.g. Lieber Georg
6) e.g. Viele Grüße
7) den 9. Februar
8) den 9.2.2011
9) e.g. Sehr geehrte Damen und Herren
10) e.g. Hochachtungsvoll
11) e.g. Ich möchte mich über Ihr Hotel beschweren.

Page 18 Listening Questions

1) C
2) C, D, E

Page 19 Reading Question

1) a) 31st July, 2 weeks
b) How many beds are in the dormitory? Do they need to take their own bedding?
c) What is there to see and do nearby? Are there are many sights or other activities for young people?

Page 20 Speaking Question

Example answer:

Was für Fernsehsendungen siehst du gern und welche siehst du nicht gern?

Meine Lieblingssendungen sind Seifenopern wie zum Beispiel EastEnders. Ich interessiere mich besonders für die miesen Leute! Komödien gefallen mir auch, weil ich sehr gern lache, aber ich kann die Nachrichten und den Wetterbericht nicht leiden — sie sind so langweilig!

Wie viele Stunden siehst du zu Hause fern?

Im allgemeinen sehe ich eine Stunde vor dem Abendessen fern, um mich nach der Schule ein bisschen auszuruhen. Dann mache ich meine Hausaufgaben. Ich mag auch am Sonntagnachmittag fernsehen, besonders wenn das Wetter schlecht ist.

Gehst du oft ins Kino?

Ich gehe vielleicht ein oder zweimal im Monat ins Kino. Ich möchte öfter dahin gehen, aber ich finde es ziemlich teuer. Es gibt ein tolles Kino in der Nähe von meinem Haus mit vielen Bildschirmen.

Was für Filme siehst du gern und welche kannst du nicht leiden?

Ich sehe besonders gern Krimis und Horrorfilme, weil sie so spannend sind. Liebesfilme finde ich furchtbar, obgleich meine Freundin sie sehr gern sieht!

Was war der letzte Film, den du gesehen hast?

Neulich haben wir „New Sun" gesehen. Das ist sowohl ein Horrorfilm als auch ein Liebesfilm, also hat er uns beiden gefallen!

Was für Musik hörst du gern?

Meine Lieblingsmusik ist Rapmusik und ich habe besonders gern Jay-Z. Ich könnte stundenlang seinen Liedern zuhören! Klassische Musik ist meiner Meinung nach uninteressant.

Spielst du ein Musikinstrument?

Als ich jünger war, lernte ich Klavier, aber ich war faul und habe nicht genug geübt! Eigentlich möchte ich Gitarre lernen und in einer Rockband spielen. Das wird prima sein!

! Was für Bücher liest du gern?

Ich lese gern Abenteuergeschichten — sie sind faszinierend. Ich mag auch gern Musikzeitschriften lesen, wenn ich genug Geld habe.

Page 21 Writing Question

Task 1 Example answer:

Nottingham, den 10. Mai

Liebe Maria,

Ich habe mich sehr gefreut, von dir vorgestern zu hören.

Ich sage dir ein bisschen über meinen Alltag.

Montags bis freitags gehe ich jeden Tag in die Schule. Ich muss um 7 Uhr aufstehen, was ich viel zu früh finde — obwohl nicht so früh wie du! Ich verlasse das Haus um ungefähr 8.05 und fahre mit dem Bus zur Schule. Ich treffe mich mit einigen Schulfreunden an der Bushaltestelle. Die Fahrt dauert eine halbe Stunde.

Der Schultag beginnt um 8.50 und die erste Stunde fängt um 9.10 an. Jede Stunde dauert fünfundfünfzig Minuten. Um 11 Uhr haben wir eine 20 Minuten lange Pause und dann noch zwei Stunden vor der Mittagspause, die sechzig Minuten lang dauert. Ich esse Butterbrot in der Schulkantine. Nachmittags haben wir zwei Stunden und der Schultag endet um 16.00. Mein Lieblingstag ist Mittwoch, weil wir den ganzen Nachmittag Sport haben.

Am Wochenende haben wir keine Stunden, obwohl man samstags oft Fußball- oder Rugbyspiele hat, wenn man Mitglied einer Schulmannschaft ist. Letztes Jahr war ich Mitglied der Leichtathletikmannschaft. Es hat viel Spaß gemacht und ich habe viele Medaillen gewonnen, aber leider hatte ich zu wenig Zeit, um meine Hausaufgaben zu machen.

Am Wochenende gehe ich oft mit meinen Freunden in den Park, um im Winter Fußball oder im Sommer Tennis zu spielen. Wir treffen uns gewöhnlich zu Mittag. Am Samstagabend gehen wir ins Kino, wenn ein guter Film läuft — die Filme fangen im allgemeinen gegen 7.30 an.

Ich möchte sehr gern mehr über deine tägliche Routine wissen.

Schreib' bald!

Tschüss

deine Sarah

Task 2 Example answer:

Ich habe neulich ein fabelhaftes Buch gelesen, das eine starke Wirkung auf mich gemacht hat. Ich möchte dieses Buch besprechen.

Das Buch heißt „A Terrible Mystery" von Darren Black und ich habe es als Geburtstagsgeschenk von meinen Eltern bekommen. Das Buch ist ein höchst spannender Krimi und ich hatte schon zwei von seinen Romanen gelesen, die sehr erfolgreich gewesen sind. Ich hatte mich schon lange auf dieses neue Buch gefreut und es hat mich gar nicht enttäuscht!

Die Hauptfigur heißt Rupert de Montfort, der an der Yale Universität in den Vereinigten Staaten arbeitet. In diesem Buch muss er mehrere Symbole finden und erklären, um seinen alten Freund, der gekidnappt worden ist, zu retten — die Geschichte ist äußerst kompliziert und manchmal ein bisschen schwer zu verstehen, aber ich konnte das Buch nicht hinlegen! Auch wenn ich sehr müde war, wollte ich immer noch einige Seiten lesen, bevor ich schlafen musste.

Was ich vor allem gut fand, war die Geschwindigkeit mit der die Geschichte sich entwickelt. Man fühlt sich ab und zu fast atemlos! Man weiß nie, was um die Ecke liegt! Von Zeit zu Zeit sind die Ereignisse ein bisschen unglaublich und es ist ein sehr langes Buch, aber sonst ist es eigentlich klasse. Ich würde dieses Buch herzlich empfehlen.

Die beiden vorigen Bücher von Darren Black, die ich gelesen habe, sind auch Filme geworden und haben viel Geld verdient. Ich hoffe sehr, dass dieses Buch auch als Film im Kino erscheinen wird. Ich weiß, dass er mir gefallen wird.

Page 29 (Quick Questions)

1) a) potato
   b) onion
   c) carrot
   d) cucumber
   e) cabbage
2) a) der Apfel
   b) die Banane
   c) die Erdbeere
   d) die Himbeere
   e) der Pfirsich
3) boiled sausage with pickled cabbage and potatoes / beef with dumplings / chicken with pasta and tomatoes
4) e.g. Ich bin Vegetarierin. Ich mag kein Fleisch.
5) e.g. Könntest du mir bitte das Salz reichen?
6) e.g. Wann isst du zu Abend?
7) We eat dinner at half past six.
8) e.g. Nein danke, ich habe keinen Hunger.
9) e.g. Das Mittagessen war lecker, danke.
10) a) viel
    b) ein bisschen
    c) ein großes Stück
    d) genug
11) a) e.g. Ich räume mein Zimmer auf.
    b) e.g. Ich muss aufräumen.
    c) e.g. Ich wische Staub.
    d) e.g. Ich muss die Spülmaschine leeren.
12) e.g. Kann ich bitte ein Handtuch haben?
13) e.g. Darf ich mich baden?

Page 36 (Quick Questions)

1) a) e.g. Ich heiße Mark.
   b) e.g. Ich bin sechzehn Jahre alt.
   c) e.g. Ich habe am 2. September Geburtstag.
   d) e.g. Ich wohne in Crewe.
   e) e.g. Ich mag Tennis.
2) a) He is medium-height and fat.
   b) She is small, has green eyes and wears glasses.
   c) He has curly red hair, blue eyes and a beard.
   d) She is tall and slim and has shoulder-length, straight, dark hair.
3) a) Mein Vater heißt Paul.
   b) Meine Stiefmutter heißt Lisa.
   c) Ich habe eine Schwester.
   d) Ich habe zwei Brüder.
   e) Ich bin ein Einzelkind.
4) a) Ich habe einen Hund.
   b) Ich habe eine Katze.
   c) Ich habe ein Kaninchen.
   d) Ich habe ein Meerschweinchen.
5) e.g. Meine Mutter heißt Helen. Sie ist mittelgroß und hat lange, braune Haare und grüne Augen. Mein Vater heißt Mick. Er ist sehr klein und hat lockige, blonde Haare und einen Schnurrbart.
6) a) sympathisch
   b) lustig
   c) freundlich
   d) blöd / dumm
   e) ekelhaft
   f) unhöflich
7) I have a little sister and an older brother. My sister is a bit annoying, but she can also be very sweet. My brother is intelligent and fairly serious, but he is very patient and always helpful. I get on well with my brother.
8) a) Er liebt Maria.
   b) Sie ist verheiratet.
   c) Er ist ledig.
   d) Sie sind geschieden.
9) e.g. In der Zukunft möchte ich in einem Verhältnis sein und vielleicht eine Familie haben. Erstens werde ich auf die Universität gehen.

Page 43 (Quick Questions)

1) a) die Obdachlosigkeit
   b) die Arbeitslosigkeit
   c) die Diskriminierung
   d) die Armut
   e) die Gewalt
2) a) e.g. Junge Leute haben ein Problem Arbeit zu finden.
   b) e.g. Ich halte Gleichberechtigung für sehr wichtig.
   c) e.g. AIDS ist ein großes Problem heutzutage.
   d) e.g. Ich denke, dass Vandalismus ein großes Problem in meiner Stadt ist.
   e) e.g. Das ist unfair. Es geht mir auf die Nerven.
3) a) the back
   b) the neck / throat
   c) the toes
   d) the knee
   e) the ear
4) a) der Kopf
   b) der Bauch / der Magen
   c) das Bein
   d) die Hand
   e) der Mund
5) a) Ich bin krank. / Mir ist schlecht.
   b) Mir ist heiß.
   c) e.g. Ich bin durstig.
   d) e.g. Ich muss ins Krankenhaus gehen.
   e) e.g. Ich muss zum Zahnarzt gehen.
6) a) My legs hurt.
   b) I have a sore throat.
   c) I have the flu and a temperature.
   d) I've cut my nose.
7) a) I only eat organic food and I do aerobics twice a week.
   b) I eat lots of fruit and vegetables and I play sport regularly.
   c) I try to avoid chips and I'm fairly active.
   d) I'm a bit overweight. I don't play any sport.
   e) I don't drink, but sometimes I smoke. I would never take drugs.
   f) I never drink, because my uncle is an alcoholic.

Page 44 Listening Questions

1) B
2) Andreas = A, Maria = C
3) a) pork
   b) cauliflower and peas
   c) raspberry gateau / tart

Page 45 Reading Question

1) a) glasses
   b) impatient
   c) businesswoman
   d) serious
   e) curly

Page 46 Speaking Question

Example answer:

Isst du gesund?

Ja, ich esse Obst jeden Tag und trinke viel Mineralwasser.

Wie könntest du besser essen?

Man sollte jeden Tag fünf Portionen Obst oder Gemüse essen. Oft esse ich nur drei oder vier Portionen pro Tag. Ich könnte das verbessern. Ich sollte auch Süßigkeiten, wie Bonbons und Kuchen, vermeiden. Aber das ist ziemlich schwer!

Bist du Vegetarier(in)? Warum/warum nicht?

Nein, ich bin nicht Vegetarier(in), weil ich Gemüse ein bisschen langweilig finde. Auch esse ich sehr gern Fleisch, besonders Wurst und Steak.

Wann warst du zum letzten Mal krank? Was war los?

Vor zwei Wochen hatte ich eine Erkältung. Ich bin zwei Tage im Bett gewesen. Aber ich bin eigentlich ziemlich gesund. Mir ist nicht oft schlecht.

Was machst du, um fit zu bleiben?

Ich gehe jeden Tag joggen, am Samstagnachmittag schwimme ich im Hallenbad im Freizeitzentrum und zweimal pro Woche spiele ich Badminton mit meinen Freunden in unserem Klub.

Trinkst du Alkohol?

Ich trinke manchmal ein Glas Wein, wenn ich mit meinen Eltern in einem Restaurant esse, aber meistens trinke ich nur Orangensaft oder Mineralwasser.

Rauchst du?

Ich rauche nie. Rauchen ist schrecklich! Meine Tante hat zwanzig Zigaretten pro Tag geraucht und ist an Krebs gestorben. Zigaretten stinken und sind wirklich teuer. Ich finde Rauchen gar nicht cool.

! Was denkst du über Drogen?

Ich hasse Drogen, weil sie so gefährlich sind. Man kann leicht abhängig werden. Glücklicherweise sind Drogen nicht so schlecht ein Problem in unserer Stadt, aber in vielen britischen Großstädten bringen die Drogen viele soziale Probleme.

Page 47 Writing Questions

Task1 Example answer:

Ich wohne in Burnley in Nordwestengland. Wir haben viele soziale Probleme in unserer Stadt, weil es nicht genug Jobs gibt. Unsere Fabriken, die vorher Kleider gemacht haben, sind jetzt zu altmodisch. Die Jobs, die unsere Eltern vor dreißig Jahren in Burnley hatten, existieren nicht mehr.

Deshalb haben die Einwohner kein Geld, ein Haus zu kaufen oder eine Wohnung zu mieten. Viele Jugendliche sind obdachlos und müssen auf der Straße wohnen. Da sie keine Arbeit haben, stehlen sie oder verkaufen sie Drogen. Man kann Drogen überall in den Diskos und Kneipen finden.

Burnley hat viele Einwohner, die aus Pakistan oder Indien gekommen sind. Sie haben vorher in den Fabriken gearbeitet und jetzt haben viele ihre eigenen kleinen Geschäfte oder Restaurants. Einige weiße Jugendliche glauben, dass diese Ausländer ihre Jobs genommen haben. Rassismus ist ein massives Problem in Burnley. Aus diesem Grund hat man leider eine rassistische Partei in Burnley.

Außerdem gibt es nichts für die jungen Leute. Wir haben keine Teilzeitjobs und wenig Geld. Es ist teuer, ins Kino zu gehen (eine Cola kostet £2.50!) oder in ein Konzert. Wenn wir mit dem Zug nach Manchester fahren, haben wir kein Geld übrig, um Kleider zu kaufen. Deshalb gehen wir in den Park und trinken Alkohol, den unsere Freunde billig im Supermarkt gekauft haben.

Um Burnley zu verbessern, muss man neue Jobs schaffen, besonders für die weißen Jugendlichen. Man muss billige Wohnungen für die Obdachlosen bauen. Die Schüler brauchen Sportzentren, die nicht zu teuer sind. Nur dann können die Einwohner von Burnley alle zusammen in Frieden leben.

Task 2 Example answer:

Ich komme gut mit fast allen Mitgliedern meiner Familie aus. Meine Eltern sind sympathisch und wir verstehen uns gut. Meine Katze ist sehr freundlich und intelligent. Ich streite mich nie mit meinem Bruder, der mir mit meinen Hausaufgaben hilft.

Aber meine Schwester...!! Meine Schwester nervt mich. Sie ist vierzehn Jahre alt und hat viele Probleme. Sie hat keine Freunde, weil sie so hässlich ist. Sie hört immer laute Musik und ihr Zimmer ist sehr unordentlich. Wir müssen die ganze Zeit auf sie warten, weil sie immer unpünktlich ist. Wenn ich könnte, würde ich meine Schwester verkaufen und eine zweite Katze kaufen!

In der Schule finde ich die meisten Lehrer gut. Wir haben einen faulen Sportlehrer, der dick und unfit ist. Er ist immer müde und launisch, da er zu viel Bier trinkt und zu spät ins Bett geht. Aber die meisten Lehrer sind hilfsbereit, geduldig und sympathisch. Nächstes Jahr werde ich in die Oberstufe gehen.

Ich komme gut mit den anderen Schülern aus. Ich habe einige Schulfreunde, die mit mir für denselben Fußballklub spielen. Auch spielen wir zusammen für dieselbe Schulmannschaft. Im Sommer werden wir nach Frankreich fahren, um Fußball mit einigen französischen Schülern zu spielen.

Am Samstagabend gehen wir immer in die BLUES-Disko. Es kostet nur £3 und es gibt viele schöne Mädchen. Ich trage meine Designerkleider und sehe unglaublich cool aus. Meine Schwester fragt immer: „Darf ich mitkommen?", aber ich sage immer: „NEIN! Du bist zu hässlich und zu uncool." Dann weint sie.

Ich kenne einige Schüler in meiner Klasse, die jeden Samstagabend allein auf dem Computer spielen oder im Internet surfen. Wie langweilig!

Mein Leben ist fast perfekt. Wenn ich eine hübsche schlanke blonde Freundin hätte, würde es vielleicht noch besser sein. Auch kennen Sie jemanden, der eine kleine vierzehnjährige Schwester billig kaufen möchte?

Page 55 (Quick Questions)

1) a) der Fußball
   b) das Badminton
   c) das Tischtennis
   d) das Squash
   e) das Hockey
2) e.g. Jeden Tag gehe ich spazieren.
3) Three from, e.g. das Fitnesszentrum, das Freibad, das Hallenbad, die Kegelbahn, der Park, das Schwimmbad, der Sportplatz, das Sportzentrum
4) a) Twice a month I play tennis with my friend in the sports centre.
   b) At the weekend I cycle in the park.
   c) I swim every day in the indoor swimming pool.
   d) In the evenings I run on the sports field.
5) a) die Geige
   b) die Querflöte
   c) die Gitarre
   d) das Klavier
6) Ich spiele Klarinette.
7) Ich bin Mitglied eines Filmklubs.
8) e.g. Ich finde Schach ausgezeichnet.
9) e.g. Das denke ich nicht.
10) e.g. Ich spiele nicht gern Squash, weil es anstrengend ist.
11) a) I like watching cartoons.
   b) I like listening to a soap opera on the radio.
   c) The news starts at 6 o'clock.
   d) The weather report ends at half past six.
12) e.g. Ich habe letzte Woche ein tolles Buch gelesen.
13) a) ein Abenteuerfilm
   b) ein Liebesfilm
   c) ein Horrorfilm
   d) ein Krimi
14) e.g. Ich habe letztes Wochenende 'The Adventures of George and Betty' gesehen. Es ist eine Komödie über einen Mann namens George und eine Frau namens Betty. Er war amüsant. Er hat mir gefallen.

Page 66 (Quick Questions)

1) a) e.g. Ich höre gern Rockmusik.
   b) e.g. Ich höre nicht gern Popmusik.
   c) e.g. Ich höre gern Rapmusik auf CD, wenn ich im Auto bin.
2) I think Karl Traumboot is totally fantastic. He is a famous German actor. Karl looks so cool and always wears black, fashionable clothes. I've seen him on stage and he was excellent. I think that he's a good role model for young people.
3) Two from, e.g. Ich chatte über MSN®. / Ich habe eine Website gemacht. / Ich hochlade meine Fotos. / Ich schreibe seit zwei Jahren ein Online-Tagebuch. / Ich mache meine Hausaufgaben auf meinem Computer.
4) a) der Computer
   b) der Drucker
   c) der Bildschirm
   d) die Tastatur
5) e.g. Ich glaube, dass Computer ausgezeichnet sind. Computer sind wirklich nützlich. Ohne Computer könnte ich meine Schularbeit nicht machen. Computer können viel Zeit sparen.
6) A text message
7) e.g. Ich werde eine E-Mail schicken. / Ich werde eine E-Mail senden.
8) e.g. Wo ist der Supermarkt, bitte?
9) e.g Um wie viel Uhr macht der Supermarkt auf?
10) The supermarket opens at half past eight.
11) a) die Bäckerei
   b) der Gemüsehändler
   c) die Metzgerei
   d) der Fischladen
   e) die Drogerie
12) e.g. Ich hätte gern mein Geld für dieses Hemd zurück.
13) e.g. Ich kaufe besonders gern Schuhe ein.
14) a) 9 euros, 95 cents
   b) 36 cents
   c) 100 euros
15) a) Ich hätte gern/Ich möchte ein Kilo Zucker, bitte.
   b) Ich hätte gern/Ich möchte ein Dutzend Äpfel, bitte.
   c) Ich hätte gern/Ich möchte eine Tafel Schokolade, bitte.
   d) Ich hätte gern/Ich möchte ein Glas Marmelade, bitte.

Page 73 (Quick Questions)

1) a) das Hemd
   b) das Kleid
   c) die Hose
   d) der Pullover
   e) der Schal
   f) ein Paar Socken
2) e.g. Dieses Kleid gefällt mir.
3) e.g. Dieses Kleid ist wirklich modisch.
4) a) I don't like this jacket. It's a bit old-fashioned.
   b) I think it's important to be individual.
   c) Brand-named clothes can be really expensive.
5) red = rot, orange = orange, yellow = gelb, green = grün, blue = blau, purple = lila
6) rosa, lila and orange
7) Ich hätte gern/Ich möchte ein Hemd aus Seide.
8) a) iron
   b) wood
   c) plastic
   d) cotton
9) e.g. Gehen wir ins Kino.

10) e.g. Ich habe nicht genug Geld. Ich würde lieber Rad fahren.
11) e.g. Kann man hier in der Nähe Rad fahren?
12) e.g. Gibt's hier in der Nähe ein Schwimmbad? Wann macht das Schwimmbad auf?
13) e.g. Wir treffen uns bei dir zu Hause.
14) a) Wie viel kostet eine Eintrittskarte?
    b) Ich möchte zwei Karten, bitte.
    c) Um wie viel Uhr fängt der Film an?
    d) Um wie viel Uhr endet er?
15) a) One ticket costs 5 euros.
    b) The film starts at half past seven.
    c) The film ends at 10 o'clock.

Page 74 Listening Questions

1) a) C
   b) C
   c) A
2) a) Sabine
   b) Fritz
   c) Katja
   d) Katja

Page 75 Reading Question

1) a) the Black Forest
   b) make-up
   c) €275
   d) trout
   e) grape juice
   f) they were on sale

Page 76 Speaking Question

Example answer:

Wie wichtig sind Computer für dich?

Sehr wichtig. Jeden Tag chatte ich mit meinen Freunden über MSN® und ich schicke viele E-Mails. Ohne Computer könnte ich meine Schularbeit nicht machen. Jede Woche surfe ich im Internet, um Antworten für meine Hausaufgaben zu finden. Computer sparen viel Zeit.

Wie findest du Computerspiele?

Ich finde Compterspiele langweilig. Meistens arbeite ich am Computer. Einige Leute sagen, dass Computerspiele einen gewalttätig machen kann, aber ich glaube das nicht.

Hast du einen Laptop?

Leider nicht. Ich möchte einen Laptop, weil sie wirklich nützlich sind, aber sie sind zu teuer und ich habe nicht genug Geld. Ich brauche einen Teilzeitjob!

Was ist deine Lieblingswebsite?

Ich spiele gern Tischtennis und meine Lieblingswebsite ist die „ETTA" - oder „English Table Tennis Association" - Website. Diese Website hat viele Informationen über Tischtennis in England.

Sind Computer schlecht für die Gesundheit?

Ja, manchmal, wenn man zu oft vor dem Computer sitzt. Man kann Rücken-, Augen-, oder Kopfschmerzen bekommen. Auch ist es ungesund immer drinnen zu sitzen. Man sollte auch im Freien herumlaufen.

Hat neue Technologie jemals Probleme für dich verursacht?

Ja, ich habe letzten Monat eine Katastrophe gehabt. Ich machte meine Hausaufgaben mit dem Computer, aber es gab einen Stromausfall. Ich hatte meinen Aufsatz nicht gespeichert und musste ihn neu anfangen.

Sind Handys in deiner Schule erlaubt?

Man darf ein Handy in die Schule bringen, aber im Klassenzimmer muss man es abschalten. Sie sind sehr nützlich, weil ich meine Eltern informieren kann, ob sie mich nach der Schule abholen müssen.

! Könntest du ohne Handy leben?

Nein, gar nicht. Ich brauche mein Handy für mein Leben außerhalb der Schule. Meine Freunde und ich simsen einander die ganze Zeit, um zu arrangieren, wann und wo wir uns treffen.

Page 77 Writing Question

Task 1 Example answer:

Am 3. März habe ich den englischen Komiker Gordon Cameron in einem indischen Restaurant in Boddley-Bibbington getroffen. Wir haben Curryhähnchen mit Reis gegessen und wir haben zwei Stunden zusammen gesprochen.

Herr Cameron, woher kommen Sie?

Ich komme aus Bumble in Sudwestengland. Bumble ist eine industrielle Stadt mit vielen Fabriken.

War es schwer, berühmt zu werden?

Es hat eine lange Zeit gedauert. Ich musste zuerst Drama an der Universität von Townchester studieren. Dann hatte ich viele schreckliche Jobs — ich habe im Supermarkt, in einer Fabrik und in einem Kino gearbeitet. Später habe ich überall als Komiker in Kneipen und Klubs gearbeitet. Endlich habe ich meine Fernsehserie „Potato Hotel" gemacht und dann bin ich ziemlich berühmt geworden.

Was ist Ihre größte Leistung?

Ich habe vier Werbungen für „Jack King's" Bier gemacht (eine Werbung im Sportzentrum, eine Werbung im italienischen Restaurant, eine Werbung im Supermarkt und eine Werbung bei meinem Großvater) und diese Werbungen sind noch sehr komisch.

Kennen Sie viele berühmte Persönlichkeiten?

Ich habe einige gute Freunde, die bekannt sind. Mein Held, als ich jung war, war der Komiker Ronnie Barker und ich habe ihn vor seinem Tod getroffen. Ich kenne auch den Komiker Al Osbourne und den Filmstar George Darling, der Doctor X in „Space Wars" gespielt hat — beide wohnen in Bumble.

Wie ist Ihr Haus?

Als Kind habe ich in einem Reihenhaus gewohnt. Jetzt wohne ich mit meiner Frau Sally und unseren zwei Töchtern in einer großen Villa in Bumble. Wir haben einen Bierkeller im Untergeschoss, wo ich gern Lederhosen trage.

Herr Cameron, was möchten Sie in der Zukunft machen?

Ich möchte eine CD mit Robbie Williams machen, aber er will nicht mit mir arbeiten, weil ich viel besser singe. Auch will ich einen James-Bond-Film machen, da James Bond und ich so ähnlich sind. Wir sind beide gut aussehend und schlank, obwohl James Bond nicht so witzig wie ich ist.

Task 2 Example answer:

Ich wohne in Blackpool, eine große Stadt an der Küste in Nordwestengland. Weil Blackpool viele Touristen anzieht, haben wir sehr viel zu tun. Erstens gibt es einen ausgezeichneten Strand und drei große Piers. Die Piers haben Geschäfte, Cafés und sogar einen Themenpark. Im Stadtzentrum gibt es den „Winter-Gardens"-Komplex; er hat einen wunderschönen Ballsaal und Theater, wo man viele Shows und Konzerte sehen kann. Die neuesten Filme kann man im modernen Kinozentrum sehen. Man kann auch Sehenswürdigkeiten wie „Sea Life Centre" oder den berühmten Turm besuchen.

Man kann auch viel Sport treiben. Blackpool hat ein großes Sportzentrum mit einem Fitnesszentrum, einem Hallenbad und vier Tennisplätzen. Auch gibt es eine Kegelbahn und eine Eisbahn in der Stadtmitte. Im Stanley-Park kann man Kricket und Minigolf spielen. Das „Sandcastle"-Zentrum ist ein fantastisches Freizeitzentrum mit einem riesigen Hallenbad, einer Sauna, einem Wellenbad, Wasserkanonen und einer Schlangenrutschbahn.

In meiner Freizeit spiele ich Fußball für Foxhall, eine sehr gute Mannschaft. Wir haben zwei Fußballplätze und Umkleideräume mit einem kleinen Café. Auch spiele ich Tischtennis in der Blackpooler Liga im „Palatine"-Zentrum. In der Schule bin ich Mitglied eines Dramaklubs, der zwei Vorstellungen jedes Jahr produziert — eine Pantomime zu Weihnachten und eine Komödie im Sommer. Der Dramaklub ist sehr populär.

Meiner Meinung nach ist Blackpool nicht typisch. Die meisten Städte haben wahrscheinlich nicht so viel für junge Leute. Aber weil so viele Touristen nach Blackpool kommen und weil sie ihre Kinder mitbringen, brauchen wir ausgezeichnete Freizeiteinrichtungen, damit sie sich nicht langweilen.

Für Jugendliche gibt es viel zu tun, aber manchmal sind die Shows und so weiter zu teuer. Auch könnte man mehr Geld in die Stadt investieren. Unsere Stadt sieht ein bisschen altmodisch aus, zum Beispiel braucht man viele Hotels modernisieren.

Page 85 (Quick Questions)

1) a) Frankreich
   b) Deutschland
   c) Dänemark
   d) Italien
   e) Spanien
   f) Polen
2) Ich bin Österreicher. Ich komme aus Österreich.
3) mein österreichischer Freund
4) Ich bin Österreicherin.
5) e.g. die Türkei, die Schweiz, die Niederlande, die USA / die Vereinigten Staaten
6) Ich komme aus der Schweiz.
7) a) the English Channel
   b) the Black Forest
   c) the Rhine
   d) the Danube
   e) Bavaria
   f) Vienna
8) e.g. Fährt ein Zug nach München?
9) e.g. Einmal hin und zurück nach München, zweite Klasse, bitte. / Eine Rückfahrkarte nach München, zweite Klasse, bitte.
10) (der) Warteraum
11) a) e.g. Ich gehe zu Fuß.
   b) e.g. Ich fahre mit dem Boot.
   c) e.g. Ich fahre mit dem Auto / dem Wagen.
   d) e.g. Normalerweise fahre ich mit der U-bahn in die Stadt.
12) a) Which platform does the fast-stopping train to Stuttgart leave from?
   b) When does the next coach to Frankfurt leave?
   c) When does the plane arrive in Berlin?
   d) Which tram goes to the airport, please?
13) e.g. Können Sie mich über die Museen in Köln informieren, bitte?
14) e.g. Um wie viel Uhr macht das Museum auf?
15) e.g. Haben Sie Broschüren über die Sehenswürdigkeiten von Köln?
16) The bus leaves at half past twelve from the bus stop.

Page 90 (Quick Questions)

1) der Urlaub
2) a) das Hotel
   b) das Gasthaus
   c) der Campingplatz
   d) die Jugendherberge
3) a) reception
   b) dining room
   c) lifts
   d) games room
4) e.g. Haben Sie Zimmer frei?
5) e.g Ich möchte ein Doppelzimmer mit Bad.
6) e.g. Was kostet es pro Nacht für zwei Personen?
7) e.g. Ich möchte einen Platz für vier Nächte, bitte.
8) e.g. Gibt es hier Trinkwasser?
9) e.g Kann man hier das Zelt aufstellen?
10) a) der Platz, die Plätze
   b) das Zelt, die Zelte
   c) der Wohnwagen, die Wohnwagen
   d) der Schlafsack, die Schlafsäcke
11) a) e.g. Wo ist der Parkplatz, bitte?
   b) e.g. Wo ist die Toilette, bitte?
   c) e.g. Wo ist das Restaurant, bitte?
   d) e.g. Wo ist das Spielzimmer/der Aufenthaltsraum, bitte?
12) a) It's outside on the left.
   b) It's downstairs at the end of the corridor.
   c) It's upstairs on the right.
   d) It's on the first floor.
13) e.g. Wann wird das Mittagessen serviert, bitte?
14) a) e.g. Die Heizung funktioniert nicht.
   b) e.g Es gibt keine Handtücher in meinem Zimmer.
   c) e.g Das Bad ist schmutzig.
15) e.g. Ich brauche neue Handtücher.
   Können Sie mein Badezimmer putzen, bitte?

Page 100 (Quick Questions)

1) e.g. Einen Tisch für vier Personen, bitte. Wir möchten auf der Terrasse sitzen.
2) e.g Darf ich bitte die Tageskarte haben?
3) a) dessert
   b) starter
   c) main course
4) e.g. Ich hätte gern/Ich möchte die Bratwurst mit Pommes.
5) e.g. Wie schmecken Spätzle?
6) e.g Herr Ober! Die Bratwurst ist verbraten.
7) e.g. Die Rechnung, bitte.
8) e.g Ist die Bedienung inbegriffen?
9) e.g Ich bin letzten Monat nach Frankreich gefahren.
10) e.g Ich war zwei Wochen lang mit meinen Freunden im Urlaub. Wir sind auf einem Campingplatz geblieben.
11) e.g. Wir sind mit dem Boot dorthin gekommen.
12) e.g Ich bin an den Strand gegangen und ich habe Tennis gespielt.
13) a) I will go to Switzerland in a month.
   b) I will stay in a hotel with my family for a week.
   c) We will get there by plane.

14) a) der Brieffreund
b) die Brieffreundin
c) ein deutscher Austausch
d) die Gastfamilie

15) a) Es regnet.
b) Die Sonne scheint.
c) Es ist heiß und feucht.
d) Es war bedeckt.
e) Es hat geschneit.
f) Es ist achtzehn Grad Celsius.

16) Today it will be wet and foggy in Germany. Tomorrow it will thunder in the south and hail in the north. In Berlin it will be cool and windy.

Page 101 Listening Questions

1) a) E
b) D
c) B

2) a) 20 to 25 °C
b) heavy cloud, showers / rain later
c) South-West Germany
d) overcast and cool

Page 102 Reading Question

1) a) 10
b) It's his favourite dish.
c) too salty
d) She's a vegetarian and there were few main courses for her.
e) delicious

Page 103 Speaking Question

Example answer:

Wohin bist du letztes Jahr im Urlaub gefahren?

Letzten Sommer bin ich mit meiner Familie nach Florida gefahren. Ich hatte die Vereinigten Staaten noch nie besucht und ich war sehr aufgeregt.

Wie bist du dorthin gekommen? Wie war die Reise?

Wir sind mit dem Taxi zum Flughafen gefahren, dann sind wir von Manchester nach Orlando geflogen. Am Flughafen haben wir ein Auto gemietet und sind zum Hotel gefahren.

Die Reise war ziemlich gut. Ich habe einen guten Film gesehen und habe drei Stunden geschlafen.

Wo hast du gewohnt?

Wir haben in einem sehr großen, modernen Hotel gewohnt. Es war klasse. Wir hatten zwei enorme Doppelzimmer mit Badezimmer, Fernsehapparat und Balkon.

Was hast du während des Tages gemacht?

Wir haben „Disney World" und „SeaWorld" besucht, wir haben uns am Freibad im Hotel gesonnt und wir sind jeden Tag an den Strand gegangen. Ich bin auch einkaufen gegangen und habe Kleidung, Parfüm und eine Sonnenbrille gekauft. Alles war sehr preiswert.

Wie war das Essen?

Wir haben im Hotelrestaurant gegessen und alles war lecker, besonders der Fisch und der Schokoladenkuchen. Es gab auch ein sehr gutes Restaurant nicht weit vom Hotel. Da waren die Steaks fantastisch!

Hattest du Probleme während des Urlaubs?

Ja, ich habe meine Handtasche in der Stadtmitte verloren. Ich bin zur Polizeiwache gegangen. Glücklicherweise hat man die Handtasche gefunden.

Was möchtest du nächstes Jahr machen?

Wir haben schon eine Reservierung gemacht — wir möchten nach Kanada fliegen, um Calgary und Vancouver zu besuchen, weil meine Cousins da wohnen. Hoffentlich werden wir Ski fahren. Meine Cousins sind ausgezeichnete Skifahrer.

! Wenn du das Lotto gewonnen hättest, wo würdest du im Urlaub fahren?

Wahrscheinlich würde ich nach Südostasien und dann vielleicht nach Australien und Neuseeland fahren. Das würde sehr schön sein!

Page 104 Writing Question

Task1 Example answer:

Am Samstagabend um elf Uhr haben wir (vierzig Studenten und vier Lehrer) unsere Schule in Kendal verlassen. Wir sind mit dem Bus nach Dover gefahren. Unterwegs haben wir Karten gespielt, einen miesen Film gesehen und nur zwei Stunden geschlafen. Um sechs Uhr sind wir mit dem Schiff nach Calais gefahren, und endlich sind wir um fünf Uhr am Nachmittag in Cochem angekommen.

Dann haben wir unsere Austauschpartner getroffen. Ich habe bei Stefan in einem Bauernhaus außerhalb der Stadt gewohnt. Jeden Tag mussten wir um sechs Uhr aufstehen, um die Tiere zu füttern!

Wir haben zwei Tage in der Schule verbracht und an den anderen Tagen haben wir Ausflüge gemacht. Wir haben einige Klassen besucht und das war wirklich interessant. Die Studenten konnten Englisch sehr gut sprechen und wir haben ihnen in ihren Englischstunden geholfen.

Cochem ist eine sehr schöne Stadt. Wir sind einkaufen gegangen, mit der Sesselbahn gefahren und im Freibad geschwommen. Auch haben wir die historische Burg Eltz, Rüdesheim (die Drosselgasse und das Niederwalddenkmal) und die Sommerrodelbahn in Altenahr besucht.

An einem Abend hatten wir ein großes Fußballspiel – England gegen Deutschland. Wir haben 3:2 gewonnen! Auch haben wir ein Rockkonzert besucht und hatten eine Disko im Jugendzentrum.

Wir hoffen, dass ihr im Juli eine gute Reise nach England habt. Unser Aufenthalt in Cochem war wunderbar – danke! Wenn ihr nach England kommt, werden wir eine Schiffsreise auf Windermere machen und eine Fabrik in Kendal besuchen, die für „Kendal Mint Cake" berühmt ist.

Task 2 Example answer:

Alice Smith, 14 Dean Court, Manchester, M12 2Q2, Großbritannien

Manchester, den 23. Juni 2009

Gasthof Wagner, 77979 Schuttertal, Parkstr. 15, Deutschland.

Sehr geehrter Herr Wagner,

meine Familie und ich haben Ihr Hotel vor zwei Wochen besucht. Wir haben eine Woche da gewohnt und anfänglich war alles gut. Das Personal war freundlich und unser Zimmer, das sauber und bequem war, hatte einen sehr schönen Blick auf der Landschaft. Dann haben die Probleme begonnen.

Es sagt in Ihrer Broschüre, dass Sie ein „beheiztes" Freibad und eine Reitschule haben. Das Freibad war gar nicht beheizt (es war zu kalt) und die „Reitschule" hatte nur zwei alte kranke Pferde. Auch war der Kinderspielplatz zu schmutzig.

Das Frühstück im Hotel war sehr gut: frische Brötchen mit Butter und Marmelade, Eier, Käse, Schinken, Obst, Orangensaft, Tee und Kaffee. Aber jeden Tag haben wir dasselbe Abendessen bekommen: frische Brötchen mit Butter, Eier, Käse, Schinken, Obst, Salat und Orangensaft oder Wein!

Es sagt auch in Ihrer Broschüre, dass das Hotel fünf Minuten von einem See liegt – fünf Minuten mit dem Flugzeug! Wir mussten dreißig Minuten durch einen Wald wandern. Als wir endlich angekommen sind, konnten wir keine Ruderboote mieten, weil es noch nicht Sommer war.

Am Abend haben die anderen Touristen immer sehr spät laute Musik im Weinkeller gespielt. Dann haben sie uns immer gestört, als sie um Mitternacht betrunken ins Bett gegangen sind. Jeden Abend haben wir sehr schlecht geschlafen.

Der Schwarzwald gefällt uns, aber das nächste Mal werden wir am „kinderfreundlichen" Campingplatz Schmidt zelten.

Hochachtungsvoll, Alice Smith.

Page 110 (Quick Questions)

1) a) die Bank
   b) die Metzgerei
   c) die Bäckerei
   d) der Bahnhof
   e) die Kirche
   f) der Marktplatz
   g) das Kino
2) a) indoor swimming pool
   b) airport
   c) hospital
   d) hotel
   e) stadium
   f) cathedral
   g) cake shop
   h) department store
3) a) e.g. Wo ist das Rathaus, bitte?
   b) e.g. Gibt es hier in der Nähe eine Apotheke?
   c) e.g. Wie weit ist es zum Verkehrsamt?
4) e.g. It's two hundred metres from here.
5) e.g. Wie komme ich am besten zum Schloss?
6) Go straight on past the church, then take the first street on the left. Go right at the lights, round the corner and it is on the left-hand side.
7) e.g. Da drüben, an der Ecke.

Page 116 (Quick Questions)

1) a) e.g. Ich komme aus Nordirland.
   b) e.g. Ich bin Nordirländer.
   c) e.g. Ich wohne in Nordirland.
2) a) I live in Newcastle in north-east England.
   b) I live in Cardiff in south Wales.
   c) I live in the countryside near Bristol.
   d) My village is in Northern Ireland next to a river.
   e) Oban is on the Scottish coast.
   f) My town is in the Welsh mountains.
3) a) e.g. Es gibt einen Markt, eine Kirche und eine Bibliothek.
   b) e.g. Die Stadt ist sauber und ruhig.
   c) e.g. Es gibt wenig zu tun.
   d) e.g. Ich wohne nicht gern in Boddley-Bibbington, weil es langweilig ist.
4) a) I live in a modern detached house.
   b) We live in an old terraced house.
   c) My flat is near the shops.
   d) The semi-detached house is near the motorway.
   e) My house has a small garden with a big tree.
5) I live in a new semi-detached house in the town centre. There is a large living room, a dining room, a kitchen, three bedrooms and a tiny bathroom. My house has a garden, but no lawn. My bedroom is small and the walls are yellow.
6) a) der Sessel
   b) die Lampe
   c) der Tisch
   d) das Bett
   e) der Kleiderschrank
7) a) e.g. Ich wohne in einem kleinen Reihenhaus nicht weit vom Bahnhof. Es gibt ein Wohnzimmer, eine kalte Küche, zwei Schlafzimmer und ein Badezimmer.
   b) e.g. Mein Haus hat einen winzigen Garten mit vielen Blumen.
   c) e.g. In meinem Schlafzimmer habe ich ein Bett, einen Kleiderschrank, einen Tisch und einen Stuhl. Der Teppich ist blau und die Tapete ist lila.

Page 122 (Quick Questions)

1) a) (das) Weihnachten
   b) (der) Heiligabend
   c) (das) Silvester
   d) (das) Neujahr
   e) (die) Chanukka
   f) (der) Ramadan
2) e.g. Wir feiern meinen Geburtstag am dreiundzwanzigsten Mai.
3) We celebrated Easter on the 4th of April.
4) e.g. Zu Weihnachten haben wir einen Weihnachtsbaum.
5) We give presents and send Christmas cards.
6) e.g. Ich feiere Neujahr mit meiner Familie und meinen Freunden.
7) Usually we have a party at home with dancing and fireworks.
8) a) the hole in the ozone layer
   b) the greenhouse effect
   c) noise pollution
   d) water pollution
   e) sulphur dioxide
   f) carbon dioxide
   g) fossil fuels
   h) rubbish
9) a) e.g. Ich halte die Umwelt für total wichtig.
   b) e.g. Jeder kann mehr umweltfreundlich sein.
   c) e.g. Wir sollten unser Altpapier recyceln.
   d) e.g. Wir sollten weniger Wasser benutzen.
10) I'm not at all interested in the environment. I am very busy and I don't have time to recycle. I never travel on public transport because I've absolutely no worries about the greenhouse effect or the hole in the ozone layer. The environment is totally boring.

Page 123 Listening Questions

1) a) C
   b) F
   c) D
2) C, D, F

Page 124 Reading Question

1) a) Vanessa
   b) Hanna
   c) Thomas
   d) Andreas
   e) Matthais

Page 125 Speaking Question

Example answer:

Wo wohnst du?

Ich wohne in Bumble in Cumbria in Nordwestengland. Bumble ist eine kleine historische Marktstadt und bekommt viele Touristen jedes Jahr.

Was für Umweltprobleme gibt es in deiner Stadt?

Wir haben schlechte Luftverschmutzung, weil die Touristen meistens mit dem Auto in die Stadt kommen. Auch ist die Stadt schmutzig, da die Touristen ihren Abfall auf die Straßen werfen.

Gibt es Umweltprobleme außerhalb der Stadt?

In Cumbria haben wir ein großes Problem mit Überflutungen. Auch haben wir Wasserverschmutzung in einigen Flüssen und die Fische sterben. Einige Leute werfen ihren Müll in die Flüsse, und manchmal fließen Chemikalien aus den Fabriken in die Flüsse.

Glaubst du, dass diese Probleme in der Zukunft verschlechtern werden?

Ja, wahrscheinlich. Zum Beispiel werden die Überflutungen vielleicht verschlechtern wegen des Treibhauseffekts. Und wenn wir die Flüsse nicht sanieren, werden mehr Pflanzen und Tiere sterben.

Bist du umweltfreundlich?

Ja, ich fahre mit dem Rad in die Schule, zu Hause trenne ich den Müll und ich dusche mich, um Wasser zu sparen.

Was macht ihr in der Schule für die Umwelt?

Wir recyceln das Altpapier und wir schalten die Lichter ab, um Energie zu sparen.

Ist Lärmbelästigung ein Problem in deiner Stadt?

Ja, besonders wenn die Betrunkenen aus den Kneipen kommen oder wenn es laute Diskos am Samstagabend gibt.

! Was kann man für die Umwelt in deiner Stadt machen?

Man kann die Autos in der Stadtmitte verbieten und eine Fußgängerzone bauen. Man kann auch die öffentlichen Verkehrsmittel verbessern.

Page 126 Writing Question

Task 1 Example answer:

Zu Weihnachten bleiben meine Eltern, mein Bruder und ich am fünfundzwanzigsten Dezember zu Hause, und unsere Verwandten besuchen uns. Wir stehen ziemlich früh (um acht Uhr) auf, um unsere Geschenke zu öffnen. Im Wohnzimmer haben wir einen großen Tannenbaum mit Kerzen und einem Engel. Zum Frühstück essen wir immer ein Speckbrot. Um zwei Uhr gibt es ein traditionelles englisches Hauptgericht: Truthahn, Bratkartoffeln, Karotten, Erbsen, usw., aber Weihnachtspudding gefällt uns nicht und wir essen immer Eis als Nachtisch.

In Deutschland feiert man den Nikolaustag am sechsten Dezember. Am Nikolaustag kommt Sankt Nikolaus (und auch sein Gehilfe, Knecht Ruprecht) mit Geschenken für die Kinder. Heutzutage kommt der Weihnachtsmann am vierundzwanzigsten Dezember auch mit Geschenken. Am Heiligabend gehen viele Deutsche in die Kirche, um berühmte deutsche Weihnachtslieder wie „O Tannenbaum" und „Stille Nacht" zu singen. Einige Deutsche essen eine Gans am Weihnachtstag (ich esse lieber Truthahn, weil ich Gans zu fettig finde).

In England haben wir einige Feste, die in Deutschland nicht existieren, z.B. „Pancake Day", wenn man Pfannkuchen isst, und „Guy Fawkes Night", die man am fünften November mit einem großen Feuerwerk feiert. „Burns Night" ist ein schottisches Fest im Januar. Man feiert den schottischen Dichter Rabbie Burns mit Whisky und „Haggis". In England feiern viele Schotten dieses Fest.

In Norddeutschland hat man „Karneval" im Februar (in Süddeutschland heißt es „Fasching" und in der Schweiz heißt es „Fastnacht"). Man feiert das Ende des Winters mit Masken, Umzügen und Partys. Im September/Oktober hat man in München das weltberühmtes Münchner Oktoberfest.

Ich kann überall in England oder in Deutschland feiern. Letztes Jahr war ich zu Ostern in Deutschland, und das hat Spaß gemacht. Der Osterhase hat bunte hartgekochte Eier und Schokoladeneier im Garten versteckt, die die Kinder finden mussten.

Mein Lieblingsfest ist mein Geburtstag. Letztes Jahr habe ich viele Geschenke bekommen, und wir sind in ein italienisches Restaurant gegangen, um Nudeln, Pizza und Eis zu essen. Es hat viel Spaß gemacht.

Task 2 Example answer:

Lieber Paul,

mein Haus liegt in einem ruhigen Vorort einer kleinen Stadt. Wir sind nicht weit von der Stadtmitte, aber wenn wir zehn Minuten mit dem Rad fahren, kommen wir aus der Stadt und auf das Land. Ich brauche zwanzig Minuten, um zu Fuß in die Schule zu gehen.

Unser Haus ist ein ziemlich modernes Einfamilienhaus mit einem Garten, einem Grillplatz, einer Terrasse und einer Garage. Im Erdgeschoss haben wir ein Wohnzimmer, eine Küche, ein Esszimmer und eine Toilette. Im ersten Stock gibt es drei Schlafzimmer, ein kleines Büro und ein großes Badezimmer mit einer Dusche.

Ich wohne mit meiner Familie. Mein Vater, der Jack heißt, arbeitet als Krankenpfleger in einem Krankenhaus, und meine Mutter, die Kate heißt, arbeitet als Mechanikerin in der Stadt. Meine ältere Schwester wohnt auch bei uns. Ihr Name ist Helen.

In meinem Schlafzimmer habe ich ein Einzelbett, ein Bücherregal, einen Schreibtisch, einen Fernsehapparat, einen Sessel, zwei Fußballposters, einen Computer und einen blauen Teppich. Die Wände sind hellblau. In meinem Schlafzimmer mache ich meine Hausaufgaben und surfe im Internet. Ich mag mein Zimmer, aber es ist nicht so groß. Wenn meine Schwester auf die Uni geht, will ich ihr Schlafzimmer in ein Billardzimmer verändern.

In der Zukunft werde ich nicht in meiner Stadt wohnen. Ich möchte einen Job im Ausland finden und ich will in Spanien wohnen. Das Wetter ist sehr heiß und es gibt viel zu tun. Ich möchte in einem Hotelrestaurant arbeiten, weil ich sehr gut kochen kann.

Tschüss, Andrew.

Page 135 (Quick Questions)

1) a) e.g. Ich mag Englisch.
   b) e.g. Ich mag Naturwissenschaften.
   c) e.g. Geografie gefällt mir mehr.
   d) e.g. Ich hasse Informatik.
   e) e.g. Französisch ist mein Lieblingsfach.
2) a) e.g. Ich gehe zu Fuß in die Schule.
   b) e.g. Ich fahre mit dem Bus in die Schule.
   c) e.g. Ich fahre mit dem Fahrrad in die Schule.
3) a) e.g. Die Schule fängt um acht Uhr fünfundfünfzig an.
   b) e.g. Die Schule ist um fünfzehn Uhr fünfundzwanzig aus.
   c) e.g. Um zwölf Uhr haben wir Mittagspause.
   d) e.g. Wir haben sechs Stunden pro Tag.
   e) e.g. Jede Stunde dauert sechzig Minuten.
   f) e.g. Wir haben im Sommer sechs Wochen Ferien.
4) e.g. Außerhalb des Stundenplans bin ich Mitglied einer Fußballmannschaft.
5) a) pencil
   b) pencil sharpener
   c) ballpoint pen
   d) fountain pen
   e) exercise book
6) a) die Aula
   b) das Klassenzimmer
   c) das Labor
   d) die Kantine
   e) die Sporthalle

7) a) Ich verstehe nicht.
   b) Können Sie das bitte wiederholen?
   c) Wie buchstabiert man das?
8) e.g. Ich lerne seit vier Jahren Deutsch.
9) 1 = very good; it's the best mark you can get.
10) a) I'm a bit worried about my grades.
    b) In my class, there's a pressure to do well.
    c) I don't want to fail.
    d) Sometimes I find the lessons quite difficult.
    e) School is stressful because I have so much homework.

Page 142 (Quick Questions)

1) I did my work experience at Volkswagen. I worked there for two weeks. The work was really interesting and my colleagues were very friendly. I felt at home. In the future, I hope to become an engineer.
2) e.g. Ich möchte das Abitur machen und dann auf die Universität gehen. Ich möchte Chemie studieren, weil ich später Apotheker werden will.
3) a) der Arzt
   b) die Lehrerin
   c) der Rechtsanwalt
   d) die Polizistin
   e) der Schauspieler
4) a) head teacher (male)
   b) hairdresser (female)
   c) architect (female)
   d) plumber (male)
   e) nurse (male)
   f) interpreter (male)
5) a) e.g. Ich will mit Tieren arbeiten.
   b) e.g. Ich will nicht mit Kindern arbeiten.
   c) e.g. Ich möchte selbständig sein.
   d) e.g. Ich möchte nicht gern Arzt sein, obwohl das Gehalt ganz gut ist.
   e) e.g. Die Arbeitszeit wäre zu lang.
   f) e.g. Ich bin lieber Bauarbeiter.
6)

Max: What will you do after 'the Abitur'/ A-levels, Claudia?

Claudia: Well, in July I'm going to go to Italy. I'd like to be an au pair. And you? Would you like to work abroad?

Max: Yes, hopefully I'm going to go to England. I'd like to travel and meet people and then work in a hotel.

Claudia: Great! That will definitely improve your English.

Page 149 (Quick Questions)

1) a) Job offer: we are looking for a chef.
   b) Would you like to work with animals?
   c) You must be responsible.
   d) You must have a driver's licence.
   e) For further details call this number: 02 34 61.
   f) We need a part-time worker. Six hours per week.
2) a) die Stellenangebote
   b) die Stellenbewerbung
   c) mein Lebenslauf
3) a) der Manager
   b) die Managerin
4) We are inviting you to an interview on Tuesday the 8th of March.
5) a) e.g. Ich möchte gern als Kellnerin arbeiten.
   b) e.g. Ich möchte gern mein Deutsch verbessern und mit anderen Leuten arbeiten. In der Zukunft hoffe ich auch als Managerin bei einem Hotel zu arbeiten.
   c) e.g. Ich habe Mathe, Englisch und Naturwissenschaften natürlich gemacht und auch Deutsch und Französisch.
   d) e.g. Ja, letztes Jahr habe ich anderthalb Wochen bei einem sehr schönen Restaurant gearbeitet. Es war ein bisschen anstrengend, aber es hat mir wirklich gefallen.
6) e.g. Hallo! Hier spricht Sarah. Meine Telefonnummer ist siebenunddreißig neunundachtzig fünfundsechzig. Kann Katja mich um 19 Uhr zurückrufen? Danke. Auf Wiederhören.
7) a) e.g. Hallo! Chris am Apparat.
   b) e.g. Warten Sie einen Moment, ich verbinde Sie.
   c) e.g. Darf ich etwas ausrichten?
   d) e.g. Es tut mir leid, falsch verbunden.
   e) e.g. Kann ich Ihren Namen haben, bitte?
   f) e.g. Sie sollten im Internet suchen.

Page 150 Listening Questions

1) a) B
   b) A
2) a) B
   b) C

Page 151 Reading Question

1) a) F
   b) T
   c) T
   d) T
   e) F

Page 152 Reading Question

2) a) A
   b) C
   c) A

Page 153 Speaking Question

Example answer:

Warum möchten Sie diese Stelle?

Ich möchte gern als Kellner(in) arbeiten, um mein Deutsch zu verbessern. Auch spare ich für einen neuen Computer. Ich werde darauf meine Hausaufgaben machen.

Was sind Ihre Lieblingsfächer?

Meine Lieblingsfächer sind Deutsch und Kunst. Ich lerne gern Deutsch, weil ich es interessant und ziemlich einfach finde. Kunst lerne ich sehr gern, weil ich ganz kreativ bin.

Haben Sie Aktivitäten außerhalb des Stundenplans?

Ja, sicher. Ich bin Mitglied einer Band und ich spiele montags und mittwochs Federball. Donnerstags gehe ich mit einer Gruppe schwerbehinderter Kinder in die Kegelbahn. Es ist wichtig anderen zu helfen, finde ich.

Haben Sie ein Betriebspraktikum gemacht?

Ja, ich habe mein Praktikum bei einer Drogerie gemacht. Ich habe eine Woche da gearbeitet. Meine Mitarbeiter waren ganz hilfsbereit und es hat mir viel Spaß gemacht, den Kunden zu helfen. Die Arbeit hat um halb neun angefangen und war erst um halb sechs zu Ende.

Haben Sie einen Teilzeitjob?

Ja, ich arbeite samstag- und sonntagabends in einem kleinen Café in meinem Dorf. Ich wasche ab, decke die Tische und nehme auch Bestellungen. Das macht Spaß.

! Essen Sie oft in Restaurants?

Ja, ich esse ziemlich oft mit meiner Familie in einem italienischen Restaurant. Das Essen dort ist lecker.

Was für Charaktereigenschaften haben Sie, um Sie für diesen Job gut geeignet zu machen?

Ich bin sehr geduldig, freundlich, fleißig und total verantwortlich.

Was für einen Beruf wollen Sie in der Zukunft machen?

Ich möchte bestimmt mit der Öffentlichkeit arbeiten. Ich möchte auch im Ausland arbeiten, vielleicht in einem Hotel in der Schweiz, weil ich gern Ski fahre und auch weil ich gern wandern gehe.

Haben Sie irgendwelche Fragen?

Ja. Wie lang ist die Arbeitzeit?

Ungefähr neun Stunden pro Woche. Sie werden Freitag und Samstag Abende von sechs Uhr bis halb elf arbeiten.

Danke schön. Das ist toll.

Page 154 Writing Question

Task 1 Example answer:

Für mein Betriebspraktikum bin ich mit einer Gruppe Klassenkameraden nach Deutschland gefahren. Zwei Lehrer haben uns begleitet und für anderthalb Wochen haben wir alle in verschiedenen Firmen in Bremen gearbeitet. Bremen ist unsere Partnerstadt, aber das war für mich das erste Mal da. Am ersten Tag bin ich zum Büro gegangen, wo ich meine Mitarbeiter kennen gelernt habe. Sie waren ganz nett und freundlich und haben mir sehr deutlich und langsam erklärt, was ich machen sollte. Um Mittag haben wir alle in der Pizzeria gegessen, weil es mein erster Tag war. Am Nachmittag habe ich versucht, einen Brief am Computer zu schreiben, aber es ist nicht gut passiert, weil die Tastatur ganz fremd war. Abends habe ich mit meinen Freunden zusammengetroffen und wir haben viel von unseren Erfahrungen erzählt.

Früh am nächsten Tag bin ich wieder mit der Straßenbahn zum Büro gefahren und ich bin an die Stadtmusikanten vorbeigekommen. Sie sahen ganz eindrucksvoll aus. Während des Tages habe ich am Computer wieder gearbeitet, aber auch am Schalter geholfen, wo ich mit den Kunden gesprochen habe. Das habe ich ein bisschen stressig gefunden, obwohl ein deutscher Mitarbeiter immer in der Nähe war.

Am Wochenende habe ich eine Stadtrundfahrt gemacht. Ich habe das alte Rathaus und die Rolandstatue gesehen, die eine Größe von fast sechs Meter hat. Fantastisch!

Am letzten Tag bin ich mit der Abteilungsleiterin nach Hamburg gefahren, um einen wichtigen Kunde zu besuchen. Wir sind mit dem IC-Zug dahingefahren. Ich habe das sehr bequem gefunden und die Reise hat nur fünfzig Minuten gedauert. Der Kunde war sehr freundlich und hat uns eingeladen, mit ihm zu Mittag zu essen. Das Essen war lecker.

Endlich sind wir alle nach England zurückgefahren. Wir waren müde, aber hatten so viel Spaß gehabt, dass niemand am folgenden Tag in die Schule wieder zurückgehen wollte. Mein Auslandsbetriebspraktikum war eine lebensverändernde Erfahrung!

Meiner Meinung nach ist Bremen eine fantastische Stadt. Ich will so bald wie möglich zurückgehen, um meine neuen Freunde zu besuchen.

Task 2 Example answer:

Meine Schule heißt die „Medway Community School" und ist eine Gesamtschule für Schüler von elf bis achtzehn, die in der Nähe von Manchester liegt. Ich besuche diese Schule seit fünf Jahren und werde nächstes Jahr in die Oberstufe gehen.

Es gibt viele Gebäude; manche sind ganz modern und neugebaut, aber zum größten Teil sehen sie total hässlich aus, weil sie in den Fünfzigerjahren oder früher gebaut wurden. Wir haben zwei Felder, wo wir entweder Fußball, Rugby oder Hockey spielen können und wo wir während der Pausen uns entspannen können. Das ist prima! Es gibt leider kein Schwimmbad oder Tennisplätze. Wenn wir schwimmen wollen, müssen wir in die Stadt fahren. Das ist nicht praktisch. Es gibt eine große Kantine, und sowohl fünf gut ausgestattete Computerräume als auch eine angenehme Bibliothek, wo wir uns bei schlechtem Wetter treffen können. Die Klassenzimmer sind leider nicht nur ziemlich dunkel, sondern auch sehr kalt im Winter und zu heiß im Sommer.

Es gibt ungefähr 1200 Schüler und Schülerinnen und dazu 120 Lehrer und Lehrerinnen. Ich denke, dass die Lehrer freundlich und nicht zu streng sind, aber manchmal geben sie uns viel zu viel Hausaufgaben. Die Sportlehrer sind besonders cool und es gibt viele Sportmannschaften. Am liebsten spiele ich Rugby.

Die Schule beginnt um Viertel vor neun und wir haben fünf Stunden pro Tag. Wenn ich Mathe oder Englisch habe, finde ich, dass die Stunden zu lang sind, aber wenn ich Sport oder Kunst habe, sind sie zu kurz! Wir tragen eine Schuluniform, damit wir nach Meinung der Lehrer und der Eltern uns immer ordentlich anziehen. Ich trage lieber meine eigenen Kleider, weil ich sie viel bequemer finde. Unsere Schuluniform ist altmodisch und kann teuer sein, und man verliert seine Individualität.

In meiner idealen Schule wären Mobbing und Drogen streng verboten. Die Toiletten wären sauber und gut gepflegt. Wir hätten bestimmt keine Uniform und wir dürften wählen, was wir in der Schule jeden Tag lernen würden.

Pages 163-164 (Quick Questions)

1) a) nominative
b) accusative
c) accusative
d) nominative
e) dative
f) genitive
g) accusative
h) nominative
i) nominative
j) accusative
k) genitive
l) accusative
m) nominative
n) nominative
o) dative
p) accusative

2) a) masculine
b) neuter
c) feminine
d) feminine
e) masculine
f) masculine
g) feminine
h) masculine
i) neuter
j) neuter
k) feminine
l) neuter
m) masculine
n) neuter
o) masculine

3) a) feminine
b) feminine
c) neuter
d) neuter
e) masculine
f) masculine
g) masculine
h) neuter
i) neuter
j) feminine
k) feminine
l) masculine

4) a) Junge
b) Jungen
c) Studenten
d) Studenten
e) Löwen
f) Herrn

5) a) die Flaschen
b) die Vögel
c) die Erbsen
d) die Biere
e) die Zoos
f) die Salate
g) die Regeln
h) die Meerschweinchen
i) die Röcke
j) die Bäuerinnen
k) die Reisebusse
l) die Felder
m) die Tücher
n) die Fabriken
o) die Museen

6) a) die Landkarte
b) der Roman
c) der Hut
d) der Keks
e) das Freibad
f) das Einkaufszentrum
g) das Kleid
h) der Kuli
i) der Käse
j) das Loch
k) die Rechnung
l) die Sehenswürdigkeit

7) a) The happy man sings a song.
b) The funny woman is wearing a hat.
c) Do you know the worried man?
d) The hungry people buy sixteen pears.
e) The proud man's car is blue.
f) The helpful man finds the important woman.
g) The stupid woman writes a postcard to the serious man.

8) a) Wrong — the verb isn't second.
Correct version: e.g. Ich fahre nach Spanien.
b) Correct
c) Correct
d) Correct
e) Wrong — the verb isn't second.
Correct version: e.g. Er hat ein neues Auto.
f) Wrong — the verb isn't second.
Correct version: e.g. Heute spiele ich Fußball.
g) Wrong — breaks the 'time, manner, place' rule.
Correct version: e.g. Ich fahre jeden Tag mit dem Rad in die Schule.
h) Correct
i) Wrong — breaks the 'time, manner, place' rule.
Correct version: e.g. Sie geht mit ihren Freunden ins Stadion.
j) Correct

9) a) e.g. Jeden Tag schwimme ich im Hallenbad.
b) e.g. Abends spielt sie Klavier.
c) e.g. Wir gehen morgen ins Restaurant.
d) e.g. Ich fahre oft mit dem Zug nach London.
e) e.g. Ich kann Tennis spielen.
f) e.g. Ich werde nächstes Jahr nach Frankreich fahren.
g) e.g. Samstag werde ich meine Großmutter besuchen.
h) e.g. Heute muss ich mit meiner Mutter in die Stadt gehen.

10) a) e.g. Er läuft jeden Tag.
b) e.g. Ich treffe meine Freunde um zwei Uhr.
c) e.g. Morgen spielen sie Tennis im Park.
d) e.g. Wir gehen nicht an den Strand, weil das Wetter schlecht ist.
e) e.g. Du musst am Montag in die Schule gehen.
f) e.g. Ich fahre jeden Tag mit dem Zug in die Schule.

11) a) e.g. Ich mag meinen Bruder, weil er lustig ist.
b) e.g. Ich bin traurig, weil mein Goldfisch krank ist.
c) e.g. Er arbeitet beim Zoo, weil Tieren ihm gefallen.
d) e.g. Ich gehe aus, weil es sonnig und warm ist.

Pages 173-174 (Quick Questions)

1) a) Ich kaufe Äpfel und Eier. / I buy apples and eggs.
b) Ich habe zwei Katzen und einen Hund. / I have two cats and one dog.
c) Ich möchte einen Apfelstrudel und einen Kaffee. / I would like an apple strudel and a coffee.

2) a) Jeden Tag schwimme oder jogge ich. / Every day I swim or jog.
b) Samstags gehe ich in die Stadt oder ins Sportzentrum. / On Saturdays I go into town or to the sports centre.
c) Ich möchte Dolmetscher oder Journalist werden. / I would like to be an interpreter or a journalist.

3) a) Ich mag Englisch, aber ich mag nicht Mathematik. / I like English, but I don't like maths.
b) Ich möchte ins Kino gehen, aber ich habe kein Geld. / I would like to go to the cinema, but I don't have any money.
c) Ich muss meine Hausaufgaben machen, aber ich will Fußball spielen. / I have to do my homework, but I want to play football.

4) 10 from, e.g. weil, während, wenn, nachdem, damit, bevor, bis, als, ob, obwohl, dass

5) a) Ich meine, dass dein Kleid fürchterlich ist.
b) Ich denke, dass du sehr unhöflich bist.
c) Heute werde ich spazieren gehen, wenn das Wetter schön ist.
d) Ich spreche gern Deutsch, obwohl es manchmal ganz schwer ist.
e) Er wäscht ab, während ich Staub sauge.

6) a) einen
b) Der
c) der
d) des
e) ein
f) eine
g) der
h) Die
i) den
j) Die
k) dem
l) einen
m) eine

7) a) Die Banane ist gelb.
b) Die Milch ist kalt.
c) Der Junge ist langweilig.
d) Das Lied ist furchtbar.

8) a) Heißer
b) Schönes
c) Gute
d) gelbe
e) seltsame
f) kleine
g) moderne

9) a) tolles
   b) junge
   c) jungen
   d) schönen
   e) schnelle
   f) kleinen
   g) interessanten
   h) seltsamen
10) a) Mein
   b) Ihr
   c) meiner
   d) Dein
   e) meiner
   f) seine
   g) unsere
   h) euere
   i) Ihrer
11) a) Welchen
   b) Welches
   c) Jedes
   d) diesen
   e) diesem
12) a) e.g. I run slowly.
   b) e.g. I run badly.
   c) e.g. He talks very loudly.
   d) e.g. You play quite well.
   e) e.g. She drives too fast.
   f) e.g. We speak a bit strangely.
13) a) I sometimes go to the cinema.
   b) I often swim.
   c) Please pay as soon as possible.
   d) Next weekend we are going out.
   e) I eat chocolate now and then.

Pages 185-186 (Quick Questions)

1) a) Hannah ist schneller.
   b) Lena ist die Schnellste.
2) a) Du bist älter.
   b) Er ist der Älteste.
3) a) groß
   b) größer
   c) der Größte
   d) gut
   e) besser
   f) die Besten
   g) nah
   h) näher
   i) das Nächste
4) a) Mia ist weniger groß als Erik.
   b) Jakob ist so groß wie Mia.
   c) Nina ist ebenso groß wie Jakob.
5) a) Maria singt lauter.
   b) Michael singt am lautesten.
6) a) Ich spiele lieber Tennis.
   b) Ich spiele am liebsten Fußball.
7) a) Ich tanze besser.
   b) Ich tanze am besten.
8) a) zu
   b) nach
   c) an
   d) zu
   e) am
   f) auf
   g) Am
   h) im
   i) aus
   j) von
   k) aus
   l) von
   m) seit
9) a) an dem
   b) in dem
   c) in das
   d) zu dem
   e) zu der
   f) bei dem
   g) von dem
   h) an das
10) a) dative
   b) accusative
   c) dative
   d) genitive
   e) accusative
   f) dative
   g) dative
   h) genitive
11) a) sie
   b) er
   c) es
   d) sie
12) a) du
   b) Sie
   c) ihr
   d) Sie
13) Ich liebe dich.
14) Er liebt mich.
15) Ich liebe ihn.
16) a) ihm
   b) ihr
   c) ihnen
17) Wie sagt man das auf Deutsch?
18) Niemand wohnt da.
19) Wer wohnt da?
20) Was wohnt da?
21) Mit wem wohnst du?
22) a) die
   b) dessen
   c) der
   d) dem
   e) den

Pages 196-197 (Quick Questions)

1) a) Du kaufst Äpfel.
   b) Er kauft Äpfel.
   c) Sie kauft Äpfel.
   d) Wir kaufen Äpfel.
   e) Sie kaufen Äpfel.
   f) Ihr kauft Äpfel.
2) a) ich segle
   b) du segelst
   c) sie segelt
   d) wir segeln
   e) sie segeln
   f) ihr segelt
3) a) ich bin
   b) du bist
   c) er ist
   d) wir sind
   e) ihr seid
   f) sie sind
4) a) ich habe
   b) du hast
   c) er hat
   d) wir haben
   e) ihr habt
   f) sie haben
5) a) er fährt
   b) sie fahren
   c) du isst
   d) ihr esst
   e) er weiß
   f) er heißt
   g) sie trägt
6) e.g. danken, folgen, gehören
   e.g. Wir danken ihm für die Kekse. / Er folgt der Katze. / Das Meerschweinchen gehört meinem Bruder.
7) a) Ich gehe schwimmen.
   b) Er geht kegeln.
   c) Sie geht joggen.
   d) Wir gehen tanzen.
   e) Sie gehen zelten.
   f) Du gehst einkaufen.
8) a) e.g. Ich werde meine Hausaufgaben machen.
   b) e.g. Er wird nach London fahren.
   c) e.g. Sie wird wirklich glücklich sein.
   d) e.g. Du wirst Rugby am Wochenende spielen.
   e) e.g. Sie wird ihren Geburtstag nächste Woche feiern.
   f) e.g. Morgen werden wir ins Kino gehen.
   g) e.g. Ihr werdet am Freitag im Restaurant essen.
   h) e.g. Diesen Sommer werden Sie nach Spanien fliegen.
9) a) e.g. Er hat mein Lieblingsessen gekocht.
   b) e.g. Ich habe das Hotel gebucht.
   c) e.g. Du hast mit der Katze gespielt.
   d) e.g. Ihr habt bei uns gearbeitet.
   e) e.g. Sie haben das Wohnzimmer geputzt.
   f) e.g. Du hast einen guten Film gesehen.
   g) e.g. Ich habe ein interessantes Paket bekommen.
   h) e.g. Wir haben kalte Limonade getrunken.
   i) e.g. Sie haben ihre Turnschuhe vergessen.
   j) e.g. Er hat sie nicht verstanden.
10) a) e.g. Ich bin in die Schule gegangen.
    b) e.g. Ihr seid nach Österreich gefahren.
    c) e.g. Er ist im Park gelaufen.
    d) e.g. Du bist mir durch die Stadt gefolgt.
    e) e.g. Wir sind am Abend gekommen.
    f) e.g. Sie sind zum Mittagessen geblieben.
    g) e.g. Ich bin sehr glücklich gewesen.
    h) e.g. Es ist sehr schnell passiert.
11) a) ich war
    b) du warst
    c) er war
    d) wir waren
    e) ihr wart
    f) sie waren
12) a) I made / did
    b) he came
    c) they drove / went
    d) she helped
    e) you drank
    f) he ate
    g) I saw
    h) you brought
    i) we pulled
    j) it gave / there was
    k) you wrote
    l) she ran
13) a) I had been playing table tennis for three years.
    b) He had been travelling by bus to school for five years.
    c) We had been running on the beach for six months.
    d) You had been staying in the hotel for three weeks.
14) a) e.g. Sie hatte ein schönes Kleid gekauft.
       She had bought a nice dress.
    b) e.g. Ich war nach Schottland gefahren.
       I had been to Scotland.
    c) e.g. Wir hatten unseres Frühstück gegessen.
       We had eaten our breakfast.
    d) e.g. Sie waren uns gefolgt.
       They / you had followed us.
    e) e.g. Du hattest meinen Geburtstag vergessen.
       You had forgotten my birthday.

Pages 210-211 (Quick Questions)

1) a) Go away!
   b) Take the baby.
   c) Give me the book.
   d) Wait here, please.
2) a) Geh um die Ecke!
   b) Kommt herein!
   c) Singen Sie lauter!
   d) Iss dein Essen!
   e) Spiel besser!
   f) Antworten Sie mir!
   g) Folgt mir!
   h) Lies diesen Artikel!

3) a) mich
b) dich
c) sich
d) sich
e) uns
f) euch
g) sich
h) sich

4) e.g. Ich sonne mich.

5) e.g. Er fühlt sich schlecht.

6) a) mir
b) dir
c) sich
d) uns
e) euch
f) sich

7) e.g. Ich wünsche mir einen Hund.

8) e.g. Ich stelle mir einen braunen Hund vor.

9) e.g. Wir haben uns schlecht gefühlt.

10) e.g. Ich habe mir einen Hund gewünscht.

11) a) I arrive at 12 o'clock.
b) Finally the music stops.
c) We should wash up.
d) He took his books with him.
e) She went out to the cinema last night.
f) I am sad because I gave the brown dog back.

12) a) Der Zug muss um zehn Uhr abfahren.
b) Gestern ist der Zug um neun Uhr abgefahren.
c) Gestern fuhr der Zug um neun Uhr ab.
d) Morgen wird der Zug um elf Uhr abfahren.

13) a) e.g. Ich höre nie Rapmusik. / I never listen to rap music.
b) e.g. Ich sehe nicht am Wochenende fern. / I don't watch television at weekends.
c) e.g. Wir schwimmen nicht mehr im Meer. / We don't swim in the sea any more.
d) e.g. Du spielst Klavier nicht gut. / You don't play the piano well.
e) e.g. Sie müssen das Abendessen noch nicht kochen. / You/they don't have to cook dinner yet.

14) a) e.g. Ich habe keinen Kuli.
b) e.g. Ich habe keine Äpfel.
c) e.g. Er treibt nie Sport.
d) e.g. Ihre Augen sind weder blau noch grün.
e) e.g. Das ist nicht mehr richtig.
f) e.g. Du hast keine Erbsen gegessen.
g) e.g. Ich habe noch niemand gesehen.
h) e.g. Du wirst nichts mehr sagen.

15) a) We must buy boiled sausages and cheese.
b) I can't find my hat.
c) You are supposed to take the first street on the left.
d) You/they can sit here in the corner.
e) He wants to work as a vet.
f) Do you like cycling?
g) May I use the toilet?
h) We want to travel to Cologne.

16) a) Wir mussten Bockwürste und Käse kaufen.
b) Ich konnte meinen Hut nicht finden.
c) Ihr solltet die erste Straße links nehmen.
d) Sie konnten hier in der Ecke sitzen.
e) Er wollte als Tierarzt arbeiten.
f) Mochtest du Rad fahren?
g) Durfte ich die Toilette benutzen?
h) Wir wollten nach Köln fahren.

17) I would go to the cinema, but I must do my homework.

18) Mia würde ins Kino gehen, aber sie muss ihre Hausaufgaben machen.

19) e.g. Ich würde Tennis spielen, aber ich habe Kopfschmerzen.

20) a) Ich möchte eine Tasse Tee.
b) Wir möchten eine Tasse Tee.
c) Möchtest du eine Tasse Tee?

21) a) Ich könnte Tennis spielen, aber ich will nicht.
b) Ich sollte Tennis spielen, aber ich will nicht.

22) If you had a brown dog, you would be very happy.

23) a) Es geht mir nicht so gut.
b) Mir geht's gut.
c) Es tut weh.
d) Es regnet.
e) Es gibt viel zu tun.
f) Es tut mir leid.

24) a) ... ohne eine Eintrittskarte zu kaufen.
b) ... um Deutsch zu lernen.
c) ... um meine Freunde zu besuchen.
d) ... um fit zu bleiben.
e) ... ohne den Zoo zu besuchen.

PRACTICE EXAM PAPER ANSWERS

Listening Paper — Page 223

Question	Answer	Mark
1 a)	C	1
1 b)	B	1
1 c)	A	1
2	Number of pitches for tents: **25** Extra charges: **electricity** and TV connections. Leisure facilities: **open air swimming pool** and a playground. Dogs welcome? **No**	1 1 1 1
3	A, C, D (any order)	3
4	B, C (any order)	2
5 a)	A	1
5 b)	C	1
5 c)	C	1
6 a)	B	1
6 b)	B	1
6 c)	C	1
6 d)	B	1
7 a)	D	1
7 b)	B	1
7 c)	A	1
7 d)	G	1
8 a) i)	fifty and sixty year olds / people in their fifties and sixties	1
8 a) ii)	moving to a different town	1
8 b) i)	racism	1
8 b) ii)	that people are nasty towards someone because they are a foreigner	1
9	1: castle 2: needs headache tablets 3: son wants to see lions 4: airport	1 1 1 1
10 a)	B	1
10 b)	A	1
10 c)	A	1
11 a)	first holiday without parents	1
11 b)	watersports	1
11 c)	to eat in evenings / to go to a restaurant	1
12 a)	C	1
12 b)	A	1
12 c)	C	1

Reading Paper — Page 232

Question	Answer	Mark
1 a)	F	1
1 b)	N	1
1 c)	T	1
1 d)	T	1
1 e)	T	1
1 f)	F	1
2	In the following order: C, E, G, D, H	5
3 a)	swimming and angling/fishing	1
3 b)	because there are so many different hobbies and sports to try	1
3 c)	you can get to know new people	1
4 a)	C	1
4 b)	B	1
4 c)	C	1
4 d)	A	1
5 a)	Georg	1
5 b)	Silke	1
5 c)	Wilhelm	1
5 d)	Ralf	1
5 e)	Leonie	1
5 f)	Georg	1
5 g)	Ralf	1
5 h)	Wilhelm	1
6 a)	C	1
6 b)	A	1
6 c)	D	1
6 d)	B	1
7 a)	D	1
7 b)	F	1
7 c)	B	1
7 d)	E	1
8 a)	She's very interested in cars.	1
8 b) (i)	He wants to be a lawyer.	1
8 b) (ii)	So he can earn lots of money	1
8 c)	He finds them quite easy.	1
8 d)	So he can decide later what he wants to do with his life.	1
8 e)	She wants to be a doctor.	1

Speaking Assessment — Page 243
Mark Scheme

It is very difficult to mark the speaking exam yourself because there isn't one 'right' answer for any of the questions. We've given sample answers for the tasks on the next page, but they're just there to give you an idea of what you could say.

Ideally you need to record the whole exam, and then use a dictionary or, even better, get someone who's really good at German to go back over it, to help you mark how well you did, using the mark schemes given here. That will give you a rough guide, but you really need a teacher, who knows the exam board's mark scheme well and has very good knowledge of the German language, to mark it properly.

The speaking tasks don't have a specific mark scheme because each person will say different things, so you can't just have one set of acceptable answers. Instead, they're marked against a series of criteria, which will be something like the ones below (Communication, Range and Accuracy of Language, and Pronunciation and Intonation). In this mark scheme, Communication is marked out of 15, Range and Accuracy of Language is marked out of 10, and Pronunciation and Intonation is marked out of 5.

Each of your two speaking tasks should be marked using these criteria, to give you a total mark out of 60 for the two tasks.

Communication	
13-15	You answer all the questions, including unpredictable and open-ended ones, fully and confidently. You speak clearly and fluently, with little or no hesitation, and interact very well with the teacher. You give detailed information, and develop and explain your ideas and points of view. You can give relevant information without being prompted, and sometimes take control of the conversation.
10-12	You answer the questions fully, and give extra information for most of them, without going off-topic. You speak confidently with little hesitation, and interact well. You explain and justify some of your opinions without difficulty.
7-9	You answer most of the questions, giving the required information. You at least attempt to answer any unpredictable questions. You give some opinions, but don't explain them all. You sometimes hesitate or have some trouble keeping the conversation going.
4-6	You mainly give only simple pieces of information and opinions, without developing many answers. You hesitate quite a lot, particularly on the unpredictable questions. You need a lot of prompting from the teacher.
1-3	You only give a small amount of relevant information. You answer slowly, hesitate a lot and don't connect your ideas. You need prompting for nearly all the questions.
0	You don't say anything that's relevant to the topic.

Range and Accuracy of Language	
9-10	You use a wide range of vocabulary. You use different tenses correctly and use complex sentences. Any mistakes you make are small, and mainly only when you're using more complex language.
7-8	You use a good range of vocabulary and sentence structures, and you use different tenses. You make a few mistakes, but always get your meaning across clearly.
5-6	Most of your sentences are simple, but you do attempt some more complicated language. Your vocabulary is straightforward and mostly predictable. You might get some of your tenses mixed up. You make mistakes, but get more right than wrong and usually get your basic message across.
3-4	Almost all your sentences are simple and your vocabulary is limited and repetitive. You make a lot of mistakes, but can still usually make yourself understood.
1-2	You mainly use simple, short phrases or individual words. Your range of vocabulary is poor. You make a lot of mistakes, which often make what you're saying hard to understand.
0	You don't say anything that makes sense or could be easily understood.

Pronunciation and Intonation	
5	Your accent and intonation are consistently good for someone who doesn't speak German as their first language, with only minor errors.
4	Your pronunciation and intonation are generally good with occasional errors.
3	Your pronunciation and accent are mainly accurate, but there are several mistakes. You sometimes sound quite English.
2	There are a lot of pronunciation errors that sometimes make it difficult to tell what you're saying.
1	You sound very English — most of your pronunciation is wrong, and it's hard to understand what you're trying to say.
0	You don't say anything that makes sense or could be easily understood.

Speaking Task 1

Example answer:

Wer ist dein Lieblingsstar im Moment?

Mein Lieblingsstar ist im Moment der Schauspieler Robert Pattinson. Er ist Engländer und ist vierundzwanzig Jahre alt. Er kommt aus London, aber wohnt jetzt in Los Angeles. Er ist ziemlich groß, mit kurzen, braunen Haaren und blaugrauen Augen.

Warum magst du diesen Mensch?

Ich meine, dass er ein sehr begabter Schauspieler ist und auch, dass er erstaunlich gut aussehend ist! Er ist immer modisch gekleidet und sein Haar ist fantastisch — unordentlich, aber ganz cool. Ich finde ihn auch überhaupt nicht eingebildet.

Erzähl mir ein bisschen über seine Karriere bis jetzt.

Also, als er jünger war, hat er als Modell gearbeitet, und später, im Alter von fünfzehn arbeitete er in einem Theater. Danach hat er mehrere kleine Rollen im Film und Theater gespielt. Im Jahre 2005 hat er die Rolle von Cedric Diggory in „Harry Potter und der Feuerkelch" übergenommen. Und drei Jahre später hat er Edward Cullen im Film des Romans „Twilight" gespielt. Es geht um Vampiren und ist auch eine Liebesgeschichte. „Twilight" hat Robert unglaublich berühmt gemacht!

Was für Interessen hat er?

Er spielt Klavier und Gitarre in der Band seiner Schwester, und ist auch Komponist. Er singt und hat einige Lieder selbst für seine Filme aufgenommen. Sportlich ist er auch — Fußball, Skifahren und Snowboarden macht er, obwohl er einmal gesagt hat, dass er lieber Snooker spielte. Er hat Tauchen für seine Rolle in Harry Potter gelernt. Er ist auch Fußballfan — seine Lieblingsmannschaft ist Arsenal.

Was hat er vor, in der Zukunft zu tun?

Hoffentlich hat Robert vor, mehr „Twilight" Filme zu machen. Vielleicht wird er auch mehr Lieder komponieren und nochmal auf der Bühne in einem Theaterstück in London erscheinen.

Ist er ein gutes Vorbild für junge Leute?

Ja, er ist ein gutes Vorbild für junge Leute, weil er sportlich ist und keine Drogen macht. Er raucht auch nicht und er ist nicht eingebildet.

Speaking Task 2

Example answer:

Was hast du mit deiner Familie oder mit deinen Freunden neulich gefeiert?

Im Sommer bin ich sechzehn geworden und ich habe eine Party gemacht. Normalerweise gehe ich nur mit Freunden aus, vielleicht ins Kino oder zur Pizzeria, aber dieses Jahr war es ein bisschen anders, weil ich sechzehn geworden bin.

Wer hat an diesem Fest teilgenommen?

Meine Eltern waren sicher da, aber auch mein älterer Bruder und seine Frau, die schwanger ist. Mein Onkel und meine Tante waren bei meinen Kusinen zu Besuch, also ist die ganze Familie angekommen. Meine Urgroßmutter, die schon zweiundneunzig ist, und meine Großeltern waren da. Meine Freunde sind erst am Abend angekommen. Ich habe viele Geschenke gekriegt und das hat viel Spaß gemacht.

Wo hat das Fest stattgefunden?

Zu Mittag haben wir in einem Restaurant gegessen. Am Nachmittag sind wir im Park spazieren gegangen, weil es so schönes Wetter gab. Dann habe ich geholfen, das Festzelt im Garten aufzustellen, damit meine Freunde und ich eine Party haben konnten.

Was habt ihr gemacht?

Wir haben im Restaurant gegessen und das Essen hat sehr gut geschmeckt. Der Kellner hat alles sehr schnell zum Tisch gebracht. Am Nachmittag nachdem wir spazieren gegangen sind, haben wir Eis gegessen oder Kaffee und Kuchen genommen. Am Abend haben wir ohne Eltern getanzt, Musik gehört und geplaudert. Das war fantastisch.

Ist etwas Komisches oder Ungewöhnliches passiert?

Meine Urgroßmutter hat sich entschieden, mit uns zu tanzen, und hat einen Walzer gemacht. Das war ein bisschen schwer, weil wir Heavy-Metal am meistens gehört haben. Mein Freund, Chris, hat mit ihr getanzt und das war ganz nett von ihm.

Was wirst du nächstes Jahr feiern?

Nächstes Jahr werden wir hoffentlich die Taufe meiner Nichte oder meines Neffen und die Silberhochzeit meiner Eltern feiern.

Wie würdest du feiern, wenn du viel Geld hättest?

Wenn ich viel Geld hätte, würde ich ein Privatflugzeug mieten, und mit meiner Familie und meinen Freunden nach Paris fliegen, wo wir die Sehenswürdigkeiten besichtigen könnten und dann würde ich in die Karibik fliegen und mich den ganzen Tag am Strand sonnen.

Writing Assessment — Page 248
Mark Scheme

Like with the speaking assessment, it is very difficult to mark the writing assessment yourself because there isn't one 'right' answer for any of the questions. There are example answers on the next page to give you an idea of what you could write for these tasks.

Make sure that you complete both tasks in exam conditions and stick to the time limit. Afterwards, you can use a dictionary or get someone who's really good at German to go back over it, to help you mark how well you did, using the mark schemes given here. That will give you a rough guide, but you really need a teacher, who knows the exam board's mark scheme well and has very good knowledge of the German language, to mark it properly.

The writing tasks don't have a specific mark scheme because each person will write different things, so you can't just have one set of acceptable answers. Instead, they're marked against a series of criteria, which will be something like the ones below (Communication and Content, Range and Use of Language, and Accuracy). In this mark scheme, Communication and Content is marked out of 15, Range and Use of Language is marked out of 10, and Accuracy is marked out of 5.

Each of your two writing tasks should be marked using these criteria, to give you a total mark out of 60 for the two tasks.

	Communication and Content
13-15	You've answered all parts of the question fully, and your meaning is always clear. You can describe things, write about what happened, give your own opinions and justify them. Your writing has a clear structure and all your ideas are linked together. Overall, it's a nice piece of writing to read.
10-12	You've answered almost all parts of the question fully, giving lots of information. You've only left out minor things and almost everything you've written is relevant. You can explain your ideas and give and justify your own point of view. Overall, your answer might be either a bit simplistic or over-ambitious.
7-9	You've answered most parts of the question, although you may have missed a few things out or written some things that are irrelevant. You can describe things and give and develop your opinions, and you've tried to link your ideas together. It might be hard to understand some of what you've written when you've tried to use complex language.
4-6	You mainly give only simple pieces of information and basic opinions, such as likes/dislikes, although you've tried to develop some of your ideas. You've left out quite a lot of information, and lots of what you've written is irrelevant or repeated. It's just about possible to understand what you've written.
1-3	You've only given a very small amount of relevant information, and your sentences aren't linked together. A native German person wouldn't really be able to understand what you've written.
0	You haven't written anything that's relevant to the topic.

	Range and Use of Language
9-10	You use a wide range of vocabulary and structures, and you write longer sentences accurately. You use different tenses correctly, and can also use things like superlatives, negatives and object pronouns.
7-8	You use a good range of vocabulary and sentence structures, and most of your longer sentences are accurate. You've tried to use a variety of tenses and object pronouns.
5-6	You've used some variety of words and structures, including some correctly linked and/or longer sentences. You've included a range of adjectives and adverbs.
3-4	You've used simple structures and pre-prepared sentences to give a basic answer to the question. You've used some adjectives, but have often made mistakes when using different tenses.
1-2	Most of the language you've used is not relevant to the question. You don't really understand sentence structure, but some of the words you've written are correct.
0	You haven't written anything that makes sense or could be easily understood.

	Accuracy
5	Your writing is very accurate, although it might have occasional, minor errors. Nearly all of your spellings, verb forms, genders and agreements are correct.
4	Generally accurate. Most spellings, verb forms and genders correct. Most mistakes are in longer sentences.
3	Your writing is quite accurate, except in more complex sentences. Most of your verb forms are correct, and it's still easy to understand what you mean.
2	There are a few correct phrases, but also lots of misspelt words, and errors with genders and verb forms which make it hard to understand what you're trying to say.
1	Very few, if any, of your verb forms are correct, and there are many incorrect spellings and genders. The large number of mistakes makes your work very hard to understand.
0	You haven't written anything that makes sense or could be easily understood.

Writing Task 1

Example answer:

Herzlich Willkommen in meiner Stadt! Die Stadt heißt Springtown und liegt in Südostengland zwanzig Kilometer von der Küste entfernt. Springtown ist eine ziemlich kleine, historische Marktstadt mit vielen alten Gebäuden, aber auch ein modernes Einkaufszentrum. Glücklicherweise scheint hier die Sonne viel mehr als im Nordengland.

Wegen des schönen Wetters können junge Leute viele Sportarten treiben. Schwimmen, Segeln, Tauchen und Kajak sind alle täglich am Wassersportzentrum verfügbar. Klettern und abseilen kann man auch. In der Stadtmitte gibt es eine neuumgebaute Kegelbahn, wo man Hamburger und Pommes nach einem Spiel in der Imbissstube essen kann. Für die kleineren Kinder gibt es mehrere Spielplätze und Grünanlagen, wo man im Freien Fußball spielen oder picknicken kann.

Erwachsene werden auch viel Spaß haben, während sie in der Altstadt bummeln oder abends im Restaurant essen. Wenn man einkaufen will, kann man entweder in das moderne Einkaufszentrum oder in die gemütlichen, kleinen Geschäfte gehen. Ausflüge an die Küste sind für Eltern und auch ihre Kinder nicht zu verpassen! Ein Kino und ein bequemes Theater haben wir auch.

Es gibt in der Stadtmitte große und kleine Hotels, wo man günstig übernachten kann. Am Stadtrand haben wir einen freundlichen Campingplatz. Es gibt auch viele Ferienwohnungen, wenn man selbst kochen will.

Um innerhalb der Stadt herumzukommen gibt es öffentliche Verkehrsmittel, zum Beispiel Busse und eine U-Bahn. Man sollte eine Wochenkarte kaufen, damit man überall entweder mit dem Bus oder mit der U-Bahn fahren kann. Taxis gibt es auch, obwohl die öffentliche Verkehrsmittel billiger sind.

Es lohnt sich, hier im August zu fahren, weil zu dieser Zeit unser internationales Festival von Jugend und Kultur stattfindet. Hier wird man Konzerte, Theaterstücke, Ausstellungen und Filme finden. Wir werden auch Feuerwerk und Straßenmusikanten haben. Letztes Jahr hatten wir das beste und größte Festival bis jetzt. Jugendliche aus vielen verschiedenen Ländern haben teilgenommen.

Writing Task 2

Example answer:

Nach den Prüfungen habe ich vor in die Oberstufe zu gehen, um Abitur zu machen. Ich möchte Deutsch, Englisch, Mathe und Informatik studieren. Nachher hoffe ich auf die Uni zu gehen, um Fremdsprachen oder Journalismus zu studieren. Ich interessiere mich für Politik und die Gesellschaft und kann im Moment mich nicht entscheiden, ob ich Journalist oder Lehrer sein möchte. Mein Vater ist Grundschuldirektor und meine Mutter war Abteilungsleiterin einer Bank, bevor sie Kinder hatte. Sie wollen, dass ich einen Beruf habe, der gut bezahlt ist.

Im Freien zu arbeiten gefällt mir nicht, weil es immer kalt und nass in Großbritannien ist. Ich würde gern mit anderen Leuten arbeiten, aber ich will nicht mit kleinen Kindern wie mein Vater arbeiten, weil sie mir auf die Nerven gehen würden. Um Arbeitslosigkeit habe ich ein bisschen Angst, deshalb muss ich trotzdem ganz flexibel sein. Bevor ich zu arbeiten beginne, möchte ich ein Jahr im Ausland freinehmen, damit ich meine Sprachkenntnisse verbessern kann. Ich weiß nicht genau wo, vielleicht in Japan oder in Spanien. Ich könnte Englisch lehren.

Ich möchte gern mich heiraten und eine Familie haben, aber ich muss vorher einen guten Job finden, damit ich mir ein Haus leisten kann. Vielleicht werde ich im Ausland wohnen, weil es ein tolles Erlebnis wäre und weil die Arbeitsmöglichkeiten häufiger sind.

Meine Freundin will Abitur nicht machen. Sie sucht lieber eine Lehre bei einem technischen Betrieb, weil sie sich sehr für Ingenieurarbeit interessiert. Sie fährt gern ins Ausland auf Urlaub, aber hat nicht vor, im Ausland zu leben. Ihrer Meinung nach schmeckt das Essen nicht gut! Sie sucht einen Beruf, wo sie Probleme löst, weil sie sehr praktisch ist. Sie denkt nicht, dass sie eine Familie haben wird, weil sie Kinder zu unordentlich findet.

Working Out Your Grade

- *Add up your marks from the Listening, Reading, Speaking and Writing exams.*
- *Look up your total in the table to see what grade you got. If you're borderline, don't push yourself up a grade — the real examiners won't.*
- *These grades will only give you a rough guide — they're no guarantee that you'll get this grade in the real exam. It's really important that you do as much practice and revision as possible to help you get the grade you want.*

Mark (out of 200)	180+	160 – 179	140 – 159	120 – 139	100 – 119	80 – 99	60 – 79	40 – 59	under 40
Average %	90+	80 – 89	70 – 79	60 – 69	50 – 59	40 – 49	30 – 39	20 – 29	under 19
Grade	**A***	**A**	**B**	**C**	**D**	**E**	**F**	**G**	**U**

Important:

- *This is a higher level paper, but it's still good practice if you're preparing for a foundation level exam. Don't be put off if you found some of the questions really difficult — they'll be more straightforward in the actual foundation exam.*

Track 1 Page 18

1) Ich finde meine Eltern prima, weil sie immer Zeit für mich haben. Ich darf meine Rockmusik sehr laut spielen und am Wochenende muss ich erst um elf Uhr nach Hause kommen. Ich brauche ihnen auch nicht viel bei der Hausarbeit zu helfen.

Track 2 Page 18

2) Morgen ist Montag und ich gehe um elf Uhr zum Friseur. Übermorgen, das heißt am Dienstag, treffe ich nachmittags ein paar Freundinnen, um einkaufen zu gehen. Am nächsten Tag muss ich meine Großmutter besuchen. Dann am zweiundzwanzigsten gehe ich am Abend mit meiner Schwester ins Kino. Am Freitag um halb acht gehe ich zum Abendessen ins Restaurant und endlich am Sonnabend ruhe ich mich aus!

Track 3 Page 44

1) Ich habe einen Bruder, der Stefan heißt. Er ist ungeduldig und launisch. Meine Eltern sind geschieden und wir wohnen bei meiner Mutter. Mein Vater wohnt bei seiner neuen Freundin in Kanada.

Track 4 Page 44

2)

M1: Ich bin im Krankenhaus. Gestern habe ich Fußball für die Schulmannschaft gespielt. Ich bin gefallen und habe mir das Bein gebrochen.

F1: Leider bin ich krank. Ich habe Bauchschmerzen und kann heute nicht in die Schule kommen. Ich habe etwas Schlechtes gegessen — wahrscheinlich die Currywurst in der Imbissstube.

Track 5 Page 44

3)

F1: Peter, das Abendessen ist um sechs Uhr. Was isst du gern?

M1: Ich esse fast alles — Hähnchen, Rindfleisch, Wurst, aber Schweinefleisch kann ich nicht leiden.

F1: Und isst du Gemüse?

M1: Ja, ich esse am liebsten Blumenkohl oder Erbsen.

F1: Möchtest du Himbeertorte oder Eis als Nachtisch?

M1: Himbeertorte, bitte.

F1: Trinkst du Cola?

M1: Nein, nur Apfelsaft, bitte.

Track 6 Page 74

1)

M1: Heidi, möchtest du am Freitagabend ausgehen?

F1: Ja, das wäre schön. Was läuft im Kino?

M1: Es gibt nur einen schlechten Gruselfilm. Möchtest du in die Disco gehen?

F1: Nein, leider kann ich nicht gut tanzen. Es gibt eine Rockband im Jugendzentrum.

M1: Ja, das wäre prima. Wo treffen wir uns?

F1: Treffen wir uns um acht Uhr am Marktplatz. Vorher können wir etwas essen.

Track 7 Page 74

2)

M1: Hallo, Fritz hier. Volksmusik gefällt mir nicht. Ich höre klassische Musik auch nicht gern. Am liebsten höre ich Rockmusik. Ich spiele Gitarre in einer Rockband. Ich sehe gern Dokumentarfilme im Fernsehen.

F1: Hallo! Ich heiße Katja. Ich finde historische Romane faszinierend. Ich gehe auch gern ins Kino, aber ich kann Krimis nicht leiden. Ich sehe nur am Wochenende fern. Seifenopern sind meine Lieblingssendungen.

F2: Hallo, mein Name ist Sabine. Ich spiele klassische Musik auf dem Klavier und gehe gern in klassische Konzerte. Ich lese gerne Liebesromane und sehe gerne Liebesfilme. Ich sehe oft fern. Meine Lieblingssendungen sind Quizsendungen.

Track 8 Page 101

1) Example:

M1: Wenn es sonnig ist, fahre ich mit dem Fahrrad in die Schule. Ich fahre Rad, um fit zu bleiben.

a) F1: Im Sommer werde ich mit dem Flugzeug nach Spanien fliegen. Wir möchten zwei Wochen in Barcelona verbringen.

b) M2: Am Wochenende fahre ich mit dem Zug nach Köln oder vielleicht Düsseldorf.

c) F2: In Berlin fahren wir immer mit der U-Bahn, weil es so schnell und billig ist.

Track 9 Page 101

2) **Die Wettervorhersage für heute:**
Norddeutschland: Windig. Ab und zu Schauer. 20 bis 25 Grad. **Ostseeküste:** Teils heiter, teils regnerisch. Temperaturen zwischen 19 und 24 Grad. **Nordseeküste:** Stark bewölkt, später Regenschauer. **Ostdeutschland:** Wolkig, aber meistens trocken. **Mitteldeutschland:** Ziemlich kühl, nebelig. **Westdeutschland:** Mehr Wolken als Sonnenschein, einige Regenschauer. **Südwestdeutschland:** Ein sehr schöner Tag! Heiß und trocken. **Bayern:** Anfangs freundlich, später Gewitter.
Die Wettervorhersage für morgen: Im Westen und Nordwesten wird es bedeckt und kühl sein. Im Süden kommen noch Blitz und Donner hinzu.

Track 10 Page 123

1) a) F1: Nimm die erste Straße rechts und es ist auf der linken Seite.

b) M1: Geh geradeaus, über die erste Kreuzung, über die zweite Kreuzung und dann immer geradeaus. Es ist auf der rechten Seite.

c) F2: Nimm die zweite Straße links, und es ist auf der rechten Seite.

Track 11 Page 123

2) Hallo, ich heiße Karl. Ich wohne in einer großen industriellen Stadt in Norddeutschland, wo die meisten Einwohner Jobs haben. Es gibt eine neue Autofabrik und ein herrliches Einkaufszentrum. Wir haben ausgezeichnete Verkehrsverbindungen. Der Flughafen liegt über zwanzig Kilometer außerhalb der Stadt, es gibt einen Hauptbahnhof, und die Autobahn ist ganz in der Nähe. Die jungen Leute haben sehr gute Freizeitmöglichkeiten — ein modernes Freizeitzentrum mit Hallenbad und Fitnesszentrum, vier Kinos und ein Sportstadion.

Track 12 Page 150

1) Hallo! Hier ist der Bernd. In der Schule ist mein Lieblingsfach Kunst. Das finde ich fantastisch, und ich bin auch sehr kreativ. Außerdem mag ich Naturwissenschaften, weil mein Lehrer so lustig ist. Ich hasse Informatik, weil das für mich nutzlos ist, und weil ich kein Interesse daran habe.

Track 13 Page 150

2)

M1: So, Katja, was hast du vor, nach den Prüfungen zu machen?

F1: Naja, ich möchte ein Jahr frei nehmen und vielleicht in Frankreich wohnen, um kochen zu lernen. Und du, Boris?

M1: Ich möchte auf die Uni gehen, um weiter zu studieren. Was willst du später machen?

F1: Ich werde mein eigenes Restaurant mit französischen Spezialitäten haben.

M1: Prima! Ich werde Tierarzt sein.

Track 14 Page 224

1) Also, ich wohne in Salzkotten in Westdeutschland. Ich wohne hier seit drei Jahren. Es gefällt mir, in Salzkotten zu wohnen, weil meine Freunde ganz in der Nähe von mir sind. Aber vorher habe ich in Hamburg gewohnt und ich habe das besser gefunden. Es gab viel mehr für junge Leute zu tun — Kinos, Sportmöglichkeiten, Jugendklubs und so weiter.

Track 15 Page 225

2) Hallo! Leider ist der Campingplatz am Waldsee im Moment unerreichbar. Wollen Sie vielleicht ein bisschen über unseren Campingplatz erfahren? Wir haben hier Plätze für zehn Wohnwagen und fünfundzwanzig Zelte. Pro Nacht kostet es pro Person sieben Euro fünfzig, und für Kinder von zwei bis vierzehn vier Euro. Strom und TV-Anschluss sind nicht im Preis inbegriffen. Ein schönes Freibad haben wir auch und einen Spielplatz für unsere jüngeren Gäste. Hunde sind hier leider nicht willkommen. Ein Restaurant und Lebensmittelgeschäft gibt es auch am Platz und Tennis und Golf finden Sie einen Kilometer entfernt. Ideal ist es auch für Rad- und Wandertouren. Bitte hinterlassen Sie Ihre Telefonnummer und Ihren Namen!

Track 16 Page 225

3)

M1: Wir sprechen heute über die Freizeitaktivitäten von Jugendlichen in unserer Stadt. So, guten Abend, Max. Kannst du uns bitte zuerst sagen, was du in deiner Freizeit machst?

M2: Ja, guten Abend. Also, Skifahren finde ich fabelhaft! Zu Weihnachten bin ich mit meiner Familie nach Österreich gefahren und war jeden Tag auf den Skipisten!

[PAUSE]

M1: Und du, Karin, ist Skifahren etwas für dich?

F1: Skifahren ist überhaupt nichts für mich! Das ist todlangweilig, finde ich! Radfahren ist meiner Meinung nach echt klasse! Und es ist auch gesund und umweltfreundlich. Im Sommer fahre ich jedes Wochenende mit meinem Vater Rad.

[PAUSE]

M1: Gut! Und jetzt Leah. Bist du auch sportlich?

F2: Sport halte ich für nötig, aber ziemlich uninteressant. Ich liebe aber Musik — Heavy-Metal bis Country-Musik und alles dazwischen! Ich kann leider kein Instrument spielen, aber ich habe jede Woche eine Gesangstunde. Ich gehe gern in Konzerte.

M1: Vielen Dank!

Track 17 Page 226

4) Ich wohne in einem modernen Wohnblock am Stadtrand. Wir haben drei Schlafzimmer. Ich habe mein eigenes Schlafzimmer, das sehr klein, aber gemütlich ist. Ich habe ein Etagenbett, so dass meine Freunde übernachten können. In meinem Schlafzimmer gibt es auch einen ganz unordentlichen Kleiderschrank, einen Sessel und eine ziemlich moderne Lampe. Ich finde mein Schlafzimmer sehr bequem, und ich mag es, weil ich darin ganz allein sein kann, wenn ich will. Leider gibt es keinen Platz für einen Fernseher oder Computer.

Track 18 Page 226

5) So, Maria. Komm mal bitte her. Ich habe dein Schulzeugnis heute Morgen bekommen und klar müssen wir ein bisschen darüber sprechen. So, deine Noten, tja, eine Zwei in Englisch hast du bekommen. Das ist ziemlich gut — der Austausch letzten Sommer war eine gute Idee, denke ich. Eine Drei in Mathe — Maria, du musst um Hilfe bitten. Und jetzt Biologie, oje, oje — hier hast du nur eine Sechs bekommen. Was hast du während des Unterrichts gemacht? Hast du nur geschlafen?

Track 19 Page 227

6) Einkaufen mach' ich so gern! Ich gehe fast jedes Wochenende in die Stadt einkaufen, und ich habe neulich ein tolles Modegeschäft in der Altstadt gefunden. Letzten Samstag habe ich da einen grüngestreiften Minirock gekauft. Den werde ich mit der neuen Lederjacke tragen, die ich diese Woche kaufen werde, um auf Giselas Party zu gehen. Gisela hat schwarze Jeans gekauft und ein sehr altmodisches weißes Hemd. Ich finde es wichtig, richtig individuell zu sein, also kaufe ich nur ungewöhnliche Klamotten. Gisela aber nicht!

Track 20 Page 228

7) **a) F1:** Ich bin Lisa und ich möchte mich einmal verloben und ein oder zwei Jahre später heiraten. Aber davor möchte ich Mathe und Informatik an der Uni studieren.

b) M1: Hier ist der Christian. Ich hoffe, einmal Rechtsanwalt zu werden. Ich möchte im Ausland arbeiten und auch eine Familie haben. Andere Pläne kann ich mir nicht vorstellen.

c) M2: Ich heiße Thomas. Im Moment weiß ich nicht genau, was ich in der Zukunft machen werde. Vor allem will ich einen Beruf, der nicht zu stressig ist. Mein Vater ist vor einem Jahr an einem Herzschlag gestorben. Und das will ich für mich nicht.

d) F2: Mein Name ist Sophia. Ich würde gerne Krankenschwester werden, aber die Ausbildung ist ziemlich lang und meine Mutter ist total dagegen, weil es so schlecht bezahlt ist. Vielleicht werde ich eine Lehre in einer Bank machen.

Track 21 Page 229

8)

M1: Arbeitslosigkeit ist ein großes Problem in unserer Stadt. Nicht nur junge Leute, sondern auch die Fünfzig- und Sechzigjährigen sind arbeitslos. Einige meiner Schulkameraden haben vor, in eine andere Stadt umzuziehen. Das wäre sehr schade!

F1: Ich meine, dass Rassismus ein größeres Problem in unserer Gesellschaft ist. Hier leben viele Leute aus aller Welt und es ist ganz unfair, böse auf sie zu sein, nur weil sie Ausländer sind. Die Gleichheit sollte die Norm sein.

Track 22 Page 229

9)

F1: Wie komme ich am besten zum Schloss, bitte? Ich muss unbedingt den alten Turm besichtigen! Ich möchte einige Fotos von oben machen.

M1: Wo ist die nächste Apotheke, bitte? Ich brauche dringend Kopfschmerztabletten! Ich kann es nicht mehr aushalten.

F2: Gibt es hier in der Nähe einen Zoo? Mein Sohn möchte die Löwen sehen. Das sind seine Lieblingstiere.

M2: Ich bin hier fremd. Wie weit ist es zum Flughafen? Mein Flug geht in zwei Stunden. Soll ich ein Taxi oder den Bus nehmen?

Track 23 Page 230

10)

M1: Guten Abend. Ich möchte einen Tisch für fünf Personen, bitte auf der Terrasse mit Blick auf die Berge. Und schnell bitte. Ich habe einen Termin.

F1: Guten Tag. Ich muss Ihnen sagen, dass ich Vegetarierin bin. Was haben Sie als Hauptgericht? Hoffentlich haben Sie eine große Auswahl.

M2: Ich muss unbedingt mit dem Geschäftsführer sprechen. Ich möchte mich beschweren und mein Geld zurück haben. Die Suppe ist nicht nur kalt, sondern auch viel zu salzig.

Track 24 Page 230

11) Letztes Jahr bin ich zum ersten Mal ohne meine Eltern in Urlaub gefahren. Ich bin mit Freunden nach Frankreich gefahren, und wir haben auf einem großen Campingplatz übernachtet.

[PAUSE]

Auf diesem Campingplatz konnte man verschiedene Wassersportarten machen, zum Beispiel Kajakfahren, Windsurfen, Segeln. Ich bin Windsurfen gegangen — das war echt spitze — und meine Freundin, Karin, hat Kajakfahren ausprobiert. Das hat sie nicht so gut gefunden, weil sie ziemlich viel Angst im tiefen Wasser hatte.

[PAUSE]

Abends haben wir entweder in der Küche auf dem Campingplatz zusammen gekocht oder sind ins Dorf gegangen, wo es einige kleine Restaurants gab. Wir haben das nicht so oft gemacht, weil das ziemlich teuer war. Aber es war praktisch.

Track 25 Page 231

12) Vor kurzem hat mein Großvater einen Computerkurs gemacht. Er ist schon achtzig und jetzt hat er auch einen Laptop gekauft. Er surft im Internet und hat eine Flugreise nach Kanada sehr preiswert online gebucht. Seine Schwester wohnt in Kanada und er will sie besuchen. Er hat ihr schon viele E-Mails geschickt und hat mich gefragt, wie das alles mit MSN geht! Lebensmitteleinkaufen macht er auch online und Fotos kann er hoch- und herunterladen. Als nächstes hat er vor, ein Online-Tagebuch für seine Enkelkinder zu schreiben. Er benutzt auch ein Online-Netzwerk, um in Kontakt mit seinen alten Kameraden zu bleiben. So was!

German–English Dictionary

KEY

m/f/n/pl: a masculine, feminine, neuter or plural noun — see p158-160
(-n), (-e) etc.: add whatever is in the brackets to make the plural
(-): plural is the same as singular (add nothing)
(-̈): put an umlaut on the stressed vowel to make the plural, e.g. Apfel → Äpfel
v: a verb — see p187
v sep: separable verb — splits into two words in the present and some other tenses — see p201-202 (verbs not labelled 'sep' are inseparable)
v ir: irregular verb (its forms are irregular in some tenses and persons, e.g. sein: ich bin)
adj: adjective — see p169-171 (has to agree with the noun it describes)
adv: adverb — see p172 (describes a verb or adjective)
prep: preposition — see p177-179 (connects the verb to a place, thing or person: 'to', 'for', 'with' etc.)
pron: pronoun — see p180-184 (replaces a noun: e.g. 'he', 'me')
conj: conjunction — see p165-166 (connects two parts of a sentence, e.g. 'but')
+ acc/gen/dat: a noun following the word should be in the accusative, genitive or dative case — see p156-157

A

ab prep + dat *from*
ab und zu *from time to time*
abbestellen v sep *to cancel*
Abend m (-e) *evening*
Abendessen n (-) *dinner, evening meal*
abends adv *in the evening*
Abenteuerfilm m (-e) *adventure film*
aber conj *but, however*
abfahren v sep ir *depart*
Abfahrt f (-en) *departure*
Abfall m (no pl) *rubbish*
Abfalleimer m (-) *rubbish bin*
abfliegen v sep ir *to take off (plane)*
Abflug m (-̈e) *take-off, departure*
Abgase n pl *exhaust gases, emissions*
abgesehen von adv *apart from*
abhängen von v sep ir *to depend on (something/one)*
abhängig adj *dependent*
abholen v sep *to collect, to meet*
Abitur n *equivalent of A-level(s)*
Abiturient/in m/f (-en/-nen) *A-level student*
abschließen v sep ir *to shut/lock, to end (studies)*
Abschluss m (-̈e) *end, final exams*
Abschlusszeugnis n (-se) *school leaving certificate*
abspülen v sep *to wash up*
Abteil n (-e) *compartment*
Abteilung f (-en) *department, section*
abtrocknen v sep *to dry up*
abwaschen v sep ir *to wash up*
Acker m (-̈) *field*
ADAC (= Allgemeiner Deutscher Automobil-Club) m *German version of AA/RAC*
Ader f (-n) *blood vessel*
Adresse f (-n) *address*
Aerobics machen *to do aerobics*
Affe m (-n) *monkey*
Afrika n *Africa*
Afrikaner/in m/f (-/-nen) *African person*
afrikanisch adj *African*
AG (= Aktiengesellschaft) f *PLC/Ltd.*
Aggression f (-en) *aggression*
ähnlich adj *similar*
Ahnung f (-en) *idea, suspicion, hunch*
AIDS n *AIDS*
Akte f (-n) *file, record*
Aktentasche f (-n) *briefcase*
aktiv adj *active*
Aktivität f (-en) *activity*
aktuell adj *current*
akzeptieren v *accept*
Alkohol m (-e) *alcohol*
alkoholfrei adj *non-alcoholic*
Alkoholiker/in m/f (-/-nen) *alcoholic*
alkoholisch adj *alcoholic*
Alkoholismus m *alcoholism*
alle pron *all, everyone*
Allee f (-n) *avenue*
allein adj *alone*
alles Gute *all the best*
allgemein adj *general*
Alpen f pl *the Alps*
als conj *as, than, when*
als ob *as if, as though*
also conj *so, therefore*
alt adj *old*
Altenheim n (-e) *old people's home*
Alter n (-) *age*
älter adj *older*
altmodisch adj *old-fashioned*
Altpapier n *waste paper*
am Anfang *at the start*
am Apparat *speaking! (on telephone)*
Amerika n *America*
Amerikaner/in m/f (-/-nen) *American*
amerikanisch adj *American*
Ampel f (-n) *traffic lights*
amüsant adj *entertaining, amusing*
amüsieren sich v *to be amused, to have fun*
an prep + acc/dat *at, to, by*
an Bord m *aboard*
Ananas f (-/-se) *pineapple*
anbauen v sep *to build on, to grow*
anbieten v sep ir *to offer*
andere/r/s adj *other*
anders adj/adv *different(ly)*
anderswo adv *somewhere else*
anderthalb adj *one and a half*
Anfang m (-̈e) *beginning*
anfangen v sep ir *to begin, to start*
Angebot n (-e) *offer*
angeln v *to fish*
Angelrute f (-n) *fishing rod*
angenehm adj *pleasant, enjoyable*
angenommen dass *assuming that*
Angestellte(r) *employee*
Angst haben *to be frightened*
ängstlich adj *anxious*
anhalten v sep ir *to stop (vehicles)*
anklopfen v sep *to knock*
ankommen v sep ir *to arrive*
Ankunft f (-̈e) *arrival*
anmachen v sep *to put on / turn on*
Anmeldung f (-en) *reception (room)*
annehmen v sep ir *to accept, to suppose*
anonym adj *anonymous*
anprobieren v sep *try on (clothes)*
Anrufbeantworter m (-) *answerphone*
anrufen v sep ir *to phone*
anschauen v sep *to look at/watch*
ansehen v sep ir *to look at*
Ansichtskarte f (-n) *picture postcard*
Anspitzer m (-) *sharpener*
anspringen v sep ir *to start (cars)*
Antwort f (-en) *answer*
antworten v *to answer*
Anzeige f (-n) *advert (written)*
anziehen sich v sep ir *to put on, to get dressed*
Anzug m (-̈e) *(men's) suit*
Apfel m (-̈) *apple*
Apfelsine f (-n) *orange*
Apotheke f (-n) *pharmacy*
Apotheker/in m/f (-/-nen) *pharmacist*
Apparat m (-e) *machine, telephone*
Appetit m (-e) *appetite*
Aprikose f (-n) *apricot*
April m *April*
Arbeit f (-en) *work*
arbeiten v *to work*
Arbeiter/in m/f (-/-nen) *worker*
Arbeitgeber m (-) *employer*
Arbeitsbedingungen f pl *terms of employment*
Arbeitserfahrung f (-en) *work experience*
arbeitslos adj *unemployed*
Arbeitslosigkeit f *unemployment*
Arbeitspraktikum n *work experience*
Arbeitszeit f (-en) *working hours*
Arbeitszimmer n (-) *study*
Architekt/in m/f (-en/-nen) *architect*
ARD *German television company*
ärgerlich adj *annoying (thing/event)*
ärgern sich v *to get angry*
arm adj *poor*
Armband n (-̈er) *bracelet*
Armbanduhr f (-en) *wristwatch*
Armee f (-n) *army*
Ärmelkanal m *the English Channel*
Armut f *poverty*
Art f (-en) *kind, sort, type*
artig adj *well-behaved*
Arzt/Ärztin m/f (-̈e/-nen) *doctor*
Asien n *Asia*
atmen v *to breathe*
Atmosphäre f (-n) *atmosphere*
attraktiv adj *attractive*
auch adv *also*
auf prep + acc/dat *up, on*
auf dem Lande *in the country*
auf die Nerven gehen *to get on one's nerves*
auf diese Weise *in this way*
Auf Wiederhören! *Goodbye! (phone)*
Auf Wiedersehen! *Goodbye!*
Aufenthalt m (-e) *stay*
Aufenthaltsraum m (-̈e) *games room*
Aufgabe f (-n) *exercise / task*
aufgeben v sep ir *to give up*
aufhören v sep *to stop (doing something)*
aufmachen v sep *to open*
aufnehmen v sep ir *to pick up / to receive / to record*
aufpassen v sep *to pay attention, watch out*
aufpassen auf v sep *to look after*
aufräumen v sep *to tidy up / clear away*
aufregend adj *exciting*
aufs Land *to the country*
Aufschnitt m (-e) *cold cut meat*
aufstehen v sep ir *to get up*
aufwachen v sep *to wake up*
Aufzug m (-̈e) *lift (elevator)*
Auge n (-n) *eye*
Augenblick m (-e) *moment*
August m *August*
Aula f (Aulen) *school hall*
aus prep + dat *out of*
ausbilden v sep *to train*
Ausbildung f (-en) *training*
Ausfahrt f (-en) *departure / exit*
Ausflug m (-̈e) *trip, excursion*
ausführen v sep *to take out*
ausfüllen v sep *to fill in (form)*
Ausgang m (-̈e) *exit*
ausgeben v sep ir *to spend (money), to give out*
ausgehen v sep ir *to go outside*
ausgezeichnet adj *excellent*
auskommen mit v sep ir *to get on with*
Auskunft f (-̈e) *information*
Ausland n *abroad*
Ausländer/in m/f (-/-nen) *foreigner*
ausländisch adj *foreign*
ausleihen v sep ir *to lend*
ausmachen v sep *to turn off*
auspacken v sep *unpack*
ausrichten v sep *pass on (message)*
ausruhen sich v sep *to have a rest*
Ausrüstung f (-en) *equipment*
aussehen v sep ir *to look (appearance)*
außen adv *outside*
außer prep + dat *except for*
außerdem adv *moreover, as well*
außerhalb prep + gen *outside*
aussetzen v sep *to abandon*
Aussicht f (-en) *view, prospect*
aussteigen v sep ir *to get out/off*
Ausstellung f (-en) *exhibition*
Austausch m (-e) *exchange*
Australien n *Australia*
Ausverkauf m (-̈e) *sale*
ausverkaufen v sep *to sell out*
ausverkauft adj *sold out*
Auswahl f (-en) *choice, selection*
Ausweis m (-e) *ID card*
ausziehen sich v sep ir *to get undressed*
Auto n (-s) *car*
Autobahn f (-en) *motorway*
Autofähre f (-n) *car ferry*
Automat m (-en) *machine*
Autovermietung f (-en) *car rental firm*

B

babysitten v *to baby sit*
Bach m (-̈e) *stream*
backen v ir *to bake*
Bäcker/in m/f (-/-nen) *baker*
Bäckerei f (-en) *bakery*
Backofen m (-̈) *oven*
Backstein m (-e) *brick*
Bad n (-̈er) *bath*
Badeanzug m (-̈e) *swimming costume*
Badehose f (-n) *swimming trunks*
baden v *to have a bath, to bathe / swim*
Badeort m (-e) *seaside resort*
Badetuch n (-̈er) *bath towel*
Badewanne f (-n) *bathtub*
Badezimmer n (-) *bathroom*
Badminton n *badminton*
Bahn f (-en) *railway*
Bahnhof m (-̈e) *station*
Bahnsteig m (-e) *platform*
bald adv *soon*
Balkon m (-e or -s) *balcony*
Ball m (-̈e) *ball*
Banane f (-n) *banana*
Band f (-s) *band, group*
Bank f (-en) *bank*
Bankkarte f (-n) *bank card*
Bär m (-en) *bear*
Bargeld n *cash*
Bart m (-̈e) *beard*
basteln v *to make (craft)*
Batterie f (-n) *battery*
Bauarbeiter/in m/f (-/-nen) *building worker/labourer*
Bauch m (-̈e) *stomach / tummy*
bauen v *to build*
Bauer/Bäuerin m/f (-n/-nen) *farmer*
Bauernhaus n (-̈er) *farmhouse*
Bauernhof m (-̈e) *farm*
Baum m (-̈e) *tree*
Baumwolle f *cotton*
Bayern n *Bavaria*
Beamte(r) *official, civil servant*
beantworten v *answer*
bedecken v *to cover*
bedeckt adj *covered, overcast*
bedienen v *to serve*
Bedienung f (-en) *service*
bedrohen v *to threaten / endanger*
bedürftig adj *needy*
beeilen sich v *to hurry up*
beenden v *to end*
befehlen v ir *to order / command*
befinden sich v ir *to be located / situated*
befriedigend adj *satisfactory*
begegnen v *to meet*
Begeisterung f (-) *enthusiasm*
Beginn m *beginning*
beginnen v ir *to begin*
begleiten v *to accompany*
begrüßen v *to greet*
behalten v ir *to keep*
behandeln v *to treat*
Behandlung f (-en) *treatment*
bei prep + dat *near, with, next to*
beide pron *both*
beiliegend adj *enclosed*
Bein n (-e) *leg*
Beispiel n (-e) *example*
beitragen (zu) v sep ir *contribute (to)*
bekommen v ir *to receive*
beleidigen v sep *to insult / offend*
Belgien n *Belgium*
Belgier/in m/f (-/-nen) *Belgian*
belgisch adj *Belgian*
beliebt adj *popular*
bemerken v *to notice, observe*
benachteiligen v *to put at a disadvantage, to discriminate against*
benutzen v *to use*
Benutzer/in m/f (-/-nen) *user*
Benzin n *petrol*
bequem adj *comfortable*
beraten v ir *to advise*
bereit adj *ready*
Berg m (-e) *mountain*
Bericht m (-e) *report*
Beruf m (-e) *job, occupation*
Berufsausbildung f *vocational training*
Berufsberater/in m/f (-/-nen) *careers advisor*
Berufsschule f (-n) *vocational school, technical college*
berufstätig adj *working*
berühmt adj *famous*
berühren v *to touch*
beschäftigt adj *busy*
beschließen v ir *to decide / resolve*
beschreiben v ir *to describe*
beschweren sich v *to complain*
besetzt adj *occupied, engaged*
besichtigen v *to visit, to see (sights)*
besitzen v ir *to own*
Besitzer/in m/f (-/-nen) *owner*
besonders adv *especially*
besprechen v ir *to discuss*
besser adj/adv *better*
Besteck n (-e) *cutlery*
bestehen v ir *pass (exam)*
bestehen aus v ir *to consist of*
bestellen v *to order*
bestimmt adv *definitely*
bestrafen v *to punish*
Besuch m (-e) *visit*
besuchen v *to visit*
Betreff m (-e) *subject (of letter / e-mail)*
betreten v ir *to enter, to step / walk on*
Betrieb m (-e) *firm, company*
Betriebspraktikum n (-praktika) *work experience*
betrunken adj *drunk*
Bett n (-en) *bed*
Betttuch n (-̈er) *sheet*
Bettwäsche f *bed linen*

prep: *preposition* **pron: pronoun** **conj**: *conjunction* **bits in brackets**: *plural ending* **(-̈)**: *plural — add umlaut*

German–English Dictionary

bevor conj *before, while*
bevorzugen v *to prefer*
bewegen v *to move*
bewerben sich um v ir *to apply for*
Bewerbung f (-en) *application*
bewölkt adj *cloudy*
Bewusstsein n *consciousness*
bezahlen v *to pay (for)*
Bezahlung f (-en) *payment*
Bezug m (¨-e) *reference*
(in Bezug auf = *with regard to, concerning)*
BH (= Büstenhalter) m *bra*
Bibliothek f (-en) *library*
Bibliothekar/in m/f (-e/-nen) *librarian*
Biene f (-n) *bee*
Bier n (-e) *beer*
bieten v ir *offer*
Bild n (-er) *picture*
Bildschirm m (-e) *screen*
billig adj *cheap*
Biologie f *biology*
biologisch adj *biological, organic*
Biomüll m *organic waste*
Birne f (-n) *pear, light bulb*
bis prep + acc *until*
bis bald/morgen/später *see you soon/tomorrow/later*
bisschen (ein) adj/adv *a little bit*
bitte *here you are, please*
bitte schön *you're welcome*
bitten v ir *to ask*
bitten um v ir *to ask for*
Blatt n (¨-er) *leaf, sheet of paper*
blau adj *blue*
Blei n (-e) *lead (metal)*
bleiben v ir *to stay, to remain*
bleifrei adj *unleaded*
Bleistift m (-e) *pencil*
Blick m (-e) *look, glance, view*
Blitz m (-e) *lightning*
blitzen v *to flash with lightning*
Blockflöte f (-n) *recorder*
blöd adj *silly, stupid*
Blödsinn m *stupidity, rubbish*
Blume f (-n) *flower*
Blumenhändler/in m/f (-e/-nen) *florist*
Blumenkohl m (no pl) *cauliflower*
Blumenladen m (¨) *florist's shop*
Bluse f (-n) *blouse*
Blut n *blood*
Bockwurst f (¨-e) *boiled sausage*
Boden m (¨) *ground, floor*
Bodensee m *Lake Constance*
Bohne f (-n) *bean*
Bonbon n or m (-s) *sweet*
Boot n (-e) *boat*
böse adj *nasty, angry*
Bowling n *(ten-pin) bowling*
Brand m (¨-e) *fire*
Braten m (-) *joint, roast meat*
braten v ir *to roast*
Bratkartoffeln f pl *fried potatoes*
Bratpfanne f (-n) *frying pan*
Bratwurst f (¨-e) *fried sausage*
Brauch m (¨-e) *custom*
brauchen v *need*
braun adj *brown*
BRD (= Bundesrepublik Deutschland) f *(Federal Republic of) Germany*
brechen v ir *to break*
breit adj *broad, wide*
Bremse f (-n) *brake*
bremsen v *to brake*
Brennstoff m (-e) *fuel*
Brief m (-e) *letter*
Brieffreund/in m/f (-e/-nen) *pen friend*
Briefkasten m (¨) *postbox*
Briefmarke f (-n) *stamp*
Brieftasche f (-n) *wallet*
Briefträger/in m/f (-/-nen) *postman/woman*
Briefumschlag m (¨-e) *envelope*
Brille f (-n) *glasses*
bringen v ir *to bring*
Brite/Britin m/f (-n/-nen) *Briton*
britisch adj *British*
Broschüre f (-n) *brochure, leaflet*
Brot n (-e) *bread, loaf of bread*
Brötchen n (-) *bread roll*
Brücke f (-n) *bridge*
Bruder m (¨) *brother*
Brunnen m (-) *well, fountain*
Buch n (¨-er) *book*
buchen v *to book*
Bücherei f (-en) *library*
Bücherregal n (-e) *bookcase*
Buchhandlung f (-en) *bookshop*
Büchse f (-n) *tin, can*
Buchstabe m (-n) *letter (of alphabet)*
buchstabieren v *to spell*
Bude f (-n) *stall, booth*
Bügeleisen n (-) *iron*
bügeln v *to iron*
Bühne f (-n) *stage*
Bundesstraße f (-n) *Federal road (= A-road)*
bunt adj *bright, multi-coloured*
Burg f (-en) *castle, fort*
Bürgersteig m (-e) *pavement*
Büro n (-s) *office*
bürsten v *to brush (e.g. hair)*
Bus m (-se) *bus*
Busbahnhof m (¨-e) *coach station*
Bushaltestelle f (-n) *bus stop*
Büstenhalter m (-) *bra*
Butterbrot n (-e) *sandwich*

C

Café n (-s) *café*
Campingplatz m (¨-e) *campsite*
Cent m (- or -s) *cent*
Champignon m (-s) *mushroom*
Charakter m (-e) *character*
chatten v *to chat (online)*
Chef/in m/f (-s/-nen) *boss*
Chemie f *chemistry*
chemisch adj/adv *chemical(ly)*
Chips m pl *crisps*
Chor m (¨-e) *choir*
Cola f (-s) *cola*
Computer m (-) *computer*
Computerprogrammierer/in m/f (-/-nen) *computer programmer*
Computerspiel n (-e) *computer game*
Couch f (-s/-en) *couch*
Cousin(e) m/f (-s,-n) *cousin*
Currywurst f (¨-e) *curried sausage*

D

da adv *there*
da drüben *over there*
Dach n (¨-er) *roof*
dafür adv *instead*
dagegen adv *against it/that*
damals adv *then (at that time)*
Dame f (-n) *lady*
damit adv *so that, with that*
Dampfer m (-) *steamer, steamship*
danach adv *after that*
Däne/Dänin m/f (-n/-nen) *Dane*
Dänemark n *Denmark*
dänisch adj *Danish*
dankbar adj *grateful*
danke (schön) *thank you (very much)*
danken v *to thank*
dann adv *then*
das heißt (d.h.) *that is (i.e.)*
das pron *that*
das stimmt *that's right*
dass conj *that*
Datum n (Daten) *date*
dauern v *to last*
DB (= Deutsche Bundesbahn) *German railway company*
Decke f (-n) *roof, ceiling, blanket*
decken v *to lay (e.g. table), to cover*
Delikatessengeschäft n (-e) *delicatessen*
denken v ir *to think*
Denkmal n (¨-er) *monument, memorial*
denn conj *then, than, because*
dennoch adv *nevertheless*
deshalb adv *therefore*
deswegen adv *therefore*
Detail n (-s) *detail*
deutsch adj *German*
Deutsch n *German (language)*
Deutsche(r)/Deutsche m/f *German (person)*
Deutschland n *Germany*
Dezember m *December*
d.h. (= das heißt) *i.e.*
Diät f (-en) *diet*
dicht adj *dense, thick*
dick adj *fat, thick*
Dieb m (-e) *thief*
Diebstahl m (¨-e) *theft*
Diele f (-n) *hallway*
Dienstag m *Tuesday*
diese/r/s pron *this*
Diesel m *diesel*
Ding n (-e) *thing*
Diplom n (-e) *degree, diploma*
direkt adj/adv *direct(ly)*
Direktor/in m/f (-en/-nen) *headteacher, director*
Disko f (-s) *disco*
Diskothek f (-en) *disco*
Diskriminierung f (-en) *discrimination*
diskutieren v *to discuss*
Disziplin f (-en) *discipline*
doch conj *yes (in opposition to what has been said before)*
Dokumentarfilm m (-e) *documentary*
Dom m (-e) *cathedral*
Donau f *the Danube*
Donner m (-) *thunder*
donnern v *to thunder*
Donnerstag m *Thursday*
doof adj *stupid*
Doppelbett n (-en) *double bed*
Doppelhaus n (¨-er) *semi-detached house*
Doppelstunde f (-n) *double period*
Doppelzimmer n (-) *double room*
Dorf n (¨-er) *village*
dort adv *there, in that place*
dort drüben adv *over there*
dorthin adv *there (to there)*
Dose f (-n) *tin, can*
Dosenöffner m (-) *tin opener*
Drama n (Dramen) *drama*
draußen adv *outside*
dreckig adj *dirty*
Dreieck n (-e) *triangle*
dreieckig adj *triangular*
drinnen adv *inside*
Drittel n (-) *a third*
drittens adv *thirdly*
Droge f (-n) *drug*
Drogenhändler m (-) *drug dealer*
Drogensüchtige(r) *drug addict*
Drogerie f (-n) *chemist's*
drüben adv *over there*
Druck m (¨-e) *pressure*
drucken v *to print*
drücken v *to press/push*
Drucker m (-) *printer*
dumm adj *stupid*
dunkel adj *dark*
dünn adj *thin*
durch prep + acc *through, by*
durchfallen v sep ir *to fail (exam)*
dürfen v ir *to be allowed to ("may")*
Durst m *thirst*
durstig adj *thirsty*
Dusche f (-n) *shower*
duschen v *to shower*
Dutzend n (-e) *dozen*
dynamisch adj *dynamic*
D-Zug m (¨-e) *express train*

E

eben adj/adv *smooth; just, precisely*
ebenso adv (+ wie) *just as*
echt adj *real, genuine*
Ecke f (-n) *corner*
egal adj/adv *the same*
(Das ist mir egal = *I don't mind)*
egoistisch adj *selfish*
Ehefrau f (-en) *wife*
ehemalig adj *former, previous*
Ehemann m (¨-er) *husband*
Ehepaar n (-e) *married couple*
ehrlich adj *honest, sincere*
Ehrlichkeit f *honesty*
Ei n (-er) *egg*
eigene/r/s adj *own*
eigentlich adj/adv *actual(ly)*
eilen v *to hurry*
eilig adj *in a hurry, hurried*
einander pron *each other, one another*
einatmen v sep *breathe in*
Einbahnstraße f (-n) *one-way street*
einfach adj *easy, single (ticket)*
Einfahrt f (-en) *entry, arrival (of train)*
Einfamilienhaus n (¨-er) *detached house*
Eingang m (¨-e) *entrance*
eingehen v sep ir *to enter*
einige pron *a few, some*
Einkäufe m pl *shopping (purchases)*
einkaufen v sep *to shop*
einkaufen gehen v sep *to go shopping*
Einkaufskorb m (¨-e) *shopping basket*
Einkaufsliste f (-n) *shopping list*
Einkaufstasche f (-n) *shopping bag*
Einkaufswagen m (-) *shopping trolley*
Einkaufszentrum n (-zentren) *shopping centre*
einladen v sep ir *invite*
Einladung f (-en) *invitation*
einmal adv *once*
einnehmen v sep ir *to take, to earn, to take up (space)*
einpacken v sep *to pack*
einrichten v sep *to furnish, to fit out*
einsam adj *lonely*
einschlafen v sep ir *to go to sleep*
einschalten v sep *to switch on*
einsteigen v sep ir *get on/in (vehicle)*
einstellen v sep *to put in, to hire, to stop, to adjust*
Eintopf m (¨-e) *stew*
eintreten v sep ir *to enter*
Eintritt m (-e) *entrance, admission charge*
Eintrittsgeld n (-er) *admission charge*
Eintrittskarte f (-n) *entrance ticket*
einverstanden adj *in agreement*
Einwanderer/Einwanderin m/f (-/-nen) *immigrant*
einwerfen v sep ir *break (window), post (letter)*
Einwohner/in m/f (-/-nen) *resident, inhabitant*
Einzelbett n (-en) *single bed*
Einzelkind n (-er) *only child*
einzeln adj *single*
Einzelzimmer n (-) *single room*
einzig adj *only, sole*
Eis n *ice, ice cream*
Eisbecher m (-) *ice cream sundae*
Eisbahn f (-en) *ice rink*
Eisdiele f (-n) *ice cream parlour*
Eisen n (-) *iron*
Eisenbahnlinie f (-n) *railway line*
Eishalle f (-n) *ice rink*
Eis laufen n *ice skating*
ekelhaft adj *disgusting*
Elektriker/in m/f (-/-nen) *electrician*
elektrisch adj *electric(al)*
Elektrogeschäft n (-e) *electrical shop*
Elektroherd m (-e) *electric cooker*
Eltern pl *parents*
E-Mail f (-s) *email*
Empfang m (¨-e) *reception*
Empfänger/in m/f (-/-nen) *recipient*
Empfangschef/in m/f (-s/-nen) *head porter*
Empfangsdame f (-n) *receptionist*
empfehlen v ir *to recommend*
Ende n (-n) *end*
enden v *to end*
endlich adv *at last, finally*
Endspiel n (-e) *final (e.g. sport)*
Energie f (-n) *energy*
eng adj *narrow, tight*
England n *England*
Engländer/in m/f (-/-nen) *English person*
englisch adj *English*
Enkel/in m/f (-/-nen) *grandson/granddaughter*
Enkelkind n (-er) *grandchild*
enorm adj/adv *enormous(ly)*
Ente f (-n) *duck*
entfernt adj *distant*
entlang prep + acc/dat *along*
entscheiden sich v ir *to decide*
entschuldigen sich v *to apologise*
entschuldigen Sie! *excuse me!*
Entschuldigung f (-en) *apology, Excuse me!*
entsetzlich adj *horrible, terrible*
entsorgen v *to dispose of*
entspannen sich v *to relax*
entweder… oder *either… or*
entwerten v *to invalidate (a ticket)*
Erbse f (-n) *pea*
Erdbeere f (-n) *strawberry*
Erde f (-n) *earth*
Erdgeschoss n (-e) *ground floor*
Erdkunde f *geography*
Erdnuss f (¨-e) *peanut*
erfahren adj *experienced*
Erfahrung f (-en) *experience*
Erfolg m (-e) *success*
erfolgreich adj *successful*
Erfrischungen f pl *refreshments*
erfüllen v *to fill, to fulfil*
erhalten v ir *to receive*
erinnern (sich) v *to remind of (to remember)*
erkälten sich v *to catch a cold*
Erkältung f (-en) *a cold*
erkennen v ir *to recognise*
erklären v *to explain, to declare*
erlauben v *to allow*
erleben v *to experience*
Ermäßigung f (-en) *reduction*
ermüdend adj *tiring*
Ernährung f (-) *food, nutrition*
ernst adj *serious*
erreichen v *to reach, achieve*
erschöpft adj *exhausted*
erst adv *first, not before, only then*
erstaunt adj *astonished*
Erste Hilfe f *first aid*
erstens adv *firstly*
erster Klasse *first class*
Erwachsene(r) *adult*
erwarten v *to expect*
erzählen v *to tell*
Erzählung f (-en) *story*
Essecke f (-n) *eating area*
Essen n (-) *food, meal*
essen v *to eat*
Essig m (-e) *vinegar*
Esszimmer n (-) *dining room*
Etage f (-n) *floor, storey*
Etagenbett n (-en) *bunk bed*
Etui n (-s) *case*
etwa adv *about, roughly, approximately*
etwas pron *something*
Euro m (-/-s) *euro*
Europa n *Europe*
Europäer/in m/f (-/-nen) *European*
europäisch adj *European*
Examen n (-/Examina) *examination*
Experiment n (-e) *experiment*

nouns — **m**: *masculine* **f**: *feminine* **n**: *neuter* **pl**: *plural* **v**: *verb* **v sep**: *separable verb* **v ir**: *irregular verb* **adj**: *adjective* **adv**: *adverb*

German–English Dictionary

F

Fabrik f (-en) *factory*
Fach n (-̈er) *subject*
Fähre f (-n) *ferry*
fahren v ir *to go, to drive*
Fahrer/in m/f (-/-nen) *driver*
Fahrgast m (-̈e) *passenger*
Fahrgeld n (-er) *fare*
Fahrkarte f (-n) *ticket*
Fahrkartenautomat m (-en) *ticket machine*
Fahrkartenschalter m (-) *ticket office*
Fahrplan m (-̈e) *timetable*
Fahrpreis m (-e) *fare*
Fahrrad n (-̈er) *bicycle*
Fahrradverleih m (-e) *cycle hire firm*
Fahrradweg m (-e) *cycle path*
Fahrschein m (-e) *ticket*
Fahrstuhl m (-̈e) *lift (elevator)*
Fahrt f (-en) *journey, drive*
fallen v ir *to fall*
fallen lassen v ir *to drop*
falsch adj *wrong, false*
Familie f (-n) *family*
Familienmitglied n (-er) *member of the family*
Familienname m (-n) *surname*
fantastisch adj *fantastic*
Farbe f (-n) *colour*
Fasching m (-e/-s) *(pre-Lent) carnival*
fast adv *almost*
faszinierend adj *fascinating*
faul adj *lazy*
Fax n (-e) *fax*
FCKWs m pl *CFCs*
Februar m *February*
fehlen v *to go wrong, to fail, to miss*
Fehler m (-) *mistake, fault*
Feier f (-n) *party, celebration*
Feierabend m (-e) *evening (leisure time)*
feiern v *to celebrate*
Feiertag m (-e) *holiday*
Feld n (-er) *field*
Fenster n (-) *window*
Ferien pl *holidays*
Ferienhaus n (-̈er) *holiday house*
Ferienwohnung f (-en) *holiday flat*
Fernsehapparat m (-e) *TV set*
Fernsehen n *TV*
fernsehen v ir sep *to watch TV*
Fernseher m (-) *TV set*
Fernsehgerät n (-e) *TV set*
Fernsehraum m (-̈e) *TV room*
fertig adj *ready, finished*
fest adj *solid, firm*
Fest n (-e) *festival, party*
Fett n (-e) *fat*
fettig adj *greasy*
feucht adj *damp*
Feuer n (-) *fire*
Feuerwehr f (-en) *fire brigade*
Feuerwehrmann/frau m/f (-̈er/-en) *firefighter*
Feuerwerk n *fireworks*
Fieber n (-) *fever, temperature*
Film m (-e) *film*
filtern v *to filter*
Filzstift m (-e) *felt-tip pen*
finden v ir *to find*
Finger m (-) *finger*
Firma f (Firmen) *firm, company*
Firmenchef/in m/f (-s/-nen) *company head*
Fisch m (-e) *fish*
Fischgeschäft n (-e) *fishmonger's*
Fitnesszentrum n (-zentren) *fitness centre*
flach adj *flat*
Flamme f (-n) *flame*
Flasche f (-n) *bottle*
Fleisch n *meat*
Fleischer/in m/f (-/-nen) *butcher*
Fleischerei f (-n) *butcher's*
fleißig adj *hard-working*
flexibel adj *flexible*
Fliege f (-n) *fly*
fliegen v ir *to fly*
fliehen v ir *to escape / flee*
Flöte f (-n) *flute*
Flug m (-̈e) *flight*
Flughafen m (-̈) *airport*
Flugzeug n (-e) *aeroplane*
Flur m (-e) *corridor, hallway*
Fluss m (-̈e) *river*
Flussufer n (-) *riverbank*
folgen v *to follow*
Forelle f (-n) *trout*
Form f (-en) *form, shape*
Formular n (-e) *form (to fill in)*
forschen v *to research*
Fortschritt m *progress*
fossil adj *fossil(ised)*
Foto n (-s) *photo*
Fotoapparat m (-e) *camera*
Fotograf/in m/f (-en/-nen) *photographer*
fotografieren v *take a photo*
Frage f (-n) *question*
fragen v *to ask*
Frankreich n *France*
Franzose/Französin m/f (-n/-nen) *French person*
Französisch n *French (language)*
französisch adj *French*
Frau f (-en) *Mrs, woman*
Fräulein(!) n (-) *Miss, young lady (waitress!)*
frech adj *cheeky*
frei adj *free*
Freibad n (-̈er) *(open air) swimming pool*
Freiheit f (-en) *freedom*
Freitag m *Friday*
freiwillig adj *voluntary, optional*
Freiwillige(r) m/f *volunteer*
Freizeit f *free time*
Freizeitaktivität f (-en) *leisure activity*
Freizeitbeschäftigung f (-en) *free time/leisure activity*
Freizeitpark m (-s) *amusement park*
Freizeitzentrum n (-zentren) *leisure centre*
Fremdsprache f (-n) *foreign language*
fressen v ir *(of animals) to eat*
Freude f (-n) *joy*
freuen sich v *to be pleased/happy*
freuen sich auf v + acc *to look forward to*
freuen sich über v + acc *to be pleased about*
Freund/in m/f (-e/-nen) *friend*
freundlich adj *friendly*
Freundschaft f (-en) *friendship*
frieren v ir *to freeze*
Frikadelle f (-n) *meatball, rissole*
frisch adj *fresh*
Friseur/Friseuse m/f (-e/-n) *hairdresser*
Friseursalon m (-s) *hairdresser's salon*
froh adj *happy*
Frohe/Fröhliche Weihnachten! *Happy Christmas!*
Fruchtsaft m (-̈e) *fruit juice*
früh adj *early*
früher adj/adv *former(ly)*
Frühling m (-e) *spring*
Frühstück n (-e) *breakfast*
frühstücken v *to have breakfast*
fühlen sich v *to feel*
führen v *to lead*
Führerschein m (-e) *driving licence*
füllen v *to fill*
Füller m (-) *(fountain) pen*
Fundbüro n (-s) *lost property office*
funktionieren v *to function, work*
für prep + acc *for*
für jetzt *for the moment*
furchtbar adj/adv *terrible/terribly*
Fuß m (-̈e) *foot*
Fußball m (-̈e) *football*
Fußboden m (-̈) *floor*
Fußgänger m (-) *pedestrian*
Fußgängerzone f (-n) *pedestrian zone*
Fußweg m (-e) *footpath*
füttern v *to feed (animals)*

G

Gabel f (-n) *fork*
Gang m (-̈e) *corridor*
Gans f (-̈e) *goose*
ganz adv *completely, quite*
ganztags adj *all day*
Ganztagsjob m (-s) *full-time job*
Ganztagsstelle f (-n) *full-time job*
gar nicht adv *not at all*
Garage f (-n) *garage*
garantieren v *to guarantee*
Gardine f (-n) *curtain*
Garten m (-̈) *garden*
Gärtner/in m/f (-/-nen) *gardener*
Gasherd m (-e) *gas cooker*
Gast m (-̈e) *guest*
Gastfreundschaft f *hospitality*
Gastgeber/in m/f (-/-nen) *host(ess)*
Gasthaus n (-̈er) *guest house, pub*
Gasthof m (-̈e) *inn*
Gaststätte f (-n) *restaurant, pub*
Gebäude n (-) *building*
geben v ir *to give*
Gebiet n (-e) *region, area*
Gebirge n (-) *mountain range*
geboren adj *born, née*
gebraten adj *roast*
Gebrauch m (-̈e) *use, custom*
gebrochen adj *broken*
Geburt f (-en) *birth*
Geburtsdatum n (-daten) *date of birth*
Geburtsort m (-e) *place of birth*
Geburtstag m (-e) *birthday*
geduldig adj/adv *patient(ly)*
Gefahr f (-en) *danger*
gefährlich adj *dangerous*
gefallen v ir *to like, to please*
Gefühl n (-e) *feeling*
gegen prep + acc *against, towards*
Gegend f (-en) *region*
Gegenstand m (-̈e) *object*
Gegenteil n *the opposite*
gegenüber prep + dat *opposite*
Gegenwart f *present (time)*
Gehalt n (-̈er) *salary*
gehen v ir *to go (by foot)*
Gehirn n (-e) *brain*
gehören v *to belong to*
Geige f (-n) *violin*
gekocht adj *cooked*
gekochtes Ei n *boiled egg*
gelb adj *yellow*
Geld n (-er) *money*
Geldschein m (-e) *banknote*
Geldstück n (-e) *coin*
Geldtasche f (-n) *money purse, wallet*
Gelegenheit f (-en) *opportunity*
gelingen v ir *to succeed*
gemein adj *nasty, common*
gemischt adj *mixed*
Gemüse n (-) *vegetable(s)*
Gemüsehändler/in m/f (-/-nen) *greengrocer*
gemütlich adj *comfortable, cosy*
genau adj/adv *exact(ly)*
Genf n *Geneva*
genießen v ir *to enjoy*
genug adj *enough*
geöffnet adj *open(ed)*
Geografie f *geography*
Gepäck n *luggage*
Gepäckaufbewahrung f (-en) *left luggage*
geplant adj *planned*
gerade adj/adv *straight, precisely / just*
geradeaus adv *straight ahead*
Gerät n (-e) *piece of equipment / apparatus*
gerecht adj/adv *just(ly), fair(ly)*
Gericht n (-e) *dish, law-court*
gern adv *with pleasure, willingly*
gern geschehen! *you're welcome, don't mention it*
gern haben v ir *to like*
Geruch m (-̈e) *smell*
Gesamtschule f (-n) *comprehensive school*
gesandt von *sent by*
Geschäft n (-e) *business, shop*
Geschäftsmann/frau m/f (-̈er/-en) *businessman/woman*
geschehen v ir *happen*
Geschenk n (-e) *present (gift)*
Geschichte f (-n) *history, story*
geschieden adj *divorced*
Geschirr n (-e) *dishes, crockery*
Geschirrtuch n (-̈er) *tea towel*
geschlossen adj *closed*
Geschmack m (-̈e) *taste*
Geschwister pl *siblings*
Gesellschaft f (-en) *society*
Gesicht n (-er) *face*
Gespräch n (-e) *conversation, discussion*
gestern adv *yesterday*
gestreift adj *striped*
gesund adj/adv *healthy / healthily*
Gesundheit f *health*
Getränk n (-e) *drink*
getrennt adj/adv *separate(ly), separated*
Gewalt f (-en) *power*
gewaltig adj *huge*
gewinnen v ir *to win*
Gewitter n (-) *thunder storm*
gewöhnen sich an v + acc *to get used to*
Gewohnheit f (-en) *habit*
gewöhnlich adj/adv *usual(ly)*
Gewürz n (-e) *spice*
Gitarre f (-n) *guitar*
Glas n (-̈er) *glass, jar*
glatt adj *smooth, straight (e.g. hair)*
Glatteis n *black ice*
glauben v *to believe/think*
gleich adv *immediately, in a moment*
gleich adj *same, similar, equal*
Gleichheit f (-en) *similarity*
Gleis n (-e) *platform, track*
global adj *global*
Glück n *happiness, luck*
glücklich adj *happy*
GmbH (= Gesellschaft mit beschränkter Haftung) *Ltd.*
Goldfisch m (-e) *goldfish*
goldig adj *sweet, cute*
Gott m (-̈er) *God*
Grad m (-e) *degree, extent*
Gramm n (-/-e) *gram*
Gras n (-̈ er) *grass*
gratis adv *free (of charge)*
gratulieren v *to congratulate*
grau adj *grey*
Grenze f (-n) *border*
Grieche/Griechin m/f (-n/-nen) *Greek*
Griechenland n *Greece*
griechisch adj *Greek*
Grill m (-s) *grill, barbecue*
grillen v *to grill, to barbecue*
Grippe f (-n) *flu*
groß adj *big, tall*
großartig adj *magnificent*
Großbritannien n *Great Britain*
Größe f (-n) *size, height*
Großeltern pl *grandparents*
Großmutter f (-̈) *grandmother*
Großstadt f (-̈e) *city*
Großvater m (-̈) *grandfather*
grün adj *green*
Grund m (-̈e) *ground, reason*
Grundschule f (-n) *primary school*
Gruppe f (-n) *group*
Gruß m (-̈e) *greeting*
Grüß Gott *hello*
gültig adj *valid*
günstig adj *favourable*
Gürtel m (-) *belt*
Gummi n or m (-s) *rubber*
Gurke f (-n) *cucumber*
gut adj/adv *good / well*
gut bezahlt *well paid*
gut gelaunt *in a good mood*
gute Nacht *goodnight*
gute Reise *have a good journey*
guten Abend *good evening*
guten Appetit! *enjoy your meal!*
guten Aufenthalt *enjoy your stay*
guten Tag *hello, good day*
Gymnasium n (Gymnasien) *secondary school for more academic pupils*
Gymnastik f *exercises, gymnastics*

H

Haar n (-e) *hair*
Haarbürste f (-n) *hairbrush*
haben v ir *to have*
Hafen m (-̈) *harbour, port*
Hafenstadt f (-̈e) *port*
Haferflocken f pl *porridge oats*
Hagel m *hail*
hageln v *to hail*
Hähnchen n (-) *chicken*
halb adj/adv *half*
Halbpension f *half board (at hotel)*
Hälfte f (-n) *half*
Halle f (-n) *hall*
Hallenbad n (-̈er) *indoor swimming pool*
Hallo! *Hello*
Hals m (-̈e) *throat, neck*
Halskette f (-n) *necklace*
Halsschmerzen m pl *sore throat*
halten v ir *to hold, to stop*
Haltestelle f (-n) *stop (e.g. bus)*
Hamburger m (-) *hamburger*
Hand f (-̈e) *hand*
Handball m *handball*
Händler/in m/f (-/-nen) *trader, dealer, shopkeeper*
Handschuh m (-e) *glove*
Handtasche f (-n) *handbag*
Handtuch n (-̈er) *hand towel*
Handy n (-s) *mobile phone*
Hansaplast n *'Elastoplast ®'*
hart adj *hard, harsh, severe, unkind*
Hase m (-n) *hare*
hassen v *to hate*
hässlich adj *ugly*
Hauptbahnhof m (-̈e) *main station*
Hauptgericht n (-e) *main course*
Hauptschule f (-n) *secondary school for vocational/practical training*
Hauptstadt f (-̈e) *capital city*
Hauptstraße f (-n) *major road, main street*
Haus n (-̈er) *house*
Hausarbeit f (-en) *housework, homework*
Hausaufgabe f (-n) *homework*
Hausfrau f (-en) *housewife*
Haushalt m (-e) *household*
Hausmann m (-̈er) *househusband*
Hausmeister/in m/f (-/-nen) *caretaker*
Hausnummer f (-n) *house number*
Hausschuh m (-e) *slipper*
Haustier n (-e) *pet*
Haustür f (-en) *front door*
Hauswirtschaftslehre f *home economics*
Hautfarbe f (-en) *skin colour*
Hecke f (-n) *hedge*
Heft n (-e) *exercise book*
heftig adj *violent, heavy (rain etc.)*
Heftpflaster n (-) *sticking plaster*
Heiligabend m (-e) *Christmas Eve*
Heim n (-e) *home*
Heimat f (-en) *home, homeland*
Heimfahrt f (-en) *home journey*
Heimleiter/in m/f (-/-nen) *warden of home/hostel*

prep: preposition **pron: pronoun** **conj**: conjunction **bits in brackets**: plural ending **(-̈)**: plural — add umlaut

German–English Dictionary

Heimleitung f (-en) person in charge of home / hostel
Heimweg m (-e) way home
heiraten v marry
heiß adj hot
heißen v ir to be called (named)
heiter adj bright (weather)
heizen v to have the heating on
Heizkörper m (-) radiator
Heizung f (-en) heating
helfen v ir to help
hell adj light, pale (colour)
Helm m (-e) helmet
Hemd n (-en) shirt
her adv (to) here
heraus adv out
Herbergseltern pl wardens (of youth hostel)
Herbst m (-e) autumn
Herd m (-e) cooker
herein! come in!
hereinkommen v sep ir to come in
Herr m (-en) Mr, gentleman
Herr Ober! waiter!
herrlich adj splendid, wonderful
herrschend adj ruling, dominant, prevailing
herum adv around
herumfahren v sep ir to travel/drive around
herunterladen v sep ir to download
hervorragend adj outstanding, excellent
Herz n (-en) heart
herzlich willkommen! welcome!
herzlichen Glückwunsch! congratulations!
heute adv today
heutzutage adv nowadays
hier adv here
Hilfe f (-n) help
hilfreich adj helpful
hilfsbereit adj helpful
Himbeere f (-n) raspberry
Himmel m (-) sky, heaven
hin und zurück adv return (ticket)
hinaus adv out
hinein adv in
hinlegen sich v sep to lie down
hinsetzen sich v sep to sit down
hinten adv behind, at the back
hinter prep + acc/dat behind
historisch adj/adv historic(al)
Hitze f (-n) heat
HIV-positiv adj HIV positive
hoch adv high
hochachtungsvoll adv yours faithfully, yours sincerely
Hochhaus n (¨er) skyscraper
hochladen v sep ir to upload
Hochschule f (-n) college, university
Hochzeit f (-en) wedding
Hockey n hockey
hoffen v to hope
höflich adj polite
holen v to fetch
Holland n Holland
Holländer/in m/f (-/-nen) Dutch person
holländisch adj Dutch
Holz n (¨er) wood
Honig m (-e) honey
hören v to hear
Hörer m (-) receiver (telephone), headphone
Horrorfilm m (-e) horror film
Hose f (-n) trousers
Hotel n (-s) hotel
Hotelverzeichnis n (-se) list of hotels
hübsch adj pretty
Hubschrauber m (-) helicopter
Hügel m (-) hill
hügelig adj hilly
humorlos adj humourless
humorvoll adj humorous
Hund m (-e) dog
Hunger m hunger
hungrig adj hungry
Husten m cough
husten v to cough
Hut m (¨e) hat

I

ICE-Zug m (¨e) intercity express train
ideal adj/adv ideal(ly)
Idee f (-n) idea
illegal adj/adv illegal(ly)
Illustrierte f (-n) magazine
im Freien in the open air
Image n (-s) image
Imbiss m (-e) snack
Imbissstube f (-n) café
immer adv always
immer noch adv still
in prep + acc/dat in, into
in Ordnung OK
inbegriffen adj included
Indien n India
Industrie f (-n) industry
industriell adj industrial
Informatik f ICT, computing
Informatiker/in m/f (-/-nen) computer scientist
Informationsbüro n (-s) information office
informativ adj informative
Ingenieur/in m/f (-e/-nen) engineer
inkl. (= inklusive) adj inclusive
Insektizid n (-e) insecticide
Insel f (-n) island
intelligent adj intelligent
interessant adj interesting
Interesse n (-n) interest
interessieren sich für v to be interested in
Internat n (-e) boarding school
Internet n internet
Internetseite f (-n) web page
Interview n (-s) interview
inzwischen adv in the meantime, meanwhile
Ire/Irin m/f (-n/-nen) Irish person
irgend- some-
irgendetwas pron something
irgendwo adv somewhere (or other)
irisch adj Irish
Irland n Ireland
Italien n Italy
Italiener/in m/f (-/-nen) Italian person
italienisch adj Italian

J

ja yes
Jacke f (-n) (casual) jacket
Jahr n (-e) year
Jahreszeit f (-en) season
Jahrhundert n (-e) century
jährlich adj/adv annual(ly)
Januar m January
je prep + acc per
jede/r/s pron each, every, everybody
jedoch conj/adv however
jemand pron someone, somebody
jene/r/s pron that
jetzt adv now
jobben v to do a job/jobs
joggen v to jog
Joghurt m or n (-s) yoghurt
Journalist/in m/f (-en/-nen) journalist
Jugendherberge f (-n) youth hostel
Jugendklub m (-s) youth club
Jugendliche m/f (-n) young person
Juli m July
jung adj young
Junge m (-n) boy
jünger adj younger
Juni m June
Juwelier/in m/f (-e/-nen) jeweller
Juweliergeschäft n (-e) jeweller's shop

K

Kaffee m (-s) coffee
Kaffekanne f (-n) coffee pot
Käfig m (-e) cage
Kakao m (-s) cocoa
Kalbfleisch n veal
Kalender m (-) calendar, diary
kalt adj cold
Kamera f (-s) camera
Kamm m (¨e) comb
kämmen v to comb
Kanal m (¨e) canal, channel
Kandidat/in m/f (-en/-nen) candidate
Kaninchen n (-) rabbit
Kännchen n (-) jug, pot
Kantine f (-n) canteen
Kanufahren n canoeing
Kapelle f (-n) chapel
kaputt adj broken
Karneval m (-e or -s) carnival
Karotte f (-n) carrot
Karriere f (-n) career
Karte f (-n) map, ticket, card
Kartoffel f (-n) potato
Kartoffelbrei m mashed potatoes
Kartoffelchips pl crisps
Kartoffelpüree m (-s) mashed potatoes
Kartoffelsalat m (-e) potato salad
Karton m (-s) cardboard box
Käse m (-) cheese
Kasse f (-n) checkout
Kassette f (-n) cassette
Kassettenrekorder m (-) cassette recorder
Kassierer/in m/f (-/-nen) cashier
Katze f (-n) cat
kaufen v to buy
Kaufhaus n (¨er) department store
Kaugummi m chewing gum
kaum adv hardly
kegeln v to bowl, to play skittles
kehren v to turn
kein pron no (= not any)
Keks m (-e) biscuit
Keller m (-) cellar
Kellner/in m/f (-/-nen) waiter/waitress
kennen v ir know (a person)
kennen lernen v to get to know
Kenntnis f (-se) knowledge
Kennwort n (¨er) password
Kfz (= Kraftfahrzeug) n motor vehicle
Kilometer m (-) kilometre
Kind n (-er) child
Kindheit f childhood
Kindergarten m (¨) nursery school
Kinn n (-e) chin
Kino n (-s) cinema
Kiosk m (-e) kiosk
Kirche f (-n) church
Kirchturm m (¨) steeple, church tower
Kirsche f (-n) cherry
Kissen n (-) cushion
Klamotten pl clothes, clobber
klar adj clear
Klarinette f (-n) clarinet
Klasse f (-n) class
klasse adj great
Klassenarbeit f (-en) test
Klassenfahrt f (-en) school trip
Klassenkamerad/in m/f (-en/-nen) classmate
Klassenzimmer n (-) classroom
klassisch adj/adv classic(al)
Klavier n (-e) piano
kleben v to stick
Klebstoff m (-e) glue
Kleid n (-er) dress
Kleider n pl clothes
Kleiderschrank m (¨e) wardrobe
Kleidung f clothing
Kleidungsgeschäft n (-e) clothes shop
klein adj small, short
Kleingeld n (small) change
Klempner/in m/f (-/-nen) plumber
klettern v to climb
klicken v to click
Klima n (-s) climate
Klingel f (-n) bell
klingeln v to ring (doorbell)
Klo n (-s) loo
klopfen v to knock
Klub m (-s) club
klug adj clever
Kneipe f (-n) pub
Knie n (-) knee
Knopf m (¨e) button
Koch/Köchin m/f (¨e/-nen) cook
Kochen n cooking
kochen v to cook
Koffer m (-) suitcase, trunk
Kohl m (-e) cabbage
Kohle f (-n) coal
Kollege/in m/f (-n/-nen) colleague
Köln n Cologne
komisch adj funny
kommen v ir to come
Kommode f (-n) chest of drawers
Komödie f (-n) comedy
kompliziert adj complicated
Konditorei f (-en) cake shop
Konferenz f (-en) conference
können v ir to be able to
Kontakt m (-e) contact
Konto n (Konten) (bank) account
Kontrolleur/in m/f (-e/-nen) (ticket) inspector
kontrollieren v to check, to supervise, to control
Konzert n (-e) concert
Kopf m (¨e) head
Kopfhörer m (-) headphones
Kopfkissen n (-) pillow
Kopfsalat m (-e) lettuce
Kopfschmerzen m pl headache
kopieren v to copy
Korb m (¨e) basket
Körper m (-) body
Korridor m (-e) corridor
korrigieren v to correct, to mark
kosten v to cost
kostenlos adj free
köstlich adj delicious
Kostüm n (-e) (women's) suit, costume
Kotelett n (-e) cutlet, chop
krank adj ill
Krankenhaus n (¨er) hospital
Krankenpfleger m (-) (male) nurse
Krankenschwester f (-n) (female) nurse
Krankenwagen m (-) ambulance
Krankheit f (-en) illness
Krawatte f (-n) tie
Krebs m (-e) cancer
Kreditkarte f (-n) credit card
Kreide f (-n) chalk
Kreis m (-e) circle
Kreisverkehr m (-e) roundabout
Kreuzung f (-en) crossroads
kriegen v to get
Krimi m (-s) crime story, thriller
Kriminalität f crime
kritisieren v to criticise
Küche f (-n) kitchen
Kuchen m (-) cake
Kugelschreiber m (-) biro, ballpoint pen
Kuh f (¨e) cow
kühl adj cool
Kühlschrank m (¨e) fridge
Kuli m (-s) biro
kümmern sich um v to take care of
Kunde/Kundin m/f (-n/-nen) customer
kündigen v to cancel, to hand in notice
Kündigung f (-en) cancellation, notice (to quit)
Kunst f (¨e) art
Kunstgalerie f (-n) art gallery
Künstler/in m/f (-/-nen) artist
Kunststoff m (-e) plastic, synthetic material
Kunstwerk n (-e) work of art
Kurs m (-e) course
Kurve f (-n) bend, curve
kurz adj short
kürzlich adv recently
Kusine f (-n) cousin (f)
Kuss m (¨e) kiss
küssen v to kiss
Küste f (-n) coast

L

Labor n (-s/-e) laboratory
lächeln v to smile
lachen v to laugh
Lachs m (-e) salmon
Laden m (¨) shop
laden v ir to load, to charge
Ladenbesitzer/in m/f (-/-nen) shopkeeper
Lagerfeuer n (-) campfire
Lamm n (¨er) lamb
Lammfleisch n lamb (meat)
Lampe f (-n) lamp
Land n (¨er) country, administrative district
landen v to land
Landkarte f (-n) map
Landschaft f (-en) landscape
lang adj long
langsam adj/adv slow(ly)
langweilen sich v to be bored
langweilig adj boring
Lärm m noise
lästig adj annoying (person)
lassen v ir to leave
Lastwagen m (-) lorry, truck
Latein n Latin
laufen v ir to go, to walk, to run
Laune f (-n) mood
launisch adj moody
laut adj/adv loud(ly), noisy
lautlos adj/adv silent(ly)
Leben n (-) life
leben v to live
lebendig adj living, lively
Lebenslauf m (¨e) CV
Lebensmittel n pl food, groceries
Lebensmittelgeschäft n (-e) grocer's shop
Leber f (-n) liver
lebhaft adj lively, busy
lecker adj delicious
Leder n (-n) leather
ledig adj single (unmarried)
leer adj empty
leeren v to empty
legal adj/adv legal(ly)
legen v to put, to lie something down
Lehre f (-n) apprenticeship, teaching
lehren v to teach
Lehrer/in m/f (-/-nen) teacher
Lehrerzimmer n (-) staff room
Lehrling m (-e) apprentice
lehrreich adj educational
leicht adj easy, light (weight)
Leichtathletik f athletics
leidtun v ir to regret, be sorry (es tut mir leid = I'm sorry)
leiden können v ir to like
leider adv unfortunately
leihen v ir to lend
leihen sich v ir to borrow
leise adj/adv quiet(ly)
Leistung f (-en) performance, achievement
Leiter/in m/f (-/-nen) manager, leader
Leiter f (-n) ladder
lernen v to learn
Lesen n reading

nouns — **m**: masculine **f**: feminine **n**: neuter **pl**: plural **v**: verb **v sep**: separable verb **v ir**: irregular verb **adj**: adjective **adv**: adverb

German–English Dictionary

lesen v ir *to read*
letzte/r/s adj *last*
Leute pl *people*
Licht n (-er) *light*
lieb adj/adv *kind(ly), likeable, nice(ly)*
Liebe f (-n) *love*
lieben v *to love*
lieber adv *rather*
Lieber/Liebe *Dear (in a letter)*
Liebesfilm m (-e) *romantic film*
Lieblings- *favourite*
Lied n (-er) *song*
liefern v *to deliver*
Lieferwagen m (-) *(delivery) van*
liegen v ir *to lie*
Liga f (Ligen) *league*
lila adj *purple*
Limo(nade) f (-s/-n) *lemonade*
Lineal n (-e) *ruler*
Linie f (-n) *line, route*
links adv *left*
Lippe f (-n) *lip*
Lippenstift m (-e) *lipstick*
Liste f (-n) *list*
Liter m or n (-) *litre*
Lkw (= Lastkraftwagen) m (-) *lorry*
Loch n (¨-er) *hole*
lockig adj *curly*
Löffel m (-) *spoon*
Lohn m (¨-e) *wage*
Lokal n (-e) *pub*
löschen v *to erase, to delete, to switch off (light), to extinguish*
Lotto n (-s) *national lottery*
Löwe m (-n) *lion*
lügen v *to tell a lie*
Luft f *air*
Luftverschmutzung f *air pollution*
Lunge f (-n) *lungs*
Lust (f) haben v ir *to feel like (doing something)*
lustig adj *funny*
Luxus m *luxury*

M

machen v *to make, to do*
Mädchen n (-) *girl*
Magen m (¨) *stomach*
Magenschmerzen m pl *stomach ache*
mähen v *to mow*
Mahl n (-e/¨-er) *meal*
Mahlzeit f (-en) *meal*
Mai m *May*
Mal n (-e) *time*
malen v *to paint*
Maler/in m/f (-/-nen) *painter*
malerisch adj *picturesque*
Manager/in m/f (-/-nen) *manager*
manchmal adv *sometimes*
Mann m (¨-er) *man, husband*
männlich adj *male*
Mannschaft f (-en) *team*
Mantel m (¨) *coat*
Margarine f (-n) *margarine*
Marke f (-n) *brand, make*
Marketing n *marketing*
Markt(platz) m (¨-e) *market (place)*
Marmelade f (-n) *jam, marmalade*
März m *March*
Maß n (-e) *measure, measurement*
mäßig adj/adv *moderate(ly)*
Mathe(matik) f *maths*
Mauer f (-n) *wall*
Maurer/in m/f (-/-nen) *builder*
Maus f (¨-e) *mouse*
Maximum n (Maxima) *maximum*
Mechaniker/in m/f (-/-nen) *mechanic*
Medienwissenschaft f *media studies*
Medikament n (-e) *medicine*
Meer n (-e) *sea*
Meerschweinchen n (-) *guinea pig*
mehr pron/adv *more*
Mehrbettzimmer n (-) *shared room*
mehrere pron *several*
Mehrfamilienhaus n (¨-er) *house for several families*
Mehrzweckraum m (¨-e) *multi-purpose room*
Meile f (-n) *mile*
mein/e/r pron *my*
meinen v *to think, to mean*
Meinung f (-en) *opinion*
meistens adv *mostly*
Meisterschaft f (-en) *championship*
Melodie f (-n) *melody*
Melone f (-n) *melon*
Menge f (-n) *quantity, load, crowd*
Mensch m (-en) *person*
merkwürdig adj/adv *strange(ly), odd(ly)*
Messe f (-n) *mass*
messen v ir *to measure*
Messer n (-) *knife*
Metall n (-e) *metal*
Meter m or n (-) *metre*
Metzger/in m/f (-/-nen) *butcher*
Metzgerei f (-en) *butcher's*
mies adj *lousy*
Miete f (-n) *rent*
mieten v *to rent*
Mikrowelle f (-n) *microwave*
Mikrowellenherd m (-e) *microwave oven*
Milch f *milk*
Million f (-en) *million*
Mindest- *minimum*
mindestens adv *at least*
Mineralwasser n *mineral water*
Minimum n (Minima) *minimum*
Minute f (-n) *minute*
mit prep + dat *with*
mit freundlichen Grüßen *yours sincerely*
mit Vergnügen! *with pleasure!*
mitgehen v sep ir *to go with*
Mitglied n (-er) *member*
mitkommen v sep ir *come (along)*
mitmachen v sep *to join in*
mitnehmen v sep ir *take (with you)*
Mittag m *midday*
mittags adv *at midday*
Mittagessen n (-) *lunch*
Mittagspause f (-n) *lunch break*
Mitte f (-n) *middle*
mitteilen v sep *to inform*
Mitteilung f (-en) *(text) message*
Mittel n (-) *means, method*
mittelgroß adj *medium/average height*
mittellang adj *medium/average length*
Mittelmeer n *Mediterranean Sea*
mitten adv *in the middle*
Mitternacht f *midnight*
Mittwoch m *Wednesday*
Mobbing n *workplace bullying*
Möbel n (-) *furniture*
Möbelstück n (-e) *piece of furniture*
möbliert adj *furnished*
Mode f (-n) *fashion*
Modegeschäft n (-e) *clothes shop*
modern adj *modern*
modisch adj *fashionable*
Mofa n (-s) *moped*
mögen v ir *to like*
möglich adj *possible*
Möglichkeit f (-en) *possibility*
Moment m (-e) *moment*
Monat m (-e) *month*
monatlich adj/adv *monthly*
Mond m (-e) *moon*
Montag m *Monday*
Morgen m (-) *morning*
morgen adv *tomorrow*
morgen früh *tomorrow morning*
morgens adv *in the morning(s)*
Mosel f *the Moselle (river)*
Motor m (-en) *engine*
Motorrad n (¨-er) *motorbike*
Motorradfahrer/in m/f (-/-nen) *motorbike rider*
müde adj *tired*
mühsam adj *laborious*
Müll m *rubbish*
Mülltonne f (-n) *dustbin*
multikulturell adj *multicultural*
München n *Munich*
Mund m (¨-er) *mouth*
mündlich adj/adv *oral(ly)*
Münze f (-n) *coin*
Museum n (Museen) *museum*
Musik f *music*
Musiker/in m/f (-/-nen) *musician*
musizieren v *to play a musical instrument*
müssen v ir *to have to*
Mutter f (¨) *mother*
Mutti f (-s) *mum, mummy*
Mütze f (-n) *cap, hat*
MwSt. (= Mehrwertsteuer) f *VAT*

N

nach prep + dat *after, to*
nach Hause *home*
nach oben *upwards, upstairs*
nach unten *downwards, downstairs*
Nachbar/in m/f (-n/-nen) *neighbour*
nachdem conj *after*
nachgehen v sep ir *to follow*
nachher adv *afterwards*
Nachmittag m (-e) *afternoon*
nachmittags adv *in the afternoon(s)*
Nachrichten f pl *news*
nachsehen v sep ir *to check, to look up, to watch*
Nachspeise f (-n) *dessert*
nächste/r/s adj *next*
Nacht f (¨-e) *night*
Nachteil m (-e) *disadvantage*
Nachthemd n (-en) *nightshirt*
Nachtisch m (-e) *dessert*
nachts adv *at night*
Nachttisch m (-e) *bedside table*
nahe adj *near*
Nähe f *nearness, vicinity*
Nahrung f *food*
Nase f (-n) *nose*
nass adj *wet*
Natur f (-en) *nature*
natürlich adj/adv *of course, naturally*
Naturwissenschaft f (-en) *science*
Nebel m (-) *fog, mist*
nebelig adj *foggy*
neben prep + acc/dat *next to*
Nebenjob m (-s) *side job*
Neffe m (-n) *nephew*
nehmen v ir *to take*
nein *no*
nennen v ir *to name, to call*
nerven v *to get on someone's nerves*
nervös adj/adv *nervous(ly)*
nett adj *nice, kind*
Netz n (-e) *net*
neu adj *new*
neulich adv *recently*
nicht adv *not*
nicht einmal *not even*
nicht mehr *no longer*
nicht nur … sondern auch *not only ... but also*
nicht wahr? *isn't it?*
Nichte f (-n) *niece*
nichts pron *nothing* (Das macht nichts = *It doesn't matter*)
nie adv *never*
Niederlande n pl *Netherlands*
Niederschlag m *precipitation*
niedrig adj/adv *low*
niemals adv *never*
niemand pron *no one*
nirgends adv *nowhere*
noch adv *still*
noch einmal *again*
noch nicht adv *not yet*
nochmal adv *again*
Nordamerika n *North America*
Norden m *north*
nördlich adj/adv *in/to the north*
Nordsee f *North Sea*
normal adj *normal*
normalerweise adv *normally*
Nostalgie f *nostalgia*
Not f (¨-e) *need, distress, trouble*
Notausgang m (¨-e) *emergency exit*
Note f (-n) *mark, grade*
notieren v *to note*
nötig adj *necessary*
Notizbuch n (¨-er) *notebook*
notwendig adj *necessary*
November m *November*
Nudeln f pl *pasta, noodles*
Nummer f (-n) *number*
nun adv *now*
nur adv *only*
Nuss f (¨-e) *nut*
Nutzen m (-) *use, usefulness*
nützlich adj *useful*
nutzlos adj/adv *useless(ly)*

O

ob conj *whether*
obdachlos adj *homeless*
oben adv *at the top, above, upstairs*
Oberstufe f (-n) *6th form*
Obst n *fruit*
Obst- und Gemüseladen m (¨) *fruit and veg shop*
obwohl conj *although*
oder conj *or*
Ofen m (¨) *heater, oven*
offen adj *open*
öffentlich adj *public, municipal*
öffentliche Verkehrsmittel n pl *public transport*
öffnen v *to open*
Öffnungszeiten f pl *opening times*
oft adv *often*
ohne prep + acc *without*
ohne Zweifel *without doubt*
Ohr n (-en) *ear*
Ohrring m (-e) *earring*
Oktober m *October*
Öl n (-e) *oil*
Öltanker m (-) *oil tanker*
Oma f (-s) *granny*
Omelett n (-e/-s) *omelette*
Onkel m (-) *uncle*
Opa m (-s) *grandpa*
Oper f (-n) *opera*
Operation f (-en) *operation (medical)*
Opfer n (-) *victim, sacrifice*
optimistisch adj/adv *optimistic(ally)*
Orangenmarmelade f (n) *marmelade*
Orchester n (-) *orchestra*
ordentlich adj *tidy*
Ordnung f (-en) *order, routine*
organisch adj/adv *organic(ally)*
organisieren v *to organise*
Ort m (-e) *place*
örtlich adj/adv *local(ly)*
Osten m *east*
Ostern n *Easter*
Österreich n *Austria*
Österreicher/in m/f (-/-nen) *Austrian*
österreichisch adj *Austrian*
östlich adj/adv *in/to the east*
Ostsee f *Baltic Sea*
Ozonloch n *hole in the ozone layer*
Ozonschicht f *ozone layer*

P

Paar n (-e) *pair*
paar (ein) adj *a few/couple*
Päckchen n (-) *packet, small parcel*
Packung f (-en) *packet*
Paket n (-e) *package, packet*
Palast m (¨-e) *palace*
Pampelmuse f (-n) *grapefruit*
Panne f (-n) *breakdown, flat tyre*
Papier n (-e) *paper*
Papiere n pl *papers, (official) documents*
Pappe f (-n) *cardboard*
Parfüm n (-e/-s) *perfume*
Parfümerie f (-en) *perfumery*
Park m (-s) *park*
parken v *to park*
Parkhaus n (¨-er) *multistorey car park*
Parkplatz m (¨-e) *parking place*
Partei f (-en) *(political) party*
Partnerstadt f (¨-e) *twin town*
Pass m (¨-e) *passport*
Passagier m (-e) *passenger*
passen v *to fit, to be suitable*
passieren v *to happen*
Passkontrolle f (-n) *passport control*
Patient/in m/f (-en/-nen) *patient*
Pause f (-n) *break*
Pech n *bad luck*
Pension f (-en) *guest house*
perfekt adj/adv *perfect(ly)*
Person f (-en) *person*
Personalausweis m (-e) *ID card*
Persönlichkeit f (-en) *personality*
pessimistisch adj/adv *pessimistic(ally)*
Pestizid n (-e) *pesticide*
Pfand n (¨-er) *security, deposit*
Pfarrer/in m/f (-/-nen) *pastor, vicar*
Pfeffer m (-) *pepper*
Pferd n (-e) *horse*
Pfingsten n (-) *Whitsun, Pentecost*
Pfirsich m (-e) *peach*
Pflanze f (-n) *plant*
Pflaume f (-n) *plum*
Pflichtfach n (¨-er) *(compulsory) subject*
Pfund n (-e) *pound*
Pfund Sterling n *pound sterling*
Physik f *physics*
physisch adj/adv *physical(ly)*
Picknick n (-e/-s) *picnic*
picknicken v *to (have a) picnic*
Pilz m (-e) *mushroom, toadstool*
Plakat n (-e) *poster*
Plan m (¨-e) *plan*
planen v *to plan*
Plastik n *plastic*
Platz m (¨-e) *place, room, seat, square, court*
plaudern v *to chat*
plötzlich adv *suddenly*
PLZ (= Postleitzahl) f *post code*
Polen n *Poland*
Polizei f *police*
Polizeiwache f (-n) *police station*
Polizist/in m/f (-en/-nen) *policeman/woman*
Pommes frites n pl *chips*
Popmusik f *pop music*
Portemonnaie n (-s) *wallet, purse*
Portion f (-en) *portion, helping*
Post f *post, post office*
Postamt n (¨-er) *post office*
Postbote/botin m/f (-n/-nen) *postman/woman*
Poster n (-/-s) *poster*
Postkarte f (-n) *postcard*
Postleitzahl f (-en) *postcode*
praktisch adj/adv *practical(ly)*
Pralinen f pl *chocolates*
Preis m (-e) *price*
Preisliste f (-n) *price list*
preiswert adj *cheap, good value*
Priester m (-) *priest*
prima adj *great*
privat adj *private, personal*
Privatschule f (-n) *private school*
pro prep *per*
pro Stunde *per hour*
probieren v *to try out*
Problem n (-e) *problem*
produzieren v *to produce*
Programm n (-e) *program(me)*
Programmierer/in m/f (-/-nen) *computer programmer*
Projekt n (-e) *plan, project*
Projektor m (-en) *projector*
Prospekt m (-e) *leaflet*
prost! *cheers!*
Prozent n (-e) *per cent*

prep: preposition **pron: pronoun** **conj**: conjunction **bits in brackets**: plural ending **(¨)**: plural — add umlaut

German–English Dictionary

prüfen v *to test, to examine, to check*
Prüfung f (-en) *exam*
Pullover, Pulli m (-, -s) *pullover*
Punkt m (-e) *point, full stop*
pünktlich adj/adv *punctual, on time*
Pute f (-n) *turkey (hen)*
putzen v *to clean*

Q

Quadrat n (-e) *square*
Qualifikation f (-en) *qualification*
Qualität f (-en) *quality*
Quantität f (-en) *quantity*
Quatsch m *rubbish (nonsense)*
Querflöte f (-n) *flute*
Quittung f (-en) *receipt*
Quizsendung f (-en) *quiz show*

R

Rabatt m (-e) *discount*
Rad n (¨-er) *bicycle, wheel*
Radfahren n *cycling*
Radfahrer/in m/f (-/-nen) *cyclist*
Radiergummi m (-s) *rubber, eraser*
Rand m (¨-er) *edge*
Rapmusik f *rap*
Rasen m (-) *lawn*
Rasse f (-n) *race (people)*
Rassenproblem n (-e) *race problem*
Rassismus m *racism*
rassistisch adj *racist*
Raststätte f (-n) *motorway services*
raten v ir *to advise*
Rathaus n (¨-er) *town hall*
Rauch m *smoke*
rauchen v *to smoke*
Raucher(in) m/f (-/-nen) *smoker*
Realschule f (-n) *secondary school*
rechnen v *to count, to calculate*
Rechnung f (-en) *bill*
recht haben v ir *to be right*
Rechteck n (-e) *rectangle*
rechts adv *right*
Rechtsanwalt/anwältin m/f (¨-e/-nen) *lawyer*
rechtzeitig adj/adv punctual, on time
recyceln v *to recycle*
Rede f (-n) *speech*
reden v *to talk*
reduziert adj *reduced*
Regal n (-e) *shelves*
Regel f (-n) *rule*
regelmäßig adj/adv *regular(ly)*
Regen m (-) *rain*
Regenmantel m (¨) *raincoat*
Regenschirm m (-e) *umbrella*
regnen v *to rain*
regnerisch adj *rainy*
reich adj *rich*
reichen v *to be enough, to reach*
reif adj *mature, ripe*
Reifen m (-) *tyre*
Reifenpanne f (-n) *puncture*
Reihe f (-n) *row (of seats etc.)*
Reihenhaus n (¨-er) *terraced house*
reinigen v *to clean*
Reinigung f *cleaning, dry cleaning*
Reis m *rice*
Reise f (-n) *journey*
Reisebüro n (-s) *travel agency*
Reisebus m (-se) *coach*
reisen v *to travel*
Reisende(r) m/f *traveller*
Reisepass m (¨-e) *passport*
Reisescheck m (-s) *traveller's cheque*
Reisetasche f (-n) *holdall, travel bag*
Reiseziel n (-e) *destination*
reiten v ir *to ride*
Reiten n *horse riding*
Reklame f (-n) *advert*
Religion f (-en) *religion, R.E.*
rennen v ir *to run*
Rennen n (-) *running, racing, race*
Rentner/in m/f (-/-nen) *pensioner*
Reparatur f (-en) *repair*
reparieren v *to repair*
reservieren v *to reserve*
Reservierung f (-en) *reservation*
Rest m (-e) *rest, remainder*
Resultat n (-e) *result*
retten v *to save*
Rezept n (-e) *prescription, recipe*
Rezeption f (-en) *reception*
Rhein m *the Rhine*
richtig adj *right, true*
Richtung f (-en) *direction*
riechen v ir *to smell*
Riegel m (-) *bar (of chocolate etc.)*
Rindfleisch n *beef*
Ring m (-e) *ring*
Risiko n (-s/Risiken) *risk*
Rock m (¨-e) *skirt*
Rockmusik f *rock music*
roh adj/adv *raw, rough(ly)*
Rollbrett n (-er) *skateboard*
Roller m (-) *scooter*
Rollschuh laufen v ir *to go roller-skating*
Rolltreppe f (-n) *escalator*
Roman m (-e) *novel*
romantisch adj *romantic(ally)*
rosa adj *pink*
Rosenkohl m (-e) *Brussels sprout*
rot adj *red*
Rücken m (-) *back*
Rückfahrkarte f (-n) *return ticket*
Rückfahrt f (-en) *return journey*
Rucksack m (¨-e) *rucksack*
rückwärts adv *backwards*
rudern v *to row*
Ruderboot n (-e) *rowing boat*
rufen v ir *to call, to shout*
Rugby n *rugby*
Ruhe f *peace, calm*
ruhig adj *peaceful, calm*
rund adj *round (shape)*
Rundfahrt f (-en) *tour (on transport)*
Rundgang m (¨-e) *tour (walking)*
Russe/Russin m/f (-n/-nen) *Russian*
russisch adj *Russian*
Russland n *Russia*

S

Saal m (Säle) *hall, ballroom*
Sache f (-n) *thing*
Sackgasse f (-n) *cul-de-sac*
Saft m (¨-e) *juice*
sagen v *to say, to tell*
Sahne f *cream*
Salat m (-e) *salad, lettuce*
Salz n (-e) *salt*
Salzkartoffeln f pl *boiled potatoes*
sammeln v *to collect*
Sammlung f (-en) *collection*
Samstag m *Saturday*
Sand m (-e) *sand*
Sandburg f (-en) *sand castle*
Sandale f (-n) *sandal*
sanft adj/adv *soft(ly), gentle/gently*
Sänger/in m/f (-/-nen) *singer*
Satellitenfernsehen n *satellite TV*
satt adj *full (having eaten)*
satt haben v ir *to be fed up with something*
sauber adj *clean*
sauer adj *sour, angry*
Sauerkraut n *pickled cabbage*
Sauerstoff m *oxygen*
saurer Regen m (-) *acid rain*
S-Bahn f (-en) *suburban railway*
Schach n *chess*
Schachtel f (-n) *small box (e.g. of chocolates)*
schade adj *(what a) shame*
schaden v *to damage, to harm*
Schaden m (¨) *damage*
schädlich adj *harmful*
Schaf n (-e) *sheep*
schaffen v ir *to create, to make*
Schal m (-s/-e) *scarf, shawl*
Schale f (-n) *skin, peel, shell*
Schalter m (-) *ticket office, switch*
schämen sich v *to be ashamed*
scharf adj *sharp, hot (spicy)*
Schaschlik n (-s) *kebab*
Schatten m (-) *shadow*
schattig adj *shady*
schauen v *to look*
Schauer m (-) *(rain) shower*
Schaufenster n (-) *display window*
Schauspieler/in m/f (-/-nen) *actor/actress*
Scheck m (-s) *cheque*
Scheckheft n (-e) *cheque book*
Scheibe f (-n) *slice*
scheiden (sich scheiden lassen) v ir *to get divorced*
Schein m (-e) *banknote*
scheinen v ir *to seem, to appear, to shine*
Scheinwerfer m (-) *headlight*
schenken v *to give (a present)*
Schere f (-n) *pair of scissors*
Schichtarbeit f *shift work*
schick adj/adv *stylish(ly)*
schicken v *to send*
schießen v ir *to shoot, to score*
Schiff n (-e) *ship*
Schild n (-er) *signpost*
Schildkröte f (-n) *tortoise*
Schinken m (-) *ham*
Schlafanzug m (¨-e) *pyjamas*
schlafen v ir *to sleep*
Schlafraum m (¨-e) *dormitory, bedroom*
Schlafsack m (¨-e) *sleeping bag*
Schlafwagen m (-) *sleeping car*
Schlafzimmer n (-) *bedroom*
schlagen v ir *to hit, to knock*
Schläger m (-) *racquet, stick, bat*
Schlagsahne f *whipped cream*
Schlagzeug n (-e) *drums*
Schlange f (-n) *snake, queue*
Schlange stehen v ir *to queue*
schlank adj *slim*
schlecht adj *bad*
schließen v ir *to close*
Schließfach n (¨-er) *locker*
schließlich adv *eventually, after all, finally*
schlimm adj *bad*
Schlips m (-e) *tie*
Schlittschuhlaufen n *ice skating*
Schloss n (¨-er) *castle, lock*
Schlüssel m (-) *key*
Schlüsselbund m or n (-e) *keyring, bunch of keys*
Schlussverkauf m (¨-e) *(end-of-season) sale*
schmal adj *narrow*
schmecken v *to taste, to taste good*
Schmerz m (-en) *pain*
schmerzhaft adj *painful*
Schmuck m (-e) *jewellery*
schmutzig adj *dirty*
Schnaps m (¨-e) *schnapps, spirits*
Schnee m *snow*
schneiden v ir *to cut*
schneien v *to snow*
schnell adj/adv *quick(ly)*
Schnellimbiss m (-e) *snack bar*
Schnitzel n (-) *(veal/pork) escalope*
Schnupfen m (-) *a cold*
Schnurrbart m (¨-e) *moustache*
Schokolade f (-n) *chocolate*
schon adv *already*
schön adj *beautiful, fine (weather)*
Schornstein m (-e) *chimney*
Schotte/Schottin m/f (-n/-nen) *Scot*
schottisch adj *Scottish*
Schottland n *Scotland*
Schrägstrich m (-e) *forward slash*
Schrank m (¨-e) *cupboard*
schrecklich adj/adv *terrible/terribly*
Schreibblock m (-s or ¨-e) *writing pad*
schreiben v ir *to write*
Schreibpapier n *writing paper*
Schreibtisch m (-e) *desk*
Schreibwarengeschäft n (-e) *stationer's*
schreien v ir *to scream/shout*
schriftlich adj *written*
Schublade f (-n) *drawer*
schüchtern adj/adv *shy(ly)*
Schuh m (-e) *shoe*
Schulabschluss m (¨-e) *school leaving certificate*
Schulbildung f *education*
Schulbuch n (¨-er) *school book*
Schulbus m (-se) *school bus*
Schuldirektor/in m/f (-en/-nen) *head teacher*
Schule f (-n) *school*
Schüler/in m/f (-/-nen) *school pupil*
Schüleraustausch m (-e) *school exchange*
Schülerzeitung f (-en) *school magazine*
Schulhof m (¨-e) *school playground*
Schulleiter/in m/f (-/-nen) *headmaster/mistress*
Schulstunde f (-n) *lesson*
Schultag m (-e) *school day*
Schultasche f (-n) *school bag*
Schulter f (-n) *shoulder*
Schüssel f (-n) *bowl*
schützen v *to protect*
schwach adj *weak, poor (e.g. schoolwork)*
Schwager/Schwägerin m/f (¨-e/-nen) *brother/sister-in-law*
schwänzen v *to skip, to play truant*
schwarz adj *black*
schwarze Johannisbeere f (-n) *blackcurrant*
Schwarzwald m *the Black Forest*
schwatzen v *to chat*
schweigen v ir *to be silent, to say nothing*
Schweinefleisch n *pork*
Schweiz f *Switzerland*
Schweizer/in m/f (-/-nen) *Swiss person*
schweizerisch adj *Swiss*
schwer adj/adv *heavy/heavily, difficult/with difficulty, serious(ly)*
Schwester f (-n) *sister*
schwierig adj *difficult*
Schwimmbad n (¨-er) *swimming pool*
Schwimmen n *swimming*
schwimmen v ir *to swim*
See f/m (-n) *sea (f); lake (m)*
seekrank adj *seasick*
Segelboot n (-e) *sailing boat*
segeln v *to sail*
sehen v ir *to see*
sehenswert adj *worth seeing*
Sehenswürdigkeit f (-en) *sight (something worth seeing)*
sehr adv *very*
Seide f (-n) *silk*
Seife f (-n) *soap*
Seifenoper f (-n) *soap opera*
sein v ir *to be*
seit prep + dat *since*
seitdem conj *since*
Seite f (-n) *side, page*
Sekretär/in m/f (-e/-nen) *secretary*
Sekretariat n (-e) *office*
Sekt m (-e) *(German) champagne*
Sekunde f (-n) *second*
selbst pron/adv *self/even*
selbständig adj/adv *independent(ly)*
Selbstbedienung f *self-service*
selten adj/adv *rare(ly), infrequent(ly), seldom*
Semester n (-) *term, semester*
senden v *to send*
Sendung f (-en) *(TV) programme*
Senf m (-e) *mustard*
sensibel adj/adv *sensitive(ly)*
September m *September*
Serie f (-n) *series (e.g. on TV)*
servieren v *to serve*
Serviette f (-n) *serviette, napkin*
Sessel m (-) *armchair*
setzen sich v *to sit down*
sicher adj/adv *certain(ly), sure(ly)*
Sicherheitsgurt m (-e) *seat belt*
Silber n *silver*
Silvester n *New Year's Eve*
simsen v *to text*
singen v ir *to sing*
Sitz m (-e) *seat*
sitzen v ir *to sit*
sitzen bleiben v ir *to repeat a (school) year*
Ski fahren v ir *to ski*
Skifahren n *skiing*
Skilehrer/in m/f (-/-nen) *ski instructor*
Slip m (-s) *briefs*
SMS f *text message*
SMV (= Schülermitverwaltung) f *school/student council*
sniffen v *to sniff/snort (drugs)*
so ... wie *as ... as*
so dass *so that*
so viel wie *as much as*
sobald conj *as soon as*
Socke f (-n) *sock*
Sofa n (-s) *sofa*
sofort adv *immediately*
sogar adv *even*
Sohn m (¨-e) *son*
Soldat/in m/f (-en/-nen) *soldier*
sollen v ir *to be supposed to*
Sommer m (-) *summer*
Sonderangebot n (-e) *special offer*
Sonnabend m *Saturday*
Sonne f (-n) *sun*
sonnen sich v *to sun oneself*
Sonnenbrand m *sunburn*
Sonnenbrille f (-n) *sunglasses*
Sonnencreme f (-s) *suncream*
Sonnenschirm m (-e) *sunshade*
sonnig adj *sunny*
Sonntag m *Sunday*
sonst adv *otherwise*
sonst nichts *nothing else*
Sorge f (-n) *worry*
sorgen für v *to take care of*
Soße f (-n) *sauce, gravy*
Souvenir n (-s) *souvenir*
sowohl ... als (auch) *both ... and*
Spanien n *Spain*
Spanier/in m/f (-/-nen) *Spaniard*
Spanisch n *Spanish (language)*
spanisch adj *Spanish*
spannend adj *exciting, tense*
sparen v *to save (up)*
Sparkasse f (-n) *savings bank*
sparsam adj/adv *thrifty, economic(al), sparing(ly)*
Spaß m *fun*
spät adj *late*
später adj/adv *later*
spazieren v *to walk*
spazieren gehen v ir *to go for a walk*
Spaziergang m (¨-e) *walk*
Speck m (-e) *bacon*
speichern v *to store*
Speisekarte f (-n) *menu*
Speisesaal m (-säle) *dining room*
Speisewagen m (-) *restaurant car*
spenden v *to donate, to give*
Spezialität f (-en) *speciality*
Spiegel m (-) *mirror*
Spiegelei n (-er) *fried egg*
Spiel n (-e) *game, match*
spielen v *to play*
Spieler/in m/f (-/-nen) *player*
Spielfilm m (-e) *feature film*
Spielplatz m (¨-e) *play area*
Spielzeug n (-e) *toy*
Spielzimmer n (-) *playroom*
Spinat m (-e) *spinach*
Spitze! *brilliant!*
Spitzname m (-n) *nickname*
Sport m *sport, PE*
Sport treiben v ir *to do sport*
Sportausrüstung f *sports equipment*
Sporthalle f (-n) *sports hall*
sportlich adj *sporty*
Sportplatz m (¨-e) *sports field*

*nouns — **m**: masculine **f**: feminine **n**: neuter **pl**: plural **v**: verb **v sep**: separable verb **v ir**: irregular verb **adj**: adjective **adv**: adverb*

German–English Dictionary

Sportzentrum n (-zentren) *sports centre*
Sprache f (-n) *language*
Sprachlabor n (-s or -e) *language lab*
Spraydose f (-n) *aerosol (can)*
sprechen v ir *to speak*
Sprechstunde f (-n) *surgery/consulting hours*
springen v ir *to jump*
Spritze f (-n) *syringe, injection*
spritzen v *to spray, to inject*
Sprudel m (-) *sparkling mineral water, fizzy drink*
Spülbecken n (-) *sink*
Spüle f (-n) *sink*
spülen v *to wash up*
Spülmaschine f (-n) *dishwasher*
staatlich adj *state*
Stadion n (Stadien) *stadium*
Stadt f (¨-e) *town*
Stadtbummel m (-) *stroll around town*
Stadtführer m (-) *town/city guidebook*
Stadtführung f (-en) *guided tour of town/city*
Stadtmitte f (-n) *town centre*
Stadtplan m (¨-e) *street map*
Stadtrand m (¨-er) *edge of the town*
Stadtrundfahrt f (-en) *guided tour of the town*
Stadtteil m (-e) *district*
Stadtviertel n (-) *district*
Stadtzentrum n (-zentren) *town centre*
Stahl m *steel*
Star m (-s) *celebrity*
stark adj *strong*
starten v *to start, to take off (plane)*
statt prep + gen *instead of*
stattfinden v ir sep *to take place*
Stau m (-e or -s) *traffic jam*
Staub saugen v *to hoover/vacuum*
stecken v *to place, to insert, to stick*
Stehcafé n (-s) *stand-up cafe*
stehen v ir *to stand, to suit someone (e.g. clothing)*
stehlen v ir *to steal*
steigen v ir *to climb, to rise, to get on*
steil adj/adv *steep(ly)*
Stein m (-e) *stone*
Stelle f (-n) *job (position)*
stellen v *to put/place*
Stellenangebote n pl *situations vacant*
Steppdecke f (-n) *duvet, quilt*
sterben v ir *to die*
Stereoanlage f (-n) *stereo*
Steward/ess m/f (-s/-en) *air steward/stewardess*
Stiefel m (-) *boot*
Stift m (-e) *pen*
still adj *quiet, peaceful*
stimmt! *right!*
Stock m (-) *storey*
Stockwerk n *storey*
Stoff m (-e) *material*
stolz adj *proud*
stoppen v *to stop*
Strand m (¨-e) *beach*
Straße f (-n) *street*
Straßenbahn f (-en) *tram*
Straßenkarte f (-n) *street map*
Straßenschild n (-er) *roadsign*
Streik m (-s) *strike*
Streit m (-e) *argument, quarrel*
streiten v ir *to quarrel*
streiten sich v ir *to argue, to quarrel*
streng adj *strict*
stressig adj *stressful*
Strom m *electricity*
Strumpf m (¨-e) *sock, stocking*
Strumpfhose f (-n) *tights*
Student/in m/f (-en/-nen) *student*
studieren v *to study*
Stück n (-e) *piece, coin*
Stückchen n (-) *(little) piece, bit*
Studium n (Studien) *(course of) study*
Stufe f (-n) *stair, level*
Stuhl m (¨-e) *chair*
Stunde f (-n) *hour, lesson*
Stundenplan m (¨-e) *timetable*
Sturm m (¨-e) *storm*
stürmisch adj *stormy*
suchen v *to seek, to look for*
Sucht f (¨-e) *addiction*
süchtig adj *addicted*
Südamerika n *South America*
Süden m *the South*
südlich adj/adv *in/to the south*
Supermarkt m (¨-e) *supermarket*
Suppe f (-n) *soup*
Surfbrett n (-er) *surfboard*
surfen v *to surf* (im Internet surfen *= to surf the internet*)
süß adj *sweet*
Süßigkeiten f pl *sweets*
sympathisch adj *nice (person)*

T

Tabak m (-e) *tobacco*
Tabakwarengeschäft n (-e) *tobacconist's*
Tablett n (-s or -e) *tray*
Tablette f (-n) *tablet, pill*
Tafel f (-n) *(black)board, bar (e.g. of chocolate)*
Tag m (-e) *day*
Tagebuch n (¨-er) *diary*
Tagesgericht n (-e) *dish of the day*
Tageskarte f (-n) *menu/dish (of the day)*
Tagesmenü n (-s) *menu of the day*
täglich adv *daily*
Tal n (¨-er) *valley*
tanken v *to fill up (e.g. petrol tank)*
Tankstelle f (-n) *petrol station*
Tannenbaum m (¨-e) *fir tree, Christmas tree*
Tante f (-n) *aunt*
Tanz m (¨-e) *dance*
tanzen v *to dance*
Tanzen n *dancing*
Tapete f (-n) *wallpaper*
Tasche f (-n) *bag, pocket*
Taschenbuch n (¨-er) *paperback*
Taschengeld n (-er) *pocket money*
Taschenlampe f (-n) *torch*
Taschenmesser n (-) *pocket knife, pen-knife*
Taschenrechner m (-) *calculator*
Taschentuch n (¨-er) *handkerchief*
Tasse f (-n) *cup*
Tastatur f (-en) *keyboard*
Taste f (-n) *key (of keyboard)*
Tätowierung f (-en) *tattoo*
Taufe f (-n) *baptism, christening*
Taxi n (-s) *taxi*
Taxifahrer/in m/f (-/-nen) *taxi driver*
Techniker/in m/f (-/-nen) *technician*
Technologie f (-n) *technology*
Tee m (-s) *tea*
Teekanne f (-n) *teapot*
Teelöffel m (-) *teaspoon*
Teil m or n (-e) *part, area, share*
teilen v *share, split*
Teilnahme f (-n) *participation*
Teilzeit f *part-time*
Telefon n (-e) *telephone*
Telefonanruf m (-e) *telephone call*
Telefonbuch n (¨-er) *phone book*
telefonieren v *to telephone*
Telefonnummer f (-n) *phone number*
Telefonzelle f (-n) *phone box*
Teller m (-) *plate*
Tellerwäscher/in m/f (-/-nen) *dishwasher*
Temperatur f (-en) *temperature*
Tennis n *tennis*
Teppich m (-e) *carpet*
Termin m (-e) *date, appointment, deadline*
Terminkalender m (-) *diary (for appointments)*
Terrasse f (-n) *terrace, patio*
teuer adj *expensive*
Theater n (-) *theatre*
Theatergruppe f (-n) *theatre group*
Theaterstück n (-e) *play*
Theke f (-n) *counter*
Therapie f (-n) *therapy*
Thunfisch m (-e) *tuna*
tief adj *deep*
Tiefkühlschrank m (¨-e) *freezer*
Tiefkühltruhe f (-n) *chest freezer*
Tier n (-e) *animal*
Tierarzt/ärztin m/f (¨-e/-nen) *vet*
Tierheim n (-e) *animal home*
tippen v *to type*
Tisch m (-e) *table*
Tischdecke f (-n) *tablecloth*
Tischler/in m/f (-/-nen) *joiner, carpenter*
Tischtennis n *table tennis*
Tischtuch n (¨-er) *tablecloth*
Toastbrot n *bread for toasting*
Tochter f (¨) *daughter*
Tod m (-e) *death*
Toilette f (-n) *toilet*
Toilettenpapier n (-e) *toilet paper*
toll adj *great*
Tomate f (-n) *tomato*
Ton m (¨-e) *tone, sound*
Topf m (¨-e) *pot, pan*
Tor n (-e) *gate, goal*
Torte f (-n) *gateau, cake*
tot adj *dead*
total adj/adv *total(ly)*
Tour f (-en) *tour*
Tourismus m *tourism*
Tourist/in m/f (-en/-nen) *tourist*
Touristeninformation f (-en) *tourist information (office)*
tragen v ir *to carry, to wear*
Tragödie f (-n) *tragedy*
trainieren v *to train, to coach*
Trainingsanzug m (¨-e) *track suit*
Trainingsschuhe m pl *trainers*
Traube f (-n) *grape*
Traum m (¨-e) *dream*
traurig adj *sad*
Trauring m (-e) *wedding ring*
treffen v ir *to meet*
Treffpunkt m (-e) *meeting place*
Treibhauseffekt m *greenhouse effect*
Treibhausgas n (-e) *greenhouse gas*
trennen sich v *to split up*
Treppe f (-n) *staircase*
Treppenhaus n (¨-er) *stairwell*
treten v ir *to step, to kick*
Trimester n (-) *term*
trinken v ir *drink*
Trinkgeld n (-er) *tip*
Trinkwasser n *drinking water*
trocken adj *dry*
trocknen v *to dry*
Trompete f (-n) *trumpet*
trotz prep + gen *despite*
trotzdem adv *nevertheless*
Truthahn m (¨-e) *turkey*
tschüss *bye*
Tube f (-n) *tube*
Tuch n (¨-er) *cloth*
tun v ir *to do*
Tunnel m *the Channel Tunnel*
Tür f (-en) *door*
Türkei f *Turkey*
Turm m (¨-e) *tower*
turnen v *to do gymnastics*
Turnen n *gymnastics, PE*
Turnhalle f (-n) *gym*
Turnschuhe m pl *trainers*
Tüte f (-n) *small bag*
Typ m (-en) *type, bloke*
typisch adj/adv *typical(ly)*

U

U-Bahn f (-en) *underground (railway)*
U-Bahnstation f (-en) *underground station*
übel adj *nasty, ill*
üben v *to practise*
über prep + acc/dat *over, above*
überall adv *everywhere*
überbevölkert adj *overpopulated*
Überfahrt f (-en) *(sea) crossing*
überhaupt nicht *not at all*
übermorgen adv *the day after tomorrow*
übernachten v *to stay the night*
Übernachtung f (-en) *overnight stay*
überqueren v *to cross*
überrascht adj *surprised*
überwachen v *to supervise*
übrigens adv *moreover, by the way*
Übung f (-en) *practice*
Ufer n *(river) bank*
Uhr f (-en) *watch, clock, o'clock*
ultraviolette Strahlen m pl *UV rays*
um prep + acc *around*
um... zu conj *in order to*
Umfrage f (-n) *opinion poll, survey*
umgeben von *surrounded by*
Umgebung f (-en) *surroundings, neighbourhood*
Umkleidekabine f (-n) *changing cubicle*
Umkleideraum m (¨-e) *changing room*
Umleitung f (-en) *diversion, detour*
Umschlag m (¨-e) *envelope*
umsteigen v sep ir *change (trains)*
Umwelt f *environment*
umweltfeindlich adj *environmentally damaging*
umweltfreundlich adj *environmentally friendly*
Umweltproblem n (-e) *environmental problem*
umziehen v sep ir *to move (house)*
umziehen sich v sep ir *to get changed*
und conj *and*
Unfall m (¨-e) *accident*
unfit adj *unfit*
unfreundlich adj *unfriendly*
ungeduldig adj *impatient*
ungefähr adv *about, approximately*
ungerecht adj *unjust, unfair*
ungesund adj *unhealthy*
unglaublich adj *unbelievable*
unhöflich adj *impolite*
Uniform f (-en) *uniform*
Universität f (-en) (Uni) *university*
unmöglich adj *impossible*
unordentlich adj *untidy*
Unrecht haben v ir *to be wrong*
unsicher adj *uncertain, insecure*
unsympathisch adj *unpleasant*
unten adv *at the bottom, below, downstairs*
unter prep + acc/dat *under*
Untergeschoss n *basement*
unterhalten sich v ir *to converse*
Unterhaltung f *entertainment*
Unterhaltungsmöglichkeiten f pl *entertainment, things to do*
Unterhose f (-n) *underpants*
Unterkunft f (¨-e) *accommodation*
unternehmungslustig adj *enterprising, adventurous*
Unterricht m *lessons, classes*
unterrichten v *to teach, to inform*
Unterschied m (-e) *difference*
unterschiedlich adj *different, variable*
unterschreiben v ir *to sign*
Unterschrift f (-en) *signature*
unterstützen v *to support*
Untertasse f (-n) *saucer*
Unterwäsche f *underwear*
unterwegs adv *on the way*
unvorstellbar adj *unimaginable*
unzufrieden adj *discontented*
Urlaub m (-e) *holiday*
usw. (= und so weiter) *etc.*

V

Vandalismus m *vandalism*
Vanille f *vanilla*
Vater m (¨) *father*
Vati m (-s) *dad*
Vegetarier/in m/f (-/-nen) *vegetarian*
verantwortlich adj *responsible*
Verantwortung f (-en) *responsibility*
verbal adj *verbal*
verbessern v *to improve*
Verbesserung f (-en) *improvement, correction*
verbieten v ir *to forbid*
verbinden v ir *to connect*
Verbindung f (-en) *connection*
verboten adj *prohibited, forbidden*
Verbrauch m *use, consumption*
Verbrechen n (-) *crime*
verbringen v ir *spend (time)*
verdienen v *to earn, to deserve*
Verein m (-e) *club, organisation*
Vereinigte Staaten m pl *USA*
Vergangenheit f *past, past tense*
vergeben v ir *to forgive, to give away*
vergessen v ir *to forget*
Vergleich m (-e) *comparison*
Verhältnis n (-se) *relationship, ratio*
verheiratet adj *married*
verhindern v *to prevent*
verkaufen v *to sell*
Verkäufer/in m/f (-/-nen) *salesperson*
Verkehr m *traffic*
Verkehrsamt n (¨-er) *tourist information office*
Verkehrsmittel n (-) *mode of transport*
Verkehrsunfall m (¨-e) *road accident*
verlassen v ir *to leave, to abandon*
verletzen v *to injure*
Verletzung f (-en) *injury*
verlieren v ir *to lose*
verloben sich v *to get engaged*
verlobt adj *engaged*
Verlobungsring m (-e) *engagement ring*
vermeiden v ir *to avoid, to prevent, to warn*
vermieten v *to rent out*
verpacken v *to pack, to wrap up*
Verpackung f (-en) *packing*
verpassen v *to miss (bus/train etc.)*
Versammlung f (-en) *meeting, assembly*
verschieden adj/adv *different(ly), various(ly)*
verschmutzen v *to dirty, to pollute*
Verschmutzung f (-en) *pollution*
verschwinden v ir *to disappear*
verspäten sich v *to be late*
Verspätung f (-en) *delay, lateness*
versprechen v ir *to promise*
verstehen v ir *to understand*
verstehen sich v ir *to get on well*
Versuch m (-e) *experiment, attempt*
versuchen v *to try*
Vertreter/in m/f (-/-nen) *representative*
verursachen v *to cause*
Verwandte(r) *relative*
verzeihen v ir *to forgive*
Verzeihung! *Sorry!*
Vetter m (-n) *cousin*
viel/e pron/adj *lots, many*
Viel Glück! *good luck*
vielleicht adv *perhaps, maybe*
viereckig adj *rectangular*
Viertel n (-) *quarter*
Virus n/m (Viren) *virus*
Vitamine n pl *vitamins*
Vogel m (¨) *bird*
Volksmusik f *folk music*

prep: *preposition* **pron: pronoun** **conj**: *conjunction* **bits in brackets**: *plural ending* **(¨)**: *plural — add umlaut*

German–English Dictionary

voll adj *full*
völlig adv *completely*
Vollpension f *full board (at hotel)*
von prep + dat *from, of*
vor prep + acc/dat *before, in front of, outside*
vor kurzem *recently*
voraus adv *in front, ahead* (im Voraus = *in advance*)
vorausgesetzt, dass *provided that*
vorbei adv *past, by*
vorbeifahren v sep ir *to go past*
vorbeigehen v sep ir *to pass by, to go by*
vorbereiten v sep *to prepare*
Vorfahrt f *right of way*
vorgehen v sep ir *to go forward, to go on ahead*
vorgestern adv *the day before yesterday*
vorhaben v sep ir *to intend, to have planned*
Vorhang m (¨-e) *curtain*
vorher adv *beforehand, previously*
vorkommen v *to occur*
Vorliebe f (-n) *preference*
Vormittag m (-e) *morning*
vormittags adv *in the morning(s)*
vorn/e adv *at the front, in front*
Vorname m (-n) *first name*
Vorort m (-e) *suburb*
vorschlagen v sep ir *to suggest, to propose*
Vorspeise f (-n) *starter*
vorstellen v sep *to introduce*
vorstellen sich v sep *to introduce oneself, to imagine*
Vorstellung f (-en) *showing, performance, idea*
Vorteil m (-e) *advantage*
Vorwahl f (-en) *area code*
vorwärts adv *forwards*
vorziehen v sep ir *prefer*

W

wachsen v ir *to grow*
Wagen m (-) *car*
Wahl f (-en) *choice*
Wahlfach n (¨-er) *option subject*
wählen v *to choose, to dial*
wahr adj *true* (nicht wahr? = *isn't it?*)
während conj *during, while*
Wahrheit f (-en) *truth*
wahrscheinlich adv *probably*
Wald m (¨-er) *forest*
Wales n *Wales*
Waliser/in m/f (-/-nen) *Welsh person*
walisisch adj *Welsh*
Wand f (¨-e) *wall*
wandern v *to walk, hike*
Wanderung f (-en) *walk, hike*
wann adv *when*
Warenhaus n (¨-er) *(department) store*
warm adj *warm*
warnen v *to warn*
warten v *to wait*
warten auf v *to wait for*
Warteraum m (¨-e) *waiting room*
Wartesaal m (-säle) *waiting room*
Wartezeit f *waiting period, wait*
Wartezimmer n (-) *waiting room*
warum adv *why*
was pron *what*
was für… *what kind of…*
Waschbecken n (-) *washbasin*
Wäsche f *washing, underwear*
waschen (sich) v ir *to wash (oneself)*
Wäscherei f (-en) *laundry*
Waschküche f (-n) *laundry room*
Waschmaschine f (-n) *washing machine*
Waschpulver n (-) *washing powder*
Waschsalon m (-s) *launderette*
Wasser n *water*
Wasserhahn m (¨-e) *tap*
Wasserski n *waterskiing*
Wasserskilaufen n *waterskiing*
Wasserverschmutzung f (-en) *water pollution*
Webseite f (-n) *web page*
Website f (-s) *website*
Wechselgeld n *change*
Wechselkurs m (-e) *exchange rate*
wechseln v *to change*
Wechselstube f (-n) *bureau de change*
wecken v *to wake someone*
Wecker m (-) *alarm clock*
weder … noch conj. *neither … nor*
Weg m (-e) *way, path*
wegen prep + gen *because of*
weggehen v sep ir *to go away*
wegwerfen v sep ir *to throw away*
wehtun v ir sep *to hurt*
weiblich adj *female*
weich adj/adv *soft(ly)*
Weihnachten n (-) *Christmas*
Weihnachtsbaum m (¨-e) *Christmas tree*
Weihnachtsmarkt m (¨-e) *Christmas market*
weil conj *because*
Wein m (-e) *wine*
weinen v *to cry*
Weintraube f (-n) *grape*
Weise f (-n) *way*
weiß adj *white*
Weißbrot n (-e) *white bread*
weit adj *far*
weiterfahren v sep ir *to continue*
weitermachen v sep *to continue (e.g. studies), to carry on*
Welle f (-n) *wave*
Wellensittich m (-e) *budgerigar*
Welt f (-en) *world*
weltweit adj/adv *worldwide*
wem pron *who, to whom*
wen pron *who, whom*
wenig pron/adj *little, few*
weniger adv *less*
wenigstens adv *at least*
wenn conj *if, when*
wer pron *who*
Werbung f (-en) *advertising*
werden v ir *to become, to get*
werfen v ir *to throw*
Werken n *handicrafts, design technology*
Werkstatt f (¨-en) *workshop, garage*
Werkzeug n (-e) *tool*
wertvoll adj *valuable*
Wespe f (-n) *wasp*
wessen pron *whose*
Westen m *the west*
westlich adj/adv *in/to the west*
Wetter n (-) *weather*
Wetterbericht m (-e) *weather report*
Wettervorhersage f (-n) *weather forecast*
wichtig adj *important*
wie adv *how, as, like*
wie bitte? *pardon?*
wie geht's? *how are you?*
wie viel(e) adv *how much/many*
wieder adv *again*
wiederholen v *to repeat*
wiegen v ir *to weigh*
Wien n *Vienna*
Wiese f (-n) *meadow*
wieso adv *why*
willkommen adj *welcome*
Wind m (-e) *wind*
windig adj *windy*
windsurfen v *to windsurf*
Winter m (-) *winter*
wirklich adv *really*
wissen v ir *to know (facts)*
witzig adj *funny*
wo adv *where*
Woche f (-n) *week*
Wochenende n (-n) *weekend*
wöchentlich adj/adv *weekly*
woher adv *where from*
wohin adv *where to*
Wohltätigkeit f *charity*
Wohnblock m (¨-e or -s) *block of flats*
wohnen v *to live*
Wohnort m (-e) *place where you live*
Wohnung f (-en) *flat*
Wohnwagen m (-) *caravan*
Wohnzimmer n (-) *living room*
Wolke f (-n) *cloud*
wolkenlos adj *cloudless*
wolkig adj *cloudy*
Wolle f (-n) *wool*
wollen v ir *to want*
Wort n (-e or ¨-er) *word*
Wörterbuch n (¨-er) *dictionary*
Wunde f (-n) *wound*
wunderbar adj *wonderful*
wunderschön adj *really beautiful*
Wunsch m (¨-e) *wish*
wünschen v *to wish, to want*
wünschen sich v *to desire, to wish for*
Wurst f (¨-e) *sausage*
Wurstbude f (-n) *sausage stand*

Z

z.B. (= zum Beispiel) *for example (e.g.)*
Zahl f (-en) *figure*
zahlen v *to pay*
zählen v *to count*
zahlreich adj *numerous*
Zahn m (¨-e) *tooth*
Zahnarzt/ärztin m/f (¨-e/-nen) *dentist*
Zahnbürste f (-n) *toothbrush*
Zahnpasta f (-pasten) *toothpaste*
Zahnschmerzen m pl *toothache*
ZDF *German television company*
Zebrastreifen m *zebra crossing*
Zeichentrickfilm m (-e) *cartoon*
Zeichnen n *drawing (subject)*
zeichnen v *to draw*
zeigen v *to show*
Zeit f (-en) *time*
Zeitpunkt m (-e) *moment*
Zeitschrift f (-en) *magazine*
Zeitung f (-en) *newspaper*
Zeitungskiosk m (-e) *newspaper stall*
Zelt n (-e) *tent*
zelten v *to camp*
Zelten n *camping*
Zentimeter n/m (-) *centimetre*
Zentralheizung f (-en) *central heating*
Zentrum n (Zentren) *centre*
zerbrechlich adj *fragile*
zerstören v *to destroy*
Zettel m (-) *piece of paper, note*
Zeug n (-e) *stuff, things*
Zeugnis n (-se) *school report*
ziehen v ir *to pull*
Ziel n (-e) *aim, goal*
ziemlich adv *quite*
Zigarette f (-n) *cigarette*
Zimmer n (-) *room*
Zimmermädchen n (-) *maid*
Zitrone f (-n) *lemon*
Zoll m (¨-e) *customs, toll*
Zoo m (-s) *zoo*
zornig adj *angry*
zu adj/adv/prep + dat *to, too (e.g. too old), closed*
zu Ende *over, finished*
zu Fuß *on foot*
zu Händen von *for the attention of*
zu Hause *at home*
Zucker m *sugar*
zuerst adv *at first, first of all*
zufällig adj *accidental, random*
zufrieden adj *satisfied*
Zug m (¨-e) *train*
Zugführer/in m/f (-/-nen) *guard (on train)*
Zuhause n *home*
zuhören v sep *to listen to*
Zukunft f *future*
zuletzt adv *at last, in the end*
zum Beispiel *for example*
zum Mitnehmen adj *take away (meals)*
zum Wohl! *cheers!*
zumachen v sep *to close, to shut*
zunehmen v sep ir *to increase, to put on weight*
zurück adv *back*
zurückfahren v sep ir *to go back, to drive back*
zurückgehen v sep ir *to return*
zurückkommen v sep ir *to come back*
zurücklassen v sep ir *to leave*
zurückrufen v sep ir *to call back*
zurückstellen v sep *to put back*
zusammen adv *together*
Zuschauer/in m/f (-/-nen) *spectator, audience*
Zuschlag m (¨-e) *supplement*
zusehen v sep ir *to look on, to watch*
zustimmen v sep *to agree*
Zweibettzimmer n (-) *twin-bed room*
zweitens adv *secondly*
zweiter Klasse *second class*
Zwiebel f (-n) *onion*
Zwilling m (-e) *twin*
zwischen prep + acc/dat *between*
zwo = zwei (telephone)

*nouns — **m**: masculine **f**: feminine **n**: neuter **pl**: plural **v**: verb **v sep**: separable verb **v ir**: irregular verb **adj**: adjective **adv**: adverb*

Index

Index